Silver Curios In the Home

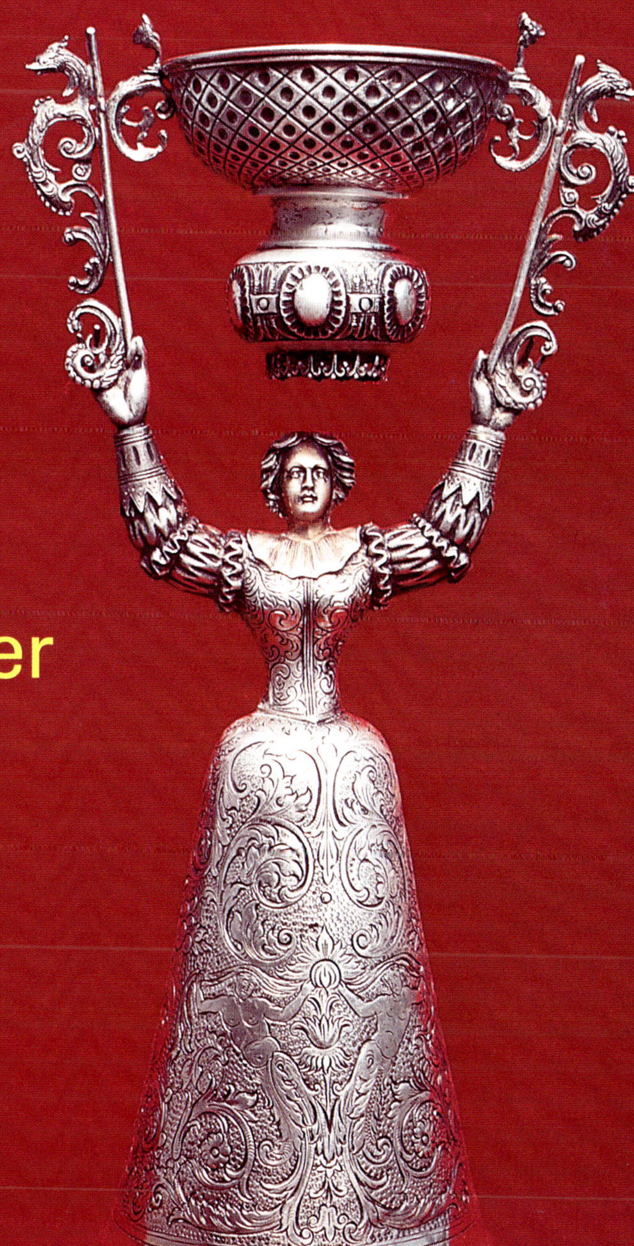

Dorothy T. Rainwater
and Beryl Frank

Schiffer Publishing Ltd
4880 Lower Valley Road, Atglen, PA 19310 USA

Dedication

To the memory of Ivan, for fifty-four years my very beloved husband, friend, and companion.

Dorothy T. Rainwater
Bowie, Maryland

Note: Neither the authors nor the publisher are responsible for the accuracy of the values listed here; they should be used as a guide *only*. Condition and demand influence both buyers and sellers in regard to the price of antiques or collectibles.

Library of Congress Catalog Card Number: 99-62924

Designed by "Sue"
Type set in Zaph Chancery Bd BT/Zurich BT

ISBN: 0-7643-0845-9
Printed in China
1 2 3 4

Published by Schiffer Publishing Ltd.
4880 Lower Valley Road
Atglen, PA 19310
Phone: (610) 593-1777; Fax: (610) 593-2002
E-mail: Schifferbk@aol.com
Please visit our web site catalog at
www.schifferbooks.com
Please write for a free catalog.
This book may be purchased from the publisher.
Please include $3.95 for shipping.

In Europe, Schiffer books are distributed by
Bushwood Books
6 Marksbury Rd.
Kew Gardens
Surrey TW9 4JF England
Phone: 44 (0)181 392-8585; Fax: 44 (0)181 392-9876
E-mail: Bushwd@aol.com

Please try your bookstore first.

We are interested in hearing from authors
with book ideas on related subjects.

Acknowledgments

There is no way one can give adequate thanks to the many friends, relatives, and even perfect strangers for their help in making this book possible. To all these our humblest and sincere thanks are offered.

It is a real pleasure to recall the many times the following people assisted us in their various ways, always with a smile: Gwen Kelso of the Rampant Lion for her ability to round up reference books when needed; Donna H. Felger who once again gave the benefit of her typing and editorial skills; photographers David Arky at Time-Life Books, Jeff Cochran, and Bruce Waters at Schiffer Publishing, all of whom brought the silver objects to life. We owe much to George B. Griffenhagen who was of much use in the pharmaceutical area.

Mere words are not sufficient to thank Connie McNally, Editor of *Silver Magazine*, who gave us permission to use material from that publication and to Vincent A. Martin, Administrative Assistant of *Silver Magazine*, who tracked down and sent photographs. Words of encouragement from Audrey Scott and Evleen Walker kept us going in spite of automobile accidents and viral infections. Marie J. Hargett's skill at proofreading is much appreciated as is her ability to see that the absent-minded member of the crew stopped for meals. We thank Phyllis J. McNeill for her efforts to prevent starvation and Robert D. McNeill, our successful fisherman on the Internet.

Dorothea Burstyn opened our eyes to the silversmiths of Hanau, Germany. For this we are eternally grateful.

Our thanks go to Antonia Moore for her generous loan of objects to be photographed and for information about them. Also thanks go to Georgia Meadows for her expertise on mourning jewelry.

The following people helped in many different ways: Edie Baker, Kevin A. Barrington, Milt Becker, David Bigoda, Betty Brinker, Charles H. C. Carpenter Jr., Marge Dearmon, Chip DeMatteo at Hand and Hammer Silversmiths, Stephen N. Dennis, Cdr. and Mrs. F. F. Duggan Jr. (Ret), and Patrick Duggan of Imperial Half Bushel, John M. Durkin for his Internet searches, Sally Fine, Alan Fortunoff, Frances E. Graves, Anne Jansen, David and Hillary Keller, Normin Koff, Henry and Jay Kupjack, Dick Lockhart, Randy Long, Ann Mahony, Lou Mello, Michael Merrill, Rosi and Dwane Miller, Pat Nelson, Helen and Peter Nowell, Betty Pavoordt, Diane Pelham Burn, Daria Phair, the staff at the Rainwater-Miles Genealogical Society Library in Bowie, Maryland, Greg Reeves, Marjorie Erp Reeves, Pat Rich, Mable Lee Rogers, Barbara and Neal Schatz, Paul Silverman, Mary Simons, Priscilla and Donald Stoffel, David L. Thomas, Margaret Vining, Robert Watkins, Don Weichert, Connie and Bud Weiser, Estelle Zalkin, and Janet Zapata.

Special thanks go to Lou Frank who, following severe injuries to one of our crew, made it possible for some work to continue. He drove many miles and listened to endless talk about silver objects with patience, enthusiasm, and encouragement.

Certainly not least is the slate of librarians who so cheerfully looked up information for us, always with a smile. They include David Beasley of the Goldsmith's Company at Goldsmiths Hall in London, and Mary Gossett, Barbara Johnson, Maureen Reefe, Leah Sparks, and Sue Stephenson all at the Bowie Maryland Library who, in spite of working under rehabilitation conditions, always found the impossible and gave it to us with a smile. It is impossible to heap too much praise on the wonderfully helpful librarians everywhere.

The guidance is real and the patience of Peter and Nancy Schiffer is almost beyond belief. Without their help, and that of Robyn Stolzfus and Jean Cline, this book could not have begun, much less have been completed.

Silver enthusiasts everywhere will cherish the memories of the work and knowledge imparted to us by the late Diana Cramer, Charles C. Williams, Richard Tousey, and Diane Zinn, all of whom were generous in sharing hard-won information as well as their words of encouragement when things were not at their best. Surely, heaven must be a happier place now that they are there.

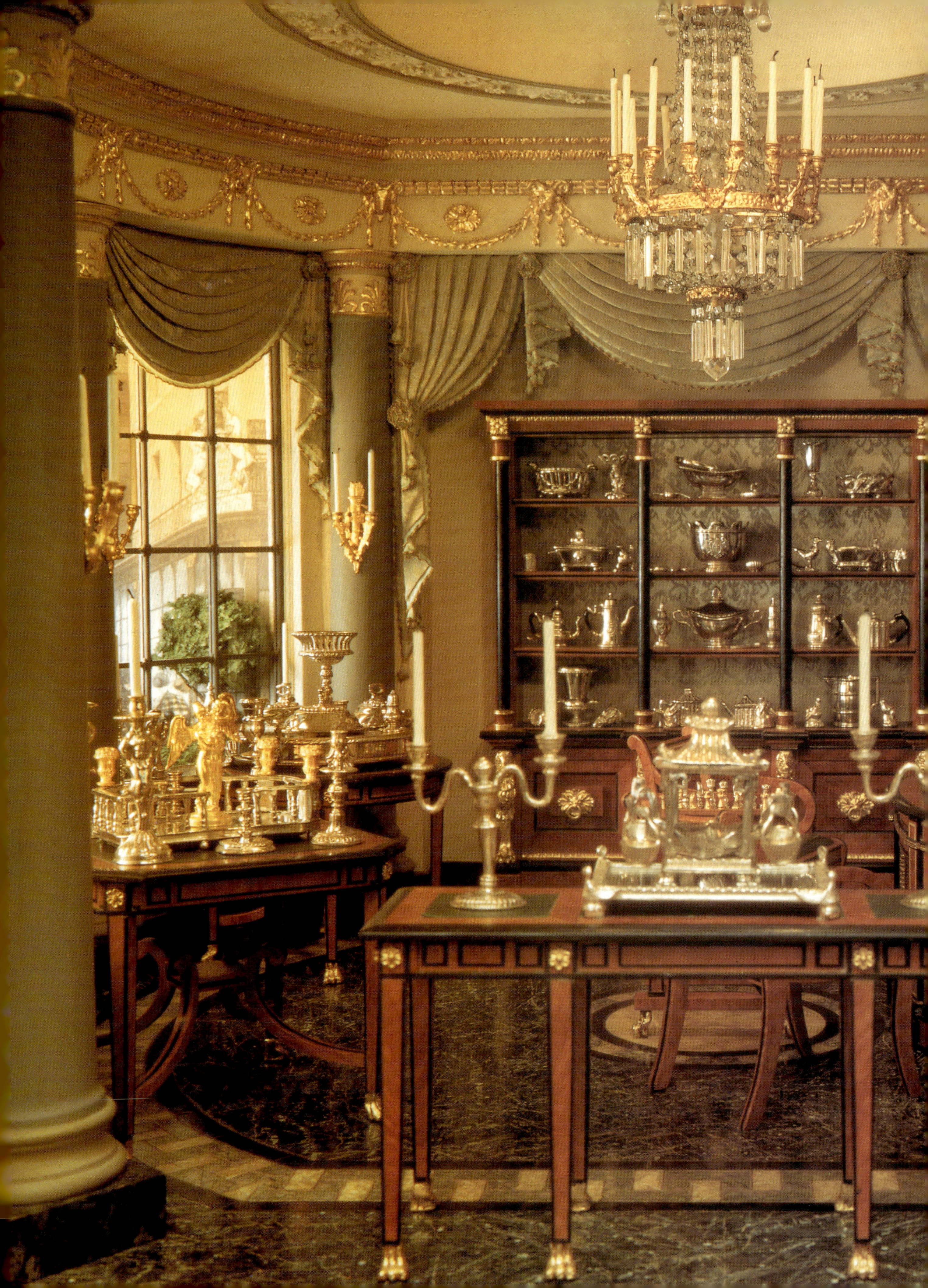

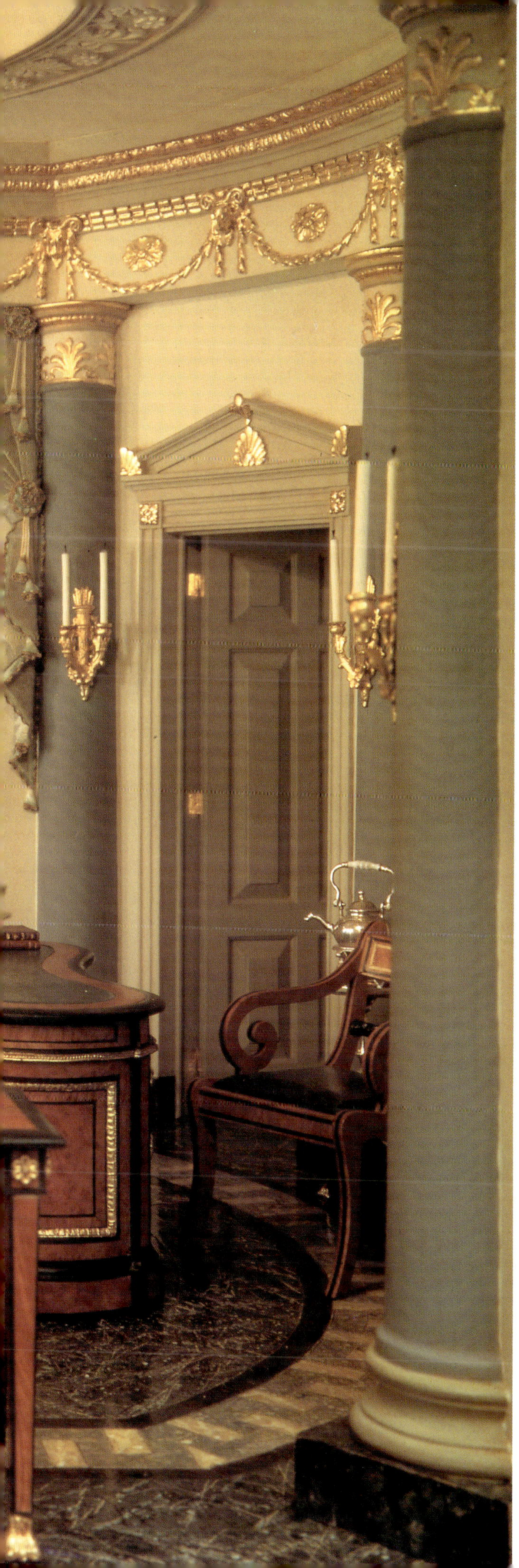

Contents

Inch to the foot scale model of an elegant silver shop of days gone by, made by Eugene P. Kupjack. *Private collection. Photo: Jay Kupjack. Copyright Kupjack Studios.*

Introduction

While studying items of silver for other book projects, small articles, some of which were from unknown sources and unknown uses, came to light. Curio cabinets became crowded with large articles, especially those of silverplate purchased specifically for illustration of a particular style or pattern. Unusual and odd pieces attracted attention, especially many small articles of unknown use which begged to be identified.

The silver curios included within these pages represent pieces that can be found in the marketplace at reasonable prices today. We have deliberately avoided the inclusion of those items far beyond the means of the average collector.

Following disastrous maneuvers in the silver market in the 1980s which elevated the price of silver temporarily, many small items turned up and were not destroyed simply because they were too small to be worth melting down for their value as bullion. The fascination in these unusual small objects was an important element in their preservation.

What makes a curio?

We may travel miles to look in awe at the tremendous size of elephants in the zoo, but scarcely anyone feels an urge to take one home. But let an adult or any normal child see a small and beautifully carved ivory elephant figure and each automatically reaches out to possess the item of curiosity. Miniature furniture, tiny silver goblets, and other small objects bring the same reaction—the urge to reach out and possess. We want to own it, to have it with us always, to make it a part of our everyday lives. This is a curio.

Some people will be surprised to learn that items of gold were made in large quantities long before those of silver. Silver is almost never found in nuggets, as is gold. Most of the silver found today is the by-product of mining for lead, copper, zinc or gold. Because silver is subject to corrosion, it is rare that really old pieces of silver are found.

Silver manufacturing begins

The manufacture of silverware began in America about 1842. Prior to that time there were no real factories in America and almost all silver was custom made with the buyer dealing directly with the silversmith. Not until the discovery of the Comstock Lode in Nevada about 1870 were large quantities of silver available at lower cost. With the rise of manufacturing goods, a new relationship developed from manufacturer to wholesaler to retailer to customer. Greater availability and lower prices were important developments in the production of the silver articles we now consider "collectible."

Museums around the world house treasures of the ages, and that is appropriate, but as museum collections grow there are fewer old originals available for private ownership. While one may be distressed at the reproduction of early designs that are intended to deceive, some reproductions are beautifully crafted in tribute to the originals and are properly marked by their actual makers. These may become the treasures of the future and be collectible themselves.

Hanau

As older silver articles have disappeared from the antique markets, silversmiths in various countries during the nineteenth century set up shops to fill the persistent demand. Among the most successful were the silversmiths of Hanau, in present-day Germany. Thought by some to be creators only of cheap, mass produced items, they actually were for many years important manufacturers specialized in highly ornate, decorative, and handmade silver items. Hanau silversmiths produced enormous numbers of marriage or wager cups, often exact copies of older originals.

From the mid-nineteenth through the early twentieth century, the silversmiths of Hanau produced silver marked with "fantasy marks." Mark stamping as practiced in Hanau would have been completely illegal in France or England, or for that matter in any German city where a guild supervised the marking. Hanau had a long tradition as a free trade city and silver production was a business proposition rather than being dependent on the grant of master status by a goldsmiths' guild or corporation. Stamping of silver wares by wardens was discontinued in Hanau by the end of the eighteenth century, and from 1874 the Hanau town mark was discontinued.

As knowledge of these pieces grows, Hanau silver is apt to become a new specialized area of interest for collectors.

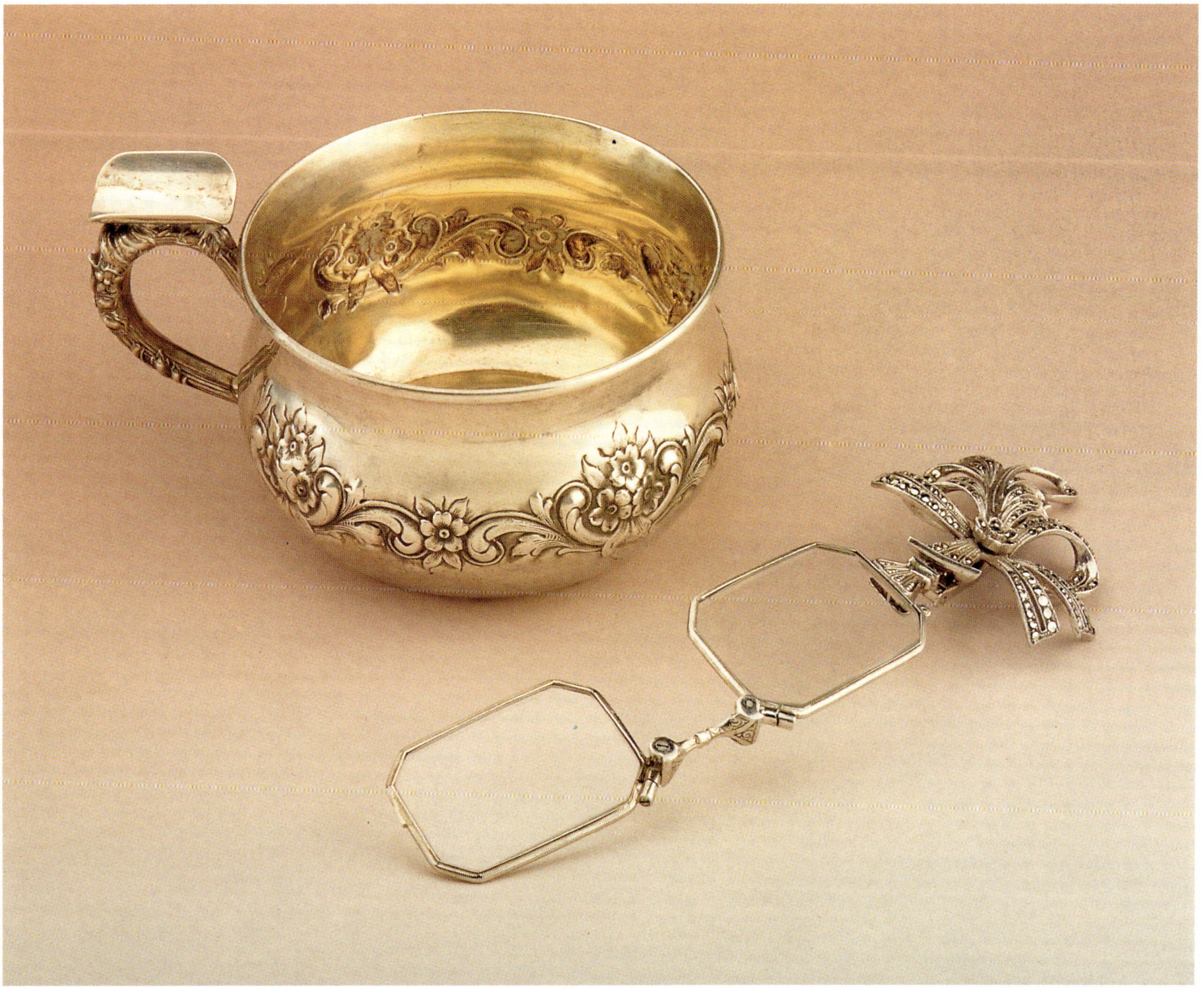

Shaving cup. Sterling with trademark of Webster Co. of North Attleboro, A.A. and 3" diameter. $225. Lorgnette/ menu reader/ pin. When the lady needs her glasses, she opens the pin at her neckline and out comes the lorgnette. Pin is silver and marcasite, no maker's mark, measures 6" extended. *Collection of Antonia Moore. Photo: Bruce Waters.* $215.

Chapter 1. Silver Curios for use...
...in the Entrance Hall

The entrance hall was the first place the visitor saw; therefore, it was impressively furnished, decorated, and lighted. Its purpose was to set the tone of the house and inform the visitor of the owner's status in the community.

In the Middle Ages and well into the sixteenth century, the hall in European noble houses was a center of all activities, an early version of the "family room." It was the meeting place for all who lived in or visited the house. It was here, twice a day, at noon and at early evening, that the head of the house and his family would meet together. According to the household, the family included not only those of blood kinship but also those who worked at the house. Here most meals were served on small tables which were moved about and set up where needed, perhaps near the fireplace in cold weather or near an open window when the weather was warm. Large furniture used for dining was not kept in position in the center of the room. Instead, wooden boards were laid across a trestle frame which was stored nearby when not in use. Not until the third quarter of the eighteenth century did dining tables about the size of present-day dining tables begin to appear.

Hall furnishings by the late nineteenth century might include a tall-case clock. Hat racks and a "hall tree" with a mirror and equipment for hanging gentlemen's hats were essential for the Victorian hall. Umbrella stands took care of umbrellas for those who ventured out in inclement weather. A seat, bench or chair were necessary for those who had to remove boots and a card receiver was always present.

Fresh flowers often lent a cheerful note in vases as did a photograph or two of family members in silver frames. One of the light and feathery type of ferns gave a softening effect.

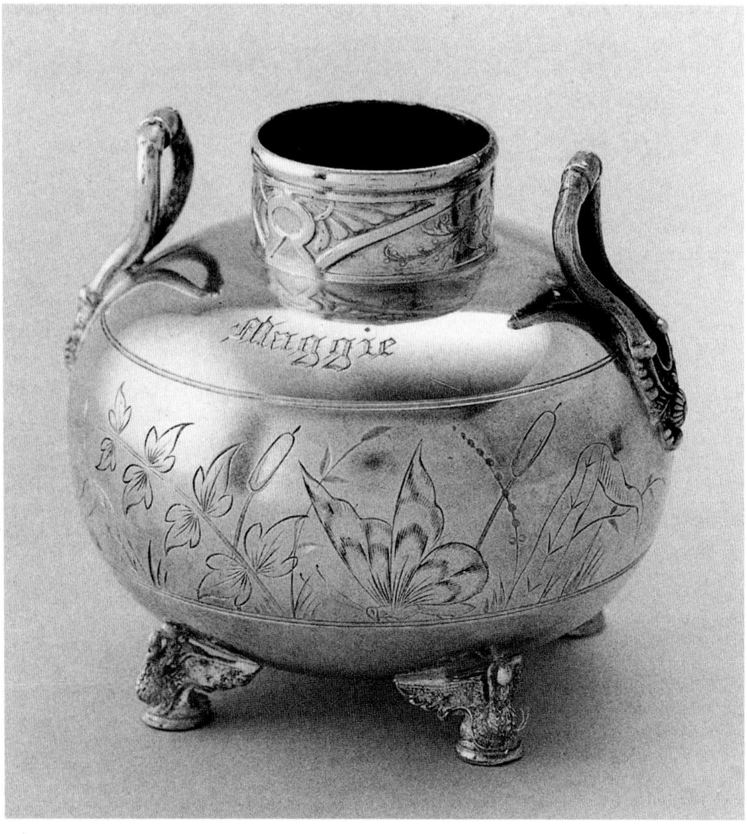

Silverplate bud vase with foot, swans under the round bowl, engraved Maggie. 3-1/2". Maker: Wilcox Silverplate Co., Meriden, CT. 1884. Suitable for bunches of violets, pansies or lily-of-the-valley. *Photo: H Ivan Rainwater.* $85.

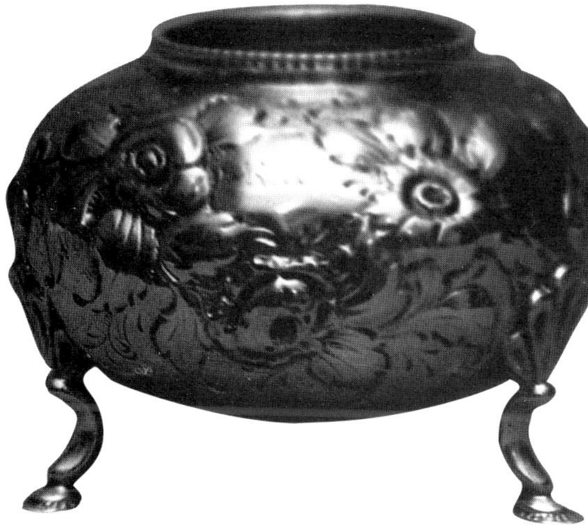

Sterling bud vase, monogrammed. Made by S. Kirk & Son Co., 1900. *Photo: H Ivan Rainwater.* $80.

Fern dish

A fern dish in silverplate, which sometimes was offered as a premium to encourage sales, might very well have been placed in the hall and been filled with growing plants. This particular premium item was offered on an eight-page list in 1903 by the Herbene Pharmacal Company of New York City. The list of premiums included everything from cake baskets to a set of nutpicks and nut cracker.

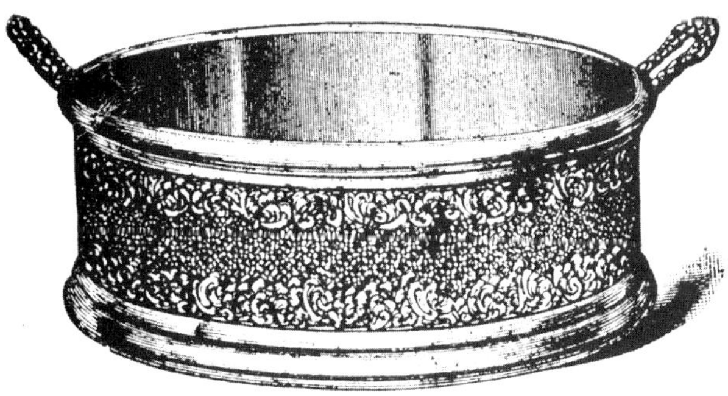

No. 23.—Fern Dish.

Fern dish, 7". Silverplate from premium list of Herbene Pharmacal Co., New York City, 1903. $45

Calling card cases

Throughout the nineteenth century engraved calling or visiting cards were essential for ladies on social occasions. Gentlemen carried business cards, as well.

American silversmiths were making card cases of silver by the 1850s. Some were quite elaborate and had chains attached for ease in carrying. Ladies' cases measured about four inches by three inches, small enough to fit in a purse or carried by its own chain. Ladies' cases were often ornate, bearing repoussé designs with high relief and intricate motifs. Some were fitted with compartments for stamps and tiny pencils and *aide memories*.

Gentlemen's cases were slimmer and smaller in size. They were plainer with no raised decoration to catch on pockets. Curved ones were made for gentlemen and these often had no lid. (See example engraved C.C.G./1900.) Cards just slipped into the card case.

Calling cards for social use have not disappeared entirely but today's emphasis is on business cards which are usually carried in plastic cases.

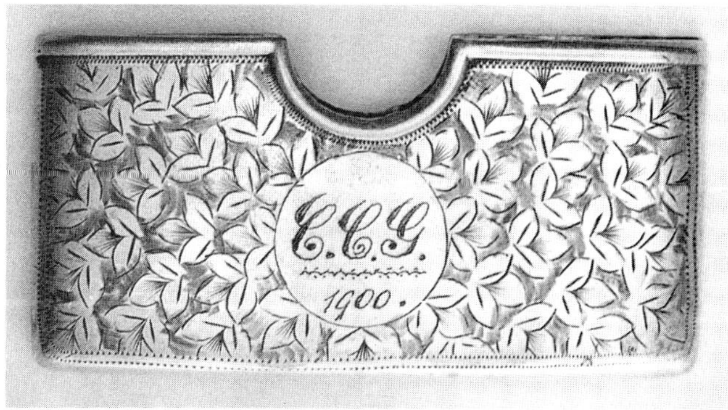

Gentlemen's curved calling card case. 3" by 1-1/2". The curve of this gentleman's case was made to fit into waistcoat pockets. *Photo: H Ivan Rainwater.* $30-120.

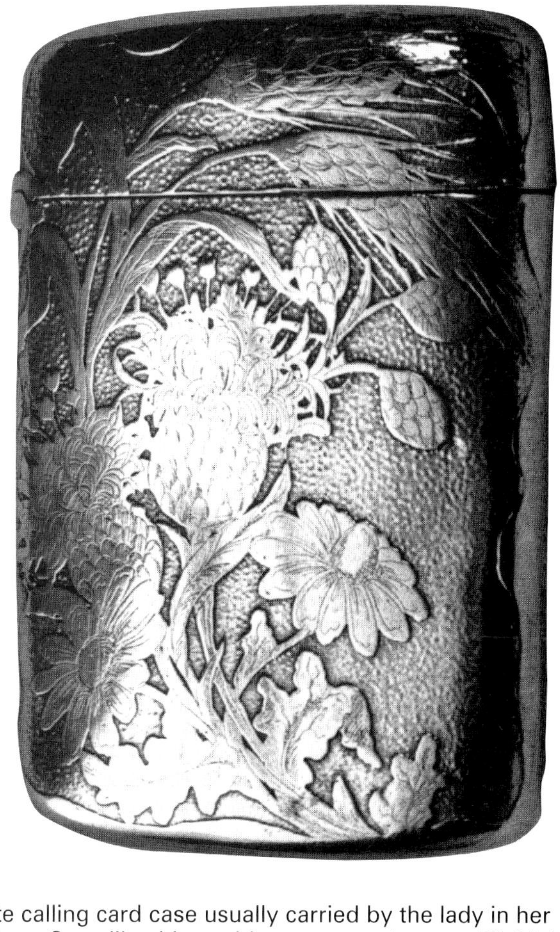

Ornate calling card case usually carried by the lady in her handbag. Ones like this could measure as large as 5". Maker: Geo. W. Shiebler & Company, 1900. *Photo: Courtesy of Silver Magazine Archives.* $30-120.

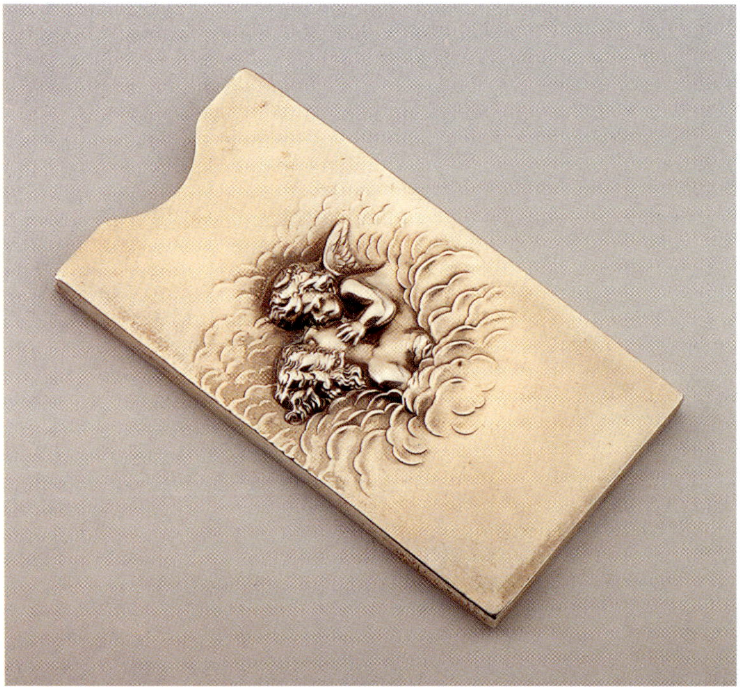

Silver calling card case marked by Unger Bros. Case measures 3-1/8" by 1-5/8". *Collection of Antonia Moore. Photo: Bruce Waters.* $30-120.

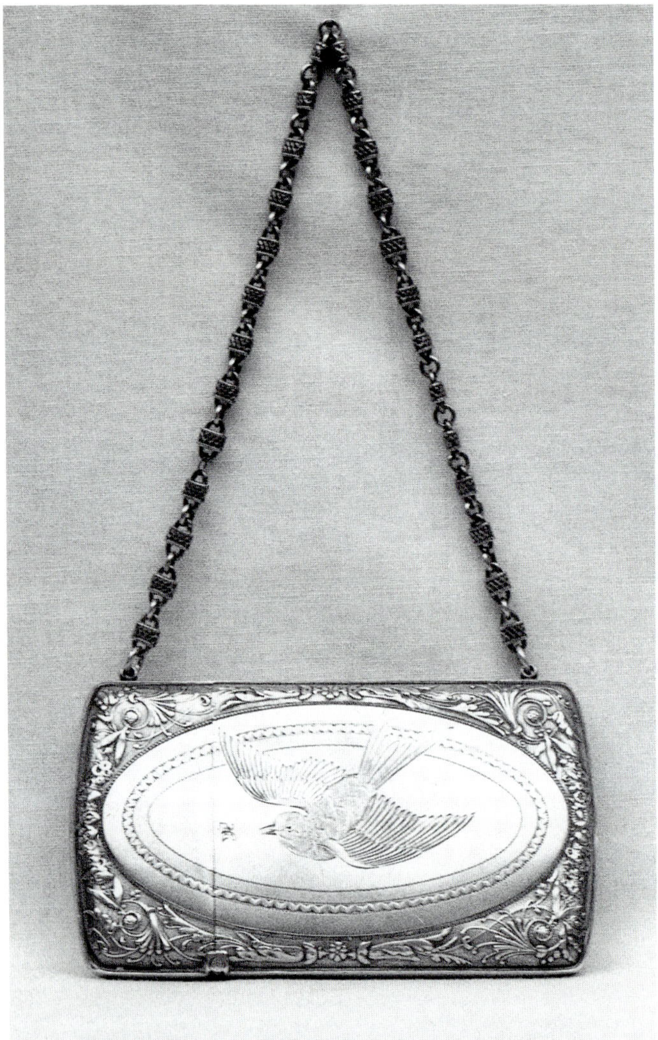

Ladies' card case on a chain, Bird motif. Unmarked. *Photo: Courtesy of Silver Magazine Archives.* $30-120.

Card receivers

The custom of leaving calling or visiting cards is one about three centuries old. During Victorian days and until World War One, the making of social calls was bound by many rules. It was the duty of the women of each household to make visits to friends to express greetings, condolence, congratulations, or to visit the sick. When making such calls, the ladies left both their husband's name cards and cards with their own name embossed.

Formal calls which included leaving name cards are seldom made today as society has become less formal. In only a few ultra-conservative communities are formal calls expected, and few are the hostesses who let it be known that they are "at home" to callers on a certain day of the week by having that day engraved on the lower left side of their personal calling cards.

To receive the calling cards of visitors, small silver trays known as card receivers were available, those in

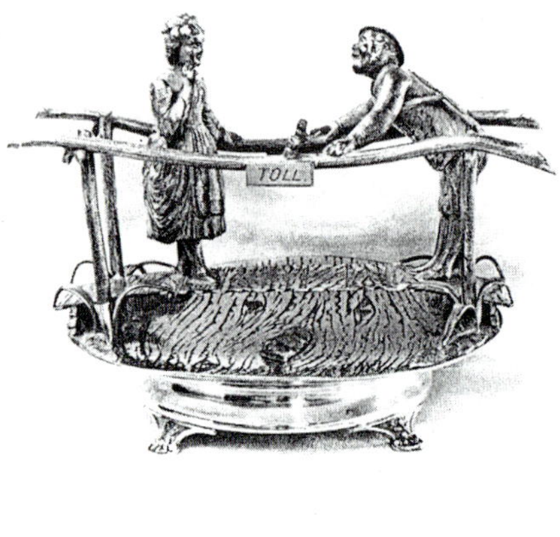

Silverplate card receiver, Middleton Plate Co. The "toll" was a kiss for the soldier guarding the bridge. *Private Collection. Photo: Diana Cramer. Courtesy of Silver Magazine Archives.* $60.

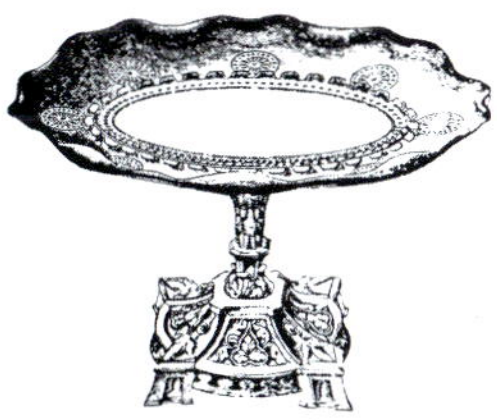

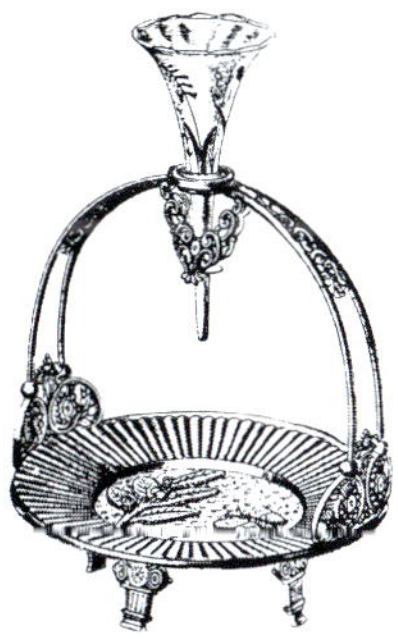

Card Receivers. Shown here are two silverplate receivers. Top: mirrored center. Bottom: bud vase for a single flower above cards. Meriden Britannia Co. catalogue, 1886. $65.

sterling silver from silversmiths the like of Tiffany and Company of New York and other fine retail stores, and in silverplate by manufacturers such as Meriden Britannia Company. Early card receivers were simple in design, consisting of a small tray about six inches in diameter mounted on a pedestal. Ornaments on card receivers were numerous and consisted of butterflies, other insects, owls, elephants, children and cherubs, swans, frogs, peacocks, storks, fruit, squirrels, cats, dogs, flowers, foliage in fantastic arrangements, and many others.

Card receivers were made by many manufacturers for a period of more than forty years. They are scarce today.

Cane and umbrella handles

When canes and walking sticks were in their heyday, a gentleman enjoyed such when his walking stick had a silver handle. Said gentlemen never went out for a walk without either that silver-handled cane, or, in bad weather, with a silver-handled umbrella.

The earliest umbrella went back to the seventeenth century when King Louis XIII of France used one to protect himself from the rays of the sun. Not until the middle of the nineteenth century did the umbrella become the fluted steel rib style which is still in use as protection from bad weather.

Both the cane and the umbrella were made with silver handles and many of these handles are found today on the antique market. Some are quite plain in design; others are decorated with hunting scenes, floral motifs and figural ones such as a dog's head or a prancing horse.

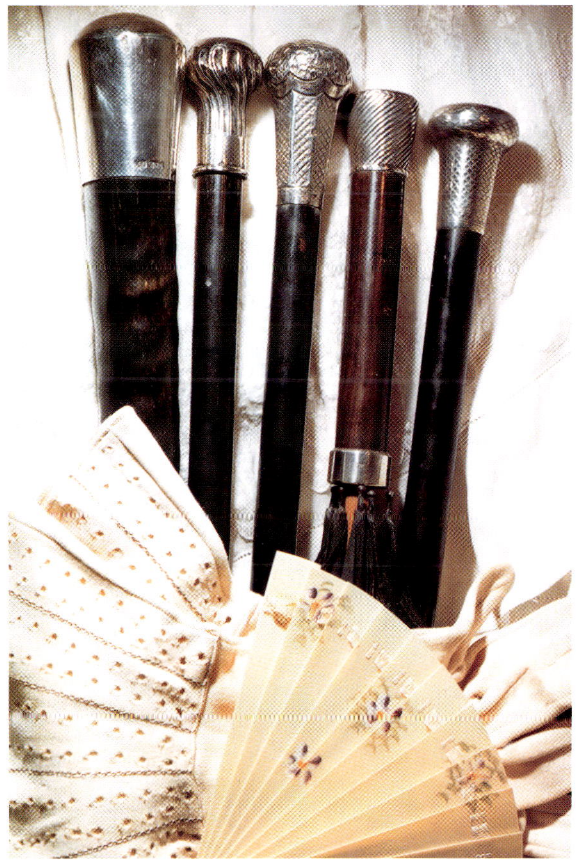

Four silver knob walking sticks and one umbrella handle. Left to right: English, 1911; Dutch, 1906-1953; English 1922; Silver umbrella cap, 1906; English walking stick, 1923. *Collection and photo: Anne Jansen.* $50 each.

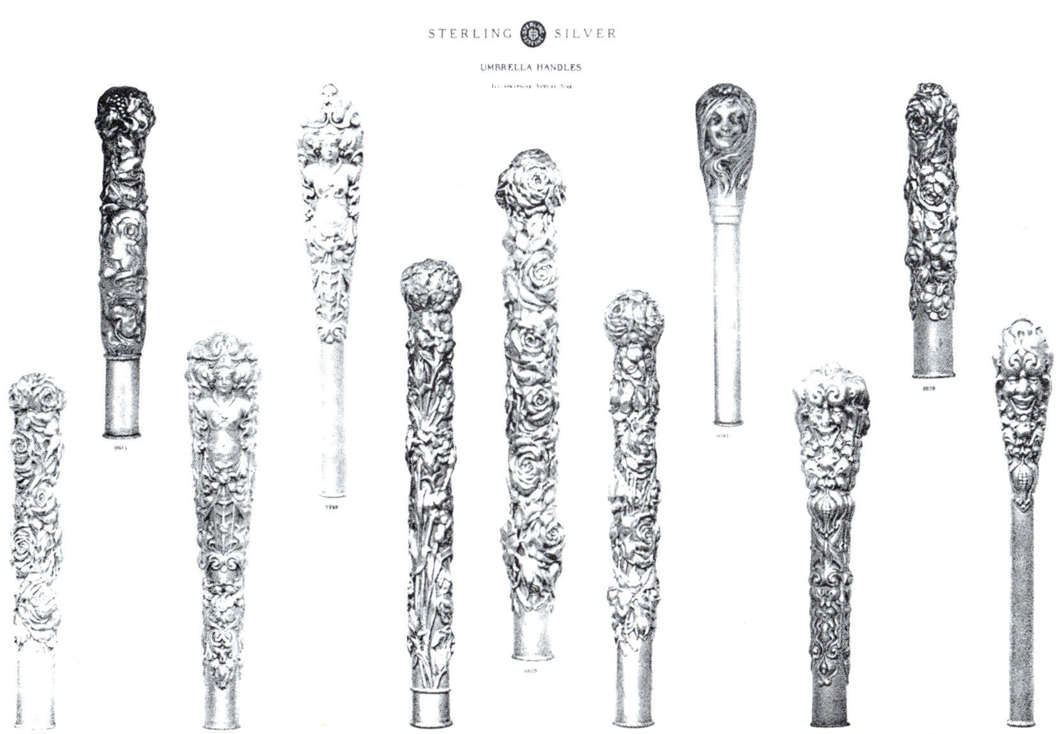

Left:
Umbrella handles made for the gentleman in a variety of designs. Unger Brothers catalogue, 1904. $75 each.

Chapter 2. Silver Curios for use...
...by Ladies

Most beautiful articles of silver have no gender connections, being regarded as the possessions of all in the household. Some appear to us as more masculine and others as definitely feminine. There are many articles of silver which are exclusively feminine, and it is with these that we are now concerned.

Numerically, dresser accessories and dresser sets lead the group in numbers. The ladies' items include glove stretchers, glove darners, hair brushes in three sizes, puff boxes, mirrors, soap boxes, nail polishers, nail files, manicure scissors, ladies combs, buttonhooks, glove hooks, shoe horns, whisk brooms, velvet brushes, infant brushes and more. All of these were included in old catalogues such as Daniel Low, Unger Bros., Gorham Mfg. Co., Meriden Britannia Company, and others. The Forbes Silver Company offered 24 designs of toilet ware in their 1914 catalogue. In 1915 the American Silverplate Company included colored porcelain miniatures to decorate their three-piece sets of combs, brush and mirror. Unger Bros., offered many sterling patterns in toilet ware as matched dresser sets.

Sweetheart Box description.

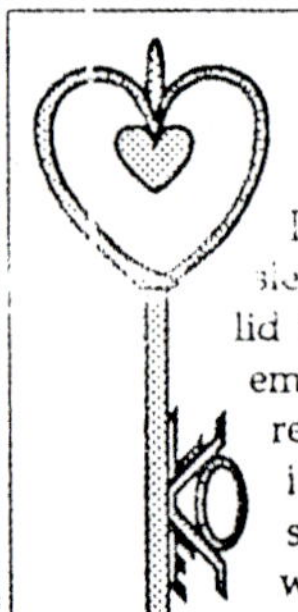

Sweetheart Box

The Sweetheart Box is a treasure chest of romance. Its basic design reflects the style of Art Nouveau; a slender profile, flowing curves and graceful shapes. The lid is more than cover. Its top surface is rippling with the emotion generated by two tiny hearts. The underside reveals a rose, symbolic of womanhood and ivy, longevity. The floor of the box shimmers with delicate flowers, soft breezes and doves. It is a fanciful backdrop for that wonderful euphoric sensation which overrides reason in early courtship. The bottom of the box is primal. It is laced with anatomical motifs which work their way up the back and mesh symbolically with the lid. Nestled within is a delicate key with concentric hearts for a crown and LOVE spelled in its teeth. Used properly, it can open most any heart. The Sweetheart Box is layered in sentiment and depicts the many facets of being in love.

R I C C I O

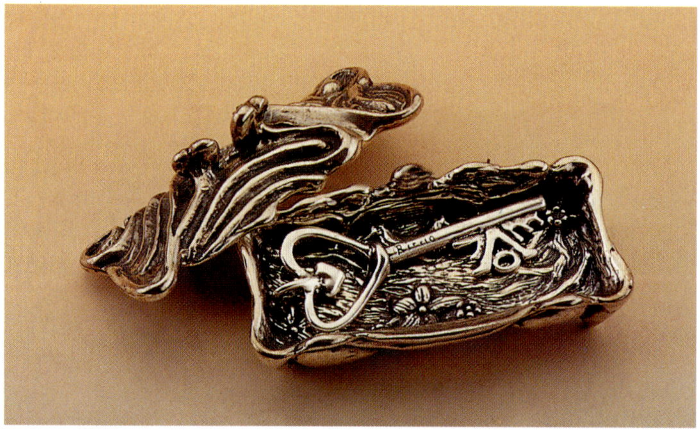

Sweetheart Box with interior key. Marked Riccio, sterling, 1988. Measures 2". *Collection of Antonia Moore. Photo: Bruce Waters.* $250.

Toilet sets were among the highly popular items which graced the feminine boudoir. Their size puts most of them beyond the scope of this book. They varied from simple, one-bottle stands holding a two ounce bottle to elaborate ones with bottles for cologne, puff box, mirror and caryatid candelabra holding six candles. Others had three bottles and a vase to match.

It is the glass vases and the glass puff or powder which attract collectors today. Decorative motifs on the glass are as varied as the designs on the silver stands. Floral designs are perhaps the most numerous but children at play, butterflies, birds and animals were also used. Great numbers of these delightful accessories were illustrated in catalogues from about 1877 until 1890. Fewer styles appeared during the 1890s and by 1900 had virtually disappeared.

Victorians loved boxes. They were a favorite for gifts. They were designed to hold gloves, sweets, handkerchiefs, jewelry, "beauty patches," cards, stamps, pins and many other things. All well-appointed ladies' dressers had at least a glove box, handkerchief box and jewel box. Highly sought among these are the ones with glass inserts and are described in old catalogues as "Rich Decorated Malachite Glass."

Victorian jewelry was plentiful, which meant that jewelry boxes were required by the ladies. Many of these were rectangular, square or round and were embossed with designs of flowers, tendrils, acanthus leaves and most desirable, scantily clad women with flowing robes and hair. Some novelty jewelry boxes were made in fanciful shapes. One novelty jewelry box was made by the Wilcox Silver Plate Co., about 1884 in the form of a hollow sphere on which Cupid raises and lowers the lid by means of a weight attached to a silverplated chain.

Dresser sets in Art Nouveau style were especially popular with the ladies when they were new and that popularity has not ceased. The female form with swirling draperies and flowing hair was one of the dominant motifs. A number of catalogues of the 1880s to c.1910 illustrated Art Nouveau dresser articles with "flowery" names like "The Birth of the Rose." This flower was difficult to adapt to the requirements of Art Nouveau because the roses' stiff stems posed a real problem. But this difficulty was overcome and the rose was incorporated into many designs by the use of asymmetrical curves which create the feeling of constant movement.

Pin trays in Art Nouveau were made in numerous designs and often with combs and nail files, polisher, cuticle knife, scissors and lotion jars to match.

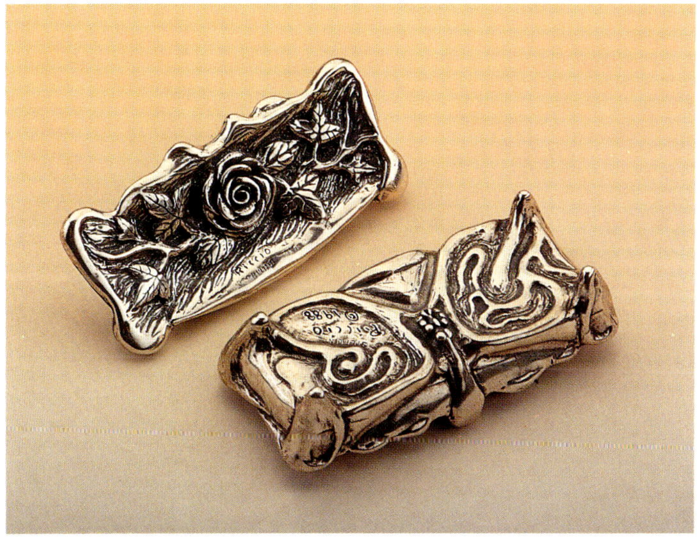

Top and bottom of a Sweetheart Box. Marked Riccio, sterling, 1988. Measures 2". *Collection of Antonia Moore. Photo: Bruce Waters.* $250.

Fans

Victorians had ways of expressing their thoughts and desires without words, but with the subtle flutter of a fan.

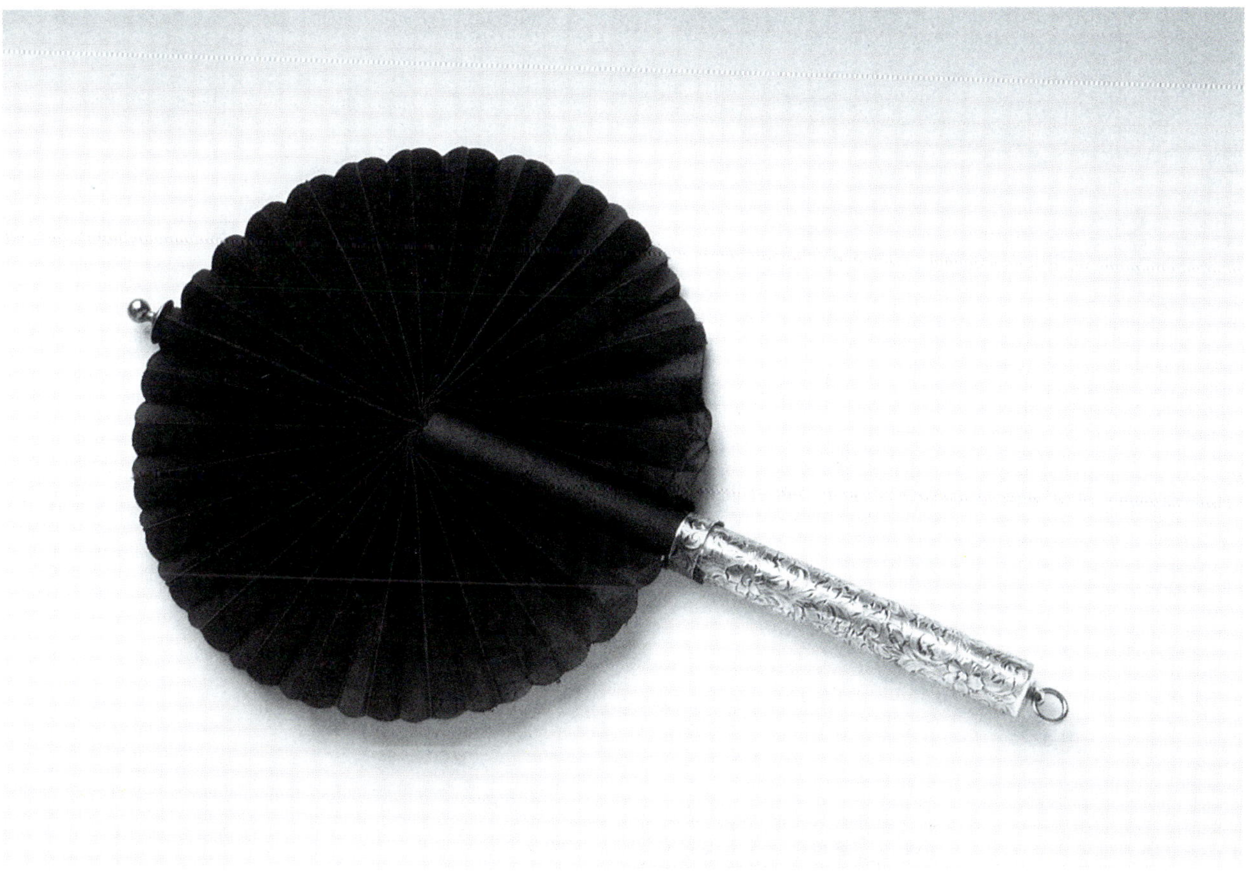

A folding silk fan with sterling handle. When the knob is pushed, the fan folds back into the silver tube. Maker: Battin & Co. Circa 1890-1900. Open, the fan measures 11". *Collection of Janet Zapata. Photo: Richard Goodbody.* $968.

Perfumers

As far back as Cleopatra in ancient Egypt, ladies have used a fresh fragrance to make themselves feel alluring. Such scents could be gathered from flowers like the tuberose, jasmine or violet.

Ladies of the nineteenth century kept *their* favorite scents of lavender or rose in a bottle on their dressing table. From this fairly unadorned glass, the perfumer for her purse could be filled by means of a perfume funnel.

Decorative perfume bottles often had a silver top over cut glass with a stopper to be used as an applicator. The scent bottle for the purse usually had an applicator so that the lady could freshen herself while away from home.

Special Lalique bottles were commissioned by Coty and the still famous Chanel No. 5 appeared on the perfume market early in the twentieth century. Earlier perfumers of cut glass with silver tops are much sought.

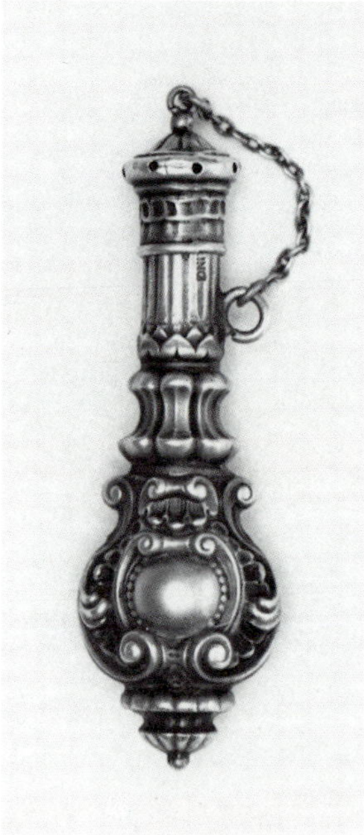

Perfumer with chain for attaching to chatelaine. Marked: Fleur-de-lis (mark in use by 1892) for William B. Kerr Co. Length 2-3/4". *Private Collection. Photo: H Ivan Rainwater.* $175.

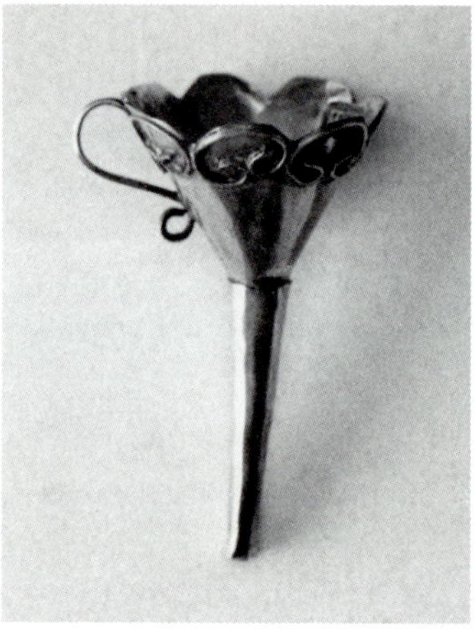

Perfume funnel used for transferring perfume to smaller container. Marked JHH. 20th century. *Private Collection. Photo: H Ivan Rainwater.* $160.

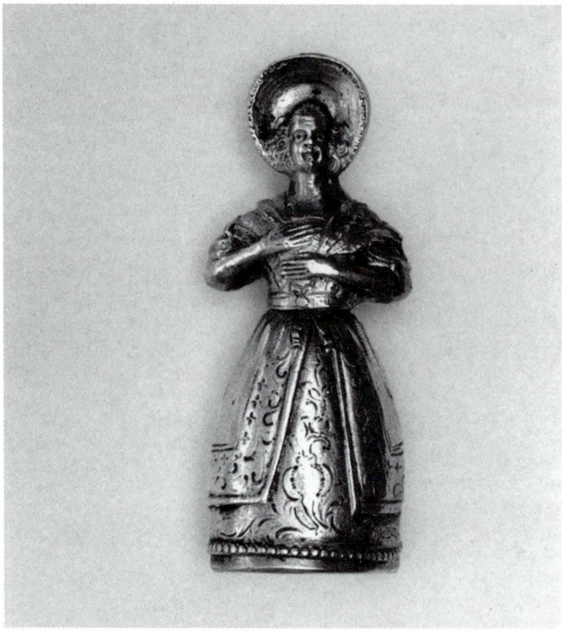

Perfumer in the form of a young girl wearing bonnet and dress with over-skirt and shawl. Marked: Crown R/800. Comes apart at waist. Length: 2-13/16". *Private Collection. Photo: H Ivan Rainwater.* $250.

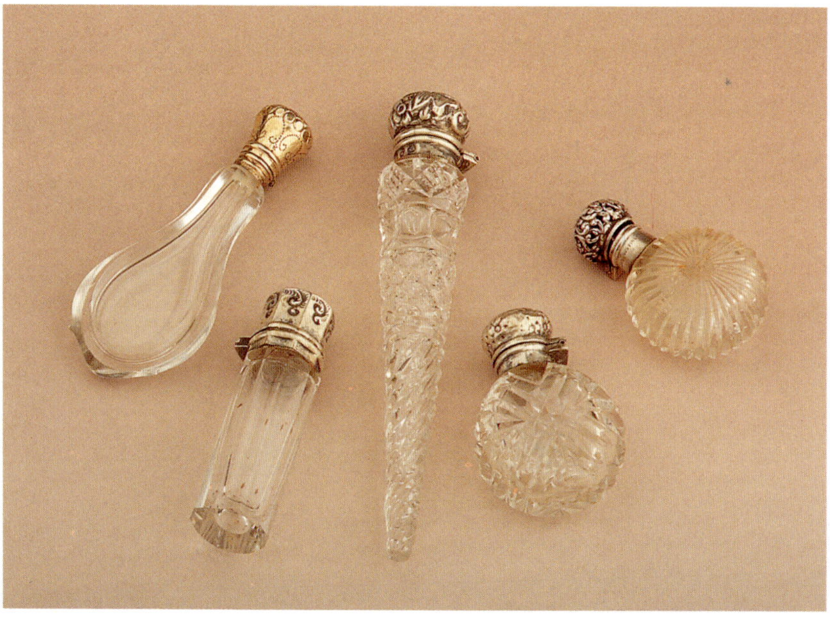

Silver topped perfume bottles. From left to right: Unusual shaped glass bottle. Silver top has no marks. 3-1/2" tall.
Sterling top with panels. 2-1/2 tall.
Made by Gorham Co. From sterling top to bottom measures 4-5/8".
Sterling mark 925 Fine plus a poorly stamped unreadable mark.
Sterling plus 925/1000 Fine. 2". *Collection of Antonia Moore. Photo: Bruce Waters.* $95-350.

Silver topped jars

"Chilly Cupids" is the name given to a design of silver in the 1901 catalogue of Daniel Low & Co. On page N76, the catalogue called it "the most unique of this season's production in sterling silver."

Both Unger Bros. and Low featured the same design. Unger Bros. named their design *Love's Dream* in their 1904 catalogue. In the 1901 Daniel Low catalogue, the same design is called *Love's Awakening.*

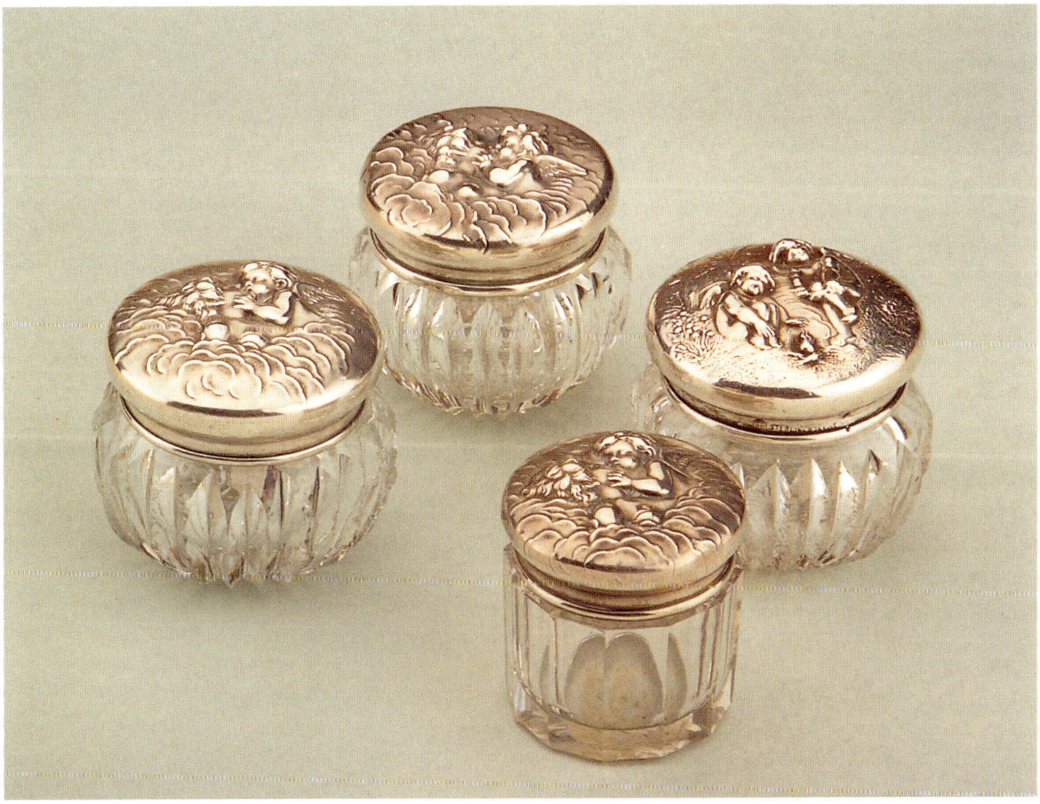

Four marked by Unger Brothers: three of the same pattern called Love's Dream in the Unger Brothers 1904 catalogue and also called Love's Awakening in the Daniel Low catalogue of 1901 One of the Chilly Cupid design. Diameters: 1-1/4" to 1-3/4". *Collection of Antonia Moore. Photo: Bruce Waters.*

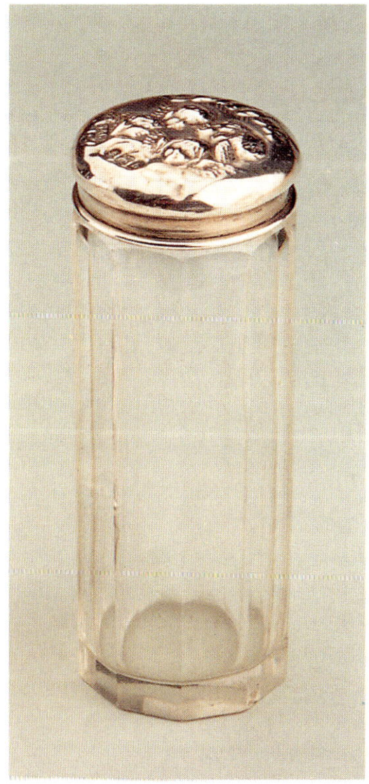

Jar used on a lady's dresser marked S & Co., possibly Spurrier & Co. of Birmingham, 1907, England. Height: 3-1/4". *Collection of Antonia Moore. Photo: Bruce Waters.* $150.

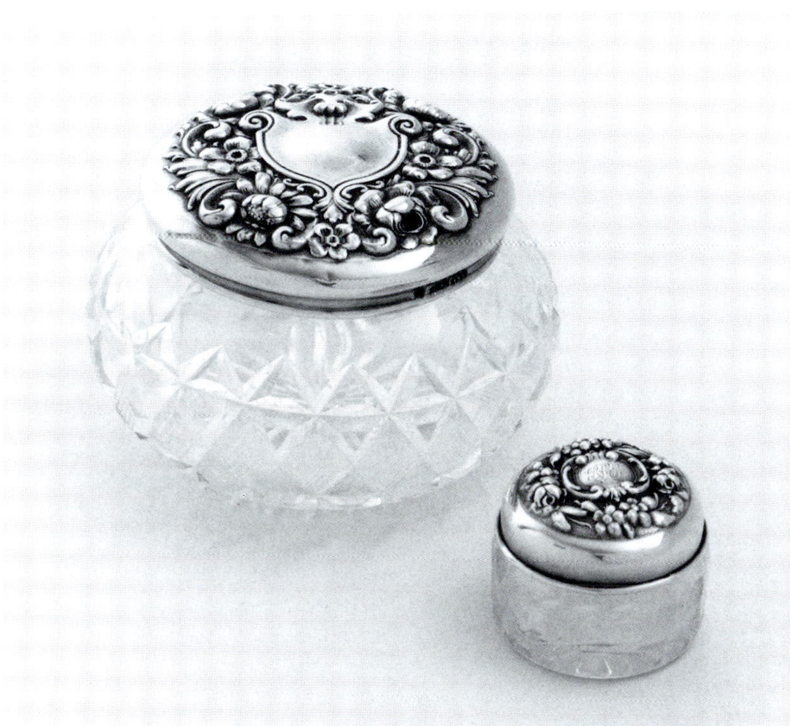

Left: cut glass powder jar marked Cloverleaf (Howard Sterling) STERLING 2533. Right: Vaseline or cream jar marked STIEFF STERLING. c.1900. *Photo: David Arky.*

Dresser trays

Dresser trays in both silver and silverplate were used by fashionable ladies of the Victorian era. They were sometimes called trinket trays, hairpin trays, pin trays, toilet trays, comb and brush trays and toothbrush trays.

Samuel Kirk & Son Co., formerly of Baltimore, Maryland, featured three pin trays in sterling in their 1914 catalogue. These ranged from 5-1/2" to 9" long and had ornate floral designs around the plain bottom of the trays. It was on the plain silver that the lady's monogram would have been added.

A hairpin tray offered in the Daniel Low catalogue of 1901 measured 2" by 5" and sold for $5.00. This oval tray had an ornate open-work edge. Simpler silver trays could be purchased for $1.50.

In the James W. Tufts catalogue of 1903, the largest silverplate dresser tray measured 12" long and cost $4.25.

The dresser tray was a frequent gift from a gentleman to his lady and was cherished by that lady for its sentiment and its usefulness.

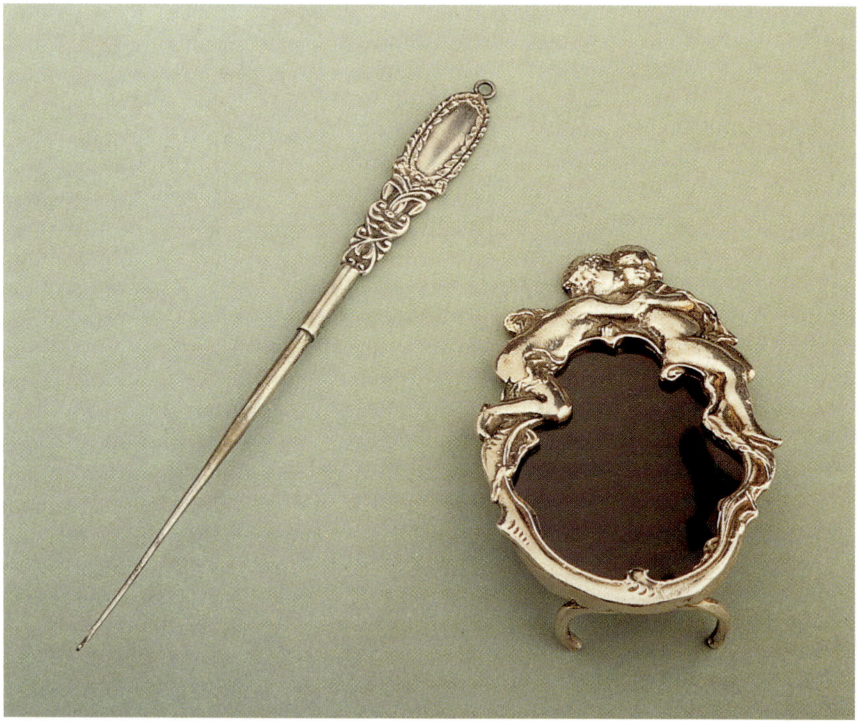

Silver crochet hook. Sterling. Measures 5" from hook to handle.
Silver picture frame for a lady's dressing table. Measures 1-7/8" by 2-7/8".
Collection of Antonia Moore. Photo: Bruce Waters. $50.

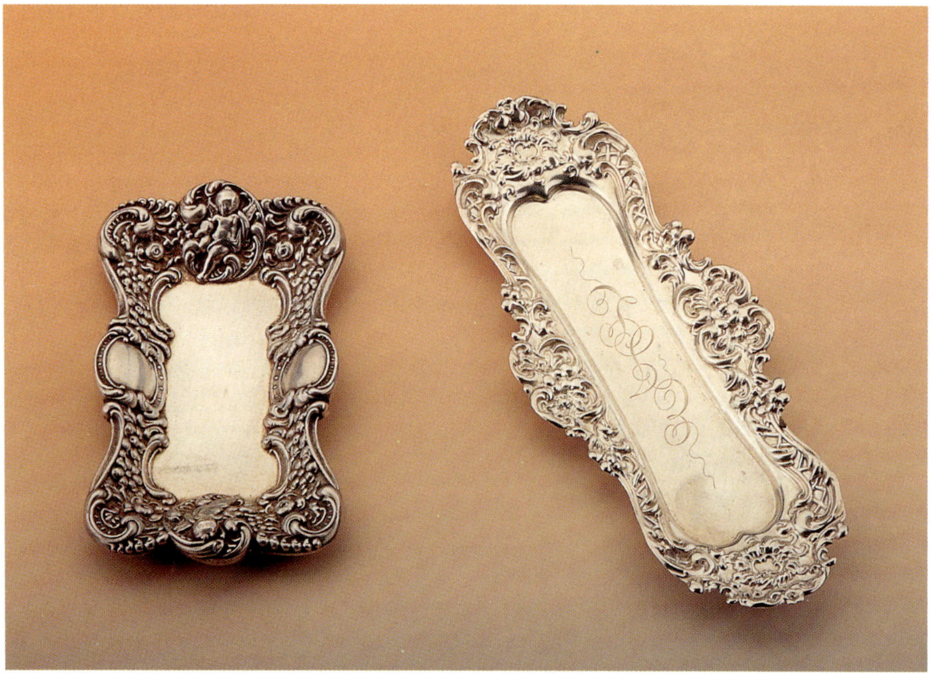

Two dresser trays. Left: Marked Unger Bros. Measures 4-9/16". Right: monogrammed pin tray with letters E J L, marked Whiting Sterling 5032 925/1000 Fine. 6-7/8".
Collection of Antonia Moore. Photo: Bruce Waters. $140-165.

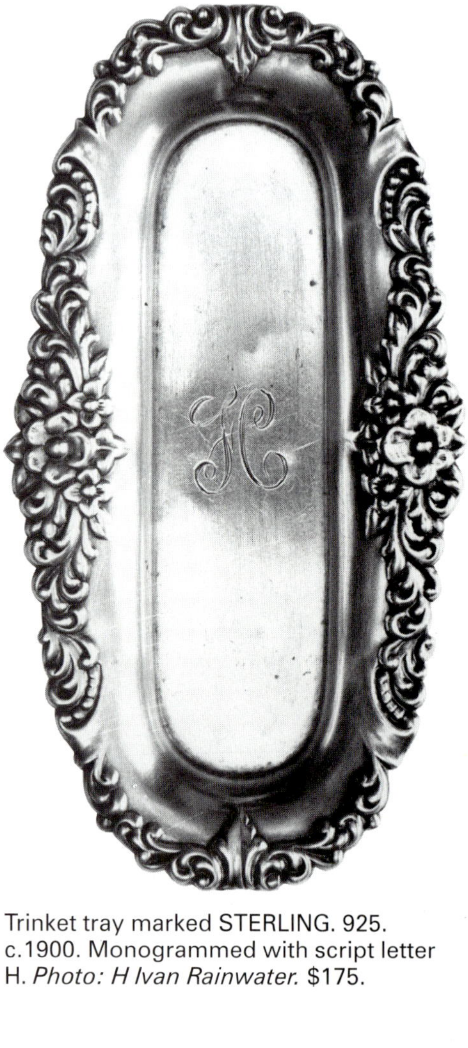

Trinket tray marked STERLING. 925. c.1900. Monogrammed with script letter H. *Photo: H Ivan Rainwater.* $175.

Curling tongs or irons

To dress a lady's hair properly toward the end of the nineteenth century, a curling set was indispensable. This set included hot curling tongs plus a means of heating them, usually the flames of a spirit stove. If the tongs were too hot, the lady might suffer a burn on her scalp or, even worse, the loss of some hair.

Many curling tongs had silver handles and were included in matched dresser sets. Such a set included ten pieces in the 1880 *Blue Book* by Tiffany & Co. In 1901, the Daniel Low catalogue offered curling tongs with silver handles for as little as $.75 to as much as $2.75 for folding tongs. The latter were convenient to carry and use when the lady traveled.

Mirrors

There can be no doubt that man first saw his own image in a quiet pool in the forest or a slow moving backwater of a small stream.

"The term 'looking glass' was the common name for a 'mirror' during the 18th and early 19th centuries, but the words were considered synonymous. By 1860, the word 'mirror' was much more commonly used. In the early 1800s, some people used 'mirror' to refer to convex or concave glass, and 'looking glass' for flat plates of reflective glass." (*Kovel's on Antiques and Collectibles*, Vol. 24, No. 12, August 1998). Used by permission.

Adornment and beautifying oneself have always been of great importance. In very early times, ladies especially spent hours before their mirrors taking great care of their appearance. People of means provided the ladies of the household with elaborate dresser sets, some sets containing as many as 30 different pieces. Among them would be mirror, ewer and basin (though less attention was given to cleanliness then than now), whisk, vases of various sizes, candlesticks of several sizes, snuffer and snuffer tray, covered jars in different sizes, pincushion, pin box, hairpin box, tooth powder box, clothes brush, hair brushes, combs, sponges, sponge box, powder box and scent bottles.

Of all these pieces, the mirror was of primary importance. So much so, that it was often the style and decoration of the mirror that determined the style and decoration of the entire boudoir.

The reflective area of mirrors of antiquity (prior to c.1200) would have been of metal. It was with the hand-mirror of late Victorian days that the silversmiths produced some of the finest expressions of Art Nouveau style. The Gorham Company was among the leaders, especially with their Martelé line. All were completely handmade with free-flowing lines characterized by an elegant interplay of undulating curves. Though these designs were fanciful, they were based on nature. It was nature as seen and expressed by the individual artist.

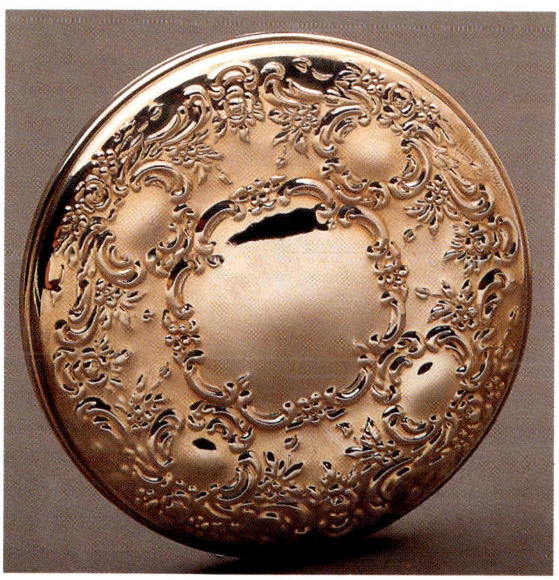

Sterling mirror marked Towle trademark/STERLING. Diameter: 3-1/4". Towle advertising reads "Beauty Marks/Exquisite Cosmetic Accessories." *Photo: Bruce Waters.* $90+.

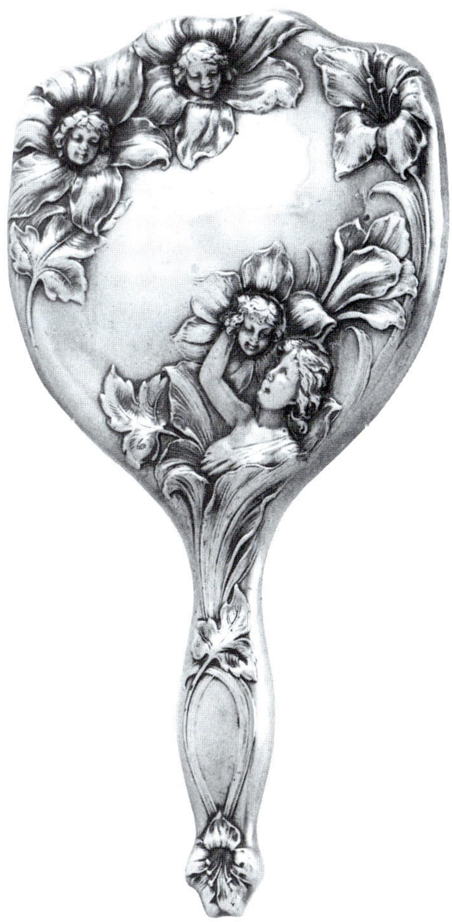

Art Nouveau mirror from a lady's dressing table set. No marks, measures 10-1/2" from top to bottom of handle, c. 1895-1910. *Privately owned. Photo: David Arky.*

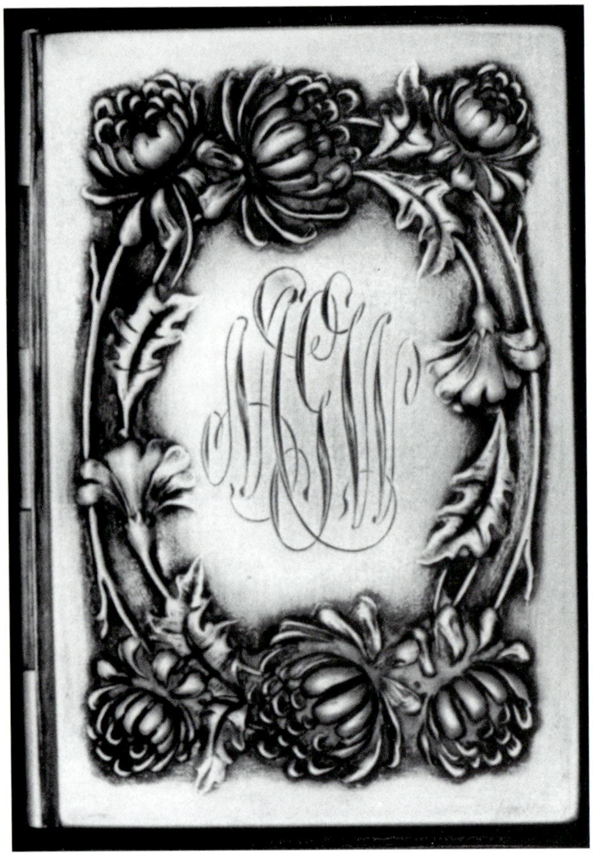

Monogrammed lady's silver notebook with ivory pages. *Photo: H Ivan Rainwater.* $75.

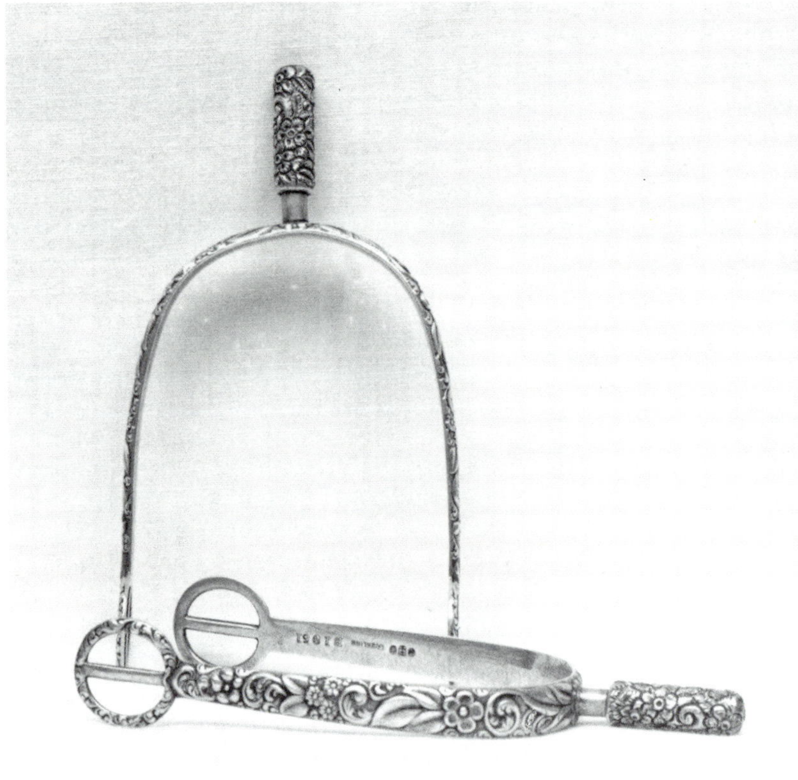

Ladies' sterling spurs spring loaded to conceal a silver spike, made by Gorham, stamped B1951, missing leather straps, 4-1/4" long, 2-3/8" wide, c.1900. *Photo: Courtesy of Silver Magazine Archives.* $300.

Glove stretchers

Are you old enough to remember when we all wore white kid gloves? One washed them carefully in Ivory soap and stretched them on glove stretchers. Glove stretchers were popular beginning c. 1880. Their popularity continued until World War I when many silver items were no longer made.

Each finger of the tight-fitting kid gloves would be pulled over the bird's beak. Pressing the large feather caused the beak to expand and stretch the wet kid glove. If allowed to dry without stretching, the kid gloves became stiff and shrunken. Gorham and Tiffany were among the many companies which made glove stretchers, some in elaborate designs. Fruit, flowers and fern designs were often used.

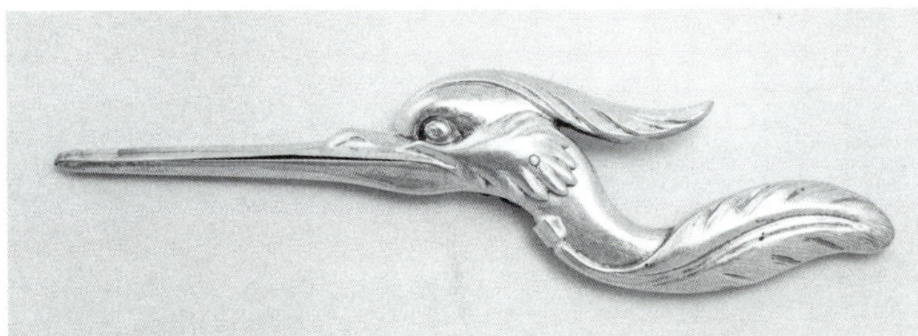

Silver glove stretcher, no marks. Length 6-3/8". *Private Collection. Photo: H Ivan Rainwater*. $90.

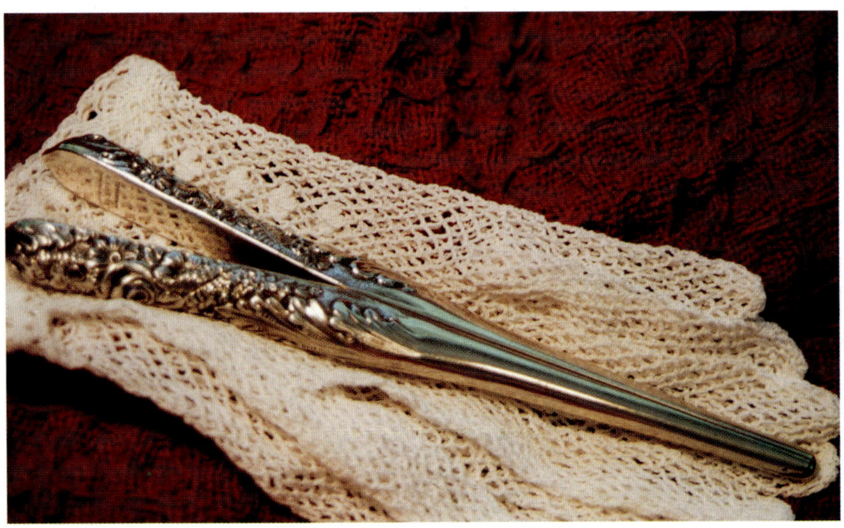

Glove stretcher marked 8261M6963/ Tiffany & Co. / Sterling Silver. 7-1/2" long. *Collection and photo: Mabel Rogers.* $120.

Glove hook

Many dressy gloves were closed with tiny buttons. For this, the lady used a glove hook to pull the button through the buttonhole. The glove hook was a small version of the buttonhook used for regular buttons, including those on shoes.

Glove darners

The glove darner helped the Victorian lady repair her precious gloves in the same way that a darner was used for darning socks. The lady put the darner into the finger of the glove and could then repair the damage with tiny stitches.

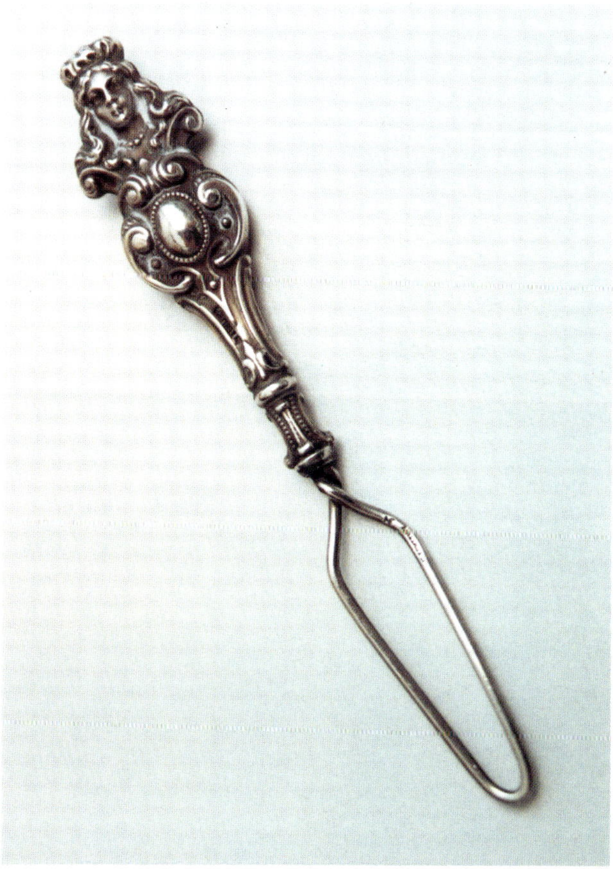

Glove hook, sterling, lady with a crown. About 4". *Collection and photo: Pat Rich.* $95.

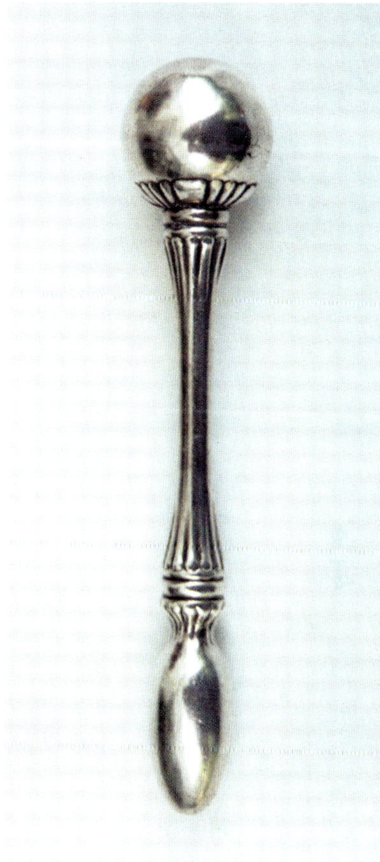

Sterling glove darner. 4" long. *Collection and photo: Pat Rich.* $75.

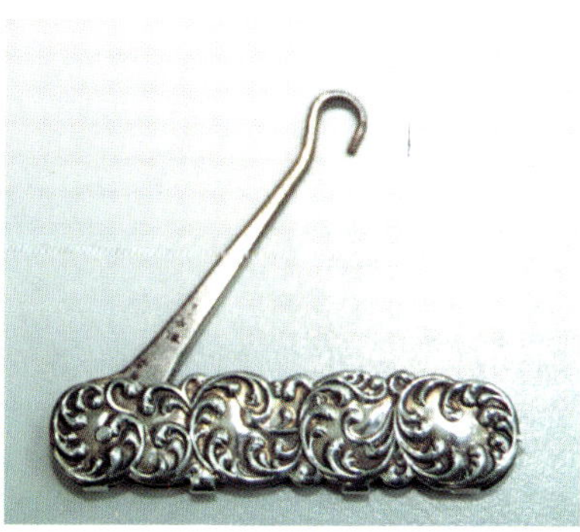

Glove hook, sterling handle with steel hook marked P & B, Paye & Baker Mfg. Co., 1890-1935. Closed, measures 1-3/4". *Collection on Edie Baker. Photo: Pat Rich.* $45.

Dresser accessories

Vanity case, powder compact, or dorine box, whatever name a lady chose to call it, this necessity of the early 1900s was carried in the lady's purse. In order to repair the lady's make-up, the case held a cake of face powder, sometimes paste rouge and a small puff Some had a mirror set into the lid, a slot for coins and even a place to store a lipstick.

These were produced in the early 1900s and continued to be used until the 1940s. They came in gold, silver and alloys. The more elegant were set with jewels and some were decorated with enamel over guilloche.

Ring trees

Ring trees are and were made to hold a ladies' rings while she washes her hands or is doing dishes. They were sometimes called "ring stands." Many ladies kept them on their dressing tables, near wash basins and near the kitchen sink. Quite a few were made in actual tree form with several branches on which rings could be held in safety. Others, of more whimsical design, were made in the form of animals. An example of this sort of whimsy is the bear holding a rifle and standing next to a tree with several branches. The slogan, "Rings and Things" of this c.1880 piece leaves no doubt of its purpose.

Another one of a baby's upraised hand was made c.1889 by the Wilcox Silver Plate Company.

Ring trees are not shown in great numbers in old manufacturers' catalogues nor in retail outlets either. Ring trees are occasionally found in present day catalogues but are mostly made of porcelain or other ceramic products.

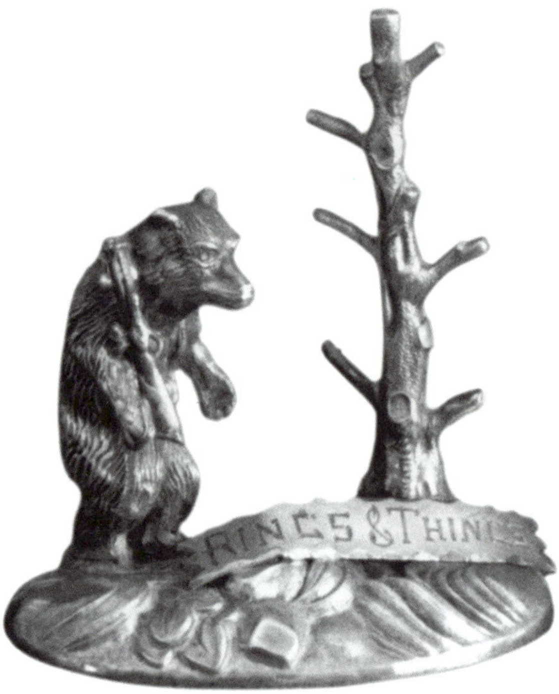

Ring tree designed as a bear with rifle, labeled on bottom Rings and Things. c.1880. *Photo: Judy Redfield.* $175-250.

Ring Tree designed as a raised hand with spread fingers, silverplate, make by Wilcox Silver Plate Co. c.1880. *Photo: Judy Redfield.* $175-250.

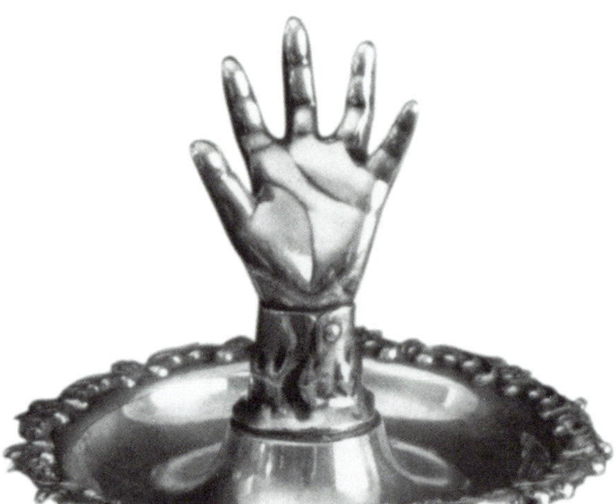

Posy holders or tussie mussies

The Victorian lady going to a ball almost always carried a bouquet of posies. If married, the lady's husband provided the flowers. If a single lady, unattached, her father or her escort provided them.

To protect the lady's hands and clothing, the flowers were most often carried in a posy holder, also called a *tussie mussie*.

These funnel-shaped devices, made of silver, silver-gilt or filigree were often richly decorated. The decoration might be gemstones, pearls, enamel, ivory or mother-of-pearl. They averaged 3" to 6" in length. Their deep funnel shape contained a damp sponge at the bottom to provide moisture for the flowers. A pin secured the tussie mussie to the lady's dress while some were equipped with a hook for attaching to the belt. Some few have a folding tripod stand which enabled them to be set on a table.

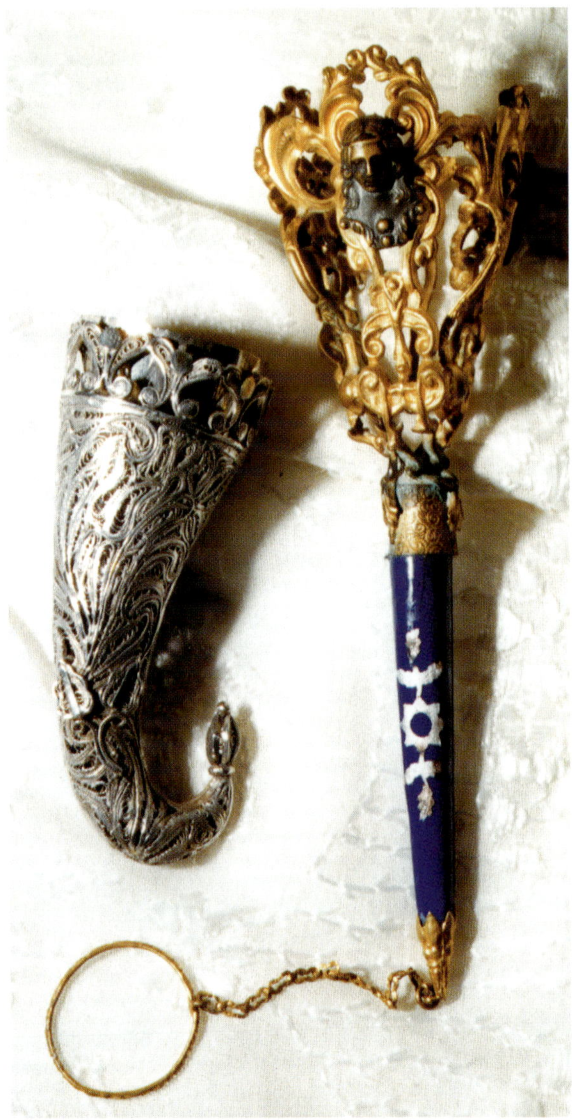

Two Victorian posy holders, c.1865. Left 2-3/4". Right: 5-1/4". The filigree is possibly Indian silver. The holder with ring attachment for the lady's finger is French. Gilt with two cameos, blue enamel handle inlaid with silver flowers. *Collection and photo: Anne Jansen.* $150-300.

In regard to the various names by which these flower holders are known, Webster's Unabridged Dictionary says, "tussie-mussie" is a variant of "Tuzzy-Muzzy" Middle English, a garland of flowers; nosegay.

Bouquet carrier is another name by which posy holders are known. Tussie mussie appears to be American terminology; tussie means a group of flowers and mussie came from the moist moss that keeps the flowers fresh. (See also page 53.)

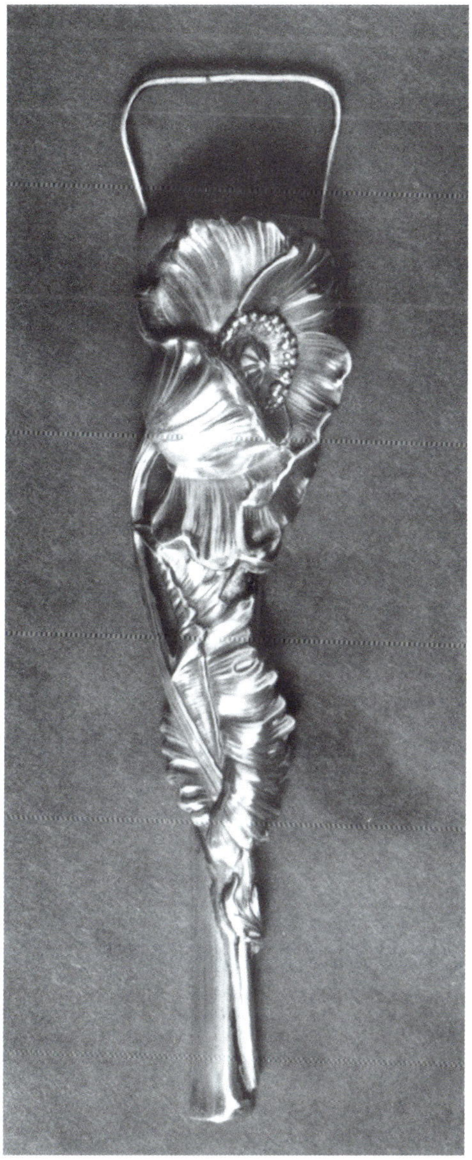

Tussie, sterling. Made by Unger Brothers, early 1900s. This type worn on a ribbon around the lady's neck. *Photo: Judy Redfield.* $150-300.

Belt buckles

Among the noted silver manufacturers who made attractive designs in belt buckles were Simons Brothers of Philadelphia, Wm. B. Kerr of Newark, and Paye & Baker of North Attleboro.

In their 1908 catalogue, Paye & Baker wrote:

> our buckle line is recognized as the leading high grade, sterling line on the market today.....The design and color scheme [referring to enamel on silver] of each piece is studied with the greatest care.....

Silver belt buckles sometimes served a dual purpose. In addition to securing the lady's belt at the waist, some could be worn as an ornamental pin on the lapel.

Paye & Baker in their 1908 catalogue featured ladies' belt buckles enameled in as many as four colors. Birds, sailing ships, flowers, stars, butterflies,

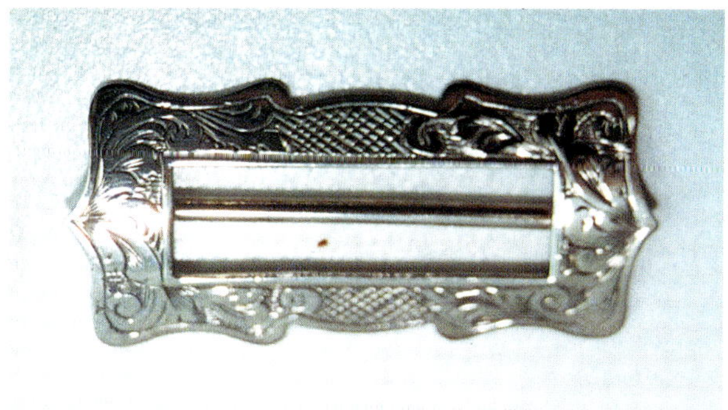

Silver belt buckle, no marks, measures 1-3/4". *Collection of Edie Baker. Photo: Pat Rich.* $90-400

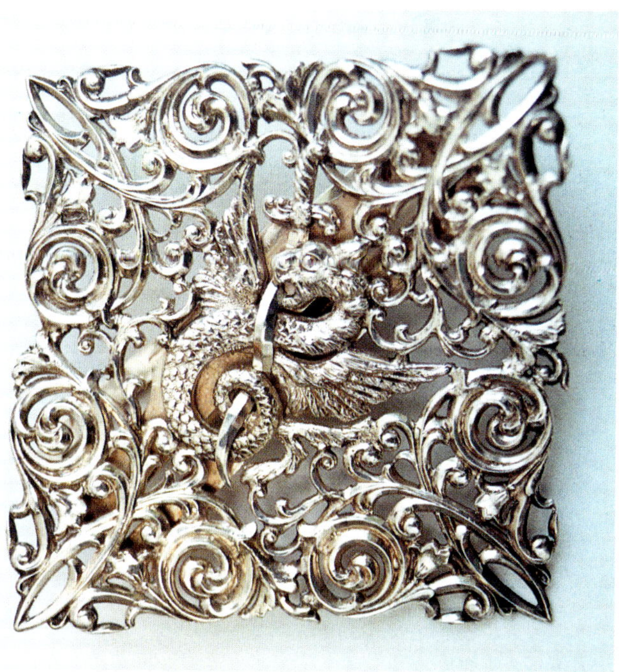

Sterling belt buckle with dragon motif, 3" square. *Collection of Edie Baker. Photo: Pat Rich.* $90-400

hearts and flowers were depicted in enamel colors. Stylized acanthus leaves and pine cones embellished some of Paye & Baker's Art Nouveau belt buckles. What seems strange to our eyes today is the number of belt buckles and other silver items which displayed the swastika. This was 1908, long before the unfortunate association with the Nazi connection. One very elaborate buckle depicts several good luck charms including a horseshoe, four leaf clover, wishbone and an old shoe, all wrapped around a swastika.

Paye & Baker devoted eight pages to belt buckles, not surprising when skirts were long and belts were cinched around the waist in an attempt to meet that idealized 18" size.

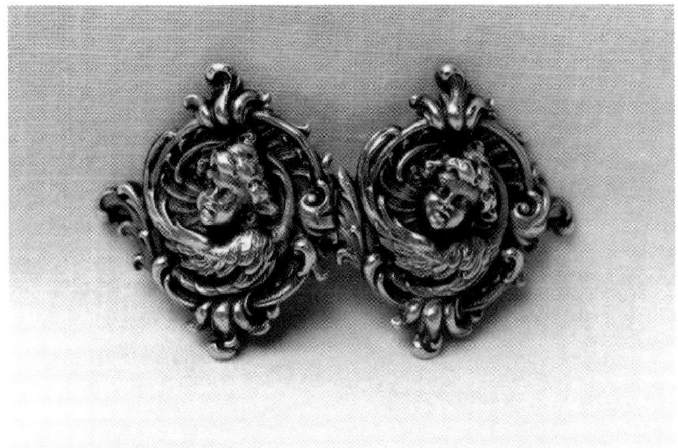

Belt buckle by Kerr with two faces framed by angel's wings, sterling. *Photo: Courtesy of Silver Magazine. Archives*. $90-400

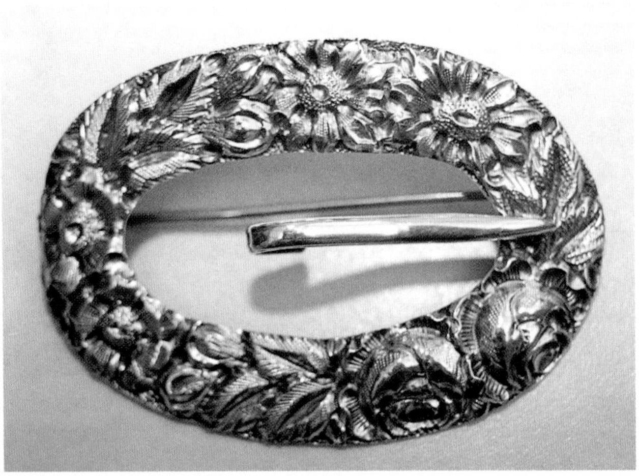

Belt buckle marked sterling which can be made into an ornamental pin for a lady's lapel, measure 3", c.1890. *Collection of Edie Baker. Photo: Pat Rich.* $90-400

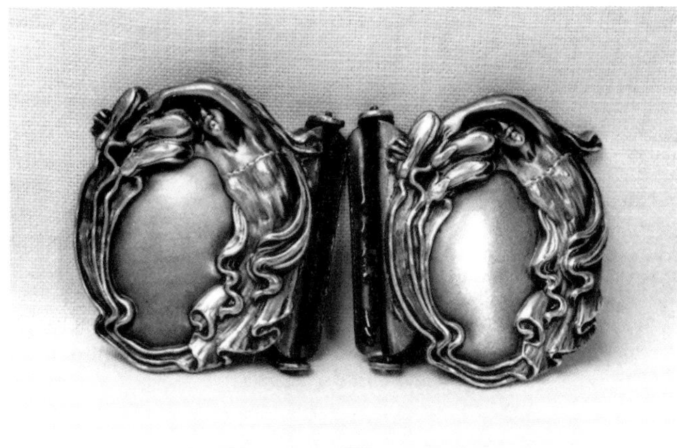

Art Nouveau belt clip, c.1900, made by Kerr prior to 1906. *Photo: Courtesy of Silver Magazine Archives*. $90-400

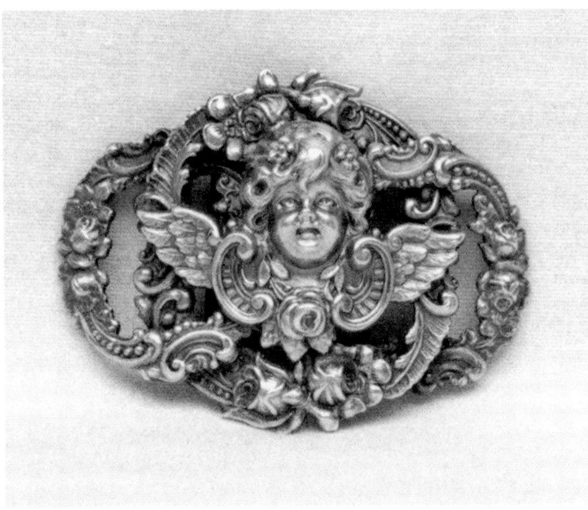

Silver belt buckle made by Simons Bro. & Co. of Philadelphia, PA. Cupid design shows cherub's face and wings, as preferred by ladies at the turn of the century. *Photo: Courtesy of Silver Magazine Archives*. $90-400

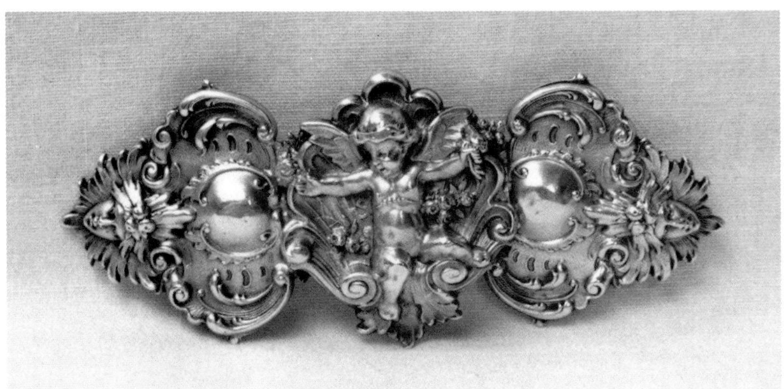

Belt buckle with winged cherub in center and one head on either end, sterling, Made by Wm. B. Kerr & Co. of Newark, New Jersey. *Photo: Courtesy of Silver Magazine Archives.* $90-400

Lorgnettes

Lorgnettes came into their own towards the end of the nineteenth century. Some were made earlier but by 1880, they were an accepted, attractive substitute for the unattractive spectacles which were previously used.

The name "lorgnette" came from the French word for spy or peep (*lorgnee*) and the English definition called them eyeglasses which could close and fold into an ornamental handle. They were made in sterling, gold and tortoiseshell and some were decorated with gem stones.

A few patterns of lorgnettes were found in jewelry catalogues around 1900. Many were advertised by opticians as well. One Rhode Island manufacturer sent out an eight-page catalogue of lorgnettes. The prices ranged from $3.25 to $4.00 for sterling. (14 karat gold cost $24.)

The elegant lorgnette was worn more often by a lady than a gentlemen. When not in use, the glasses could be folded and conveniently carried in the lady' s purse. Some had a clip or a chain which could be fastened to her dress and only opened when needed.

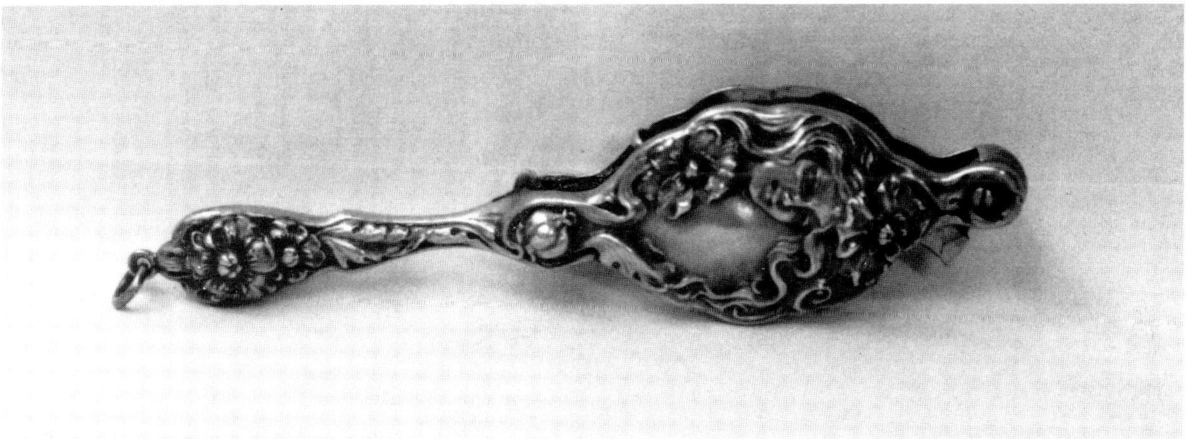

Silver lorgnette, a pair of eye-glasses which fold into the ornamental handle when not in use. Length 5", c.1890. Possibly made by Unger Bros. *Photo: Courtesy of Silver Magazine Archives*. $175.

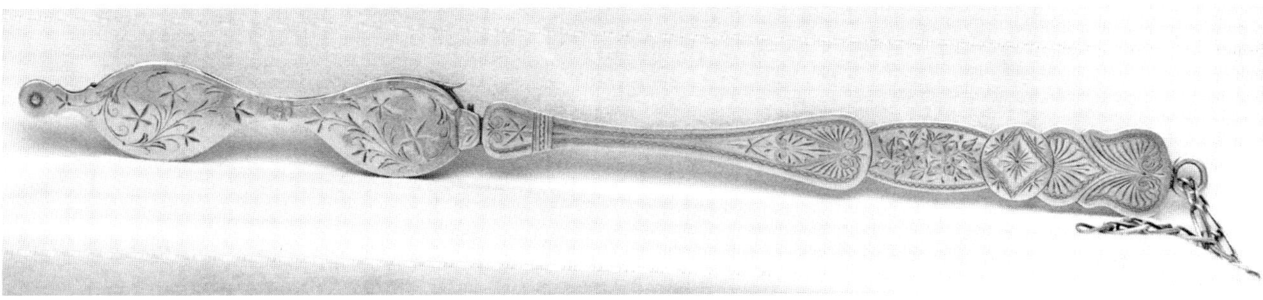

Unmarked coin silver lorgnette, as illustrated in 19th century opticians' advertisements. *Photo: Courtesy of Silver Magazine Archives*. $165.

Silver overlay

Examples of silver overlay include cologne bottles, inkwells, vases and drinking mugs. This technique of decoration was sometimes called silver deposit or American overlay (although it was not exclusively an American technique). It was a specialty of prominent silver companies including, Alvin, Gorham, La Pierre Manufacturing Company and Scharling & Co., Inc.

The technique of silver overlay begins with glass. The glass blower makes the shape desired of clear or colored glass. The pattern for the design is sketched out with a stylus. Flux is applied where the designer wants the silver to adhere. The piece is then placed in a plating vat and remains there until the desired thickness is deposited. When the piece is removed from the vat, that silver which was not on the flux flakes off, leaving only the design in silver.

Silver overlay was applied to glass and to ceramics. A three-piece tea service c.1905 was made by the Willets Manufacturing Company of New Jersey. The ceramic is white Belleek porcelain with the same silver overlay pattern on all three pieces. Lenox also used silver overlay on some of their china and later the process was applied to cut glass.

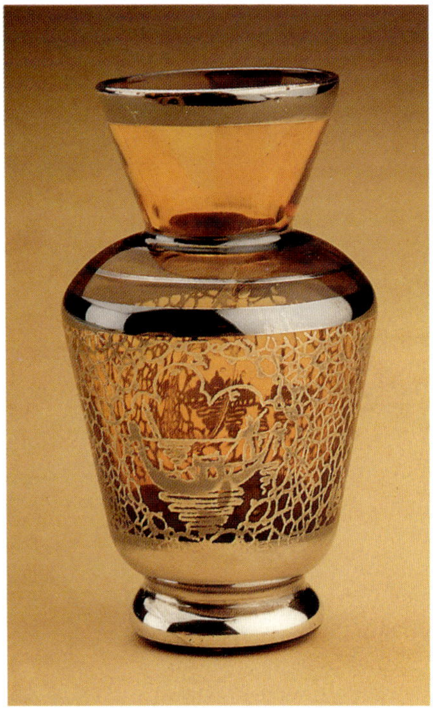

Amber glass vase with silver overlay (also called silver deposit), height 3". *Photo: Bruce Waters.* $60-150

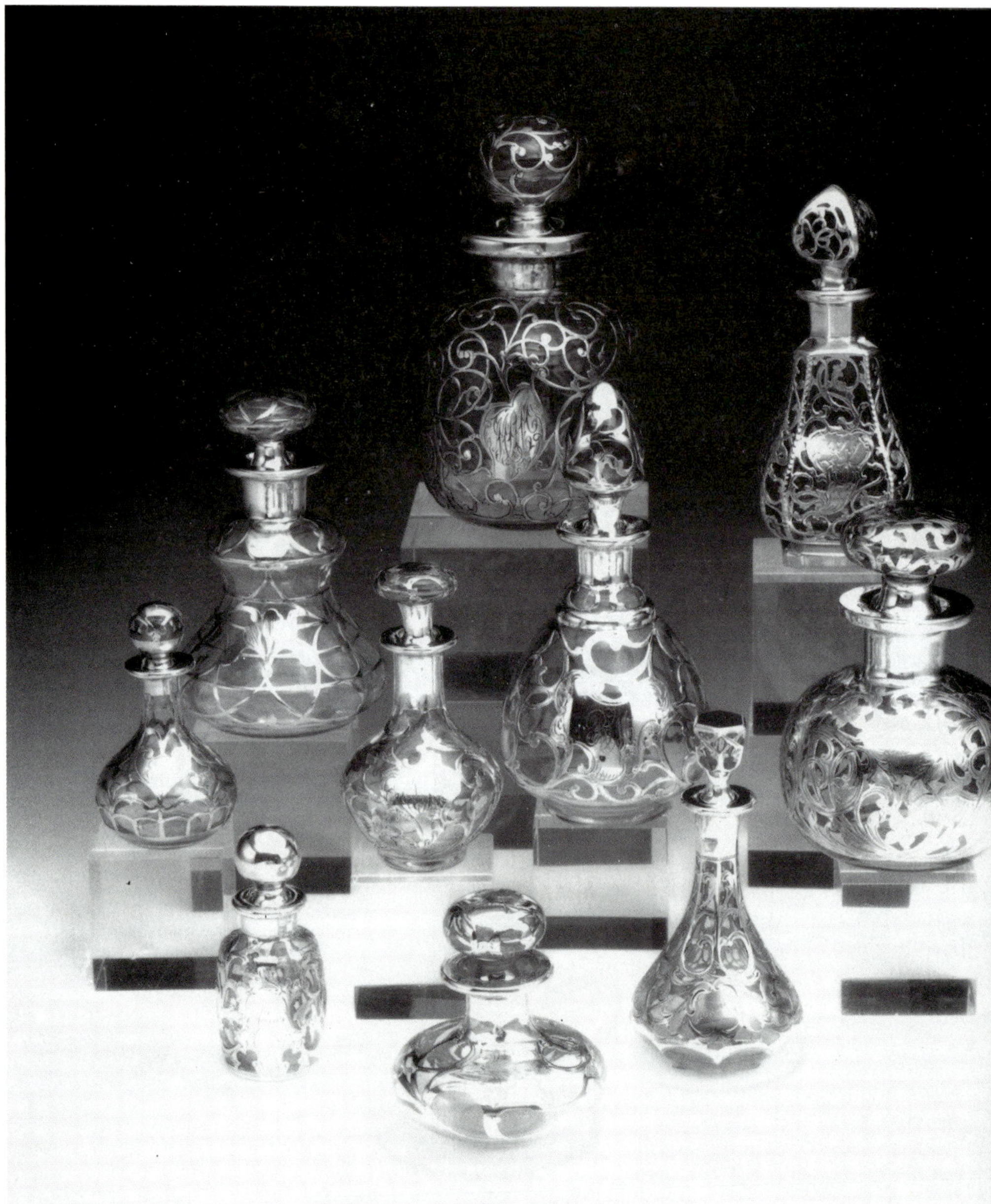

Perfume bottles decorated in silver overlay ranging in size from 3" to 7-1/2" tall. Alvin & Co. and Gorham & Co. were two of the most famous makers of this technique. *Collection of Nelson & Nelson, New York, NY. Photo: Noel Allum.* $60-150

Buttonhooks

As Victorian styles dictated more use of buttons, buttonhooks became a necessity. They were included in a lady's dresser set and often in a set of toiletries for the gentleman as well. If these sets were made of silver or silverplate, the buttonhooks had a handle which matched the pattern of the other articles in the set.

Exactly what was a buttonhook? It usually had a shank made of a piece of steel with a rounded hook on one end. The curved hook went through the buttonhole, around the button itself and then pulled the button through the buttonhole. The straight end of the hook was fitted into the handle. The handle might have been made of many different metals. Although there are some buttonhooks made entirely of silver, most had steel hooks.

Buttonhooks were made in a wide range of sizes. Some measure 24". Some are as small as 1". The very long buttonhooks were usually for boots and high button shoes. The small ones were used to fasten gloves. In between, some sturdy hooks might be used to lace up ladies' corsets. A small waist was considered the sign of a lady and a buttonhook helped make those laces tighter.

Silver marks on silver buttonhooks depended upon where the hooks were made. Silver buttonhooks made in England were marked with English hallmarks. It is fairly easy to identify those of English origin. In the United States, hooks usually had the word *Sterling* as well as the maker's mark. While some buttonhooks were made in France, Germany and Japan, most found today were made in England or the United States.

Souvenir and commemorative buttonhooks make a specialized collection as could figurals. Figural hooks in silver ran the gamut from goddesses in Grecian robes to long-haired *Art Nouveau* ladies. Animals such as a dog, teddy bear, long-necked swan and the wise old owl were used. One figural used a golf club for a handle. Still another collection might be of the smaller glove hooks, sometimes called buttoners, which resemble buttonhooks in all ways except size.

In the 1880s gift sets were presented in plush cases with satin linings. Some included hammered silver buttonhooks, a hammered silver shoehorn and a glove buttoner all in the same pattern.

Close fitting garments, high button shoes and 'way-above-the-elbow-gloves required the use of buttonhooks. All through the Victorian era everyone used buttonhooks. Some of the most beautiful were made of silver.

Today, buttonhooks are seldom if ever used. They give us a glimpse of domestic life at the end of the nineteenth century when ladies and gentlemen used buttonhooks to help fasten the many buttons they wore.

While the slide fastener, forerunner of the modern zipper, was invented by Whitcomb L. Judson and patented by him August 29, 1892, it was twenty years later before the idea was developed into a marketable product and another ten years before it was readily accepted by the public. Many folks were still "buttoning up" and even bending over to button their shoes and boots throughout the first quarter of the twentieth century. Buttoned shoes were first popular about 1860 but it was not until about seven years later that some inventive genius got around to devising the buttonhook.

First the zipper, and later Velcro, threaten the existence and usefulness of buttons and buttonhooks.

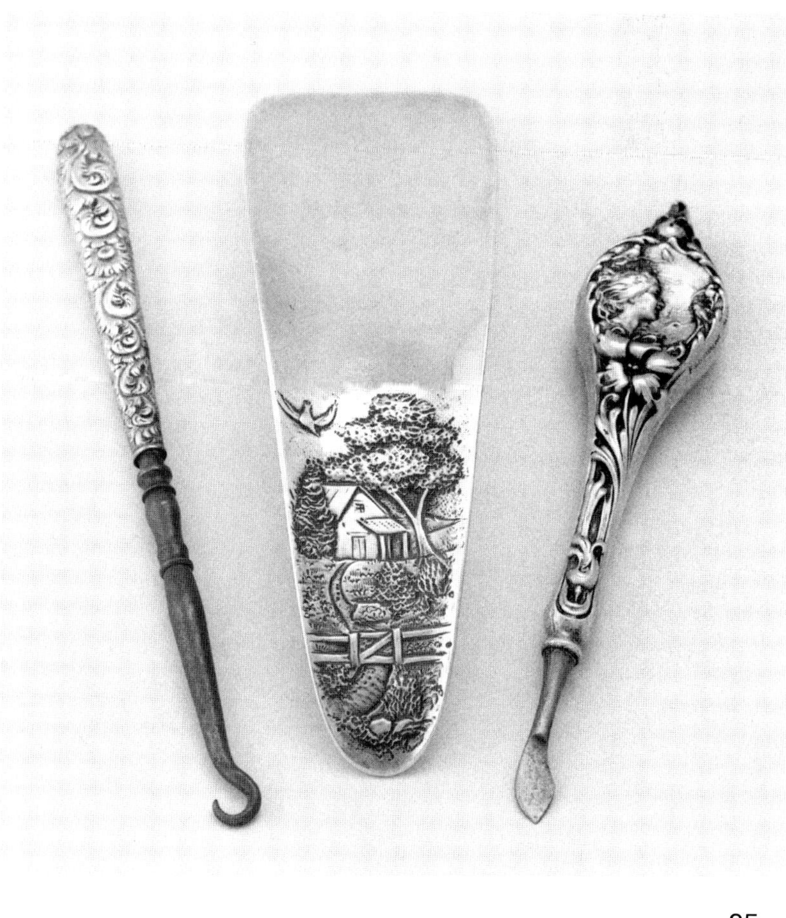

Left: buttonhook marked Gorham. Oddly, the Gorham mark is on the base metal of the hook, 6-1/8".
Center: Shoe horn marked S. Kirk & Son Co. 925/1000, length: 6".
Right: cuticle knife marked F & B (Foster & Bailey) STERLING Pat'd. 5-5/8", all c.1890-1900. *Private Collection. Photo: David Arky.*

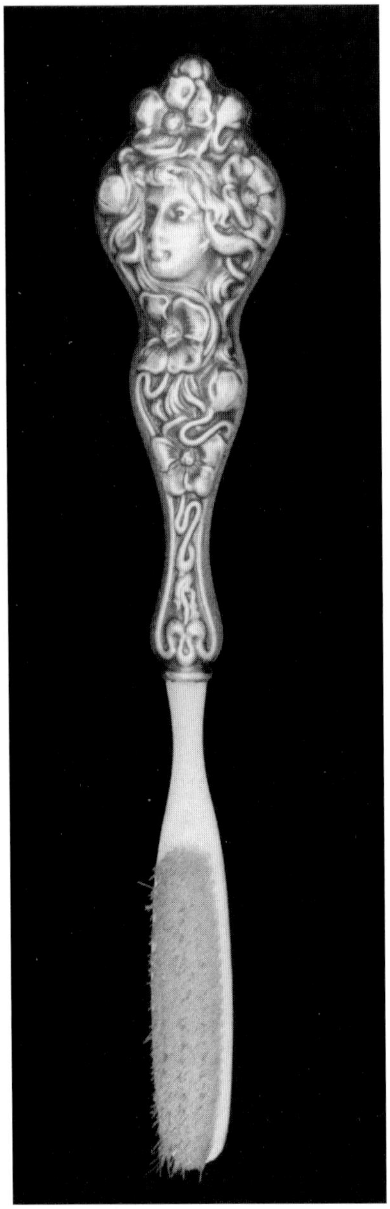

Art Nouveau toothbrush marked STERLING. 6-3/4". *Photo: H Ivan Rainwater*. $60.

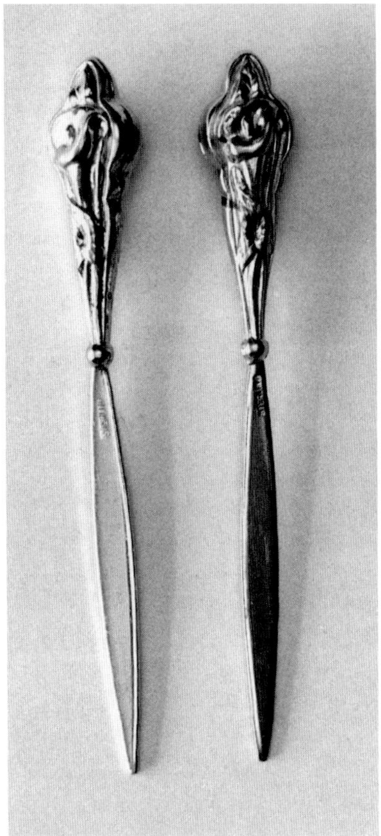

Nail files marked STERLING on the blades below the silver handles, length 7". *Photo: H Ivan Rainwater*. $75+.

Sterling backed hair brushes by Unger Bros. Entire toilet sets could be purchased in various designs. Left: Dawn. Right: Love's Dream. *Unger Bros. catalogue 1904.* $95-125.

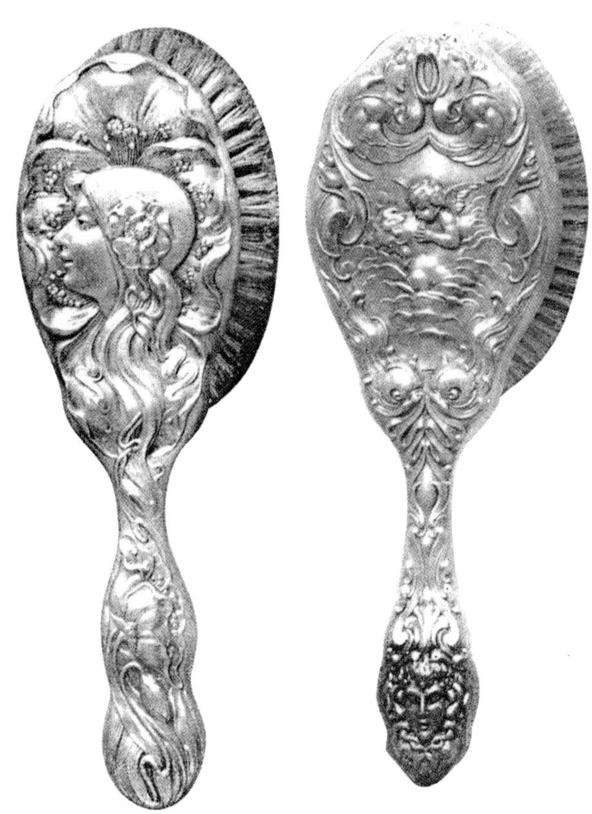

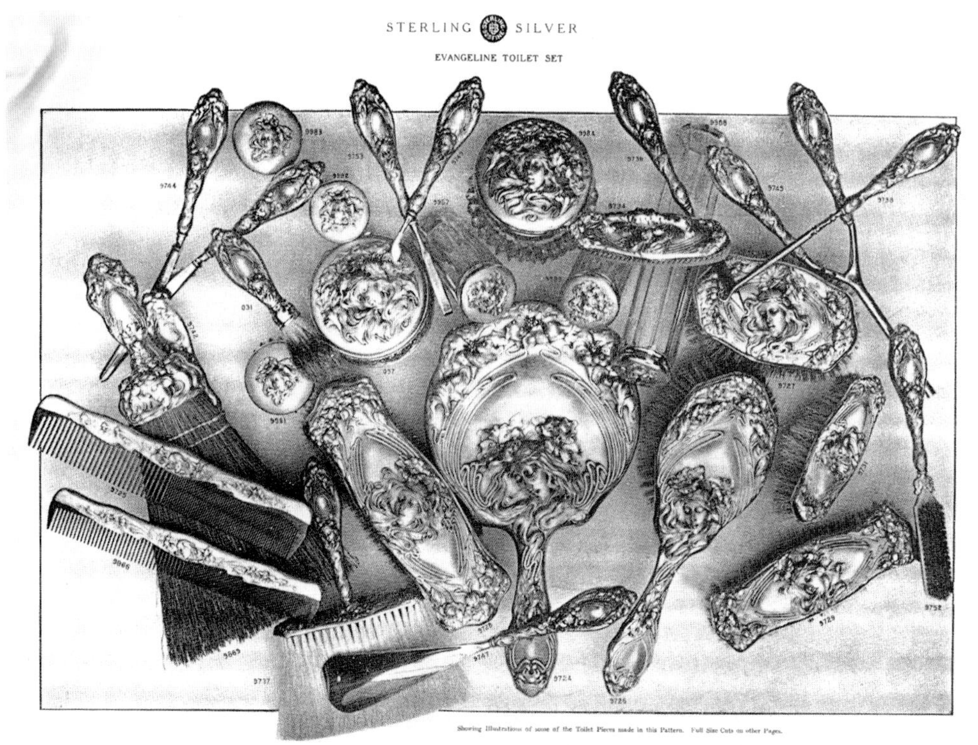

Typical pieces for the lady' s dressing table made in the pattern called Evangelize by Unger Bros. Each piece was made in sterling silver.

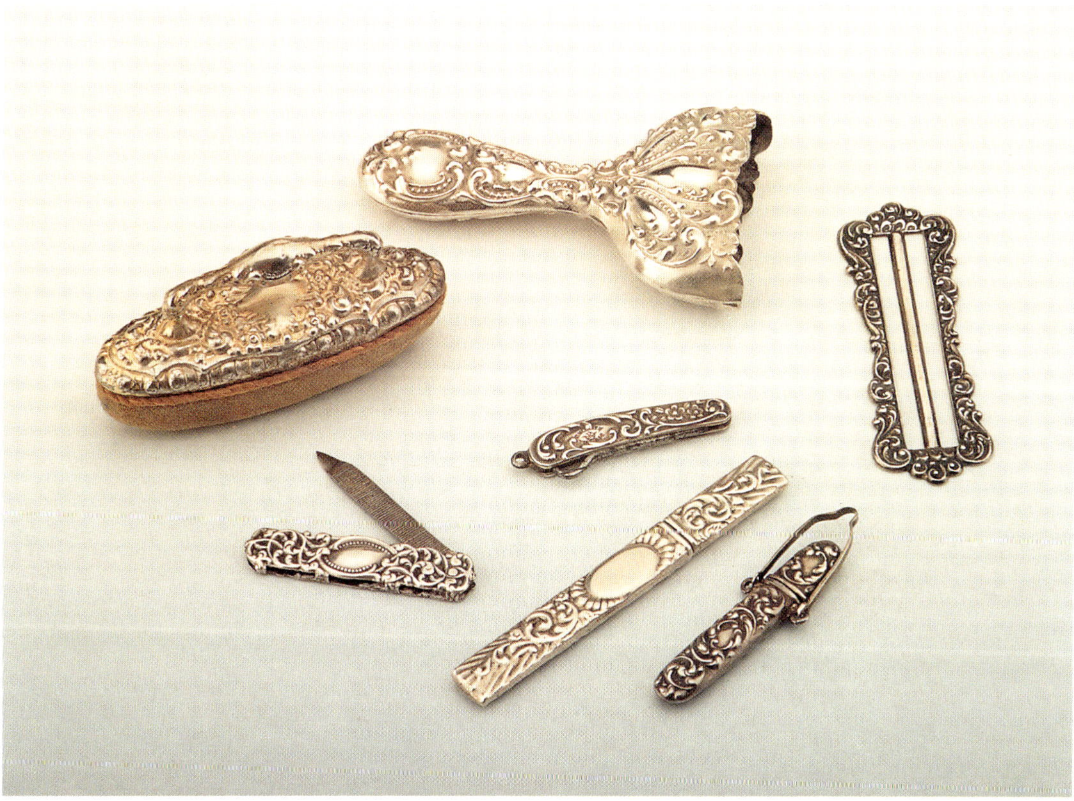

Group of seven pieces: Sterling buckle. Maker: Weaves & Sillcock. Measures 2-9/16". The word "buckle" comes from the Latin *bucca, buccola* meaning helmet strap or fastener.
2. Silver clothes brush holder. Measures 3".
3. Fingernail buffer with sterling handle and top. 2-3/4".
4. Sterling needle case by Unger Bros. 1-9/16".
5. Sterling nail file case. Measures 2-7/8".
6. Sterling folding glove hook. Maker: Redd & Co., Inc. Newark, NJ. Closed measures 1-5/8". Open 2-3/8".
7. Silver nail file. 1-5/8".
Collection of Antonia Moore. Photo: Bruce Waters.

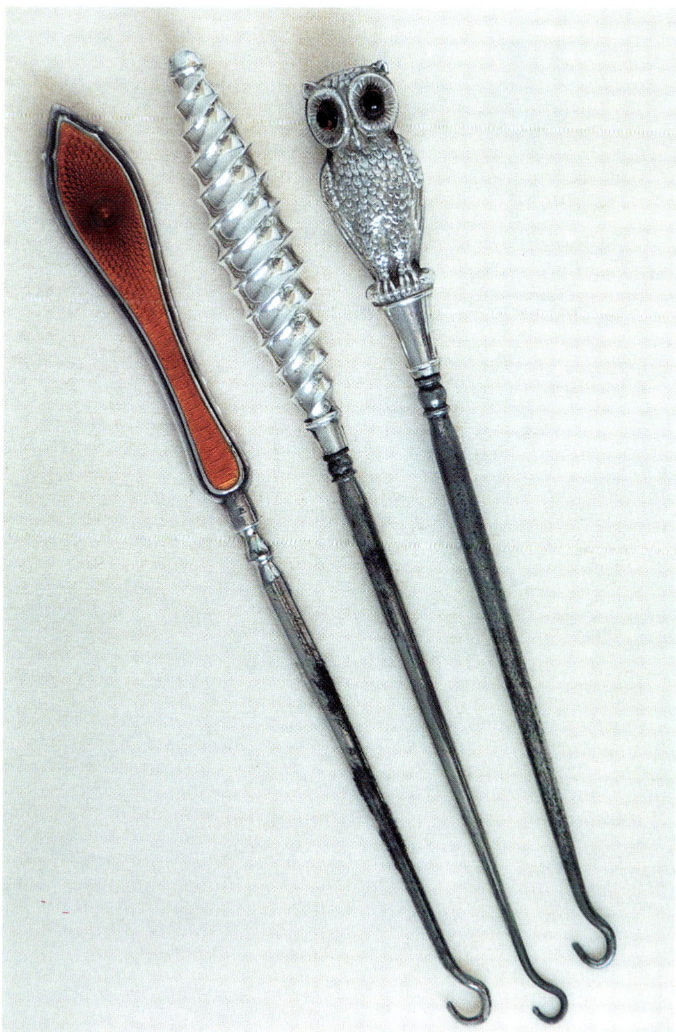

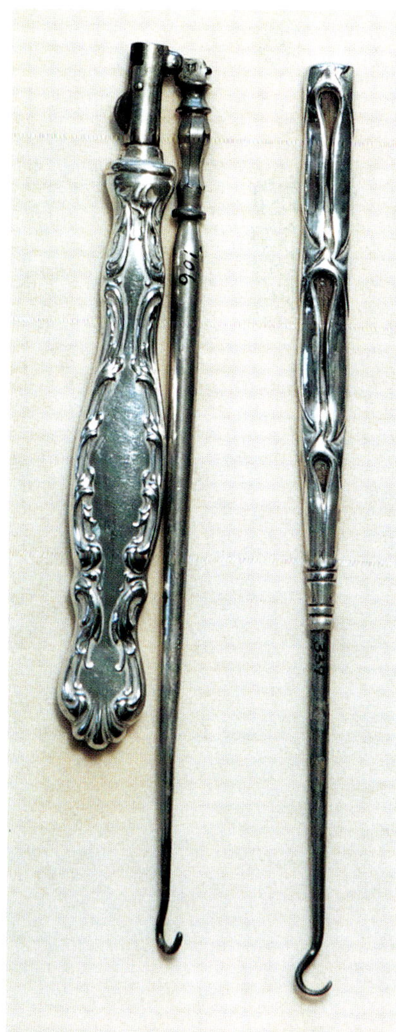

Right:
Buttonhooks, English, dating from left to right: rust red enamel on silver, 1934. Twist hook, 1893. Owl with red stone eyes, 1906. *Photo: Don Stoffel.* $55-110.

Far right:
Left: folding buttonhook with mechanism from Germany, c. 1910. Completed by Frank M. Whiting Mfg. Co. U.S.A. Right: Buttonhook made by Frank M. Whiting Mfg. Co. c.1910. *Photo: Don Stoffel*. $55-110.

Right:
All of the hooks shown here were made in the same pattern and for sale from the Meriden Britannia Co. catalogue, 1886. $55-110.

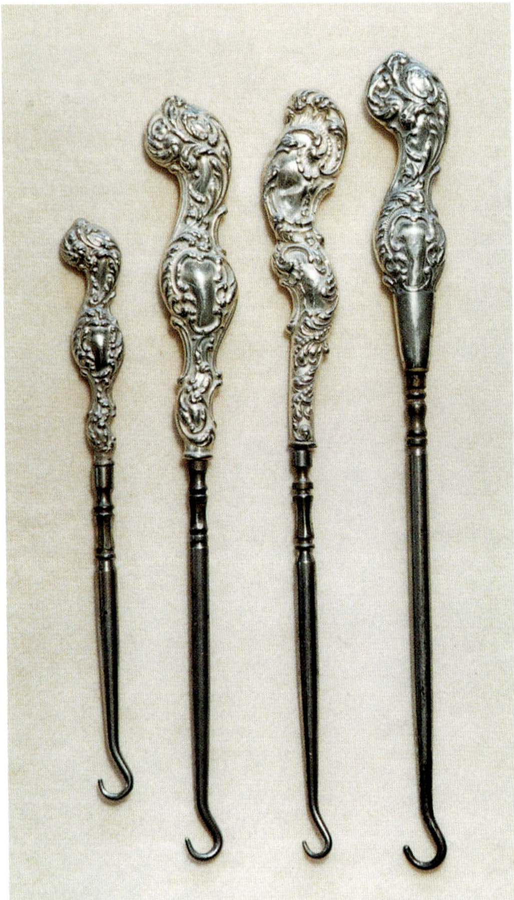

American buttonhooks made by Unger Bros. ranging from 5-3/4" to 8" in length. The two on the left are the same pattern in different sizes. *Photo: Don Stoffel.* $55-110.

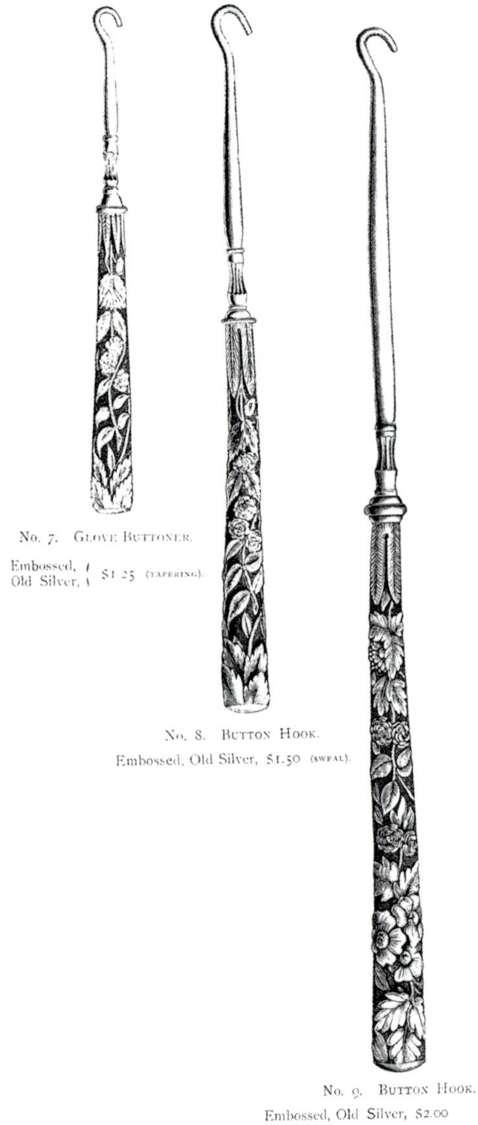

82. Meriden Britannia Co. catalog, 1886.

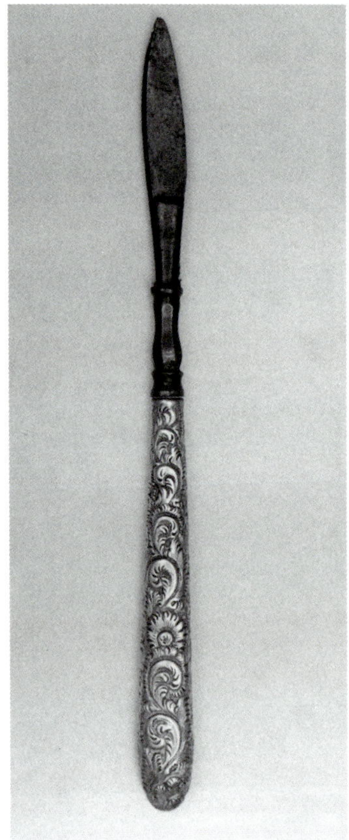

Silver handled buttonhook and scalpel. The Gorham marks are on the steel rather than the silver handles. Hook measures 6". c.1895-1900. *Photo: H Ivan Rainwater*. $55-110.

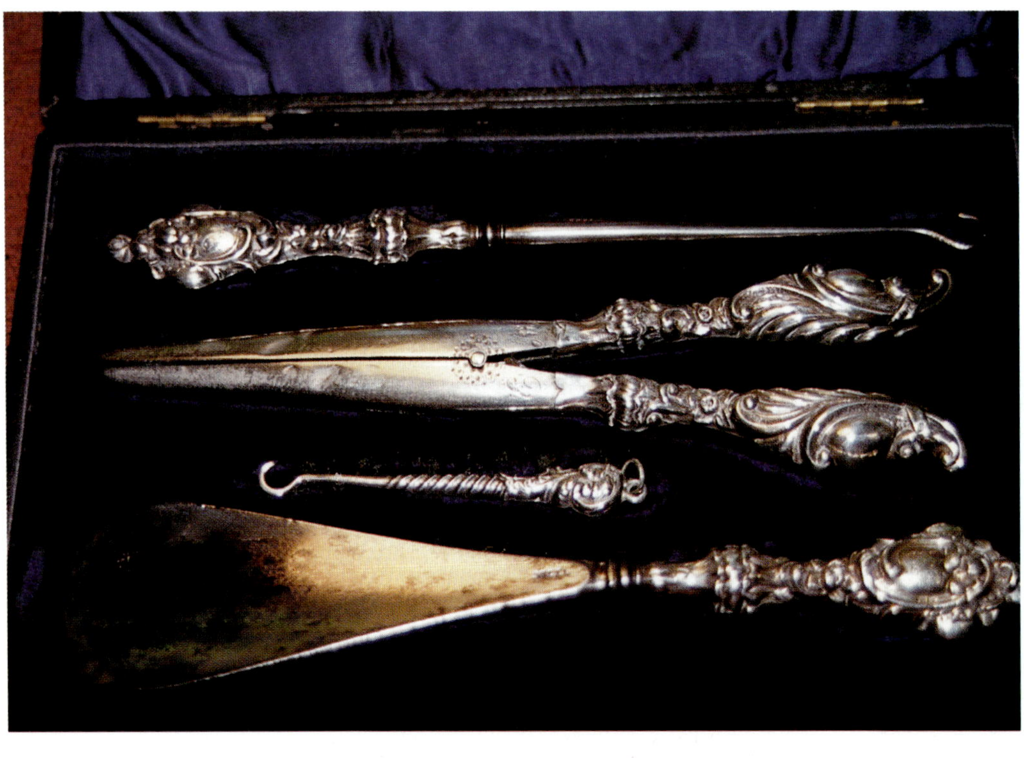

Lady's personal box including buttonhook, glove stretcher, glove hook, and shoehorn. Script monogram on all pieces. English, silver, Birmingham, 1897. Box measure 8-1/4" by 5-1/4". Satin lined box top reads J. H. Potter, Manufacturing Silversmith & Outler, Sheffield. *Collection and photo: Mabel Rogers.*

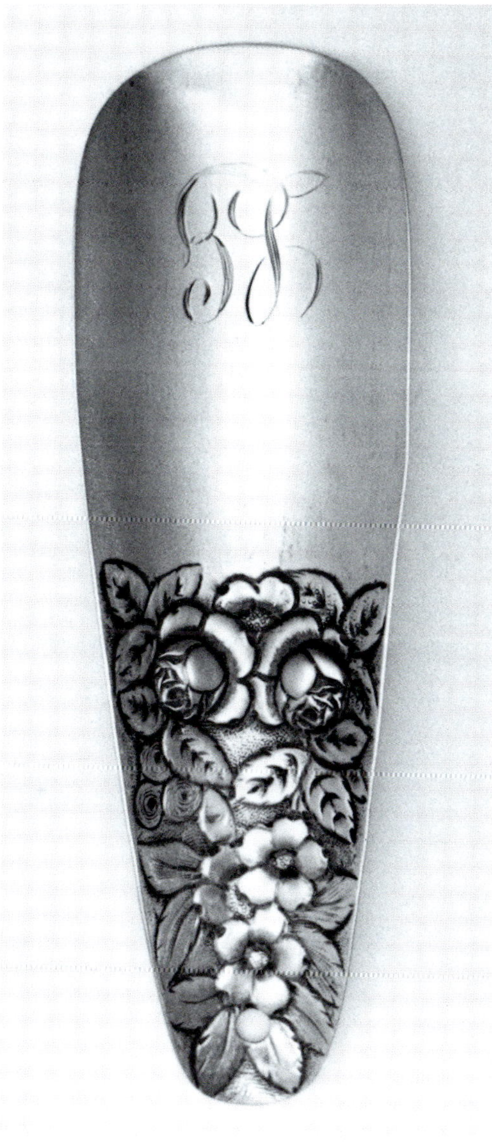

Monogrammed shoe horn marked 925/ STERLING/1000, 5-1/2", late nineteenth century. *Private Collection. Photo: H Ivan Rainwater*. $100.

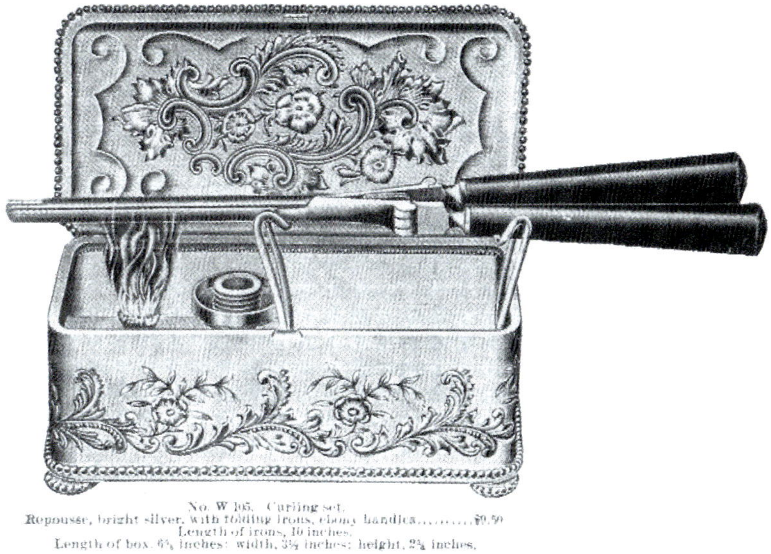

Curling set from Carson, Pirie, Scott & Co. of Chicago, Illinois, catalog, 1898-1899.

Skirt lifters

Skirt clips (English), skirt lifters (American), or *Porte-jupes* (French), were all for the same purpose—to lift skirts out of the grime on the streets.

Skirts were long in the nineteenth century and streets were not only unpaved, they were constantly soiled by the excrement of horses and other animals. Life was difficult for ladies who wished to keep their finery unsullied.

Fashionable gowns were often edged with a tough woolen braid or an edging of a "brush braid" that literally swept the streets. Skirts with a train sometimes had a loop of the dress fabric attached to the back seam. This loop could be caught up with one hand and held by the wearer as she danced.

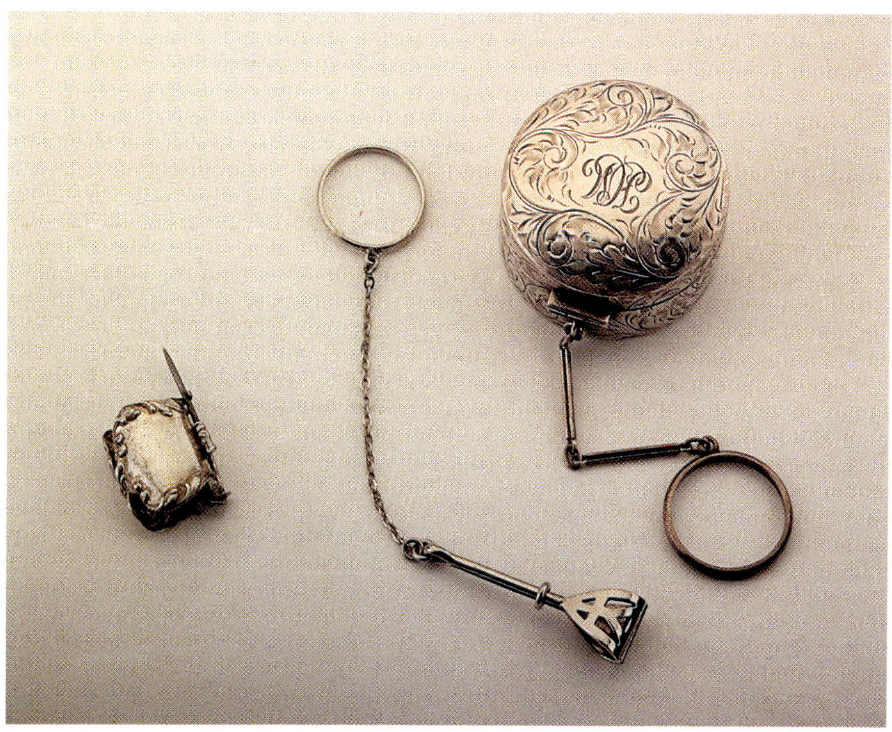

Left: A tiny violet holder measures 3/4", maker: Unger Brothers, ca. 1904-05. $45 and up.
Center: Sterling skirt lifter. Maker: Foster & Bailey, the largest American manufacturer of silver between 1878-1898. Measures 2-1/2". *Collection of Antonia Moore. Photo: Bruce Waters.*
Right: Dorine box. Sterling with monogram on front. 1-1/2" diameter. *Collection of Antonia Moore. Photo: Bruce Waters*. $150 and up.

Several gentlemen, always aiming to please the ladies, came up with numerous devices designed to keep the ladies' skirts out of the mud. Illustrated here is a skirt clip by Thomas Johnson of England. This Victorian skirt clip was both practical and decorative. Made in 1876, the pin was attached to the body of the skirt and the hem was clipped up whenever necessary.

Crinoline skirts could be fitted with a series of internal cords which were used to pull up skirts all around—especially useful for ladies playing croquet.

The Miller Brothers of Newgate Street, London, advertised a "Lover-lock Dressholder" which they claimed was suitable for valuable and delicate fabric.

Fyfe's patented device of 1876 consisted of a pair of rubber padded tongs and a sliding cast butterfly clasp which was pulled up to hold the tongs closed. Fyfe's 1880 patented skirt clip was known for its extra strong spring. There was a cast ornament fitted to a chain to a bangle on the wrist.

The efficiency of all these gadgets arouses doubts. In true American fashion came Blackwood's Magic Skirt Elevator for which the claim was fashionably with one easy pull: it lowers itself."

None of these devices did more than lift the outer skirt; under-skirts were simply ignored.

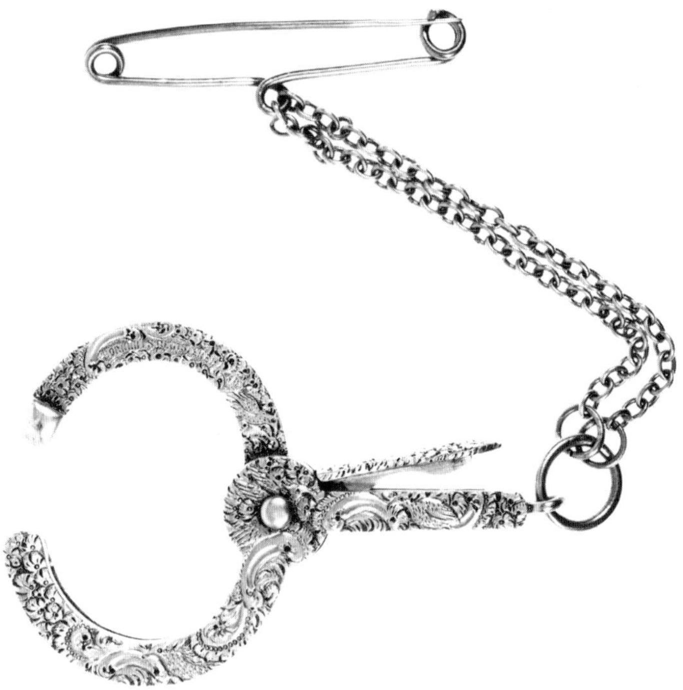

Victorian skirt clip made in 1876 by Thomas Johnson of England. Pin was attached to the body of the skirt, raising the length of the hem. *Photo: N. Bloom & Son, London.*

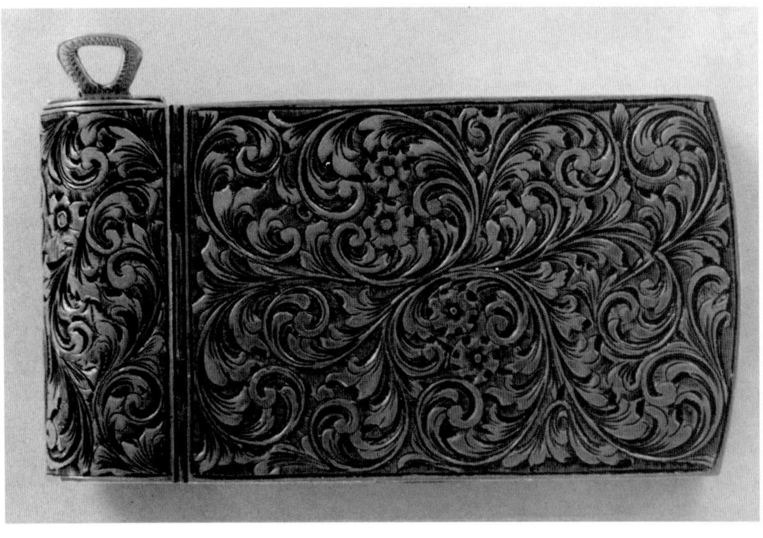

Silver vanity case. Large compartment holds powder plus two coin slots for "mad" money. Left side holds a lipstick. Marked 800. c.1910. Measures 4-1/2" in length. *Private Collection. Photo: H Ivan Rainwater*. $150 and up.

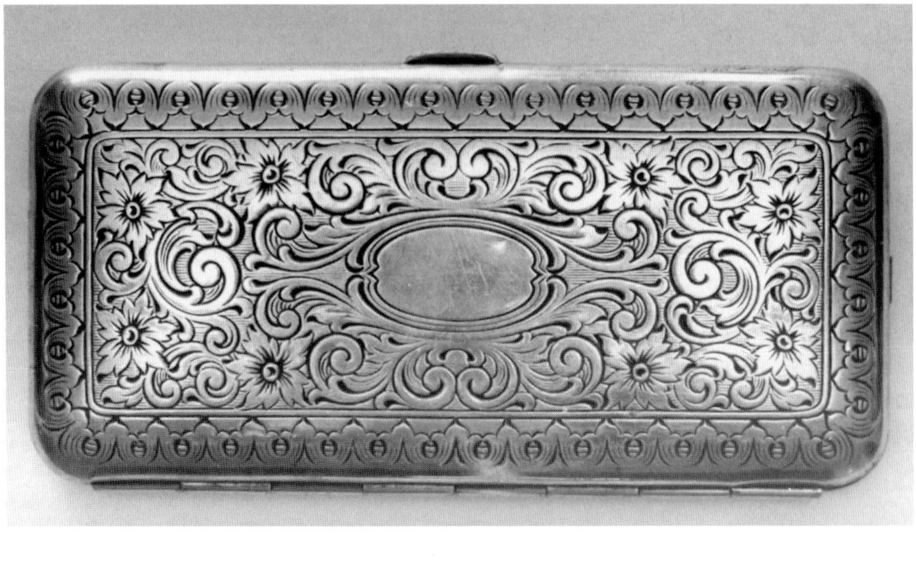

Vanity case with German silver mark. Holds loose powder and two coin slots. Length: 4-1/2" c.1910. *Private Collection. Photo: H Ivan Rainwater*. $150 and up.

Chapter 3. Silver Curios for use...

...as Jewelry

Since the beginning of time people have adorned themselves. When the first mortal female looked upon the first mortal male, there was born a desire to make herself more attractive. It was then that our first prospective customer for the jewelers' trade was created. Conversely, when the first mortal male looked upon the first mortal female, there was born in him the desire to please and to add something to make his personage more attractive. So, it was then that the first prospective buyer of gifts, jewelers patron and personal shopper was born.

Articles for their personal adornment may have been only colorful feathers or blossoms in their season. Those first people were never to know the pleasure of giving nor of receiving the gift of shining new silver jewelry. Nor did they experience the joy of receiving handed-down family silver jewelry that has through the years acquired that characteristic and beautiful patina.

Long before Europeans arrived in America, the native peoples had learned to use gold which they fashioned into personal adornments. Jewelry of gold was made and survived in greater quantity than silver. Silver is almost never found in nuggets as is gold. Though silver is only somewhat resistant to oxidation, and because of its scarcity and beauty, silver is highly regarded for personal ornament. Discoverers of gold associated its yellow color with the sun and related the brilliant white of silver to the moon.

Very little silver jewelry exists today that was made and worn in the eighteenth century or earlier. Most of the jewelry worn in America in colonial times was imported, but there were a few gold and silversmiths capable of making "bespoke" articles of all sorts. The ladies could count on local workers to make beads, necklaces, brooches, rings (especially mourning rings) and watches and many other items, even in colonial days.

Early nineteenth century ladies would find ear knobs, rings, hair combs, decorative pins of all sorts, lockets, charms and gold beads all readily available. The desire of every woman, it seems, was a string of gold beads. To satisfy that longing, jewelers made gold beads in a variety of styles and fineness.

America's silver jewelry industry begins

The establishment of jewelry making as an industry in America, with the production of jewelry as a stock-in-trade, was begun in Providence, Rhode Island. It was there that Seril Dodge (1759-1802) eventually settled. Seril was born in Pomfret, Connecticut, and went to Norwich, Connecticut, with his brother Ezra (1766-1798) who was a silversmith. Seril was apprenticed to Thomas Harland (1735?-1807). Seril Dodge went to Providence in May of 1784 where he set up his small shop two years later on North Main Street. There he did a thriving business in the production of shoe buckles. Just as the ladies aspired to gold beads, the gentlemen seemed to desire silver shoe buckles.

Six years after Seril Dodge established himself, Nehemiah Dodge (1795-1807), his nephew, opened his small shop farther up on North Main Street as "Goldsmith and jeweler and watch-maker." He is considered the real pioneer in establishing the manufacturing jewelry business in Providence. Nehemiah Dodge had learned the trade from a jeweler in Norwich, Connecticut. Dodge's first shop on North Main Street was on the Roger Williams estate.

Four years later, in 1798, Nehemiah moved to a new location nearer the Market Square. Here he worked in 18k gold, making to order only gold necklaces, knob earrings and twists, gold rings, and miniature cases. While working here, he conceived the idea of increasing his clientele by introducing a cheaper grade of jewelry. Some of these goods were made from a crude quality of gold plate and others from a composition of metals that was gilded. This less expensive line was immediately successful.

Among Nehemiah Dodge's apprentices was Jabez Gorham who became a journeyman silversmith. According to legend, young Gorham went about town with his little basket of spoons and sold them house-to-house. He had the reputation of making spoons of real silver and his designs were of fine character. Very early he established the Gorham reputation for quality.

Perhaps it was Dodge's immediate success with the less expensive lines of jewelry which inspired the establishment in 1805 of four more manufacturing jewelers; John C. Jencks (1776-1852); Ezekiel Burr (1765-1846); Pitman & Dorrance, Saunders Pitman (1732-1804) and Samuel Dorrance (1778-1815).

Figures for the early years of the jewelry manufacturing industry are meager but by 1810 about 100 workmen were employed in Providence in the manufacture of $100,000 worth of jewelry. The industry continued to grow and in 1812 about 125 were so employed, producing products valued at $300,000.

The jewelry industry, more than many others, is especially vulnerable to financial crises which affect the country at large. The War of 1812 had a paralyzing effect. The country was flooded with cheap European jewelry and jewelry manufacture in Providence practically ceased. By 1815 the number of workers engaged in the production of jewelry had not increased. But, it revived in 1818 and by 1820 the value of jewelry produced reached $600,000 and 300 workmen were employed.

Other years in which there were financial crises were 1857 and 1861-1864. The latter were the Civil War years when the number of firms dwindled from 86 to 56, though some firms found it profitable to make brass buttons, belt clasps, and other metal articles called for by the government.

Another financial panic occurred in 1873 and its effect was felt by the jewelry industry. The effects of the panic of 1873 and the general business depression of 1893-1897 were offset somewhat by the lower market price for silver bullion.

In the twentieth century, both World Wars have depressed the jewelry industry. A lack of materials for the production of jewelry and the needs of the nation for war materials have caused many manufacturers during war times to turn to the production of military emblems and medals, surgical instruments, electronic components, precision instruments for aircraft, and close proximity fuses for rockets and shells, to mention a few.

The Depression of the 1930s brought about massive layoffs, and marginal firms floundered; some did not survive. The imposition of first a ten percent and then a twenty percent luxury tax during the 1940s also placed a severe burden on the industry.

Other factors influencing the jewelry industry have been the increase in the quantity used and the type of jewelry findings, the introduction of more efficient machines which reduce hand labor, and changes in styles and fashion.

People of today have the same desire to make themselves more attractive, more appealing to others. Wearing silver jewelry is one of the many devices still used.

The Alfred Jewel

Many things of interest and occasionally even real treasures turn up at the world-famous Portobello Road Market held every Saturday morning in London. Just such a piece is this silver-gilt adaptation of the priceless Alfred Jewel, the original of which is now one of the featured treasures of the Ashmolean Museum in Oxford, England. Housed in a free-standing pedimented case, it draws the attention of school children as well as adults.

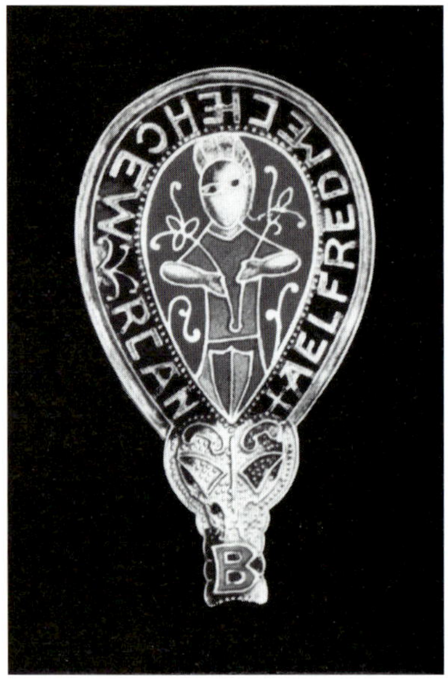

The Alfred Jewel adaptation. Maker: James Fenton, Birmingham, 1926. Length: 2". Sterling and gilt with non-safety catch. *Photo: H Ivan Rainwater.*

The real Alfred Jewel is famous as a work of art and because of its probable association with Alfred the Great, England's best-known Saxon king. It was discovered in Newton Park, near North Petherton, just four miles from Athelney in Somerset, in 1693 by Sir Thomas Wrothe, lord of the manor. The Isle of Athelney is where Alfred withdrew in 878 to plan his attack on the Danes and received the scolding known to every school child from a peasant's wife for allowing her cakes to burn.

The Alfred Jewel consists of a pear-shaped panel of enamel, just under 2-1/2" in length and protected by a layer of rock crystal. It depicts the head and shoulders of a man carrying two curved stems which blossom into flowers above his shoulders. From the time that the jewel was first known it has been the subject of much speculation, especially in regard to its uses and to the identity of the figure. This figure has been described variously as Christ, the pope, Alfred himself or a saint, preferably that of St. Neot or St. Cuthbert, Alfred's two favorite saints. It is probably none of these. Dr. Egil Bakka (*Antiquaries Journal*, xlvi,

277-892, 1966) explains that the figure is probably symbolic of Sight, one of the Five Senses. This is based on the similarity to an Anglo-Saxon ninth-century silver brooch on which there are five figures representing Taste, Smell, Touch and Hearing with Sight bearing two plant-like stems, very much like the Alfred Jewel figure.

The design is in cloisonné enamel on gold. The enamel colors are white for skin tone, gray hair, light green tunic, reddish brown for the belt and blue background. The setting of the jewel is a deep band of gold filigree around which runs the inscription: AELFRED MEC HEHT GEWYRCAN (Alfred ordered me to be made). The frame terminates in an animal head holding an open tube in its mouth. The socket in the animal's mouth is about 1/2 by 3/16" in diameter, crossed by a stout gold pin suggesting that the jewel was once attached to a stem of some perishable material, perhaps wood or ivory. The reverse side of the jewel is of gold ornamented with an elaborate tree-like scroll on a basket-work background.

When the first description of the jewel was published in 1698 by Dr. Musgrave, he called it an amulet. An account written in the first quarter of this century says that, "The jewel, worn in the front of his [King Alfred] helmet, would be known to his friends and enemies alike, so it is supposed that, lest it should betray him, he buried it." If such a case, surely Alfred would have returned himself or sent someone to retrieve it. Perhaps the true purpose may never be known. One other logical use has been proposed, that is, that it was the terminal of an abbot's *aestel*, or pointer, used to follow the lines of a manuscript to prevent it being soiled by the fingers of the reader.

For twenty-five years after its discovery, the Alfred Jewel remained in the possession of Sir Thomas Wrothe's uncle, Colonel Nathaniel Palmer, of Fairfield House, Stoke Couray. The Colonel had attended Trinity College, Oxford University, and after his death in 1717 this precious relic was presented to his alma mater. Its arrival in the Ashmolean Museum is recorded under the date 1718 in the Museum's earliest *Book of Benefactors*.

The modern adaptation of the Alfred Jewel is slightly smaller than the original, being fitted with a non-safety catch. The figure, the floral stems and the blue enameled background are fairly faithful copies of the original except that the reddish brown belt of the original has been replaced by a divided shield, the left half (from the viewer's standpoint) is reddish brown and the right half is green. Applied to the lower section of the animal's head is a letter "B" done in blue enamel and outlined in silver-gilt. There is also a variance in the inscription. The modern jewel reads, "AELFRED MEC CEWRCAN." The letter "T" has been dropped from the original "HEHT," the "G" in GEWYRCAN has been replaced by a "C" and the "Y" dropped and a decorative floral motif inserted in its place.

Inquiries concerning the silver-gilt adaptation of the Alfred Jewel were made to the Birmingham Assay Office and also to the Ashmolean Museum. The latter being the owner, it was assumed that permission would have been necessary in order to copy the design. Neither institution had any records showing the occasion for the modern jewel, nor the significance of the blue enameled "B." What is known about it, from the hallmarks, is that it was made in sterling (gilt) by James Fenton of Birmingham in 1926. James Fenton first registered his mark at the Birmingham Assay Office on the 5th of April 1851 and continued up to the 6th of March 1885 when the firm was taken over by Ernest Bowker and Allan Howard Elkington who continued to trade under the name of James Fenton. The last record the Birmingham Assay Office has of the company was in November 1927.

So, the mystery of the Alfred Jewel continues. Nobody is absolutely certain that the "Alfred" on the ancient jewel referred to Alfred the Great, nor can we be certain of its intended use. In spite of the gracious assistance of S.E.F. Beechey, Assay Master, Birmingham Assay Office, Birmingham and of Arthur MacGregor, Assistant keeper of Western Art at the Ashmolean Museum, the mystery of the "B" on the modern jewel continues as well.

Faithful reproductions of the Alfred Jewel have been made. One writer about 1930 wrote, "When the Ashmolean Museum was founded the Alfred Jewel was handed over to its keeping, and there it is today for all to see, with exact duplicates in gold and enamel that anyone of us may buy. One copy lies before us as we write."

Chatelaines

Chatelaines as waist-hung articles go back in history to 2000 B.C. During Roman times they were worn by men and women. Those early ones were made of bronze with three chains attached which held keys. Saxon chatelaines were attached to a girdle and were sometimes made of ivory. They held keys and often a dagger as well. More festive occasions might be anticipated in the presence of the chatelaine wearer of medieval times as theirs often carried a nutmeg grater and corkscrew as well as the keys to the liquor cabinet.

By the eighteenth century chatelaines were worn only by women. Silver toothpicks, pin cushions—some with silver mountings—scissors and perfume bottles were among the items attached.

Chatelaines of the 1840s were somewhat larger than earlier ones. By the 1850s the fashion of wearing chatelaines had subsided but was revived in 1871 by Princess Alexandra of Wales who wore one. They remained in vogue for another 20 years.

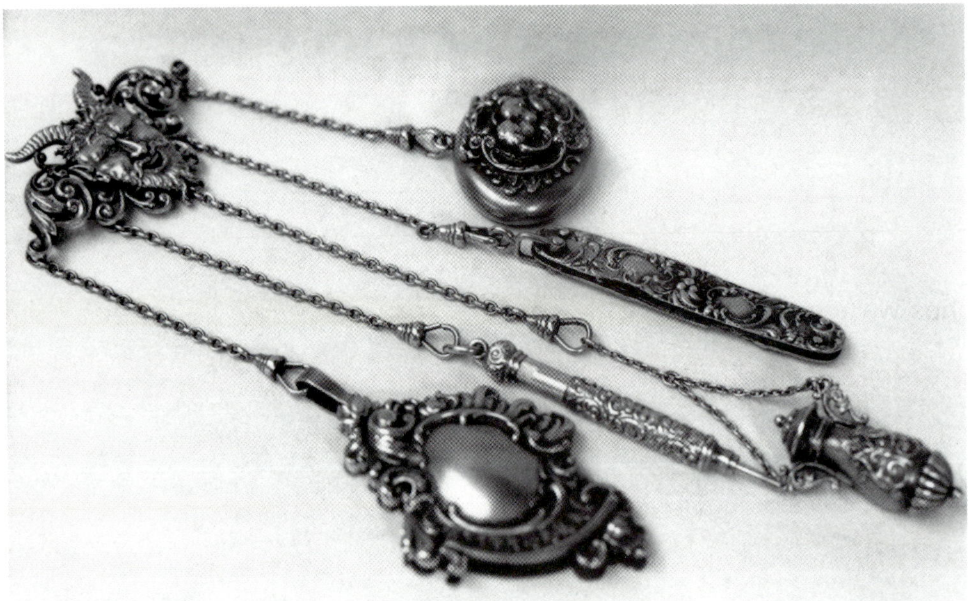

Chatelaine of silver with five tools attached, made by William B. Kerr, Co., c.1880. *Photo: Silver Magazine*.

In Victorian times the waist chain was replaced by a deep hook which was attached over the waist band. A shaped plate from which chains with swivel ends dangled were used for suspending scissors, thimble cases, small scent bottles and other trifles.

Some silver manufacturers advertised "Chatelaines to Suite the Wearer." For instance, chatelaines for the needlewoman might include books of needles, scissors, thimbles, pin cushions and a thimble case. Or, a religious chatelaine might have a rosary and a prayer book, a hymnal and other trinkets, a miniature fan and a tiny watch.

The term "chatelaine" was first applied to the wife of the castellan—the mistress of a chateau or other large household. By association, it came to be applied to the item itself. The word chatelaine is derived from *Chabelaine* or warden, whose duty it was to carry the keys of a castle.

Chatelaines were worn in England in the seventeenth century, and flourished in the eighteenth and early nineteenth. By c.1850 they declined in popularity in England when they were no longer regarded as fashionable jewelry and were worn only for their practical uses. Today they are valued mainly for their collectibility as examples of yesterdays fashions.

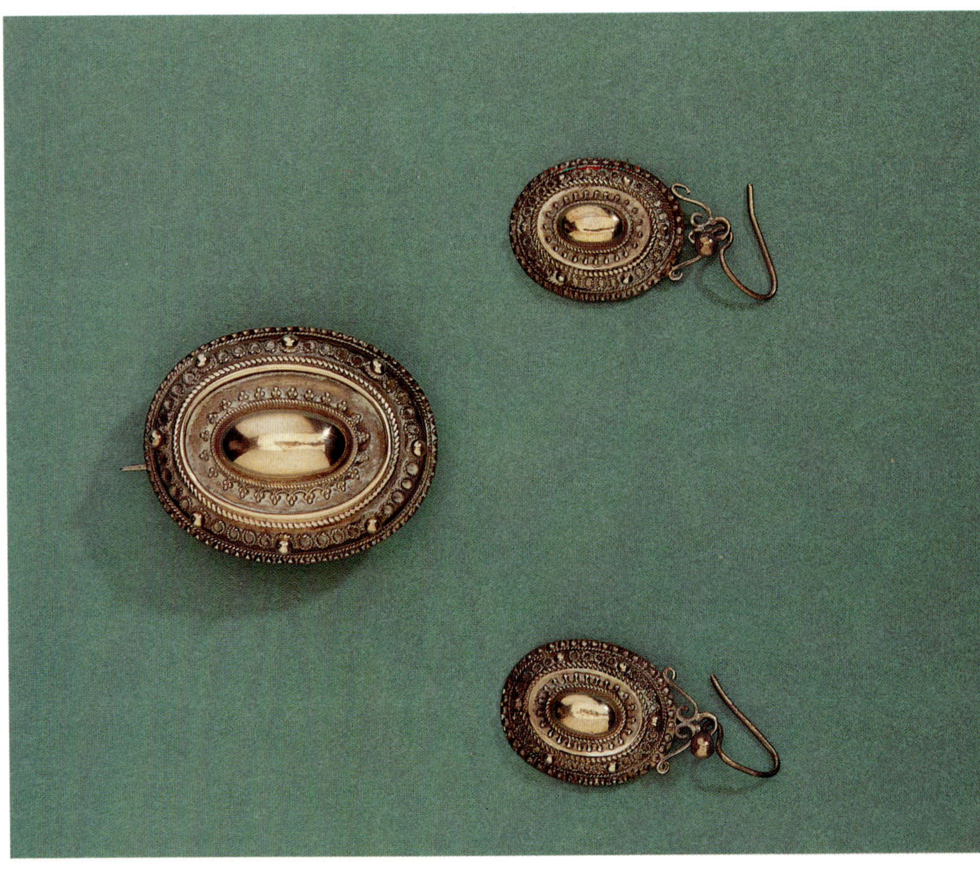

Silver brooch with matching earrings, unmarked, probably European. All three pieces have granulations in lacy geometric pattern. On the back of the brooch is a glass enclosed memento cavity. c.1860. *Private collection.*

Scottish jewelry

The penannular (means almost a ring) brooch was made by Ward Bros., Birmingham, England, 1917, and is a well-known Celtic design. The stone is cut crystal. penannular pin brooches were invented independently by the Celts in Britain during the Early Iron Age (1st millennium B.C.). Other jewelry of that period included beads of amber, jet and glass but metalwork was featured. Anannular (means a complete ring) pin brooches were made of gold, silver, bronze and electrum (a pale yellow natural alloy of gold and silver—much used to mount articles of jewelry made of amber).

The heart-shaped pin is silver with red and green stones set in the outline of the heart. The thistle blossom in the center is formed from an amethyst, unmarked, c.1900.

The oval pin contains a faceted cairngorm surrounded by the oak leaf motif. Unmarked, c.1900. The repoussé oak leaf refers to the Boscobel Oak where Charles II hid in 1651 after his defeat by Cromwell at Worcester.

The cairngorm is a variety of quartz, a clear brown which takes its name from the Cairngorm Mountains of the Scottish highlands. Originally found on Cairn Gorm, a mountain in Scotland, and much used in Scottish jewelry. The original sources are near depletion. Present-day stones may come from Arran, the Swiss Alps, or Colorado. Heat-treated amethysts from Brazil may also be used.

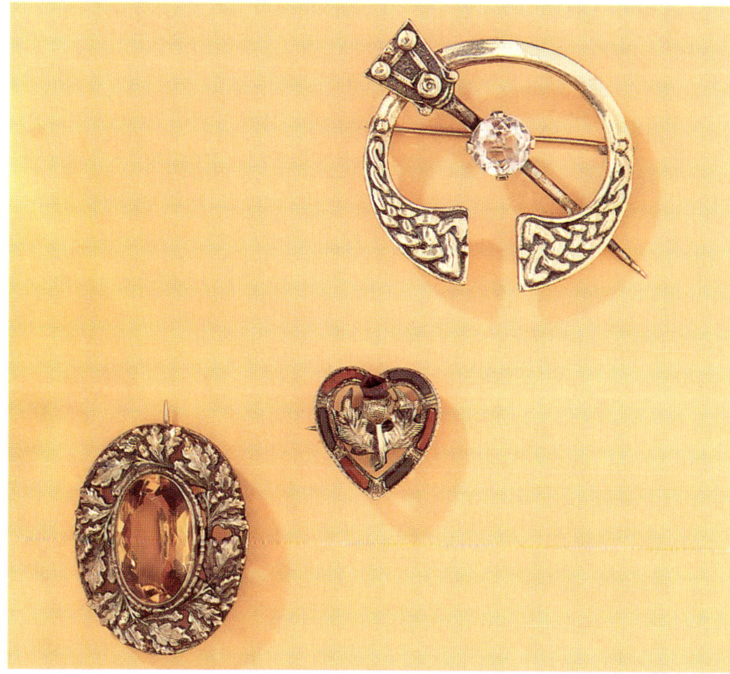

Three pins of Scottish design. From left to right: 1. Penannular brooch, sterling with cut crystal. 1917.
2. Heart pin of silver with thistle design, amethyst, red and green stones. c.1900.
3. Scottish brooch with faceted cairngorm and silver repoussé oak leaf decoration. *Private collection.*

"Baltimore" style jewelry

The repoussé decoration so closely related to the city of Baltimore and its oldest silversmith, Samuel Kirk, is actually a "Baroque-revival" with Caroline features. While generally attributed to Samuel Kirk, it was made by several other Baltimore silversmith as well.

The repoussé style of the 1820s was well suited to Victorian taste so it is not surprising that it had "one of the longest runs of any style in the decorative arts remaining popular and essentially unchanged for at least one hundred years." (Jennifer F. Goldsborough, *Silver in Maryland*, p. 13-15.)

Careful study of Baltimore repoussé silver discloses more variations than first thought. Early pieces were comprised of a variety of small or romantic Gothic "Tuscan" buildings amidst birds and flowers—called "Etruscan" by the makers. Fern fronds were added to the floral designs of the 1870s and 1880s. Large scale roses adorned the early twentieth century silver. The 1840s and 1850s saw the introduction of "Chinoisserie" scenes of actual buildings on "bespoke" services.

Some of the finest examples of Baltimore repoussé silver are the custom-made and presentation pieces. So many Baltimore silversmiths adopted these repoussé style that it is virtually impossible to be sure of the maker of a particular piece without consulting the marks.

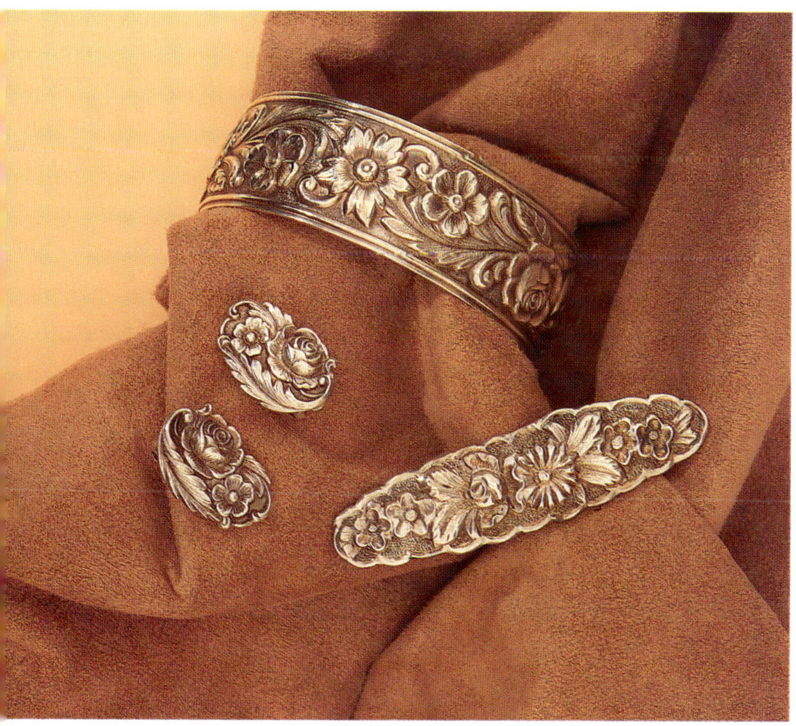

Bracelet, pin and earrings in floral repoussé designs made by S. Kirk & Son, Baltimore, MD. Pin c.1900. Bracelet and earrings c.1964. *Private Collection.*

Novelty jewelry

Dragonfly clips and pins became popular around 1870 with the creation of mass-produced novelty jewelry. They became popular accents for day dresses in the late nineteenth century and continued to be made and worn in various forms throughout the 1950s as lapel pins. Very lightweight dragonfly pins were traditionally used to keep mourning veils in place.

Right: Link bracelet and pearl earrings set in silver. Marked: STERLING. From Hawaii c.1950.
Left: Bracelet of silver floral links with jade balls. Maker: Wall and Dougherty, Honolulu, Hawaii. c.1950. *Private collection*.

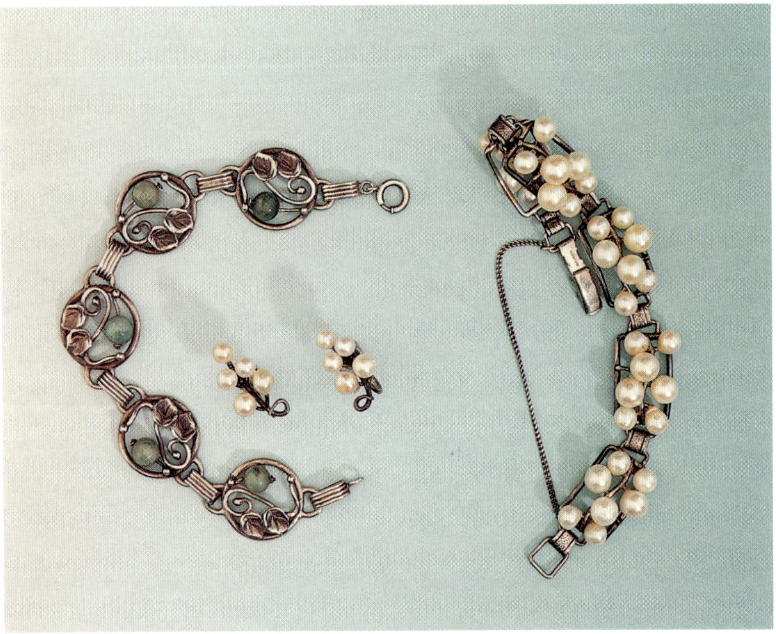

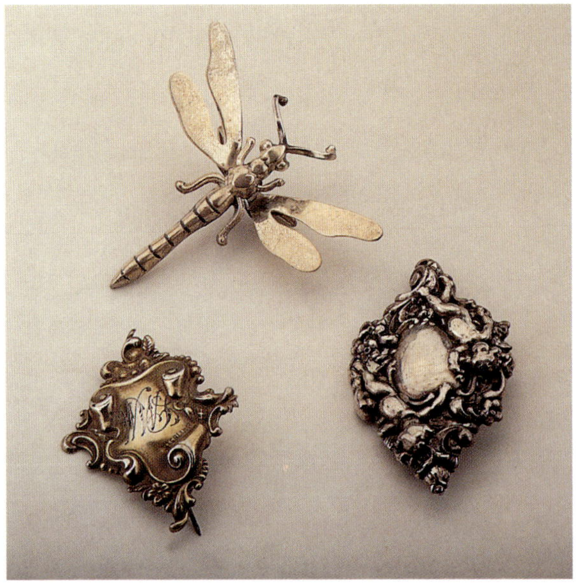

Dragonfly pin, c. 1880.
Sterling Art Nouveau pin, unmarked, with initials inscribed on the smooth front. The straight stick pin on the back indicates this is an original of the period 1895 to 1905. 1 3/8" long.
Sterling Art Nouveau pin with cherubs design. Safety catch on the back indicates this is a later reproduction of the style first popular c. 1885 to 1910. 1-3/4" long. *Collection of Antonia Moore. Photo: Bruce Waters*.

Below:
Earrings depicting the rabbit in the Mad Hatter's Tea Party story from the book *Alice in Wonderland.*
Silver owl tie tack. Maker: Unger Bros. Measures 9/16". Bracelet with heart.
Sterling lapel pin designed as a dancer. 2 3/4" long. *Collection of Antonia Moore. Photo: Bruce Waters.*

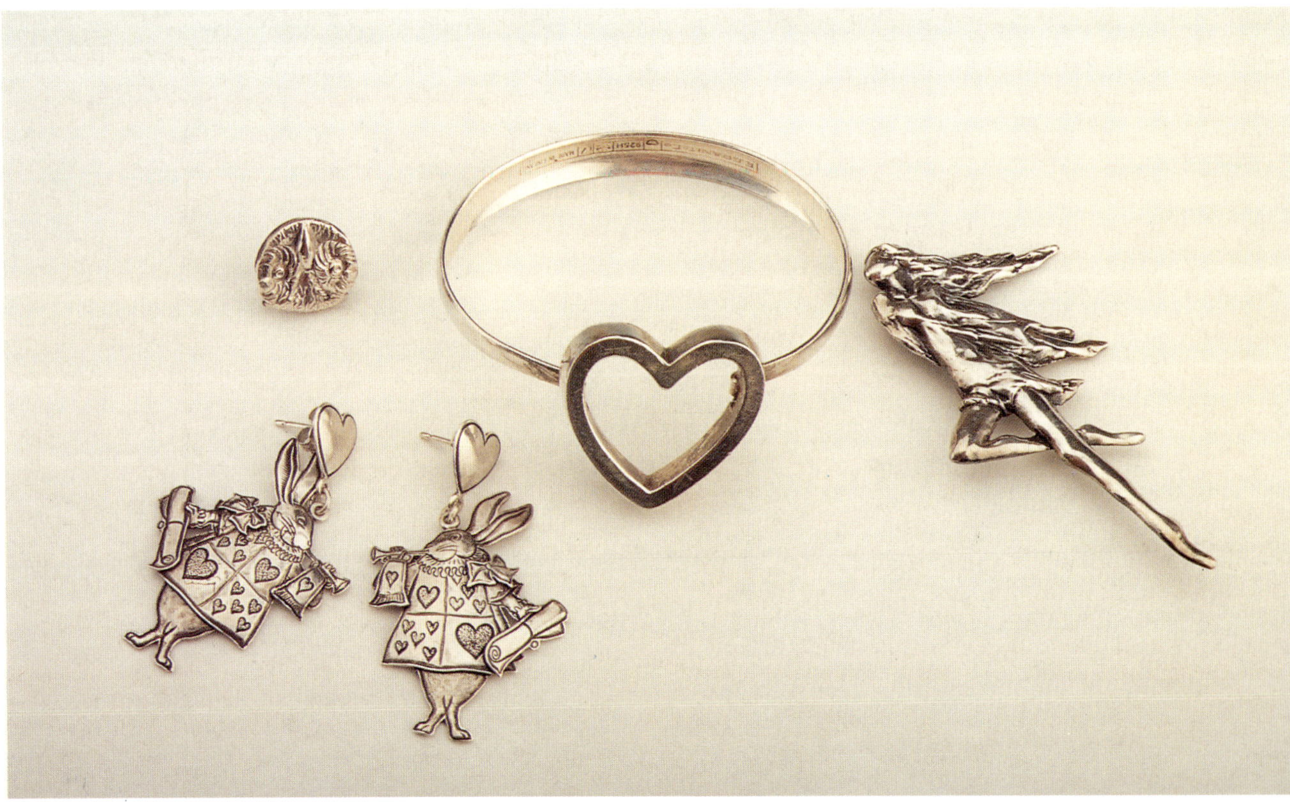

Charm bracelets

Novelty jewelry of the late Victorian period led to the development of charms for charm bracelets, which are gold or silver chain bracelets from which small trinkets are suspended. Among the favorite trinkets are figures of animals and miniatures of important historical buildings and articles associated with a particular place, person or event. Charm bracelets became popular about the middle of the nineteenth century and, though the popularity has varied from time to time, they continue to be sold, especially in resort areas and any place travelers and tourists gather. Some charm bracelets are assembled with all the charms of a single place or theme. Others are assembled one-by-one as people travel. Such bracelets are especially appreciated by the stay-at-home members of the family. They are proof that the traveler has been thinking of the ones left behind. Being so small and easily carried, they are ideal mementos of travels and happy days.

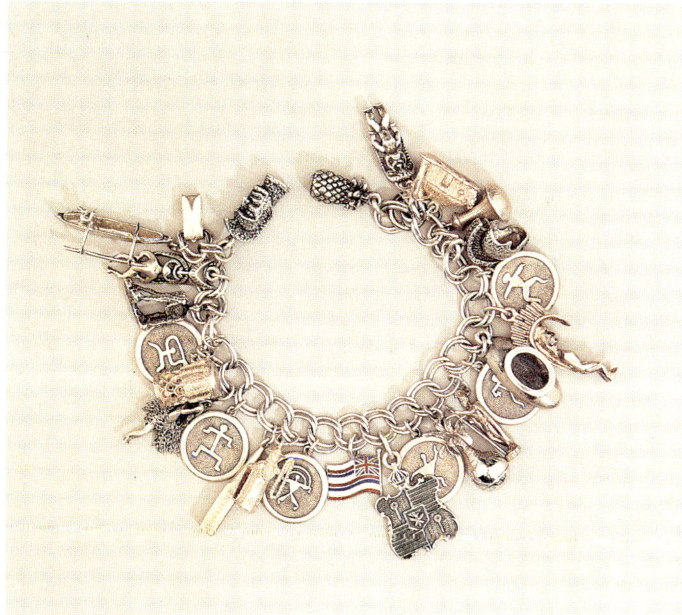

Sterling charm bracelet with double link chain and twenty-five charms. Six discs, designed by Dorothy Rainwater after Hawaiian petroglyphs c.1950. Other charms include an outrigger canoe, hula dancer, British colonial flag of Hawaii, Hawaiian royal coat of arms. *Private collection.*

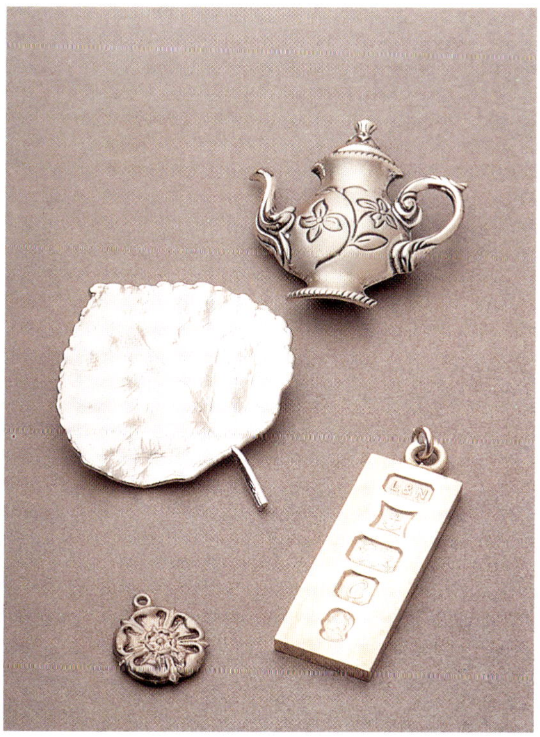

Private collection. Photo: Bruce Waters.

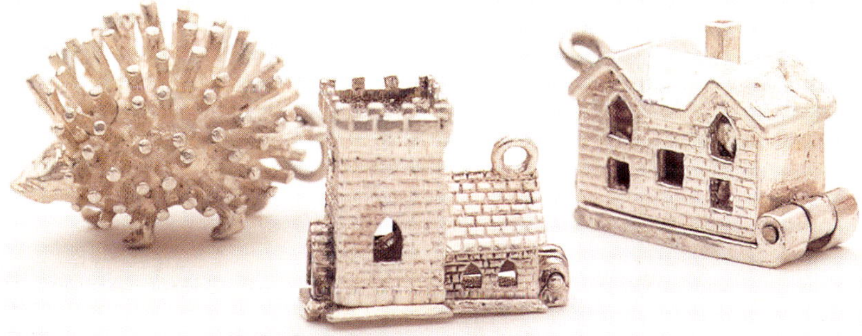

Private collection. Photo: Bruce Waters.

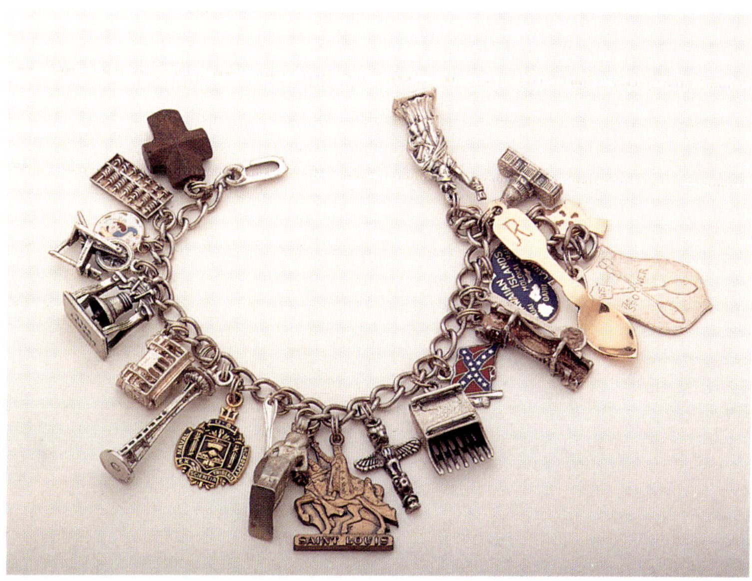

Charm bracelet. Most of the charms are sterling. They include: West Virginia Fairy Cross; abacus; enameled Amish peacock; spinning wheel; Liberty Bell; cable car (a Stanhope—hold to the light and see a picture of the Golden Gate Bridge); Seattle Space Needle; Naval Academy logo; silver spoon; Egyptian statue; St. Louis statue; totem pole; cranberry scoop; Confederate Flag; Golden Gate Bridge; silver ladle; Hawaiian map; 14K gold spoon; Statue of Liberty; U.S. Capital; Celtic Cross; ID membership in spooners' club. *Private collection. Photo: Bruce Waters.*

Gibson Girl jewelry

American illustrator Charles Dana Gibson drew the first of his famous Gibson Girl images in 1885. He was born in Roxbury, Massachusetts, on September 14, 1867, and was brought up in modest circumstances. One of his ancestors was William Lovert of Boston, a noted painter of miniatures. Gibson's artistic talent was noted early in his life and he was apprenticed to the sculptor Augustus Saint-Gaudens, but the arrangement did not prove congenial. With the encouragement of illustrator Dan Beard, Gibson enrolled at the Art Student's League in New York, where he spent two years.

In 1886 Gibson sold a drawing to John Ames Mitchell for the humor magazine *Life*, and that year he visited London. Upon his return to New York he illustrated stories for the magazines *Harper's*, *Scribner's*, and *Century*. His special type of illustration placed an emphasis on people from the upper middle class, and they were gently satirical. He continued to contribute drawings to *Life* and other publications. While Gibson illustrated magazines of many different types, it was his drawings of Gibson Girls that brought him lasting fame. He spent the later part of his life painting portraits in oils and died in New York City on December 23, 1944.

Gibson Girl illustrations became the epitome of what was most desirable in a girl in the 1885-1900 era, and it did not matter that she was not real. Even today just to mention her name is to hear sighs from men too young to have known her. She lacked many of the skills for which present-day young ladies are known favorably; she could not cook or manage a large household, but, like the "people's princess," she was idealized as a "lady." Her actions were not always politically correct, but her sympathy for and understanding of those less fortunate made her, like Diana, a princess for the world. A Gibson Girl lived in a world among socially prominent people— people of wealth and position. Against this glittering background the Gibson Girl drew the adoring attention of all who saw her. Her way of doing her hair was copied. Her clothing was admired and copied. Manufacturers labeled shirtwaists with the "Gibson pleat" running from shoulder to waist in a tapering line. Shirts, skirts, and hats were given her name. Spoons, cups, and mugs, etc. were imprinted with her face. While she graced the tennis court and appeared on the beach in a modest bathing suit, her demeanor was such that her presence at un-chaperoned situations between the sexes was unquestioned.

Who were the models for Charles Dana Gibson's girl on the red velvet swing? One was the beautiful Evelyn Nesbit who posed for him many times, including for the pin shown here and for Gibson's painting "The Eternal Question." Then, at the tender age of sixteen, she became the mistress of Sanford White, the distinguished architect. White had made a hobby of seducing young girls and for his amusement would have them put on little girls' dresses and cavort on a red velvet swing in a heavily curtained, lavishly decorated miniature Taj Mahal. At the age of nineteen, Evelyn left White to become engaged to Henry Thaw, whom she married the following year. Thaw enticed young girls to his apartment where he whipped them— a treatment he also inflicted on his young bride. Thaw beat her until she "confessed" her past "sins" with Sanford White. Thaw was insanely jealous and while attending a dinner theater Thaw shot White. Many felt that White deserved being shot and spoke in Thaw's defense. Thaw was eventually declared criminally insane and was imprisoned for life in a mental institution. Finally released in 1922, having been declared sane, he roamed the world, spending his millions until his death in 1947. Evelyn Nesbit continued to appear in vaudeville for many years and later took up a career in ceramics in California.

And the meaning of "The Eternal Question?" Why, of course, though it is seldom voiced out loud, it is simply, "Will she—or won't she?"

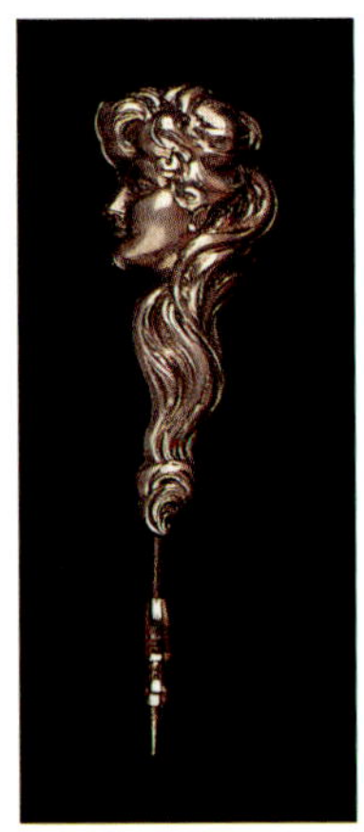

Sterling silver stick pin after an illustration by Charles Dana Gibson. A woman's hair swirls to form a question mark. In 1885, American illustrator Gibson drew an idealized woman, for which Evelyn Nesbit was the model. She became known as a "Gibson Girl." She was the epitome of what was most desirable in women's appearance at the time. (See p. 65, *Bell's Gold Jewelry*). 1-3/4" long, unmarked. *Private collection Photo: Bruce Waters.*

Bracelets of Hawaiian design

Hawaii's mild climate meant that the people's clothing needs were minimal. The celebrated feather capes and cloaks of Hawaiian dress were essentially indications of social standing rather than practical clothing.

Everyday clothing for men consisted of a *malo* or loin cloth. They were about twelve inches wide and three to four feet long. Women's kapa cloth skirt was called a *pa'u.* Ordinarily, only women wore the *pa' u* but both men and women wore them while dancing the hula. The *pa' u* was about thirty inches wide and three to four yards long. The *pa' u* was simply wrapped around the waist.

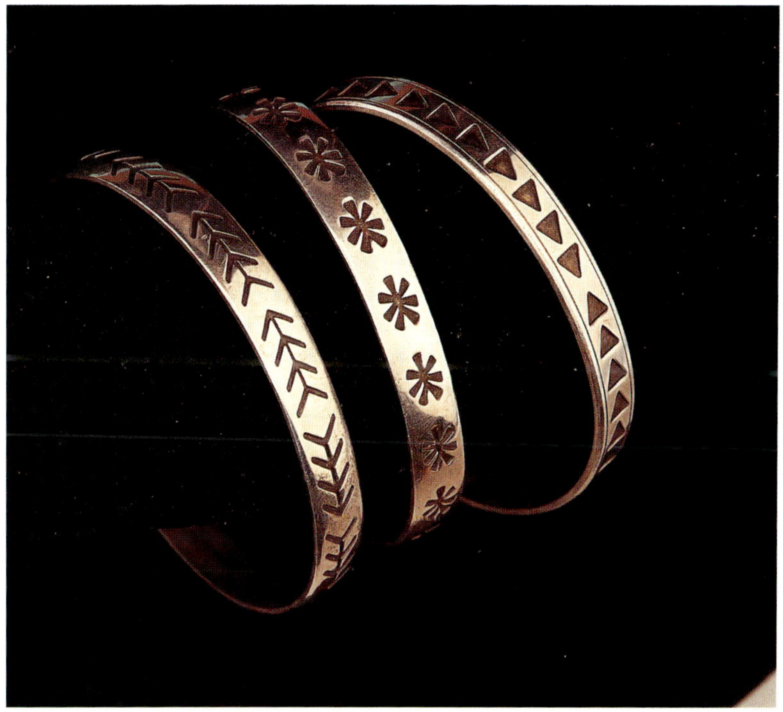

Three silver bracelets with designs based on ancient Hawaiian kapa cloth. Designed by Dorothy Rainwater for the E. J. Towle Company, Seattle, Washington, c.1955-1960, and sold by the Bishop Museum, Honolulu, gift shop. *Private collection.*

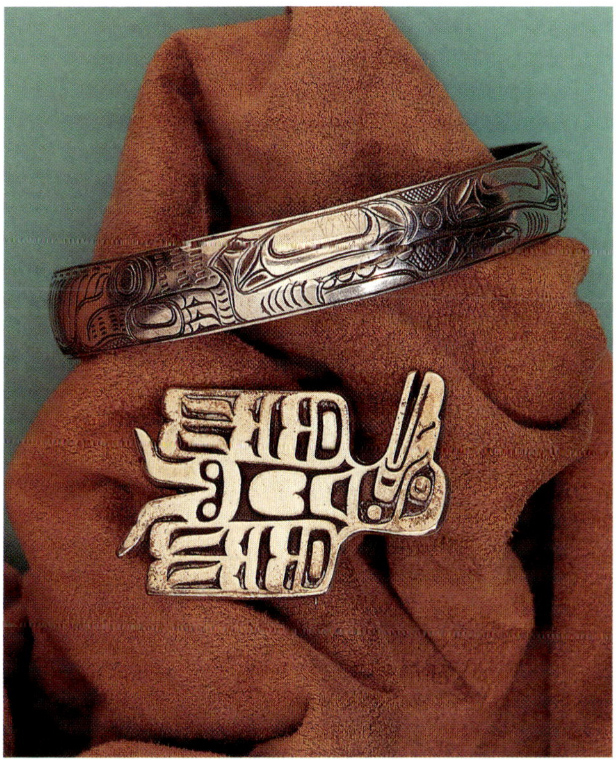

Incised bracelet of silver with early overlapping clasp. Unmarked. c.1940. Made by a Pacific Northwest coast native craftsman.
Sterling pin with raven design. Marked "A". Pacific Northwest coast craftsman (possibly Alaska). *Private collection.*

Kapa cloth was made from several types of the inner bark of trees and shrubs. The paper mulberry (*Wauke*) was the favored source for kapa cloth. Making kapa was women' s work though the men cut the trees or bushes and the women stripped off the bark. After the bark was stripped from the trees, it was soaked in sea water for a week or two to make it soft and pliable. The strips of bark were beaten, then set aside to bleach in the sun. Several beatings were done to produce the soft *kapa*. The final beating was done with a wooden beater with a geometric pattern which left a design akin to the watermark on fine paper. It was from some of these beaters that the designs on the bracelets were found.

Maple leaf pin

The maple leaf has long been accepted as a symbol of Canada. The decision to adopt the maple leaf flag was reached in 1965 only after the longest debate in Canadian parliamentary history. The leaf pin shown here was made by G. Cini about 1960.

Guglielmo Cini grew up in Florence, Italy. He was trained as a jewelry designer there. He came to the United States in 1922 already an accomplished creator of fine jewelry. He created handwrought jewelry in 1922. He established his own business producing silver jewelry in Boston, Massachusetts, and worked there until 1957 when he relocated to Laguna Beach, California. Many of his designs include flowers with realistic detail. His jewelry is sold by specialty shops such as Gumps of San Francisco. His jewelry was sold by specialty shops, for many years.

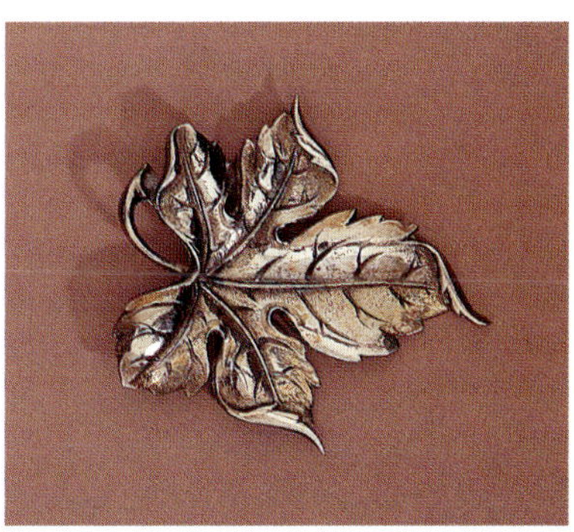

Sterling maple leaf pin. Maker: Guglielmo Cini, United States c.1960. *Private collection.*

Hand & Hammer jewelry

Third generation silversmith Chip DeMatteo designs hundreds of jewelry articles. Many of them are custom designed. Unlike many of today's silver jewelry and collectibles made by machine, DeMatteo and the members of his workshop prefer the handmade. They also feel that the intrinsic value of the silver matters less to silver lovers than its beauty and amazing physical properties. Silver is the most reflective element known to man. Its unmatched conductivity of heat and electricity make it invaluable in industry and science and its incredible malleability and ductility make it the perfect medium for the artist and craftsman.

Recently, with the encouragement of his wife, Ann, DeMatteo and his workers have designed a line of equestrian jewelry. This tremendous new collection includes close to fifty brooches, chains, earrings, key rings and pins with an equestrian theme. "Man's Best Friend," the dog, is well represented in some forty sterling silver pins. Their hundreds of other designs include florals, Nantucket basket, crosses, hearts, angels, snowflakes, Celtic crosses, wreaths, animals, butterflies, birds and much more.

In addition to Hand & Hammer's extensive line of handmade jewelry, they are also exclusive suppliers of keys to initiates of the prestigious Phi Beta Kappa Academic Society. Their commercial and corporate clients include Tiffany & Co., A.T.&T., Pepsi Co., and many others. Nearly every major museum and many smaller ones in the country are customers for Hand & Hammer Silversmith's specially designed and custom made jewelry and collectibles.

Chip DeMatteo, the third generation silversmith, learned silversmithing from his father, William L. DeMatteo, who was best known to the public as a silversmith at Colonial Williamsburg. He had been commissioned to design and make presentation pieces for every American president since J. F. Kennedy. The White House and Department of State were among his clients.

Three of Hand & Hammer's present designs are illustrated here. Peter Rabbit peeks out of his watering can. He can be a Christmas tree ornament or a brooch. The Fabergé egg ornament may also be worn as a brooch. The Angel with Star is a tree ornament or a brooch. While the emphasis here is on silver, several of the designs may also be vermeil.

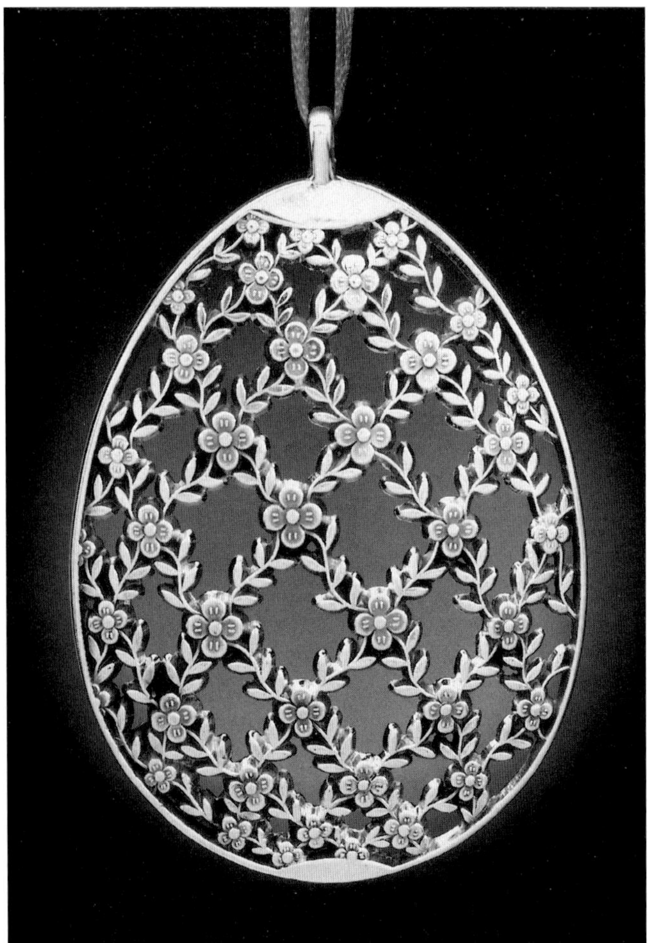

Fabergé egg ornament or pendant of sterling silver made by Chip DeMatteo. *Courtesy of Hand & Hammer. Photo: Mark Gulezian.*

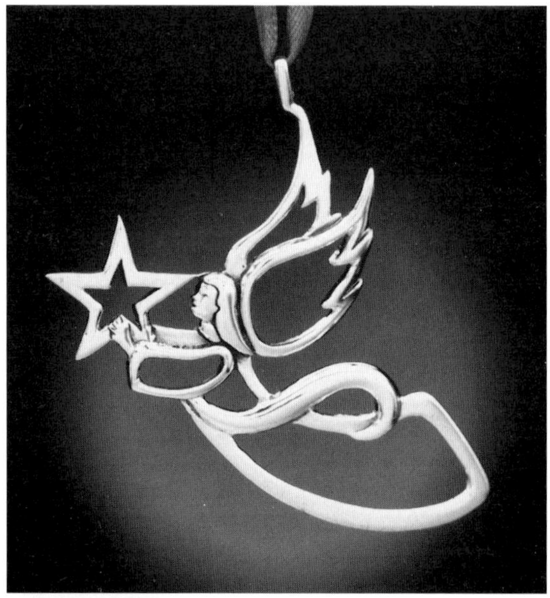

Angel with star tree ornament or pendant of sterling silver made by Chip DeMatteo. *Courtesy of Hand & Hammer. Photo: Mark Gulezian.*

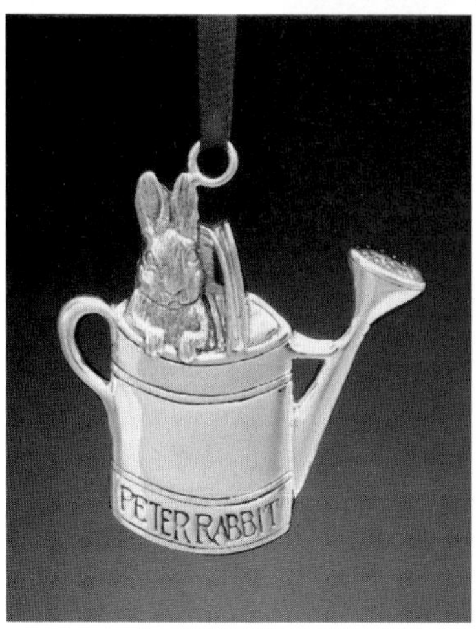

Left:
Peter Rabbit tree ornament or pendant of sterling silver made by Chip DeMatteo. *Courtesy of Hand & Hammer. Photo: Mark Gulezian.*

Greg Reeves

Silversmith, goldsmith, and jeweler Greg Reeves of Annapolis, Maryland, has chosen to create custom designed and handmade silver and jewelry, such as belt buckles, pendants, and pins. His hand engraved switch plates are truly "jewels for the home." Much of his sterling silver jewelry reflects his interest in the equestrian world as this is "horse country" as much as are parts of Kentucky and Virginia.

Greg Reeves was born in Colville, Washington, on January 14, 1956 to Marjorie Erp Reeves and Edgar B. Reeves, Jr. In 1962 the family moved to the suburban Washington, D. C. area where Edgar Reeves was employed by the 4-H Foundation and Department of Agriculture. His parents' backgrounds were English, Welsh, Scottish, and German; they were just a typical "all American" family. Up to this time Greg had not exhibited any special artistic interests or talents.

Greg graduated from Largo, Maryland, High School and started working for Jaguar car specialists in the metal division in Bladensburg, Maryland. He found he was much interested in working with metal, especially this particular type of metal work. Greg's older brother, Mark, was doing leather work manufacturing tack for the Quarterhorse trade. Greg went to Reno, Nevada, to the Silver State Silver Company where he was to work for three months without pay; in time a decision would be made. After only one month, Greg showed such skill and promise that he was put on the payroll immediately. This company specializes in making silver buckles, Indian turquoise jewelry, and other jewelry in a Western theme, notably silver-mounted leather goods.

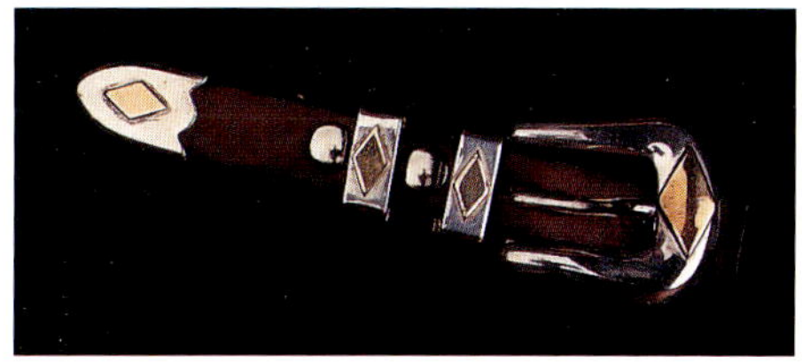

Western style buckle, loops and tip marked Precious Annapolis Metals, Sterling, buckle 1-7/8" long X 1-5/8" wide, designed and made by Greg Reeves. $250.

Mark Reeves moved to Albuquerque, New Mexico, to make saddles with silver mountings. He needed a silversmith, so Greg joined him. Together, they created many of the silver-mounted saddles for which that part of the country is well known. Later, they de-

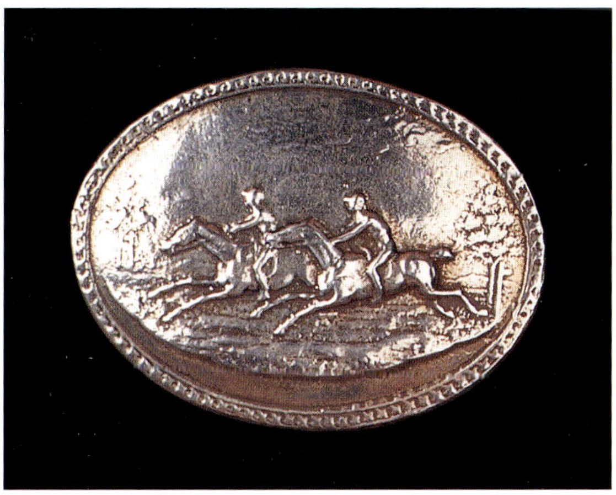

Left:
Small Steeplechase buckle marked Sterling, 2-3/8" long X 1-3/4" high, designed and made by Greg Reeves. $200.

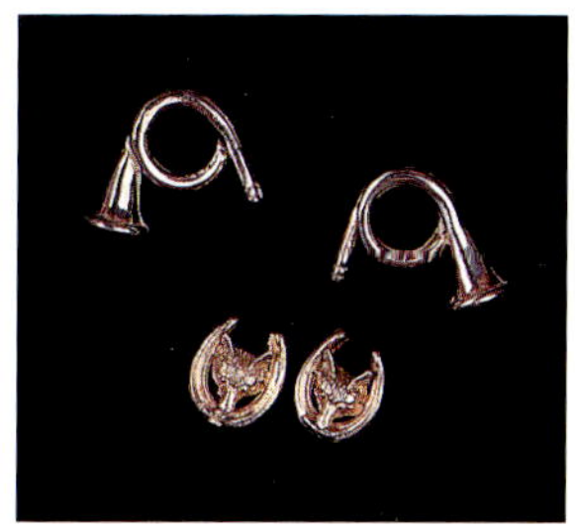

Small fox mask and horseshoe earrings, 5/16" long, designed and made by Greg Reeves. $25.
Small hunting horn earrings, 9/16" long, designed and made by Greg Reeves. $25.

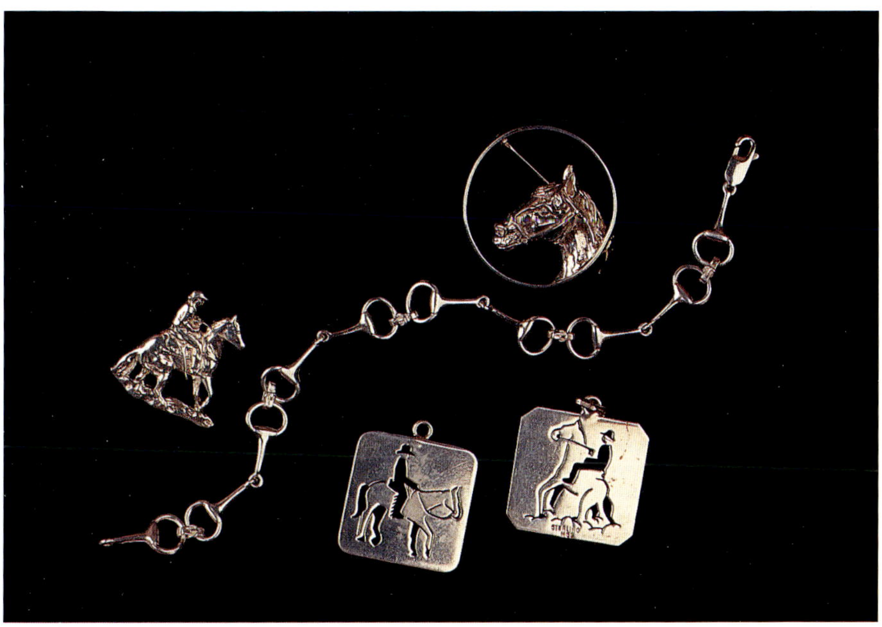

Left:
Hinged Bit bracelet, 7-1/2" long. $85.
Running Horse slide, 1" wide X 1-1/8" long. $35.
Running Horse cutout charm marked Sterling MST, 1" square. $65.
Western Pleasure Horse cutout charm marked Sterling MST, 1" square. $65
All the above designed and made by Greg Reeves.
Circle pin with horse head marked Beau Sterling. $75.

cided to return to Maryland to set up shop in their parents' basement. There they made their wares which they took to horse shows to sell.

In 1978, the Reeves brothers established their first real shop in Gambrills, Maryland, near Crofton. For about ten years they made custom saddles and tack for the Quarterhorse trade. They produced silver on saddles, halters, bridles, personal attire, belts, belt buckles, and name plates. Gradually they developed a line of equestrian jewelry with venders serving the English Riding circuits.

Their next move was to Annapolis, Maryland, where the Reeves brothers continued to work together. In 1988 Greg decided to have his own shop for sterling items and without saddlery. He opened Annapolis Precious Metals where he designs, makes, and sells custom articles. In 1999 he modernized the shop and created space to display more of his own work as well as pearl and precious and semi-precious-set jewelry.

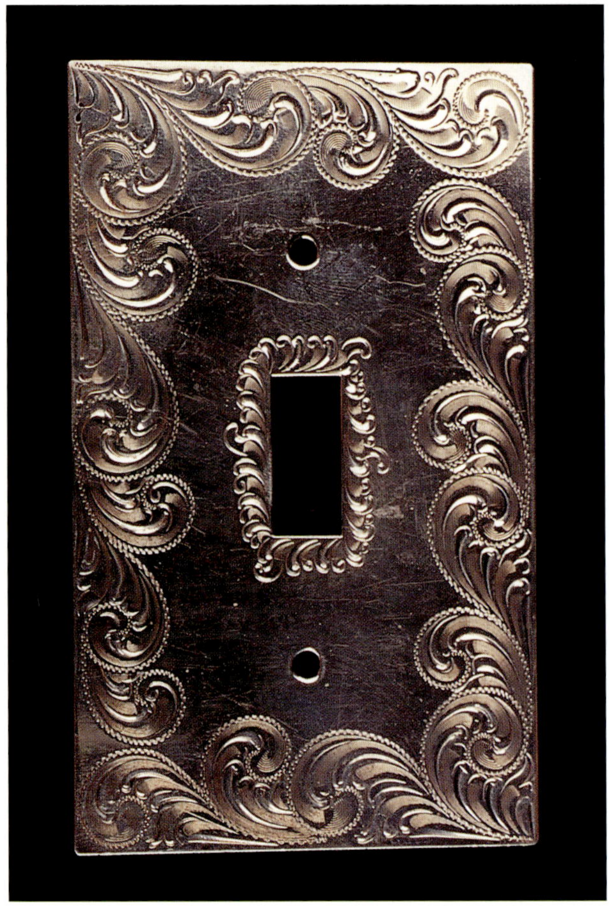

Switch plate with engraved scrolled leaf design, 2-3/4" wide X 4-1/2" high, designed and made by Greg Reeves. $125.

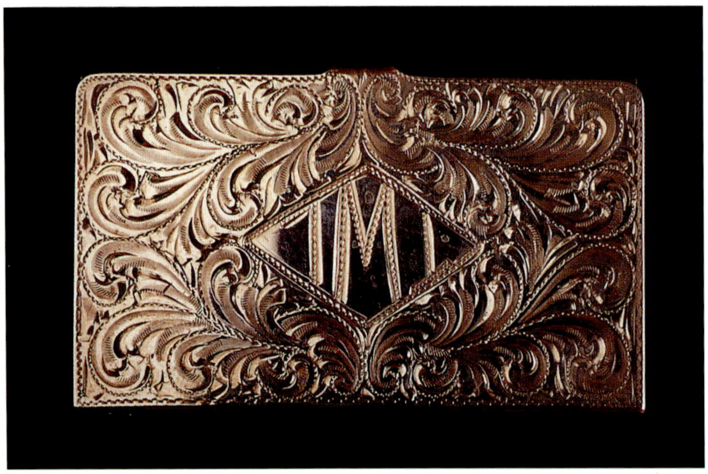

Card case engraved with initials TWL and scrolled leaf design and marked Handmade Sterling, 3-3/4" long X 2-1/4" high, designed and made by Greg Reeves. $275.

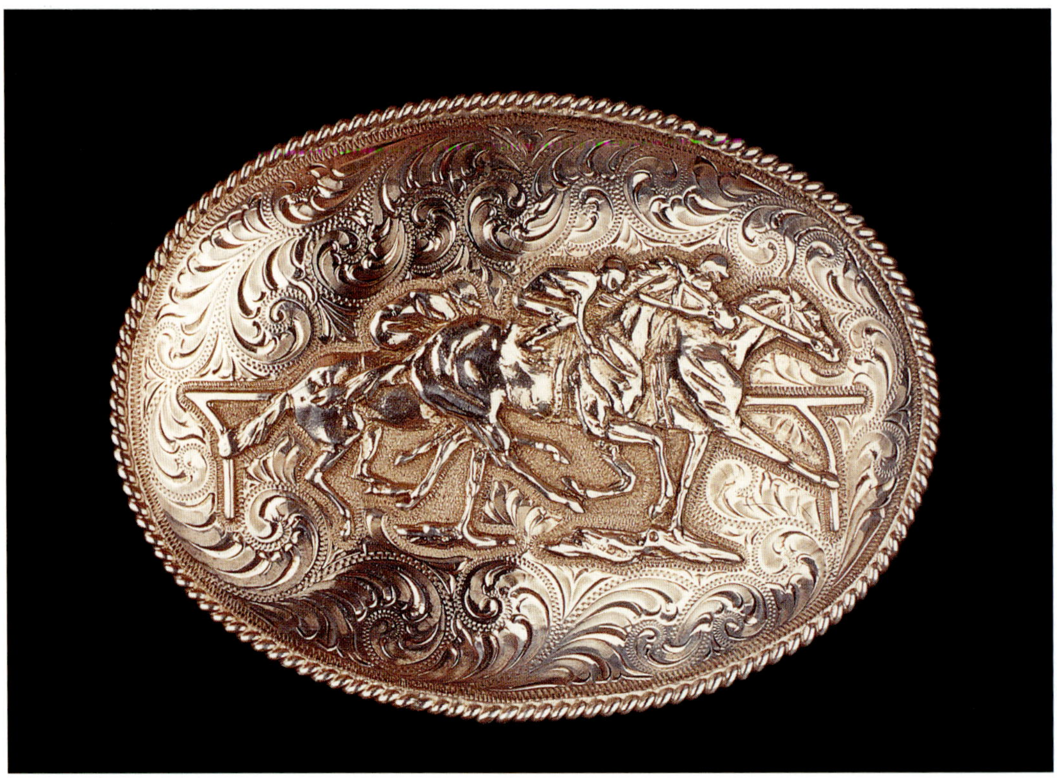

Large Racing Scene buckle marked Marks Saddlery Handmade Sterling, 5 1/4" long X 3 7/8" high, designed and made by Greg Reeves. $597.

Chapter 4. Silver Curios for use...
...by Gentlemen

According to the Tiffany *Blue Book* of 1880, a gentleman's personal items ranged from collapsible drinking cups to "Segar Lighters" to silver trowels "for use at ceremonial laying of corner-stones." Those are only a few of the many personal items made in silver and silverplate for the gentleman.

A dresser set on his dresser might have included a pair of military brushes with silver backs, many and assorted shaving needs such as an ornate shaving cup for the lightly scented shaving soap or a silver watch stand for the precious pocket watch. If the gentleman smoked in his bedroom, he might have an ash receiver there.

Other necessities for the gentleman might have included a good shaving brush with silver handle, a silver shoe horn and a silver collar box. Much depended on the occupations of the gentleman in question. The business man or banker probably had more silver articles on his dresser than his less affluent brothers.

Most of the purely personal items for the Victorian gentleman were in use every day. That is why they were found on his dresser in the bedroom. From belt buckles to clothes brush, the late nineteenth century gentleman had a wide array of personal items all adorned with silver.

The fastidious gentleman also included a cloth brush for his suits, a brush for his velvet coat collar and a hat brush. These often came in matched sets with sterling silver backs.

Flasks

Silver makers of quality included silver flasks for gentlemen toward the end of the nineteenth century. Shown in American catalogues of 1900 to 1910 were several different types of flasks. All were intended for alcoholic liquid refreshment.

Pocket or hip flasks were curved to fit into the gentleman's back pocket. Flasks with a flat bottom and being a little larger were used on a dinner table or desk. Still others were included as part of a matched toilet set.

While surely producing some of the finest silver flasks. Tiffany and Gorham were by no means the only places to buy a flask. Catalogues used by Unger Bros., Daniel Low & Co., Baird-North, Sears Roebuck and many others showed flasks in different styles and prices.

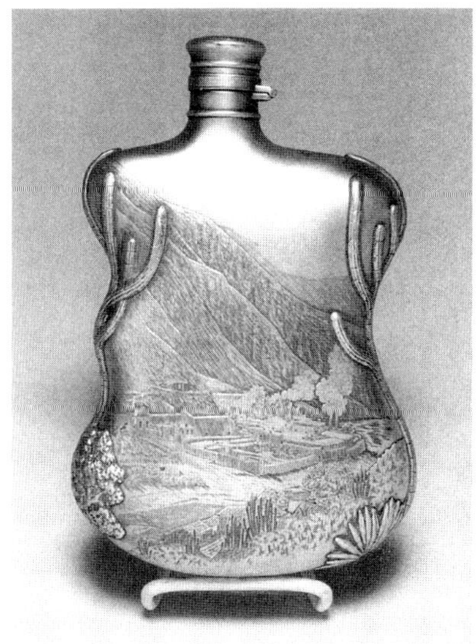

Gorham silver flask dated 1888. Forty-six flasks special ordered to present to investors of the Batopilas Silver Mine, Chihuahua, Mexico. Height: 7-1/2". Width: 5-1/2". *Collection of David and Hillary Keller, New York City.* $350-$700.

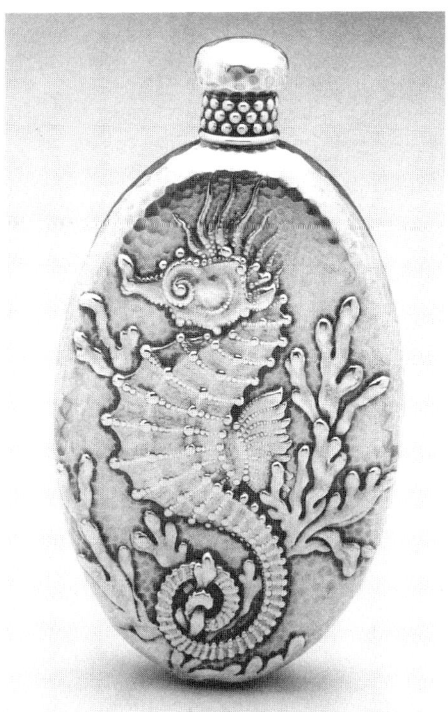

Sterling hip flask by Tiffany & Co., circa 1873-1891. Sea horse pattern with half round pearl shaped accents to make a third dimension of the background water. Pearls are also around neck of the flask. Height: 5-3/4". Width: 3". *Collection of David and Hillary Keller, New York City.* $350-$700.

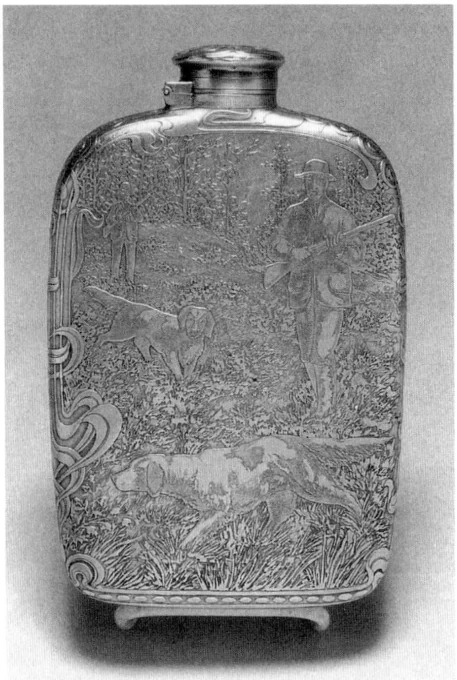

Left:
Very rare sterling flask called "Hunting" by Tiffany & Co. Made 1891-1902. The perspective of both dogs and hunters shows a third dimension in the scene. Height: 6-3/4". Width: 4-1/2". *Collection of David and Hillary Keller, New York City.* $350-$700.

Right:
Silver hip or pocket flask made by Tiffany & Co. circa 1891-1902. Called "Tennis Match." Note the perspective of the players. Height: 6". Width: 4". *Collection of David and Hillary Keller, New York City.* $350-$700.

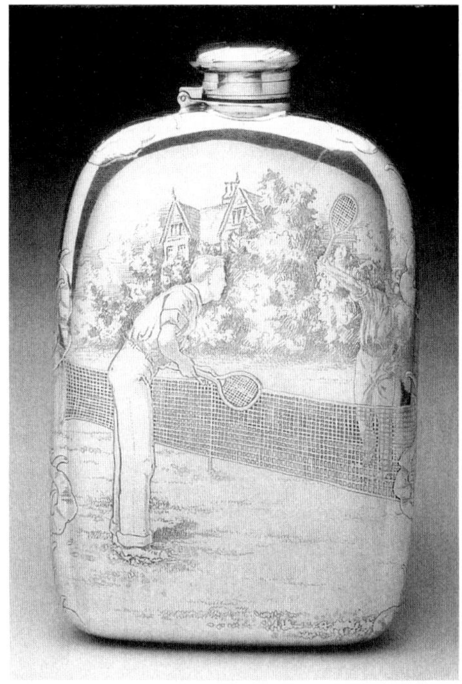

For the man who shaved

If a gentleman of the Victorian era had a well-filled wallet, he might never have wrestled with the problem of shaving himself at home. Instead, a part of his daily routine was a trip to the barber where he was shaved and shined from shoes up to a hair trim or cut, if needed. His personal shaving cup was lined up with the cups of other regular customers and the barber used a fresh razor for every shave given.

The average gentleman did *not* go regularly to the barber and so had to take care of his shaving himself. For this ritual, he required a sharp razor, a shaving mug, a shaving brush and a mirror or shaving stand. The latter came in two styles—a stand which could sit on top of a dresser or a larger floor model. Both types were complete with a drawer which could hold the necessities of shaving and, of course, the indispensable mirror.

Although some safety razors were made prior to 1900, it was not until 1906 that the Gillette Safety Razor began to replace the straight razor. Today, that safety razor has been replaced with the electric shaver. What will tomorrow bring for the gentleman who shaves?

On the mustache

Mustaches were particularly stylish from about 1860 to 1900. The oil paintings of that time showed gentlemen sporting a heavy upper lip of hair, which was usually waxed. For this reason, the gentleman who enjoyed his first cup of coffee while he shaved usually drank from a mustache cup.

Said mustache cup had a guard which prevented the mustache from getting wet and helped to keep the wax from melting.

The particularly proud mustache wearer required a special comb. Many times this mustache comb was carried in a handy pocket to be used at any time of the day to spruce up the gentleman's looks. Some mustache combs had silver mountings and a few were carried in silver mounted leather cases.

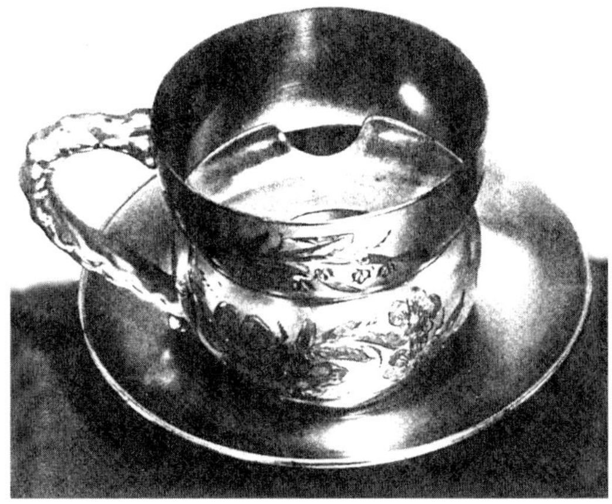

Mustache cup designed to protect the gentleman's mustache from getting in his cup. *Maker: Wilcox Silver Plate Co., 1895.* $95.

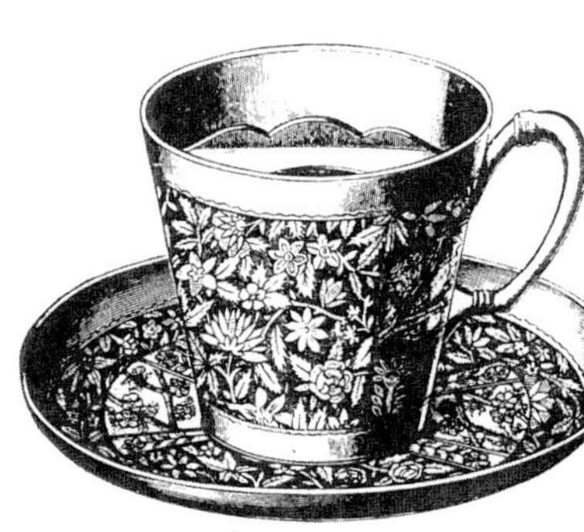

Mustache cup in choice of patterns either Satin or Brocade. Chased; both with gold lined cups. Meriden Britannia Co. catalogue, 1882. $135.

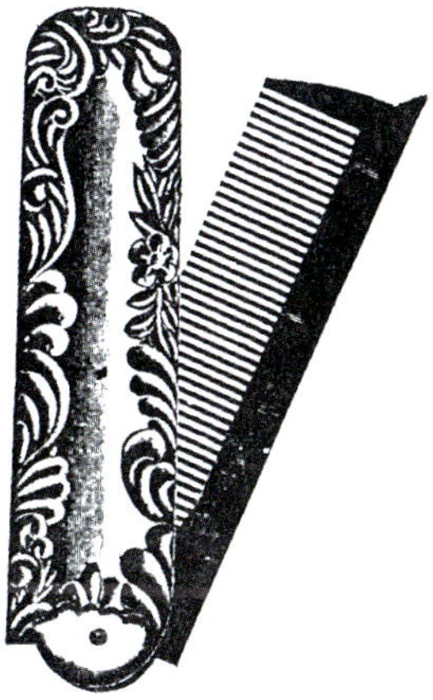

Mustache Comb, rococo edge

Sterling mustache comb with rococo edge. *From A. I. Hall and Sons, San Francisco, California, 1895-1896.* $50.

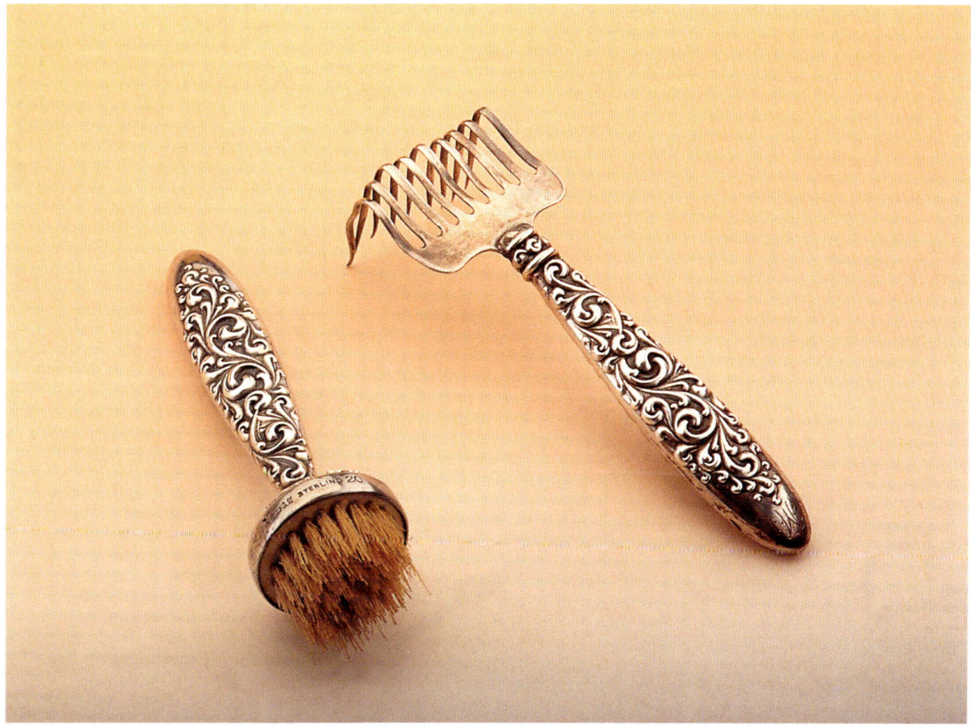

Wig styling set for gentleman's grooming. c.1860. Includes rake for cleaning the wig and the curling brush for the gentelmen's long white curls. Mark: RWS sterling 20 (R. Wallace & Sons). The rake measures 4". *Collection of Antonia Moore. Photo: Bruce Waters.* $410.

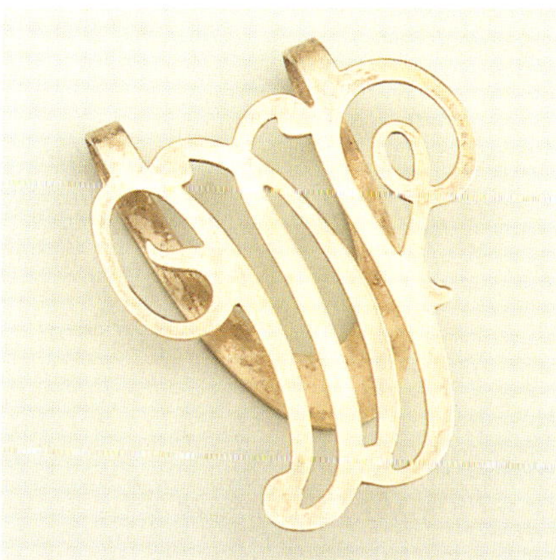

Money clip in sterling for the gentleman's pocket. Monogrammed. Maker: P.L. Measures 1-3/4". *Collection of Antonia Moore. Photo: Bruce Waters.* $30.

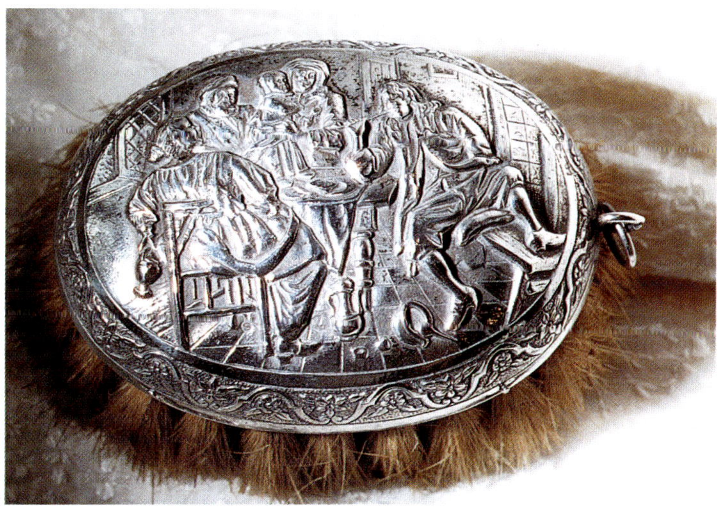

Dutch silver clothes brush marked 833. 4-1/4" long. Date: 1828. Scene depicts 19th century family in their cups. *Collection and photo: Anne Jansen.*

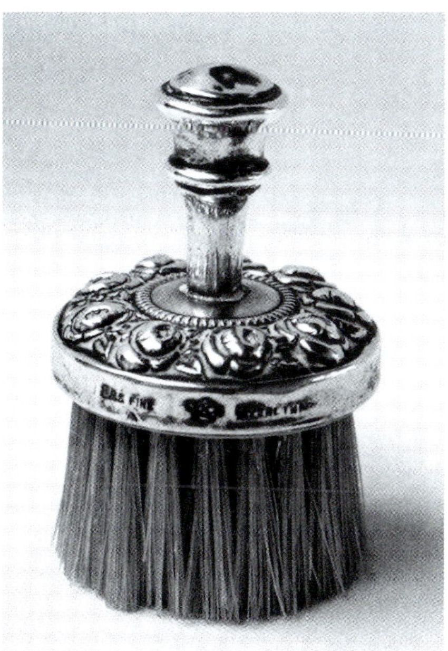

Silver clothes brush for the fastidious gentleman or his valet to use. Marked Sterling. *Photo: Courtesy of Silver Magazine Archives.*

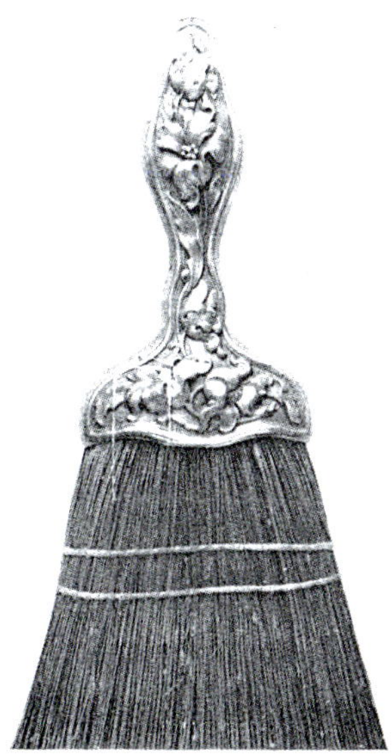

Sterling handle whisk broom for the gentleman' s clothing in an ornate pattern called Tulip. *Unger Brothers catalogue, 1904.* $75.

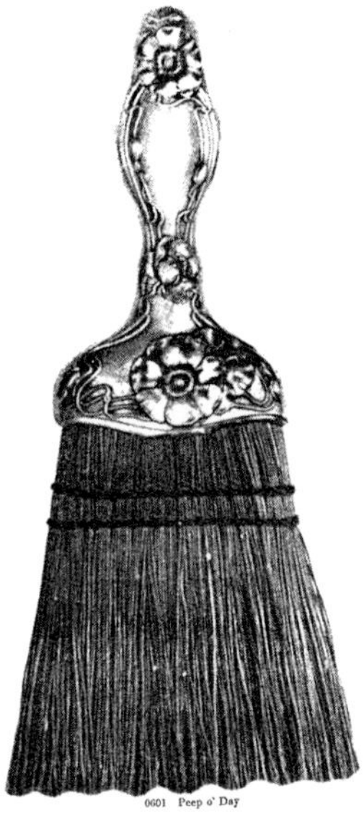

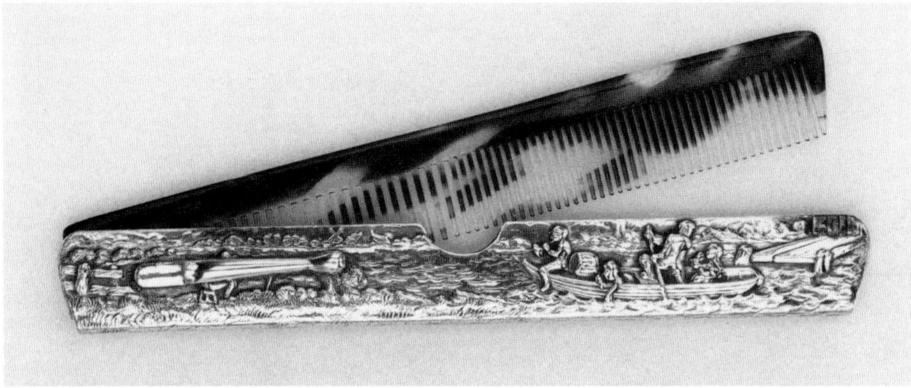

Silver pocket comb from the Netherlands. Note windmills in background and men in the boat. *Collection of Diane Zinn. Photo: Robert Watkins.*

Sterling handle whisk broom in Peep o' Day pattern used to whisk lint off clothing. *Unger Brothers catalogue, 1904.* $75.

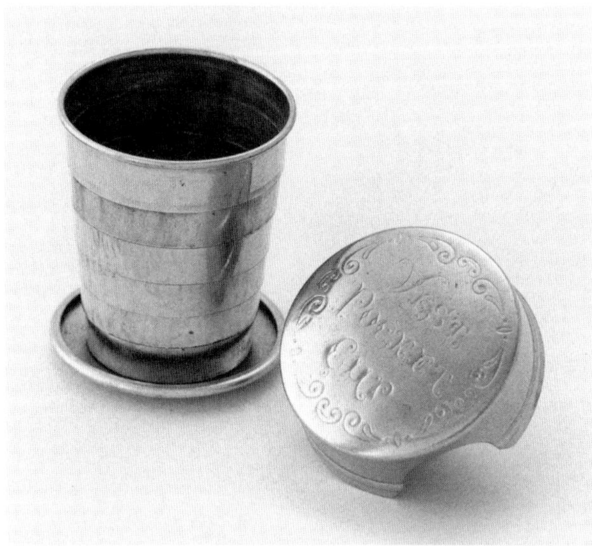

Gentleman's collapsible Vest Pocket Cup. Measures 2-1/4" round and stands 2-1/2". c.1880. *Photo: H Ivan Rainwater*. $65.

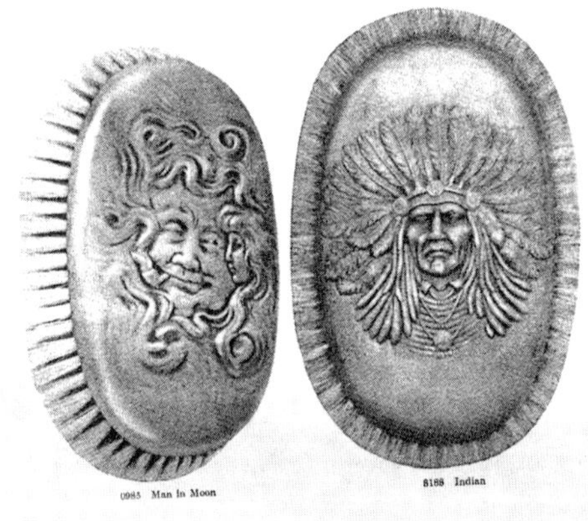

Two patterns of sterling military brushes, French gray finish. Maker: Unger Brothers. To left, Man in Moon pattern. To right, Indian pattern. Both c.1900.

Collar-Box, Cuff-Box and Glove-Box

SET OF THREE PIECES

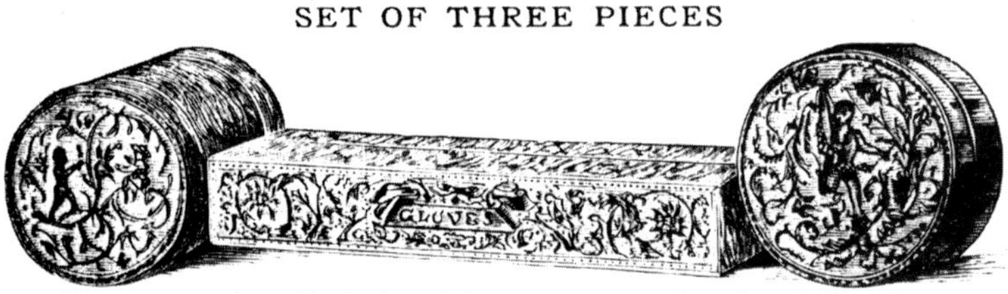

To any one who will, before July 1st, 1891, send us One Dollar for a new Yearly Subscriber (not their own name), we will forward by mail (ten cents extra must be sent us to prepay the postage) the set we show, including a Collar-box, Cuff-box and Glove-box. The latter is 12 inches long, 3¼ inches wide; the Collar and Cuff Boxes are of proportionate sizes. All the pieces are handsomely embossed in an artistic imitation of antique leather—a most acceptable present for either a lady or gentleman. Don't forget the extra money for postage.

The price at which we sell the three pieces is very low—65 cents, postpaid. We cannot break the set.

Supplement to June Number, 1891. *The Ladies Home Journal*.

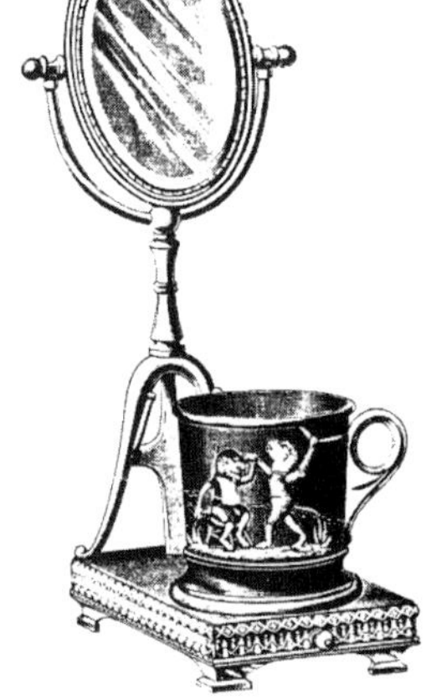

Right:
Silverplate shaving set with drawer for razor. Meriden Britannia Co., 1886. $130.

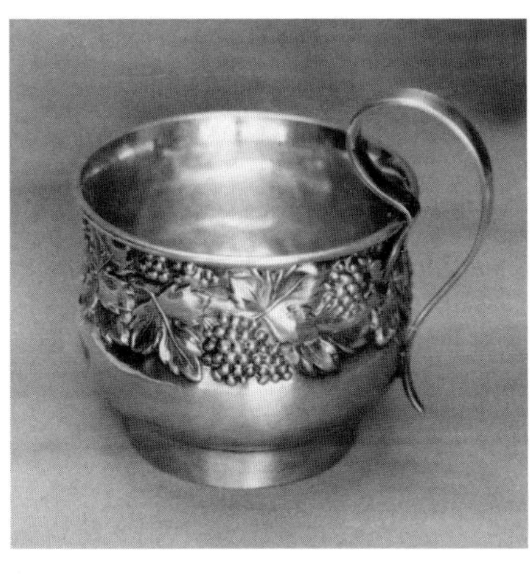

Silver shaving mug inscribed "H. A. Roby" and "March 11th 1841." Marked Kirk SK 11. Grape and leaf design. *Private Collection. Photo: H Ivan Rainwater*. $125.

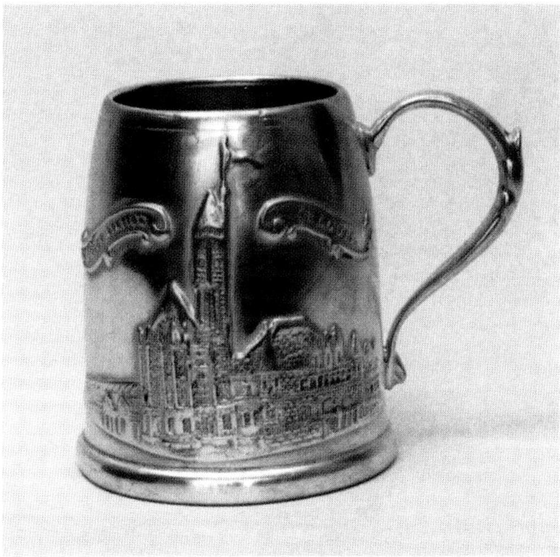

Silver plate cup memonto of the St. Louis Exposition of 1904. The view shown here is of Union Station in St. Louis, Missouri. *Photo: H Ivan Rainwater*. $95.

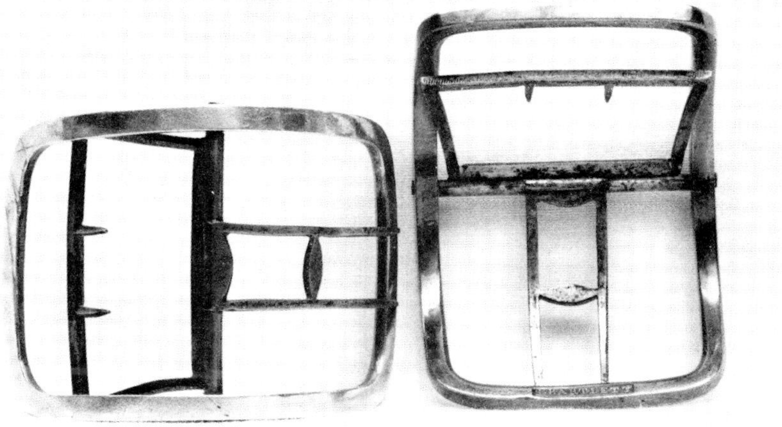

Men's shoe buckles. Maker: Samuel Bartlett (1752-1821) of Concord and Cambridge, Massachusetts. Buckles have been used since Roman times made of silver, gold and other metals. Silver on copper with steel fittings. Height: 2-1/8". Width: 2-3/4". *Photo: Courtesy of Silver Magazine Archives*.

Watch stands

His pocket watch was a proud possession of the man who lived during Victorian days. He usually wore it with a chain which stretched from the watch in one vest pocket to the watch fob in the other. It was easy to take out the pocket watch and note the hour. While pocket watches are a collectible in themselves today, the watch stand, sometimes called a watch holder, is a collectible, too.

The watch stand appeared in such catalogues as Samuel Kirk, 1913, and even in an earlier Daniel Low, 1901. The stands were usually just a bit larger than the pocket watch for which they were designed, measuring about 3" tall. Others made by the George W. Shiebler Company and Gorham measured only 2-3/4". Some watch stands were decorated with cherubs and flying ribbons on either side. Others were a simple heart shape with a hook at the top on which the watch was hung. Designs varied from the heavily ornate to the vary simple.

Where did the watch stand wait when not in use? In all probability, it had a place of honor on the gentleman's dresser and the working hours of the watch stand were from evening when the watch was placed there until the next morning when the watch was returned to the vest pocket of its owner.

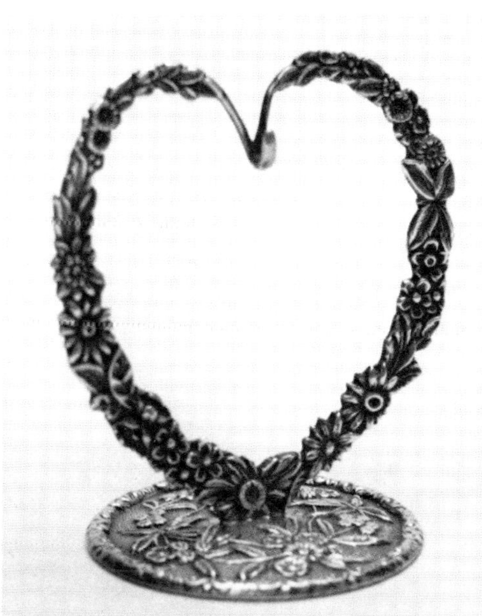

Sterling watch stand. 3-5/8" tall. Maker: S. Kirk & Son Co. Baltimore, MD. Pictured in 1914 catalogue but may have been made earlier. *Photo: H Ivan Rainwater*. $300+.

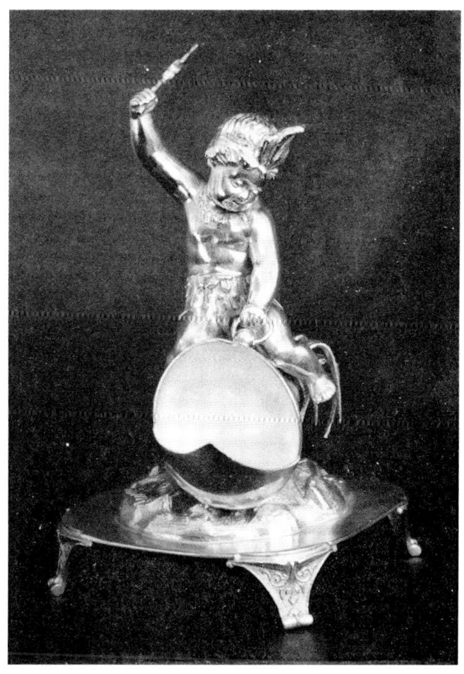

Silver watch stand with young boy holding tomahawk and wearing an Indian headdress. c.1870. Made by B. J. Mayo, Newark, NJ. Measures 6" tall by 4-1/4" square. *Photo: Judy Redfield*. $300+.

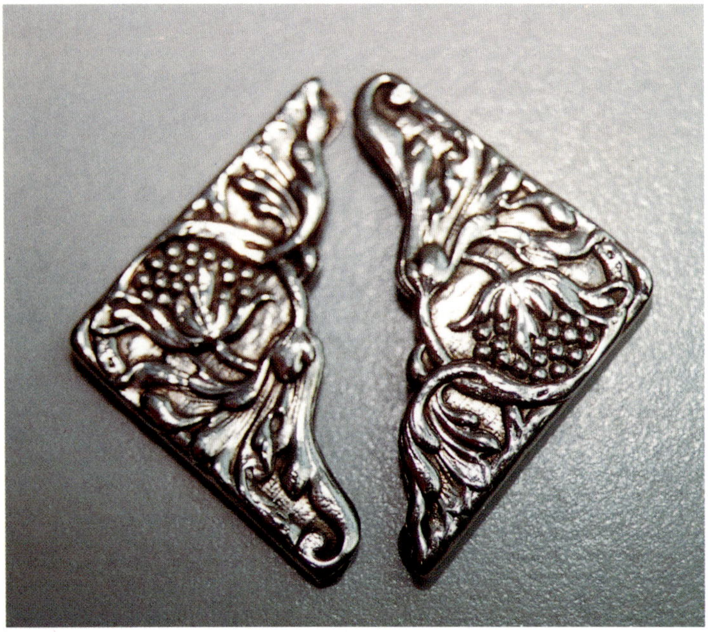

Silver corners usually found on a blotter or gentleman's billfold and other leather goods. They served as a protection for the leather at the point of wear. Maker: Gorham Mfg. Co. Copyright 1880. *Collection of Edie Baker. Photo: Pat Rich.*

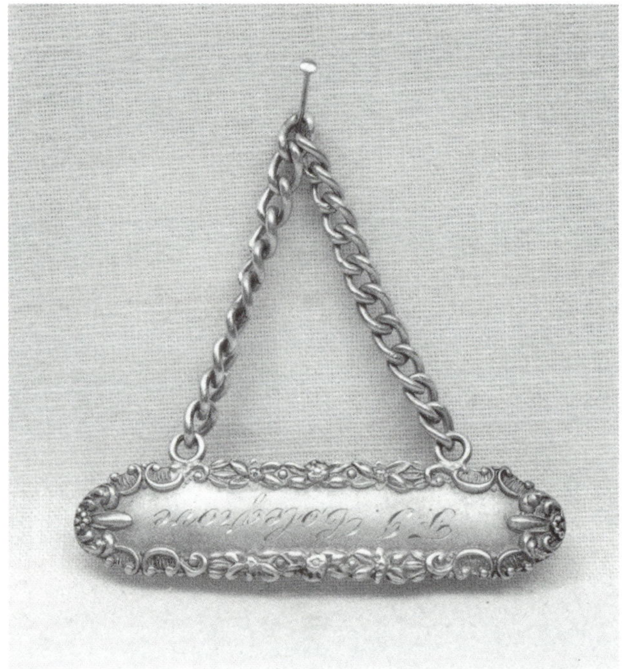

Coat Hanger. Maker: D. S. Spaulding of Mansfield, MA. 2". Note that the owner's name is engraved upside down. *Photo: Courtesy of Silver Magazine Archives.*

Coat hangers and hat marks

Silver coat hangers for the gentleman's coat were advertised in many catalogues from 1890 into the early 1900s. One description said they were small loops in the neck of coats to hand them by. Silver coat hangers did have a chain for hanging. However, another description said they were light in weight and indicated ownership of the coat rather than for hanging. Whichever your prefer, the coat hangers in sterling had a place on the front to put the gentleman's name or initials.

Catalogue prices for silver coat hangers ranged from as little as $.75 to as much as $2.00 each. They were included in such mail order catalogues as Baird-North's of 1913 and C. H. Lane of Portland, Maine, c.1890. The Sears Roebuck catalogue of 1897 listed one "solid sterling silver coat hanger" at $.75 pulse two cents postage.

There were three different styles of *hat marks* for the gentleman to choose from. One used prongs to fit into the hatband. A second style had *hinged* prongs to fit more easily and the third style was a slip-on triangle which was even easier to fit into the hatband.

Hat marks were less expensive than coat hangers, ranging fro m $.20 plus two cents postage from Sears Roebuck 1897 to as much as $1.25. All were of sterling and the heavier one cost more than those lighter in weight.

Gentleman's silver hat mark. Inscribed J.W. Wilmore. *Photo: Courtesy of Silver Magazine Archives.*

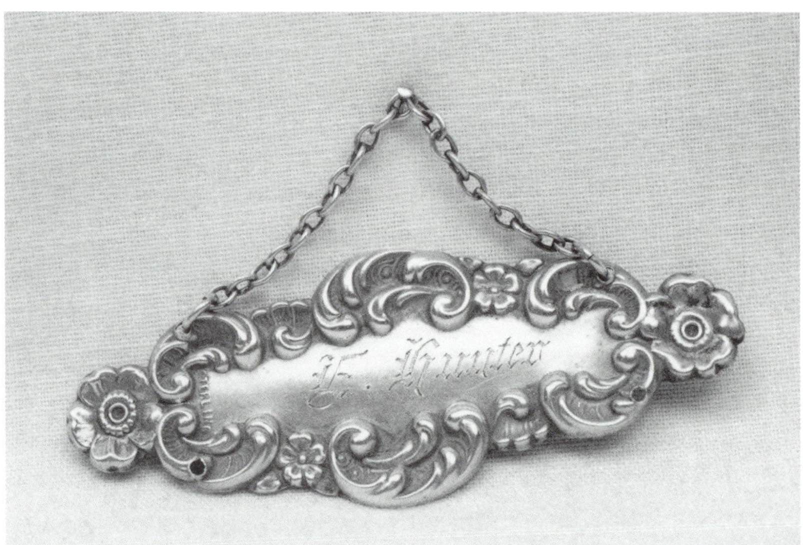

Coat hanger. Sterling but no maker's mark. Ornate design. Measures 2-11/16". *Photo: Courtesy of Silver Magazine Archives.*

Chapter 5. Silver Curios for use...
...in the Sewing Room

Sewing articles, as we know them, date back to the time of the Pharaohs in Egypt; the Egyptians did sew. But the beginning of sewing as a skill might go as far back as the cave dwellers who laced animal skins together to use as clothing. Their sewing articles might have been splinters of shell, bone and large thorns. Later, sewing tools of iron, bronze and brass were produced. These, however, were rare and expensive.

Silver sewing implements were practically unknown until the sixteenth century. Prior to that time, base metal sewing articles were considered so valuable that they were included in wills and inventories of those days.

Sewing tools dating back to the sixteenth century were made by metal specialists who belonged to guilds. Early silver sewing tools became an indication of wealth and status, but there was a second benefit which comes into the twenty-first century. Silver was and is kinder to the skin than base metals. This was particularly true of thimbles.

The eighteenth century saw a tremendous change in silver sewing articles. The development of new manufacturing techniques led to mass production. All sewing tools became more widely available for almost every lady who stitched a seam or cut a thread.

The beginning of the nineteenth century showed a decided difference in the style of silver sewing articles. They became more ornate even as they became more affordable. Indeed, there is no better place to look for the style of the Victorian era than in sewing articles. Elegant *etuis* were fitted out with silver tools.

Silver thimbles, in particular, were being made in Germany, France, the Netherlands, as well as England. Embroidery scissors may have had blades of steel but their handles were marked "sterling." Thread winders, spool holders, needlecases and hem gauges, to mention just a few sewing articles, were all made in silver.

Many modern sewing tools are found in twentieth century stores, but today's collectors find more pleasure in specializing in silver sewing tools from days gone by.

Bodkins

Bodkins, thread needle, ribbon threader, drawing needle. Some mail order houses of days gone by even called them *tape needles*. Whatever name you give them, bodkins go back a very long way. They were used 4000 years ago in ancient China and popular tools in the days of Julius Caesar.

One type of bodkin resembles a needle with an enlarged eye through which tape, ribbon or elastic can be drawn. It usually measures 3" or less in length. This needle-like tool has a blunt end while a needle has a sharp one.

Another type is the flat bodkin with an eyelet in one round end and a rectangular slot in the other. This, too, would pull a ribbon, tape of elastic through a loop or hem and also measured 3" or less in length.

The flat bodkin was used in Victorian times. Frequently, they came in sets of three or four different sizes and many times were enclosed in a silk-lined case. Such a set might have been given by a gentleman to his lady.

Since they came in gold, silver and baser metals, bodkins have been offered for sale in jewelry stores and mail-order catalogues, as well.

Knitting or yarn ball

Lucky is the twentieth century lady who finds time to do fine sewing. Her Victorian sister was almost always seen with some form of needlework at hand.

One item that she used was a yarn or knitting ball, so called because the lady could put her yarn inside the silver ball, thread it through the top and then release what she needed as she worked.

Since yarn and wool were usually wound in small balls for wool and small spools for yarn, they could be protected by using the silver ball. In addition, this was a convenient way to keep yarn from getting tangled in the sewing box or bag.

The knitting ball is not usually in today's sewing bag. A beautiful silver ball from 100 years ago is now a treasure.

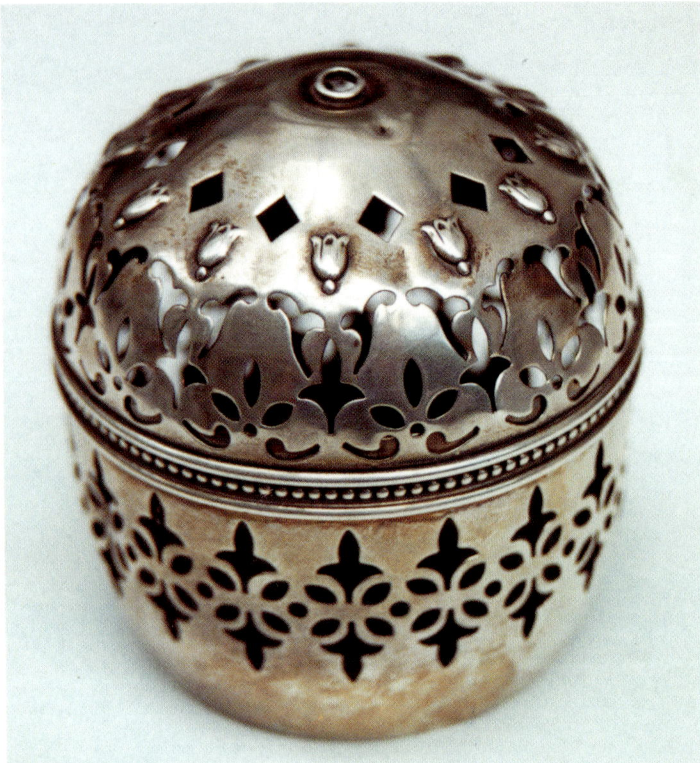

Sterling knitting ball. Maker: Gorham. Measures 3" by 3". c.1875. *Collection and photo: Pat Rich*. $260.

A bird with many names

They have been called *sewing birds, hemming birds, grippers and sewing clamps*. Whatever they were called, they were a vary useful device. Clamps for holding needlework were made of metal as early as the eighteenth century and of wood at least a century earlier.

Sewing birds, as they are called today, are fastened to the edge of a table by a clamp. The beak of the bird is opened by pressing the tail feathers together, the material to be sewed is inserted and the beak closed by a spring when the tail feathers are released.

Charles Waterman of Meriden, Connecticut, took a patent on sewing birds on February 15, 1853. In the first price list of the Meriden Britannia Company for 1853, sewing birds were listed showing that they were sold even before that patent. When that first patent expired, many manufacturers made sewing birds. Most were made of silverplate but some were made of silver.

With the advent of the sewing machine, ladies no longer needed to use sewing birds because the sewing machine was able to stitch long seams. While collectors may find sewing birds on the antique market today, they are no longer in common use in the sewing corner.

Buttons

The early use of buttons, in particular silver buttons, was ornamental rather than functional. If you see a picture of a gentleman from the eighteenth century, he might have buttons on his sleeves, his cuffs or elsewhere on his costume. These buttons were decorative. They might enhance the gentleman's costume but were not a means of closing clothing until later.

Originally, buttons were small knobs or disc attached to clothing. They were decorations found in ancient Egypt and Persia. They were used in China to denote high rank. It was not until the end of the eighteenth century that buttons became functional. At that time, they began to be made in large quantities in both England and the United States.

Then, as now, two kinds of buttons are made. One is the pierced button with two or more holes to sew directly onto the fabric. The other type has a shank through which thread is passed to secure the button to the fabric. The second type is what was generally used for silver buttons. This allowed the ornamental face of the button of show. It also permitted such scenes as a pastoral setting, a scene of the hunt or a coin's face to decorate the button without the distraction of the thread.

Throughout the eighteenth century, buttons were made in sets of from as few as five to as many as thirty-five. They were often sold in elegant satin-lined jewelry boxes. These were expensive and treasured.

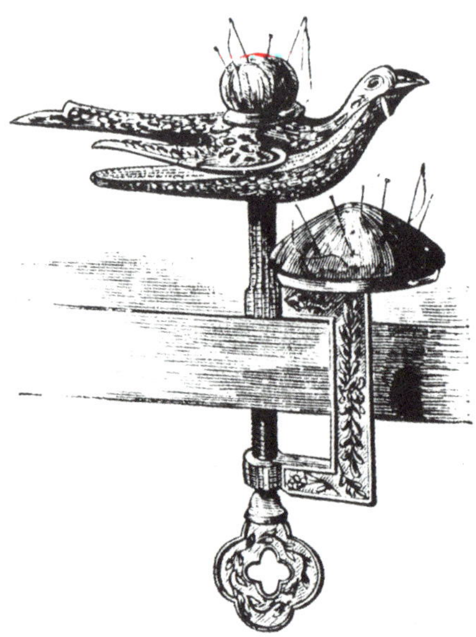

Silverplate sewing bird or clamp. Meriden Britannia Co. catalogue, 1867. $35-80.

England was not far ahead of the United States with the manufacture of buttons. English silver buttons are usually hallmarked and can, therefore, be dated. American-made buttons many times have a maker's mark but this does not provide exact dating, only an approximate time of manufacture.

Silver buttons were used in the United States from as early as 1796 for political campaigning. A gentleman running for office may have changed the original buttons on a jacket or vest for silver buttons with the candidate's picture on them. This was certainly the forerunner of the modern campaign button and can form a historical collection of great interest to the history buff.

By the end of the nineteenth century and into the twentieth, coin buttons which were actually made of coins, heraldic uniform buttons, and Mexican silver buttons were all being made. Many of these can still be found on the button market today.

Very unusual and fun to find would be a button made from an Elizabeth I coin. Although the coin may date to the Queen's reign from 1558 to 1603, the button was more likely made in the early 1900s.

Collecting silver buttons is an education in itself. One can learn history, metallurgy and clothing styles at the same time and most of all, have fun at antique shows and fairs.

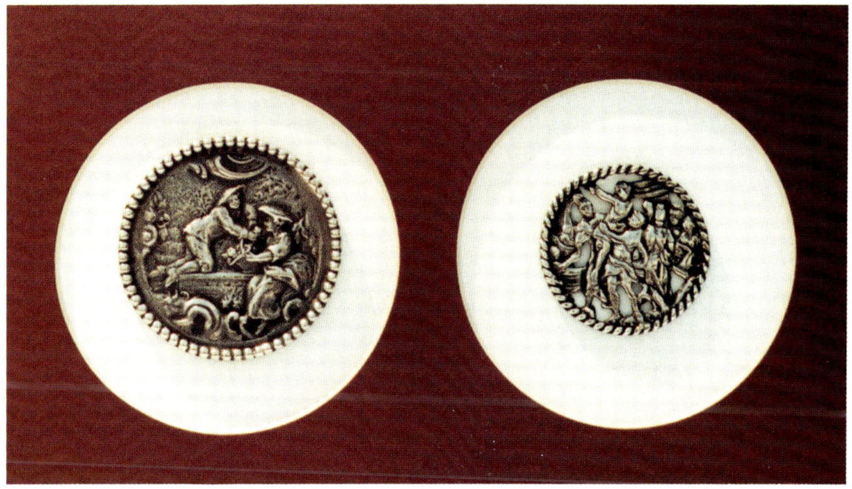

Left: Continental silver, c.1918, beaded border. Scene shows pastoral couple. Measures 13/16".
Right: English scene called The Rape of Watlean. *Collection of Marge DeArmon and Connie Weiser.* $15-100 per button.

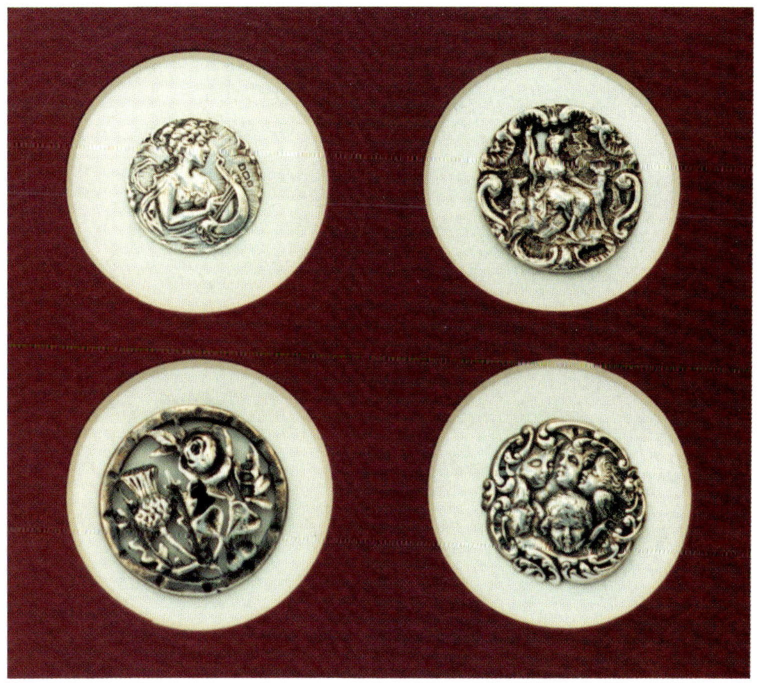

Top left: represents Euterpe, muse of music, with her harp.
Top right: Diana the huntress with her dogs.
Bottom left: floral design of thistle, rose and three-leaf clover.
Bottom right: five cherub heads. largest button here is 1-1/4". All have English hallmarks. *Collection of Marge DeArmon and Connie Weiser.* $15-100 per button.

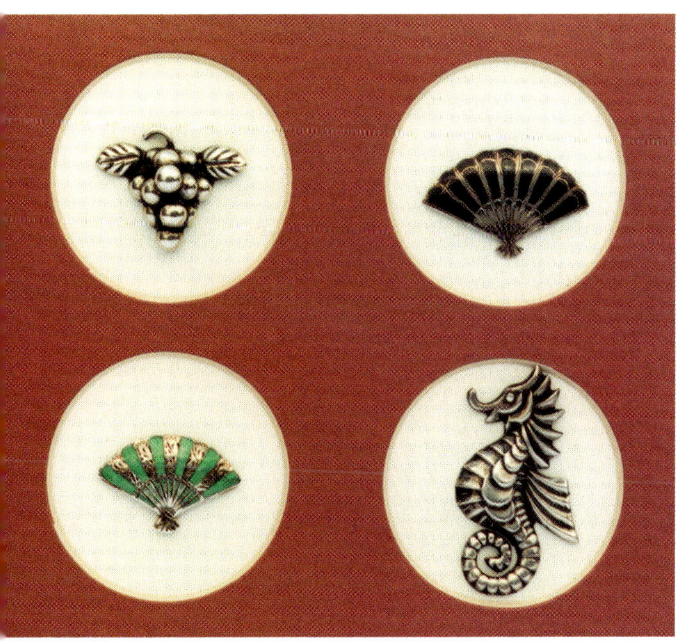

Top left: grapes with leaves. Marked: Sterling Taxco, Mexico.
Top right: fan using niello and silver from Siam.
Bottom left: silver fan with green enamel. Marked: Thainakon.
Bottom right: seahorse marked sterling from Mexico. *Collection of Marge DeArmon and Connie Weiser*. $15-100 per button.

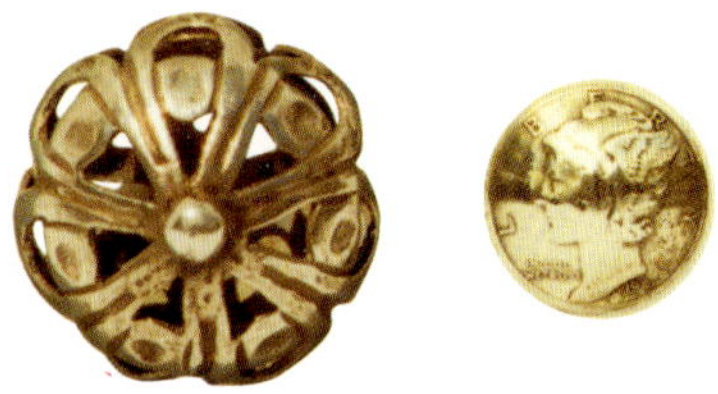

Left: coin button made with an American Mercury dime, 1941. Right: toggle button in modified ball shape. Called pierced or Bird Cage design. *Collection of Marge DeArmon and Connie Weiser.* $15-100 per button.

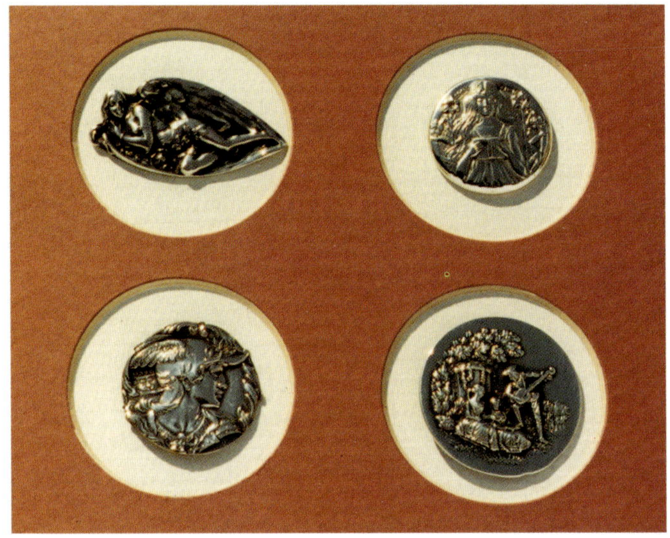

Top left: Art Nouveau style with reclining angle. Top of leaf is the angel's wing. English.
Top right: a girl reading her book in the garden. English.
Bottom left: head of Mercury (Hermes) messenger of the gods and patron of thieves and merchants. English
Bottom right: Gentlemen playing a mandolin for two seated ladies. Date 1896. English. *Collection of Marge DeArmon and Connie Weiser.* $15-100 per button.

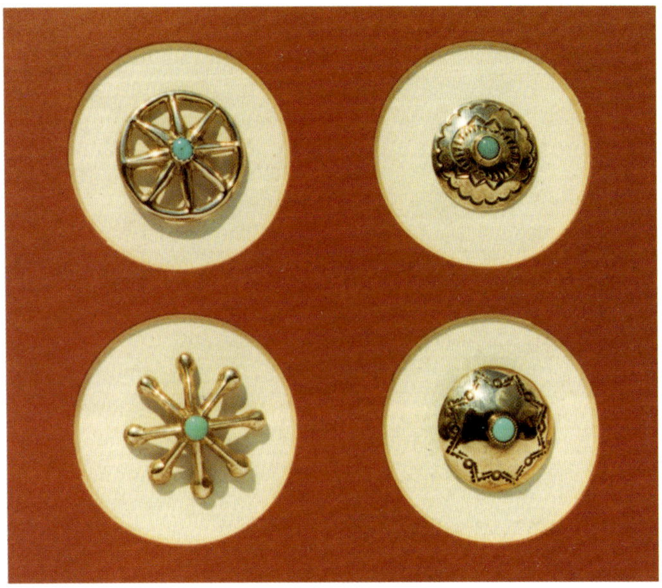

Four examples of buttons made by modern Navajo Indians in Arizona, the largest being 1". Silver and turquoise. *Collection of Marge DeArmon and Connie Weiser.* $15-100 per button.

Hem gauges

At the end of the nineteenth and into the twentieth century, hem gauges were used as an aid to the needlewoman who had a wide skirt to shorten. Hemming was tedious then as now and the small hem gauge was more convenient to use than a ruler. It was an accurate guide to an even hem all the way around the skirt. Some hem gauges had sterling ornamental heads while steel was used for the measuring unit. Others were made entirely of silver.

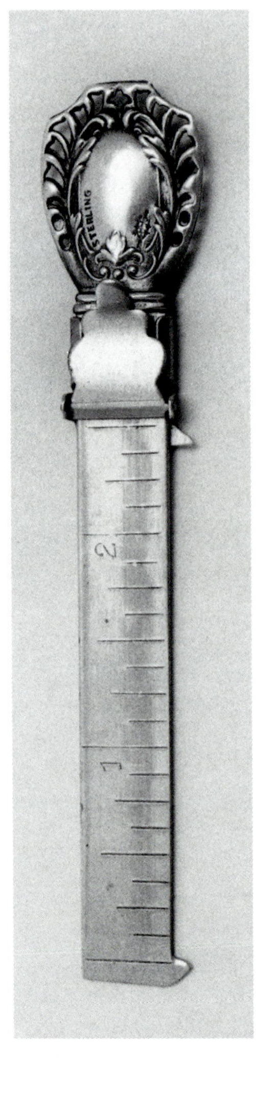

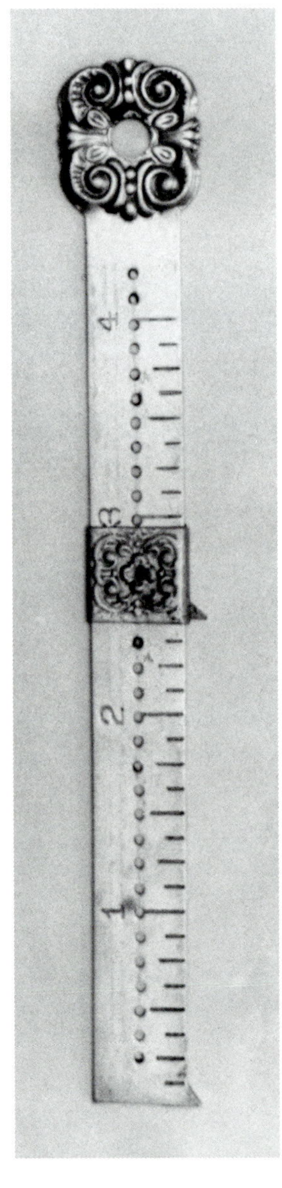

Right:
Two hem gauges. Both made by Webster Company c.1910. Note the ornate designs on each. *Photo: H Ivan Rainwater*. $100 each.

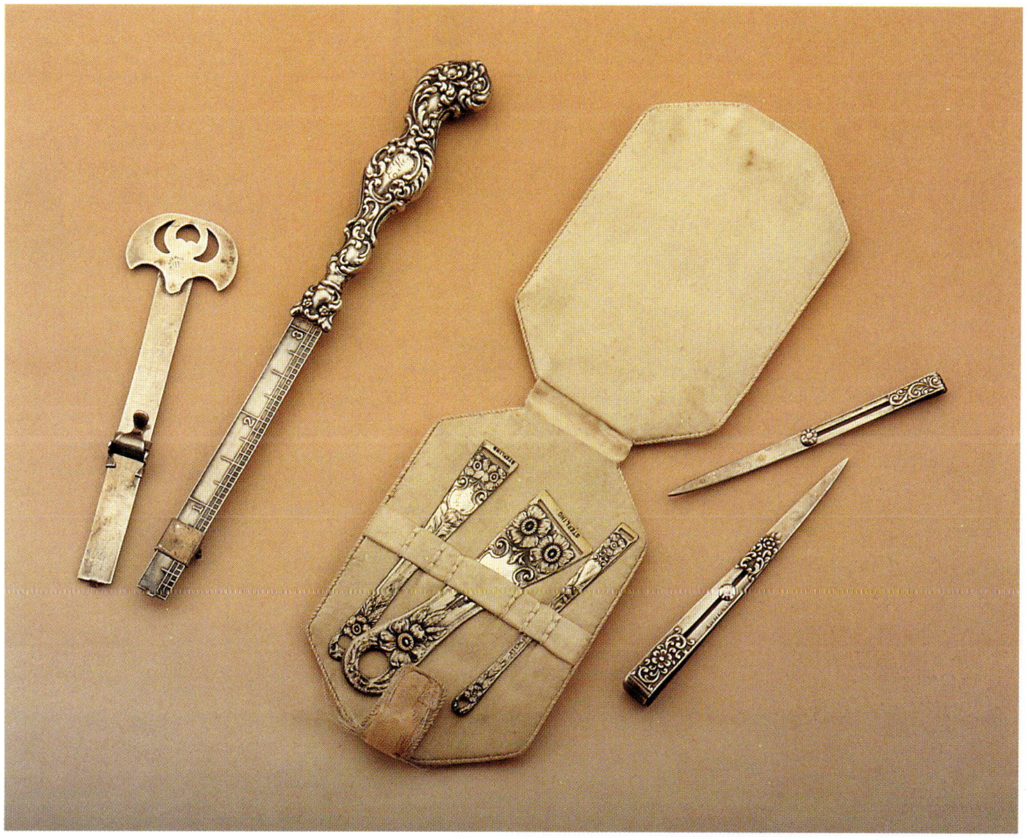

Left: hem gauge in Lotus motif by Unger Bros. Sterling. Locks length in place. Measures 4". Center: sterling hem gauge also with lock. Initialed E. K. Maker: Unger Bros. Measures 6-3/8". Right: three flat bodkins in case. Marked sterling by Unger Bros. Most popular during Victorian days.
Far right: two needle-shaped bodkins with vertical openings for the tape. Also, sterling by Unger Bros. *Collection of Antonia Moore. Photo: Bruce Waters.* $30-50 each.

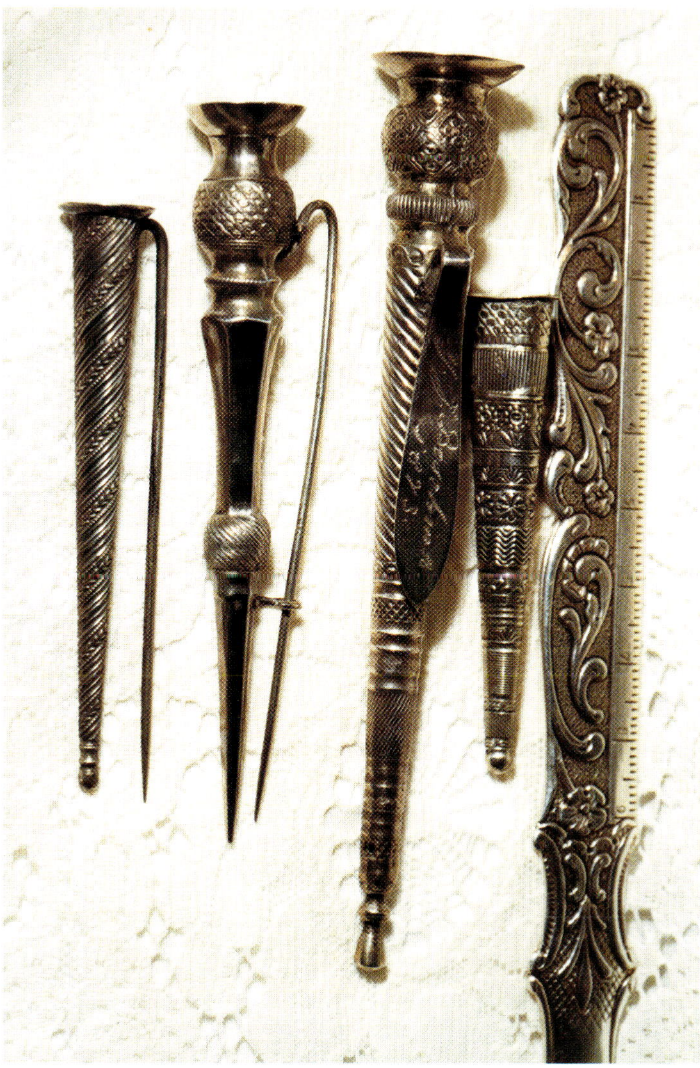

Three posy holders, a needle sheath, and a ruler, all of Dutch silver. Late 19th century. Third from left is engraved and dated 1873. Scale on right shows the dimensions. *Collection and photo: Anne Jansen.*

Knitting needle sheaths

In the days of Queen Victoria, knitting needles did not have knobs on the end as they do today. The knitting needle sheath, or holder as it was sometimes called, served two important functions for the knitter.

Since knitting needles measured about 9 inches (23cm) and were open ended, the knitter had to have help keeping the stitches from falling off the back end of the needle. Also, the knitting sheath took some of the weight off the needle, allowing the knitter to free up the right hand to throw the thread. The sheath attached to the knitter's belt on the right hand side to aid the work in progress and helped the knitter gain great speed in the project.

(Knitting sheaths should not be confused with knitting guards. The latter always came in pairs and were used on the front end of the needle when the work was put aside.)

Needlecases

Because silver needles were very precious in the early nineteenth century, the lady who sewed (and most ladies did), kept her needles in a special needle case. These were made of silver, mother-of-pearl, enamel, ivory and wood, to name just a few.

Silver needlecases were made in France, Germany, Italy, the United States and, of course, in England. The Redditch needle factories of England turned out millions of needles a day. These were shipped all over the world. Redditch needles were carefully protected by placing them in a needle case. The cases measured about 2-1/2 to 3 inches.

In the early days of the twentieth century, needles were sold in paper packets according to the size of the needles. They are still packaged that way today. But the lady of yesterday who kept her needles in a silver needle case had a piece of sewing equipment which was both useful and lovely to own.

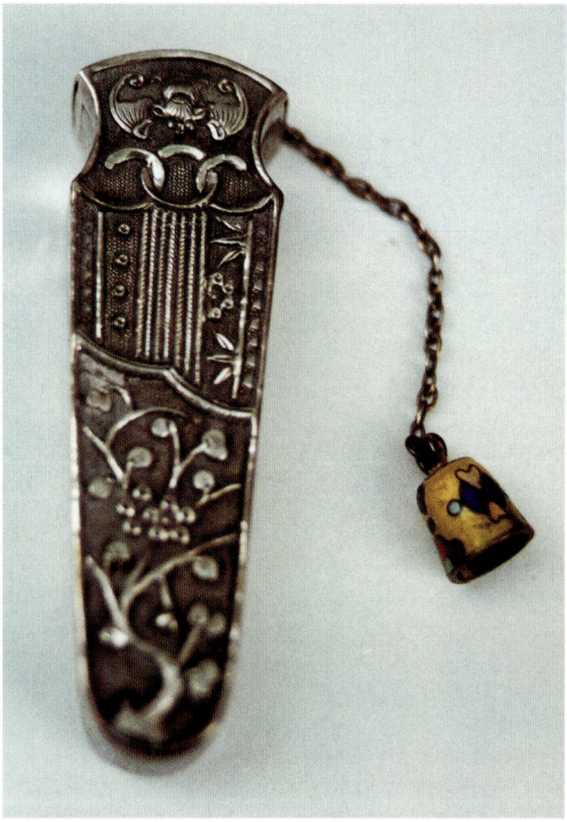

Chinese needle case with enamel thimble on chain. Measures 2-1/2″ by 3/4″. *Collection and photo: Pat Rich*. $50.

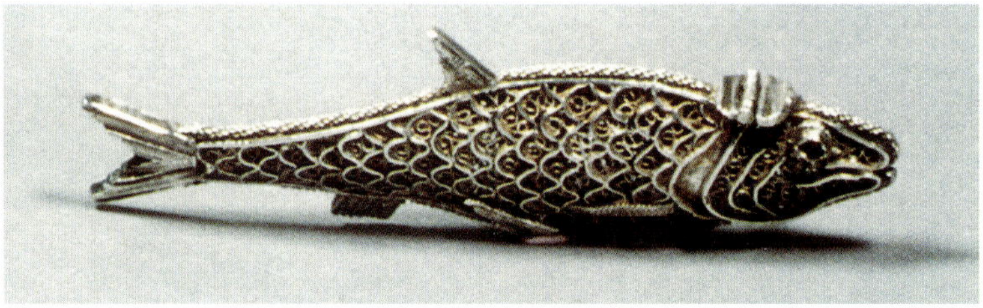

Needle case in form of a fish. Dutch silver filigree. The head lifts up to put in the needles. A similar specimen can be seen at Frans Hals Museum in Harlem. c.1812. Measures 2-1/2″. *Collection and photo: B.V.D. Pavoordt.* $100.

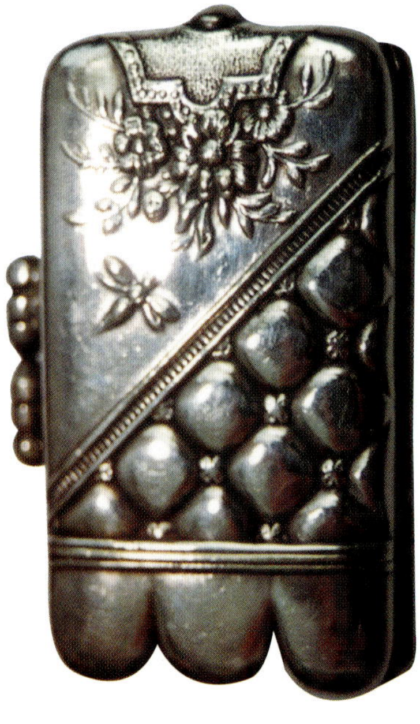

French silver needle case, closed. Repoussé design. Opened view of this case shows celluloid interior and velvet needle cushions. *Collection of Edie Baker. Photo: Pat Rich*. $95.

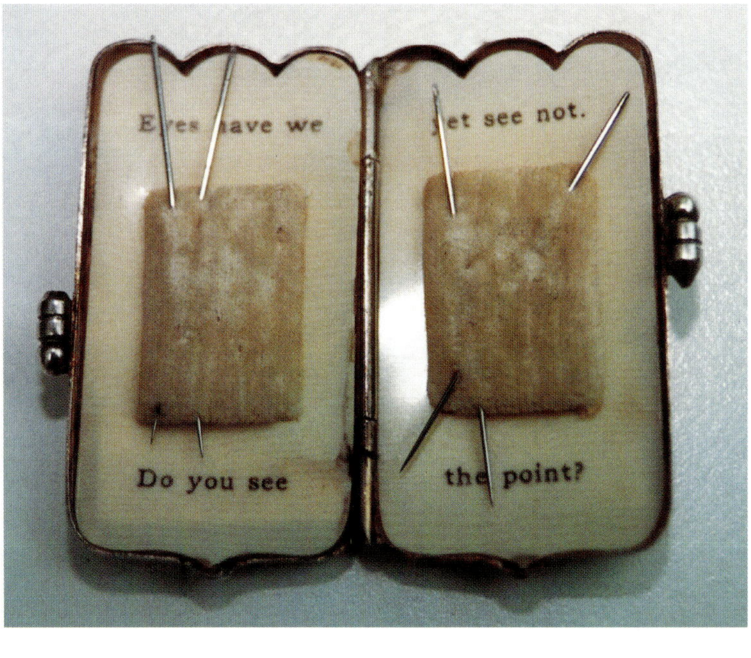

Thimble pencil case

A pencil of some kind was often used when sketching patterns but this novelty collapsible pencil which fit into a thimble may or may not have proved useful. When opened, the thimble measured 1 inch and could be used to protect the finger from needle pricks. The pencil measured 5 inches when opened for use.

The London firm of Sampson Mordan was known for its production of silver and gold pencils, many of them novel in concept. The thimble pencil case was one of Mordan's designs. Although the silver thimble was made by Samuel Foskett, the novelty was completed by Mordan.

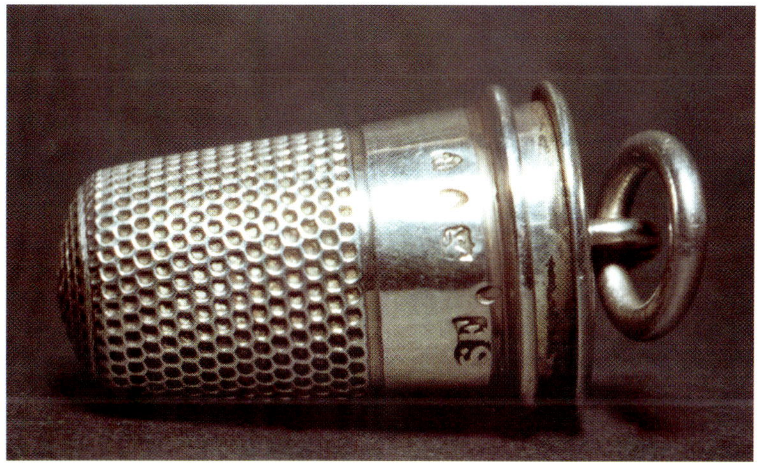

Silver pencil case in shape of thimble. Made by Samuel Foskett, London. c.1892. *Collection and photo: B.V.D. Pavoordt.*

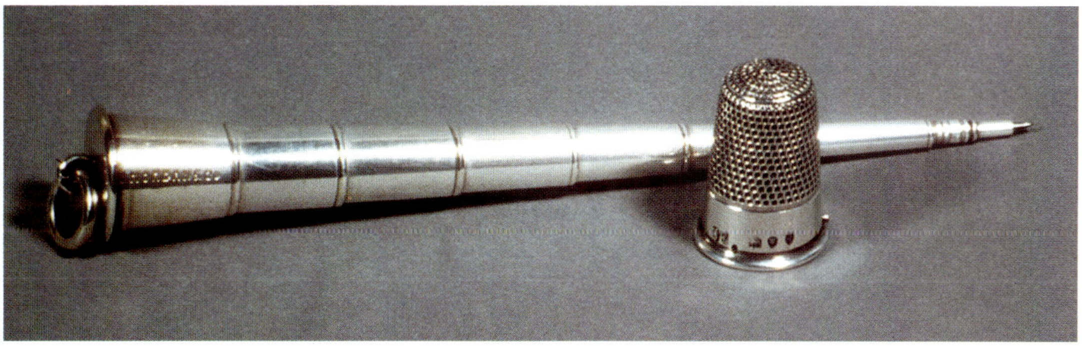

The collapsible silver pencil measures 5" when in use and fits inside the thimble when closed. Novelty made by Samuel Foskett, London, 1892. *Collection and photo: B.V.D. Pavoordt.*

Pin and thimble holder

A combination pin and thimble holder in a walnut would not have been unusual in the last quarter of the nineteenth century. A lady needed both pins and her thimble available and so she carried such a combination in her purse or on her chatelaine.

Many kinds of pincushions can be found in silver ranging from small pin poppets, which were usually round to two silver rectangles with pins pushed into the velvet between the two pieces of silver.

Thimble holders were also made in silver as the thimble was a precious tool. The variety of thimble holders still found range from beautifully hand stitched thimble slippers to silver, ivory and alabaster.

With the emphasis on preserving the precious pins and keeping the equally precious thimble (it might have been an engagement gift!), pin and thimble holders were elegant parts of the Victorian scene.

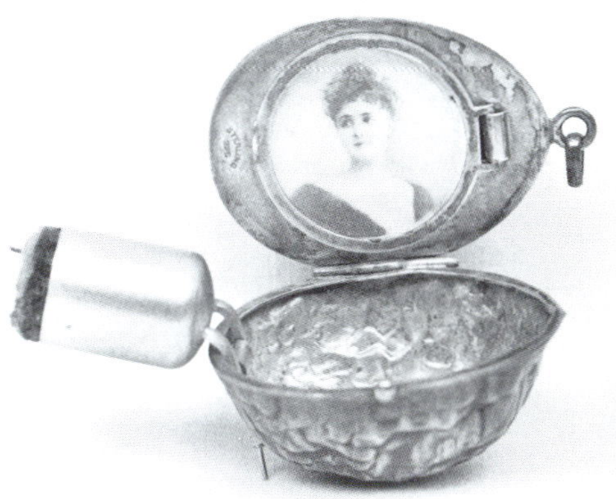

Silver walnut pin and thimble holder with lady' s picture in top of shell. Pins fit into the capsule on the bottom and thimble fits on top of the pins. *Photo: Courtesy of Silver Magazine Archives.*

Thimble holder shaped like a strawberry. Sterling. Tiffany & Co. c.1900. *Photo: Courtesy of Silver Magazine Archives.*

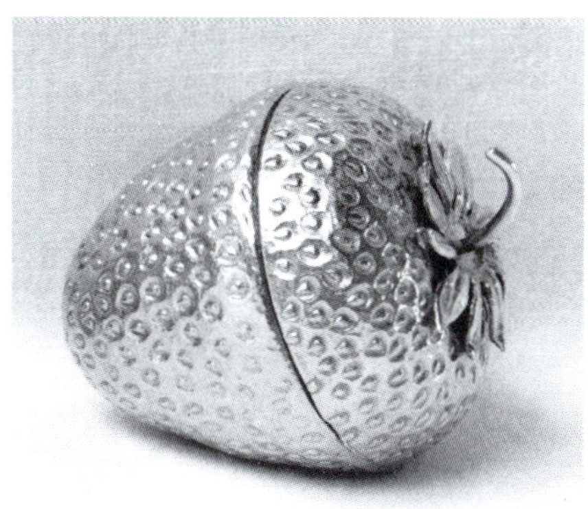

Pincushions

Before the days of mass production of pins, the lady who sewed needed to keep her precious pins safe. For this purpose, the pincushion was an important part of the sewing basket.

Pincushions range from small round pin poppets to a variety of silver animals; elephants and camels to pigs and frogs and swans. Silver *animal* pincushions were generally made in England c.1900-1910.

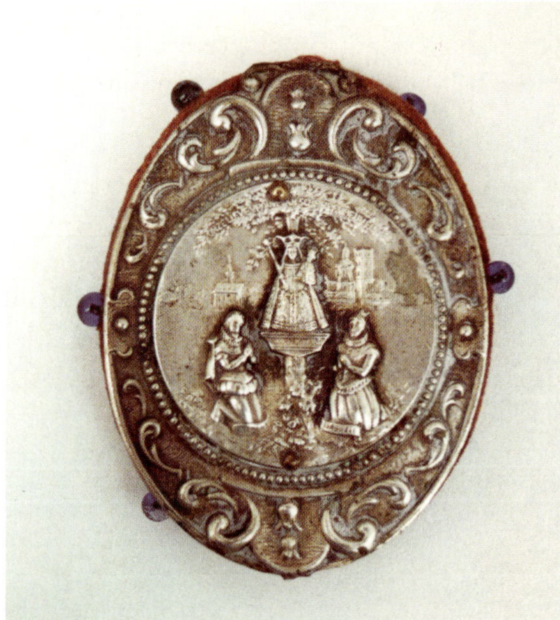

Religious pincushion. Albert and Isabella kneeling to the Virgin and Baby Jesus. 2-3/4". Spanish or Portuguese. *Collection and photo: Pat Rich*. $40-100.

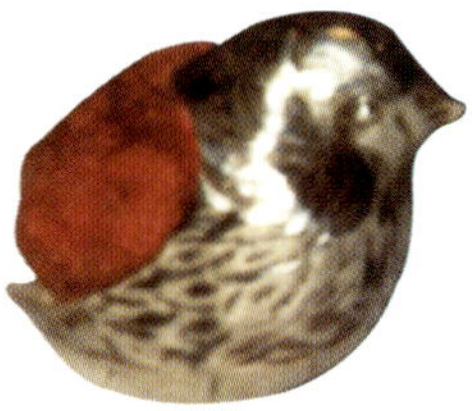

Pincushion in shape of small bird with a red velvet cushion. c.1900 Measures 7/8" tall by 1". Possibly Sampson Mordan, London, 1924. *Photo: Don Weichert.* $40-100.

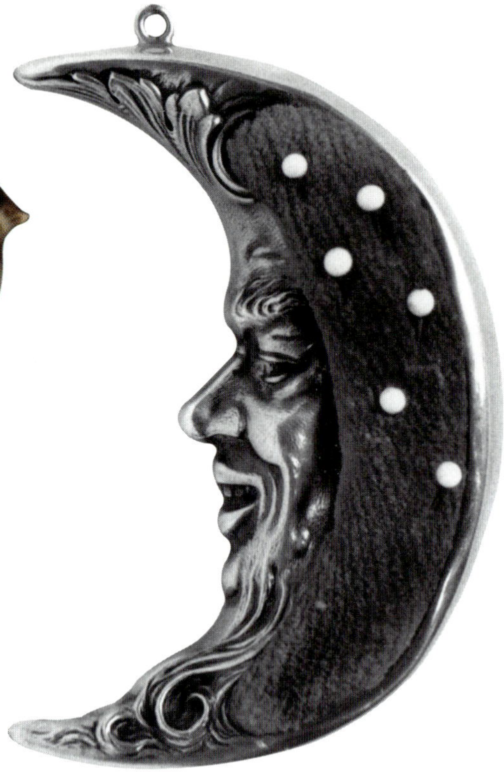

Left:
Pincushion measures 3-1/4". Art Nouveau man-in-the-moon face. Maker: William B. Kerr & Co. c.1900. *Photo: Courtesy of Silver Magazine Archives*. $40-100.

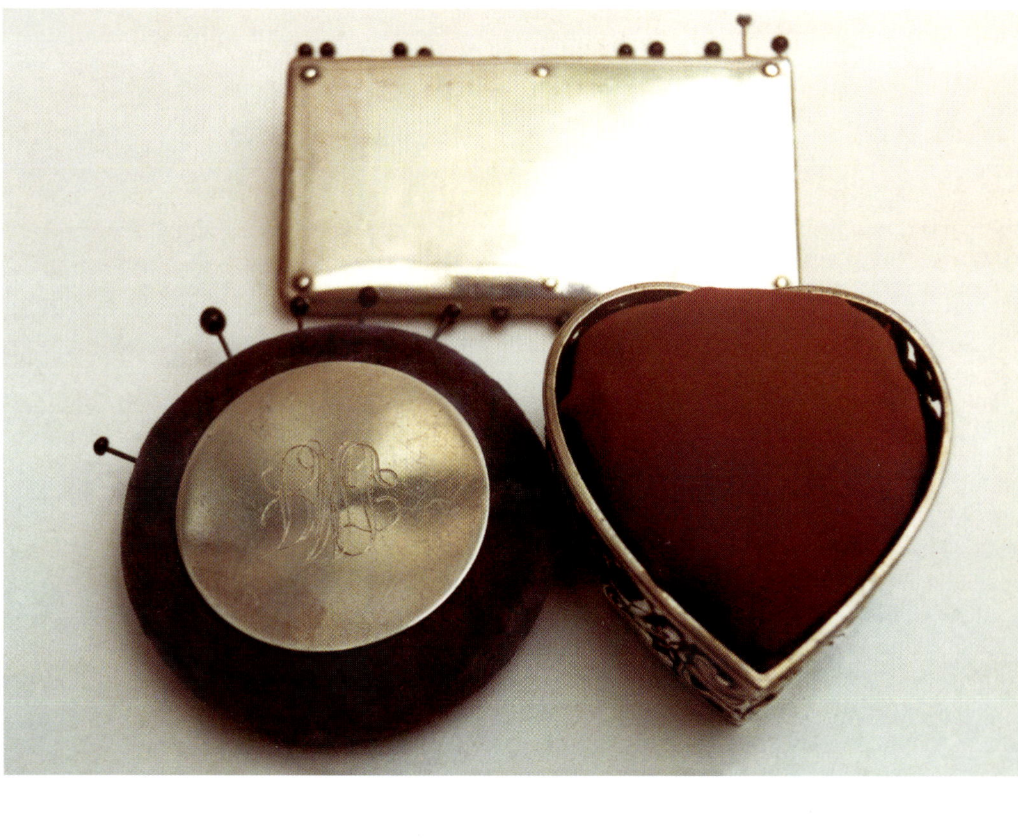

Pincushions. Front left: monogrammed. Marked on back "Leonore Doskow, Sterling." Top: sandwich panel pincushion. Sterling. Maker: Battin & Co. 2-3/4" by 1-3/4". Right: heart shaped with dragon motif. Unreadable mark. *Collection of Edie Baker. Photo: Pat Rich.* $40-100.

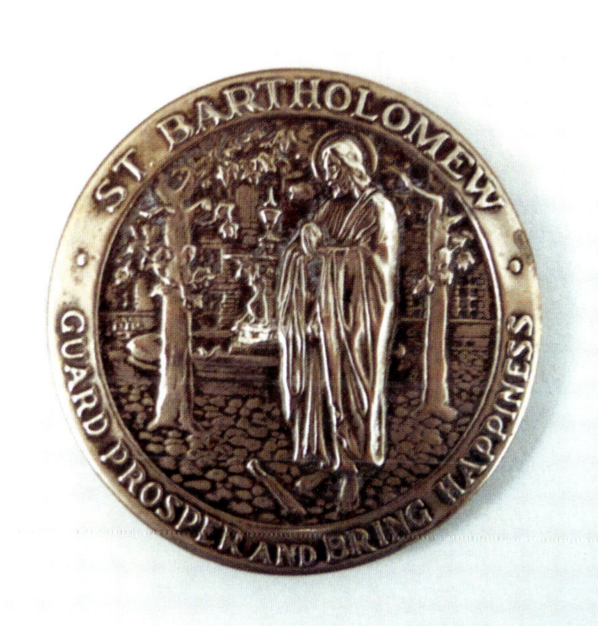

St. Bartholomew pincushion saying "Guard, Prosper and bring Happiness." Measures 2-1/2". *Collection and photo: Pat Rich*. $40-100.

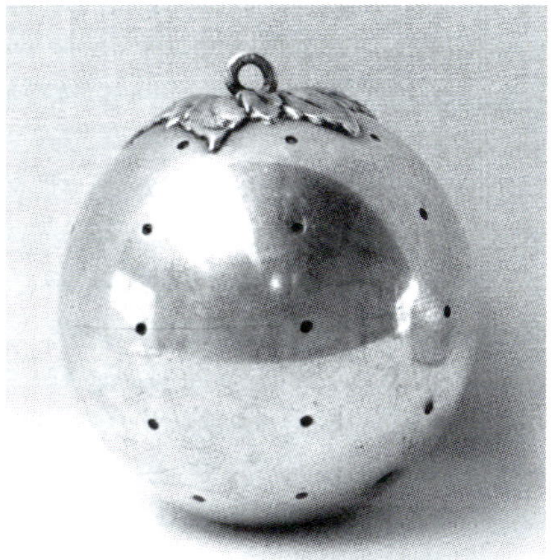

Sterling pin ball (first cousin to a pincushion) with applied leaves at top. 1-1/2" diameter. *Photo: Courtesy of Silver Magazine Archives*.

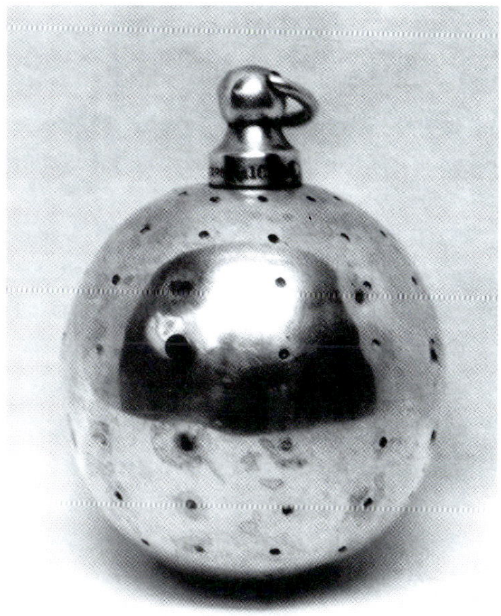

Lebkuecher & Co. of Newark, New Jersey, made this pin ball c.1910. *Photo: Courtesy of Silver Magazine Archives*.

Sewing sets

Whether you called them sewing sets, embroidery tools, compendiums or fitted needlework cases, these were wonderful for the nineteenth century ladies who used them. They were small enough to fit into a purse and the tools were meant to be used for fine stitchery.

Materials in the fitted needlework cases ranged from gold and silver to mother-of-pearl. While most were for embroidery, some were fitted for such specialized work as crocheting.

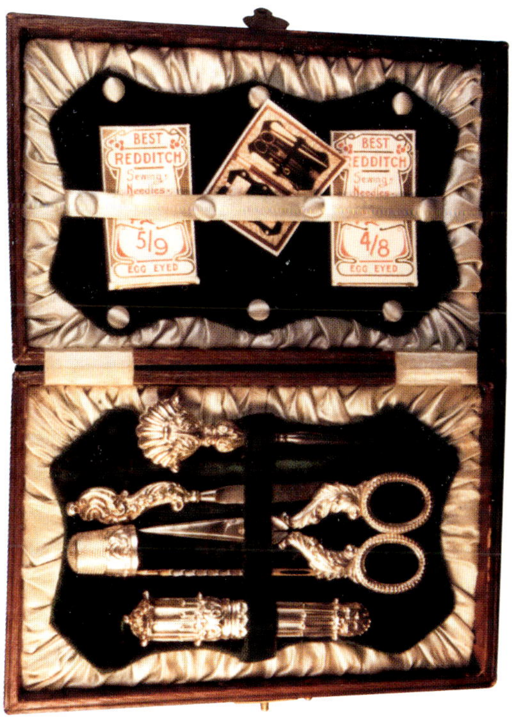

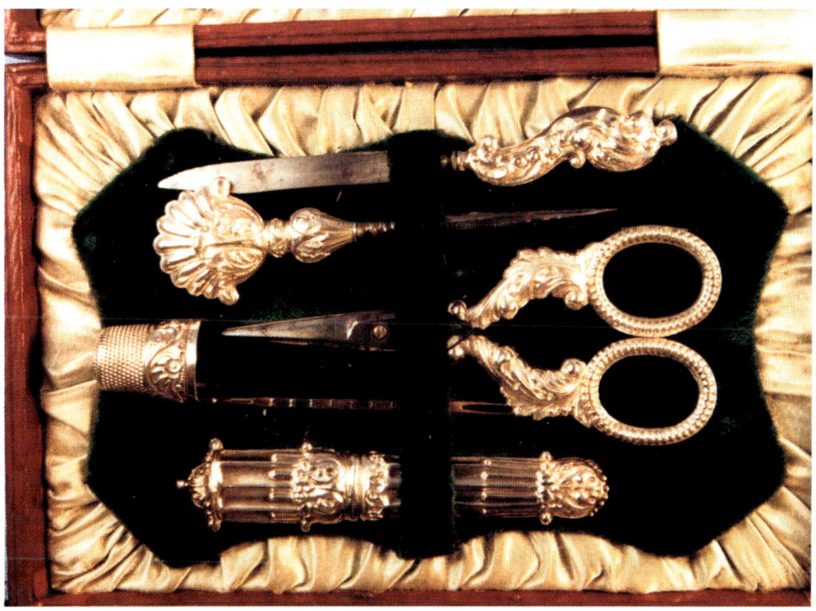

This matched set of French sewing tools rests upon velvet surrounded by satin. The tools include a stiletto, a thimble, a pair of scissors and a needle case. *Collection and photo: Frances Graves.* $150+.

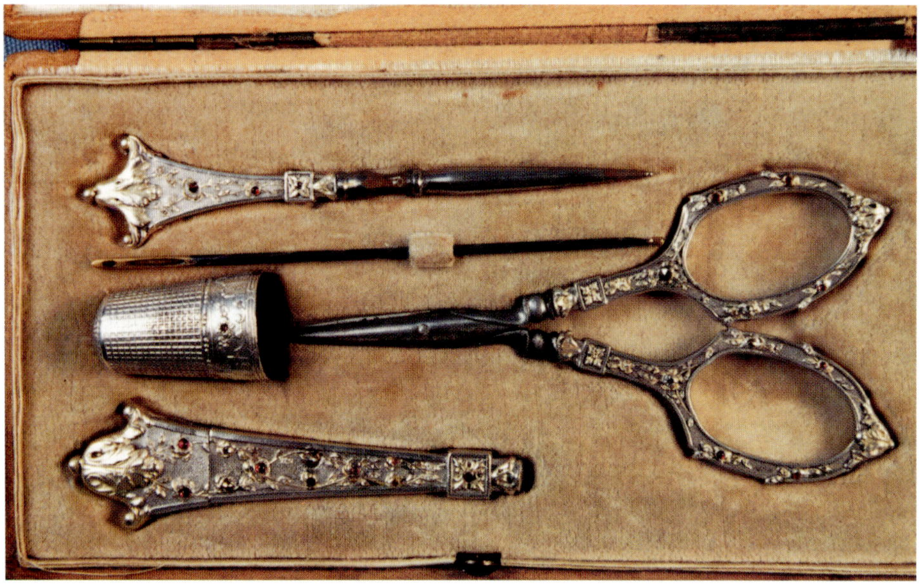

This set of French sewing tools resting on velvet has a rose motif set with red stones. Marked H. L. *Collection and photo: Frances Graves.* $400.

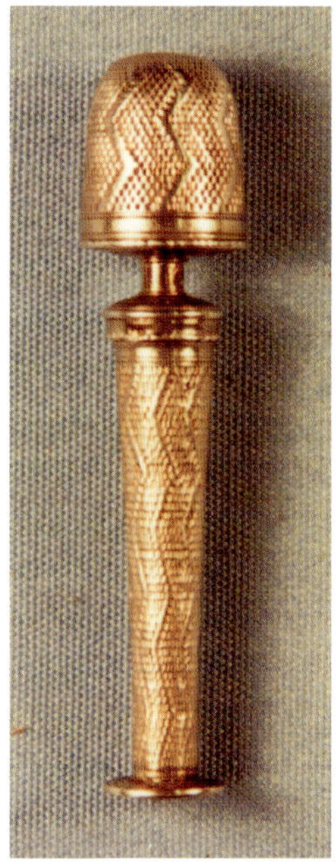

Silver compendium has the Dutch tax mark used from 1831 to 1893. It includes thimble on top, thread reels within and a needle case. Stands 2-3/4". *Collection and photo: Frances Graves.*

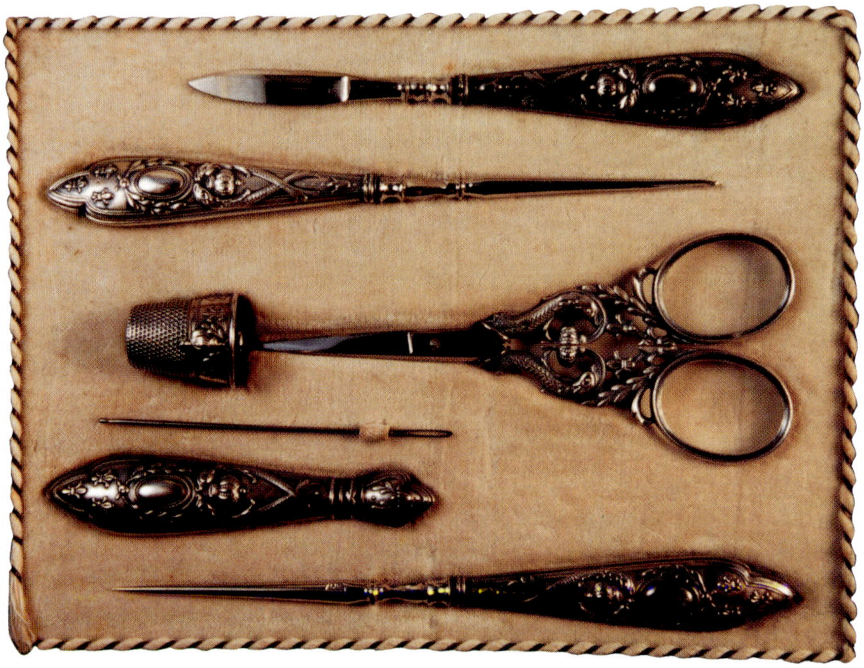

These embroidery tools are signed H. B. with German mark of the crown and the crescent. The ornate pattern is clearly worked on each silver piece. *Collection and photo: Frances Graves.*

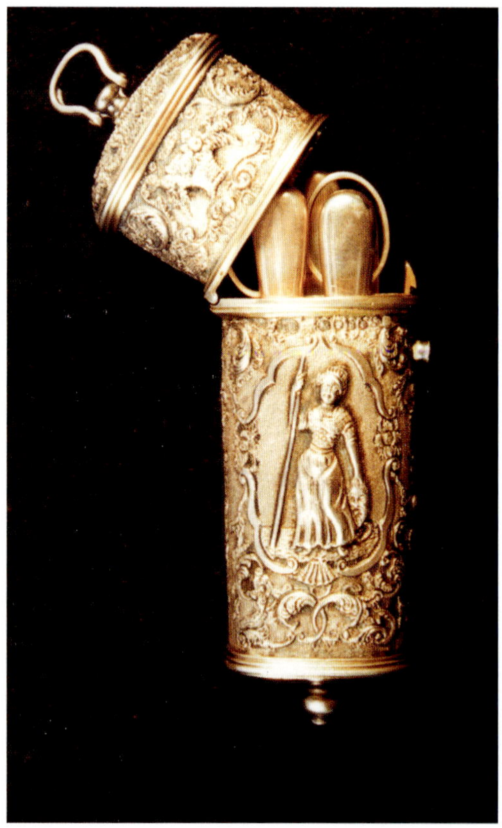

English etui signed T. J. Marked London, 1873. contains scissors, punch, crochet hook, bodkin and needle case. Measures 3-1/2". Depicts Salome with the head of John the Baptist. *Collection and photo: Frances Graves*.

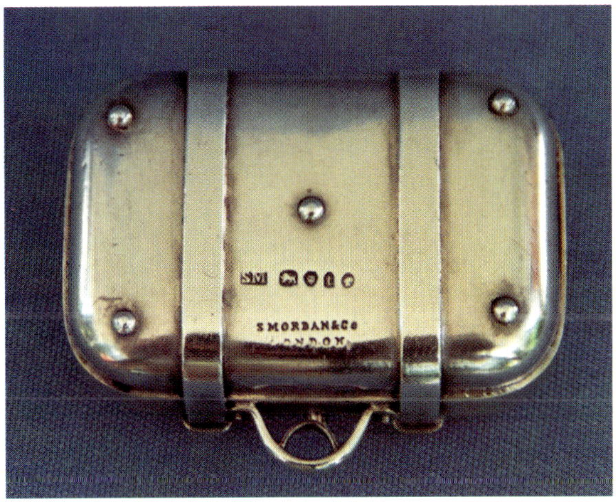

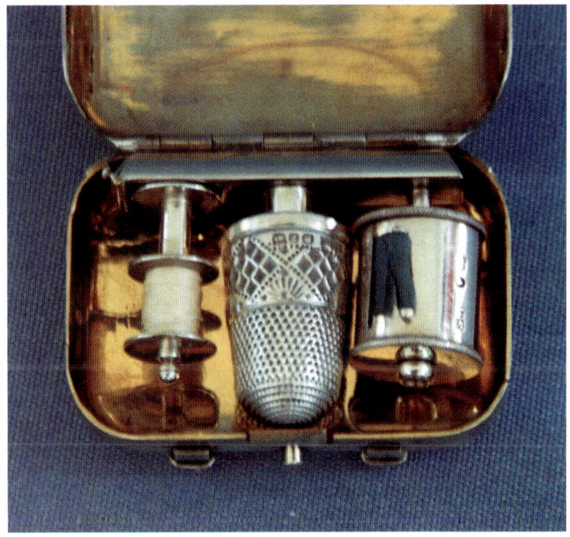

A suitcase with retaining straps is the form of this silver compendium. Bears the London mark for 1874. Maker: Sampson Mordan & Co. Inside view of the suitcase shows a tape measure, thimble, thread bobbin and almost at the hinge is a needle holder. Closed, the case measures 2-1/4 by 2-3/4." *Collection and photos: Frances Graves.* With matching tools $750.

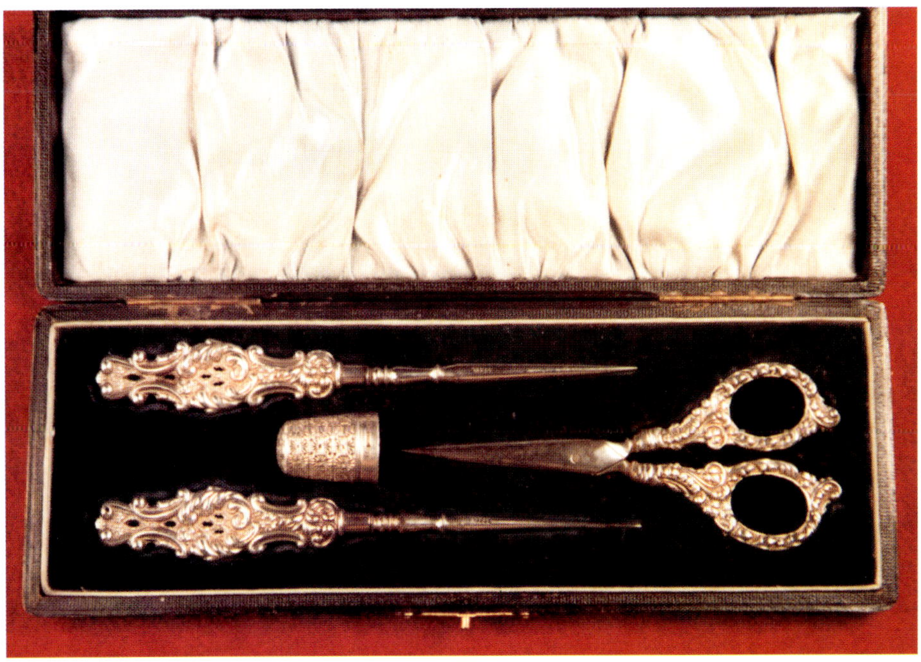

The English crochet set is on black velvet. Marked Birmingham, 1899 and signed A. & L. Ltd. Includes a stiletto, scissors, thimble and crochet hook. *Collection and photo: Frances Graves.*

Spool holder

When closed, a spool holder reminds one of a silver thimble holder or a silver emery case. When opened, the spool holder has just enough room to hold one spool of thread. The size of the spool holder is determined by the size of the spool of thread.

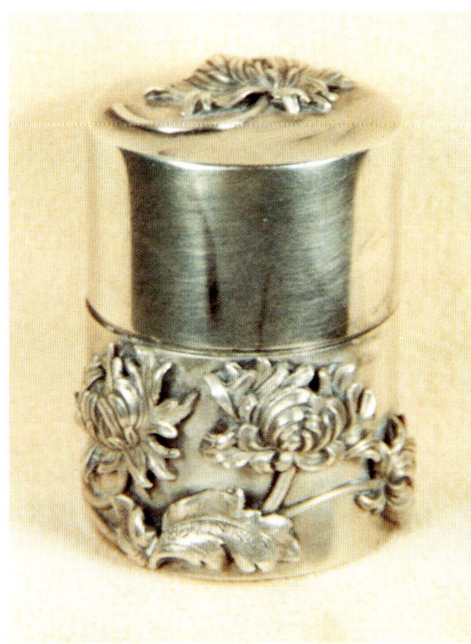

Spool holder made by Shiebler & Co., c.1900. The design is applied chrysanthemums on sides and top. *Collection and photo: Frances Graves.* $250.

Spool knave

The spool knave (sometimes called *reel holder*) was used when a continuous thread was needed for a chain stitch or tambour work. The ball of thread fitted over the horizontal bar. The most conventional type hooked comfortably over the lady's waistband. With the spool knave so placed, the sewer's hands were free for stitching. This was a nineteenth century convenience for ladies who carried their fine work with them into the parlor.

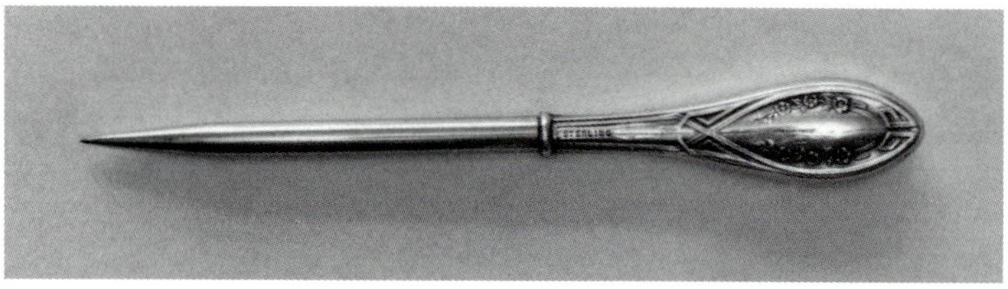

Stiletto marked sterling. Used to make holes in fabric for delicate embroidery work. *Photo: H Ivan Rainwater*. $45.

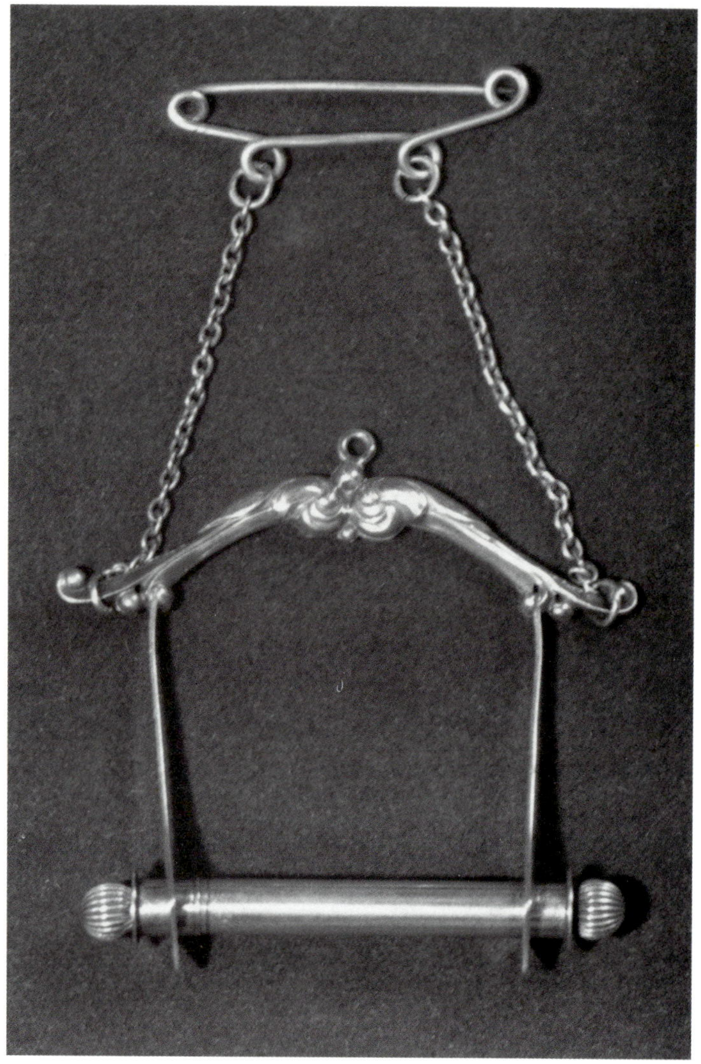

Spool knave. Measures 4" from top to bottom. *Photo: Diane Pelham Burn.* $275.

Tape measures

Sylvia Groves, in her book *Needlework Tools,* shows a picture of what she called "silver yard measures." She also shows yard measures made of ivory, bone, ebony and Tunbridge ware. These were all called yard measures as the ribbon used to measure was one yard long.

> "Ribbon measures winding into small receptacles were in use in the early part of the seventeenth century and were thought of sufficient importance to be named among minor bequests." said Miss Groves.

Silver tape measures were made in England and the United States. The hey-day for production of tape measures was from the late Victorian era up to the 1930s. Novelty tapes were made in Germany and Austria as well as the English speaking countries.

Not all tape measures showed inches on the tape. Some showed centimeters as well. With the advent of the spring activated retractor, the tape no longer needed hand winding, although many hand wound tape measures can still be found.

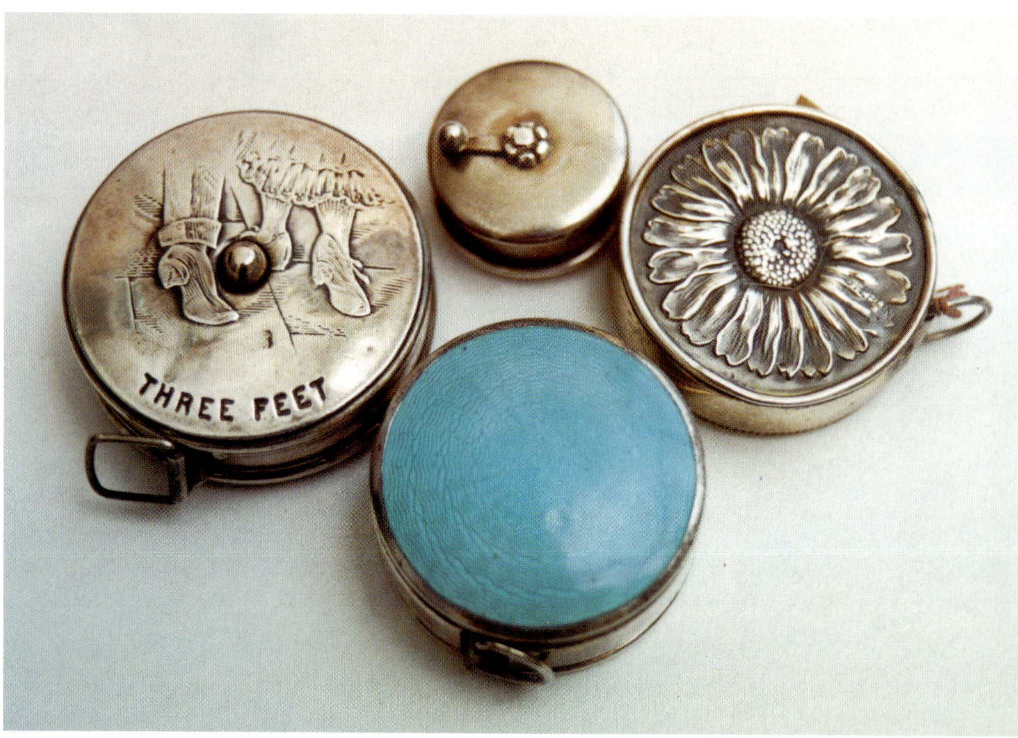

American tape measures from left to right: 1. Three feet, clearly marked in the 1930s.
2. Small tape with handle for winding.
3. Daisy tape.
4. Enamel and sterling. Maker: Webster & Co. Diameters range from 1-1/2" to the smallest 3/4". *Collection of Edie Baker. Photo: Pat Rich.* $65+.

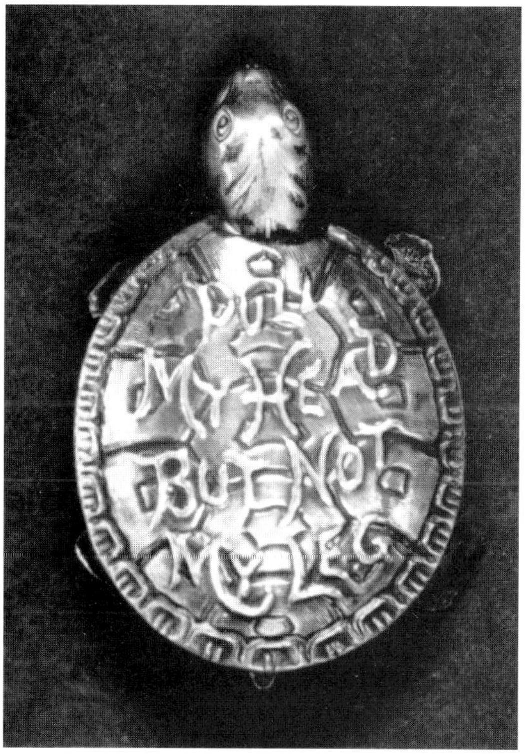

Turtle tape measure. Written on turtle's shell, "Pull my head but not my leg." silverplate. c.1880. Price listed in a 1913 Baird-North catalogue was just 35 cents. *Photo: Judy Redfield.* $120.

Thimbles

After Columbus discovered the New World, many explorers sailed back to Europe with their ship holds filled with silver. These explorers had found rich deposits of silver in the New World from Mexico to Peru. Where silver had once been rare and expensive, it now became more affordable.

But the availability of silver was not the only reason sewing tools began to be made of silver. Silver tools, particularly thimbles, were kinder to the skin than iron or brass. Although silver was soft and had to be combined with copper, once this was done, the silver thimble would outlast a thimble made of other metals.

From where did the name thimble come? Was it always called a "thimble?" According to Mr. Edwin F. Holmes in *A History of Thimbles*, the word thãma was the old English word for thumb. From that word came *thymel*. As early as 1000 AD, the thymel was used to protect an injured thumbnail. the word thymel was then changed to thimble and the thimble became a protector for the finger when sewing. By the time of Queen Elizabeth I, thimble was the accepted name for this very useful sewing device.

By the middle of the seventeenth century, silver thimbles were so affordable in England that most women who sewed had one. What was true for England was also true of the other countries of Europe. From Sweden to France, thimbles and other sewing tools were made of silver. Each country had its own style.

To recognize the country of origin for a silver thimble, a knowledge of marks plus a strong magnifying glass are essential. In England, the Lion Passant denotes silver content of a thimble. Sweden uses three crowns and the letter S. American thimbles use the word sterling which indicates .925 parts silver. A study of silver marks becomes essential for the thimble collector.

A silver thimble may have been made originally to protect the finger from the prick of a needle. At the end of the twentieth century, they still serve the same purpose. Thimbles are found in museums all over the world. A beautiful silver thimble is also a work of art.

The tallest thimble shown here is 1". All are silver. Front row left to right: 1. Sweden, green stone top.
2. England, thistle design.
3. Iran, lovebirds.
4. France, Lily-of-the-Valley motif.
Back row: 1. India, all over floral design.
2. United States, well known Cupid.
3. German souvenir. *Photo: Diane Pelham Burn.* $55-200.

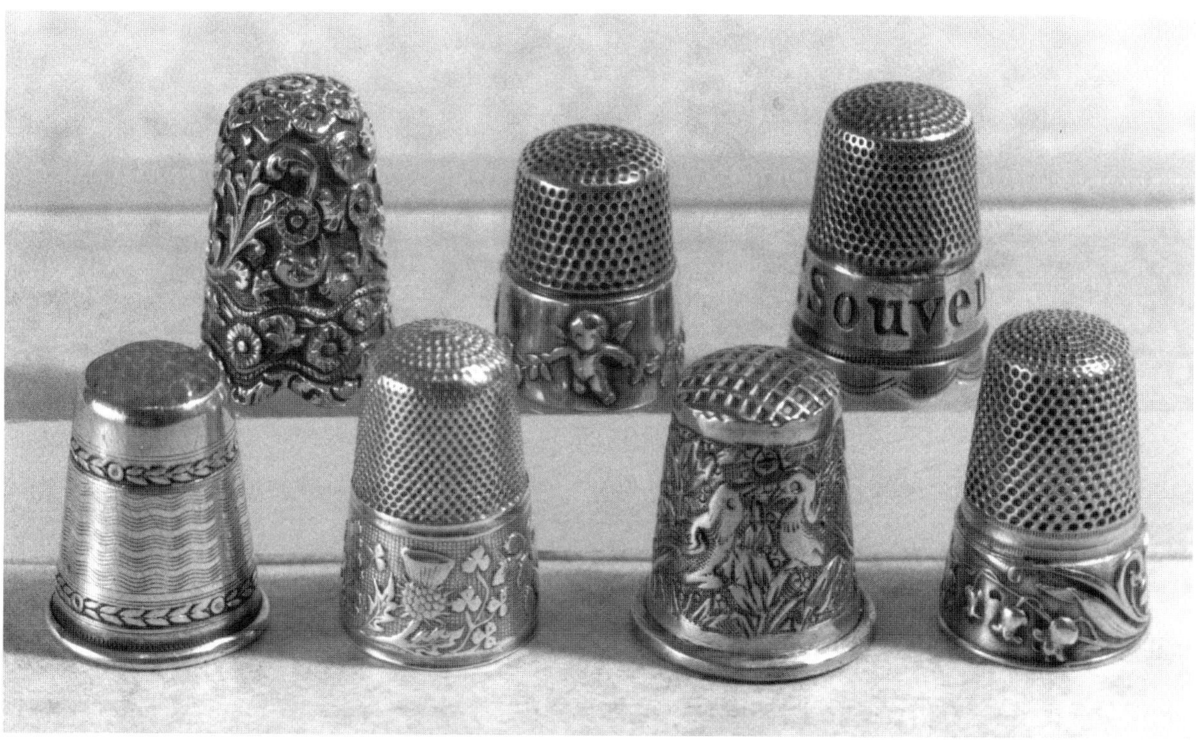

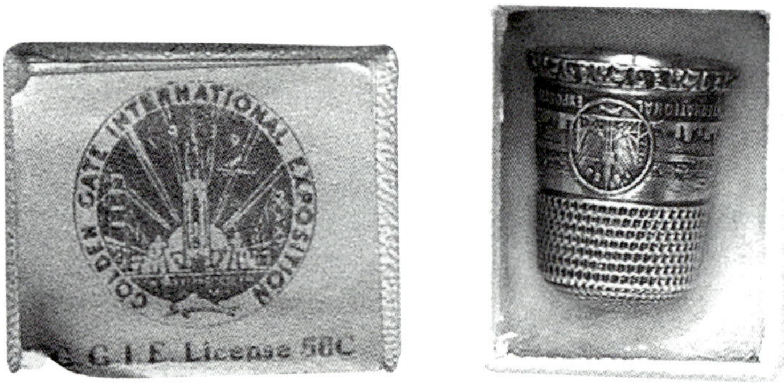

Souvenir silver thimble in original box from the Golden Gate International Exposition, 1939. Maker: Simons Bros. Co. The center of thimble band is Tower of the Sun, exposition logo. Both San Francisco-Oakland and Golden Gate bridges are part of the design. *Photo: H Ivan Rainwater*. $95.

Thread winders

Ladies have been using thread winders for more than two centuries. By definition, a thread winder was a flat grooved surface on which thread could be wound. They varied in size from 1 inch or smaller for silk thread to more than 3 inch for heavier cotton or linen thread.

As early as 1830, both silk and cotton threads were sold in skeins. In order to keep this thread form tangling or breaking, the lady who sewed had to wind the thread from a skein onto her thread winder. The winder than became a very convenient way to keep the thread untangled.

But, says the astute collector, thread winders were made of every material from sturdy cardboard to sterling silver. This is true, but *silver* winders were the ones most used during the nineteenth century.

Many silver thread winders were marked indicating their country of origin. They were made in England, France, the United States and the Netherlands, to mention a few. Winders were included in sewing work boxes which came from the Far East.

In addition to being an attractive piece of silver, thread winders were a convenient method of storing thread. Today, they are a collector's joy to own.

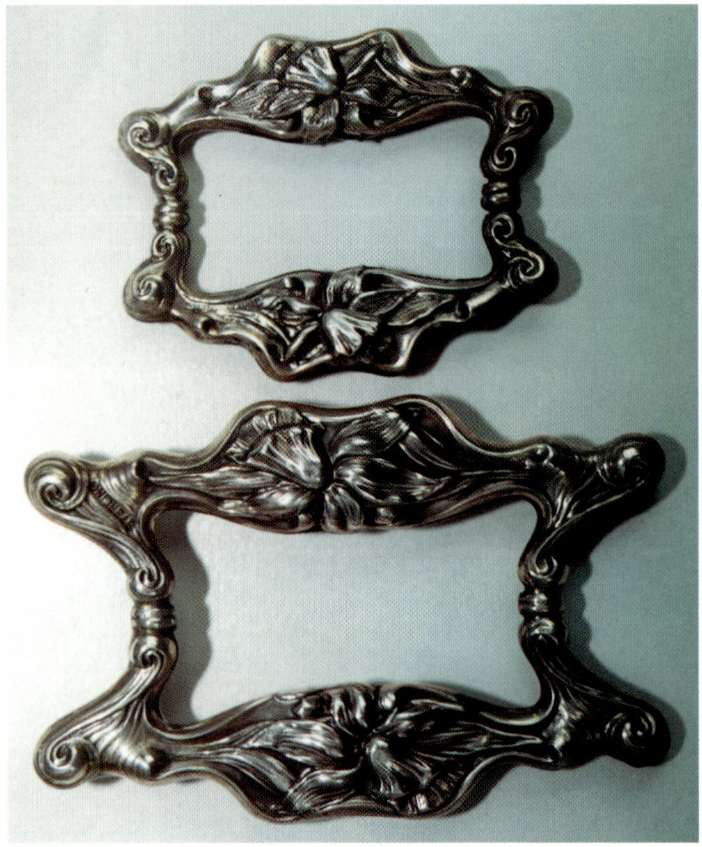

Art Nouveau thread winders. American. Sterling. Smaller winder measures 2" by 1-1/2". Larger measures 3" by 1-3/4". *Collection and photo: Pat Rich*. $125-250.

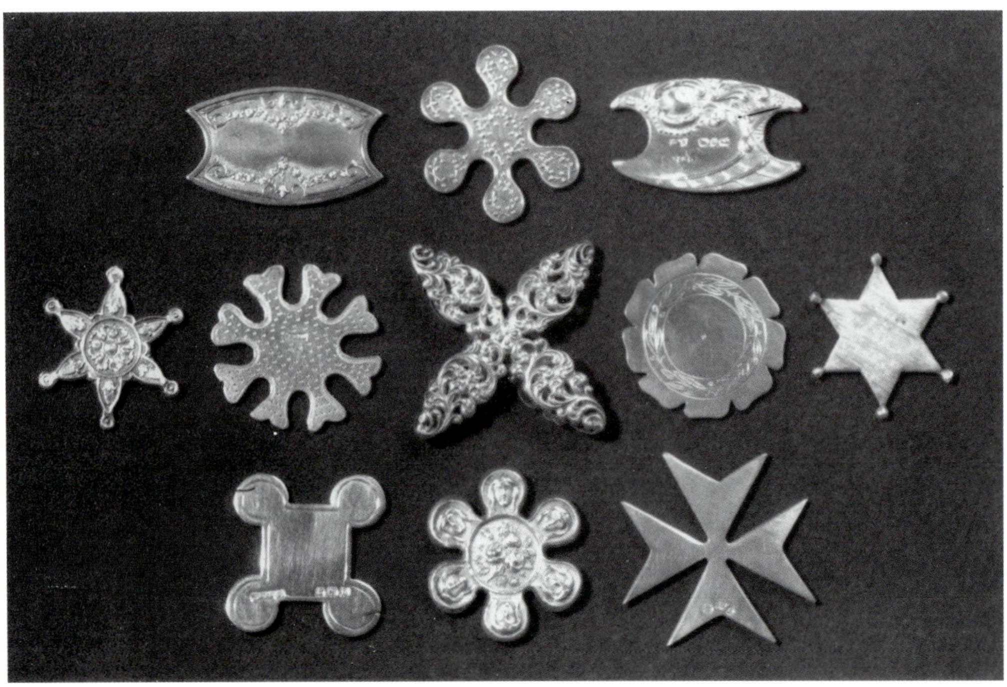

Silver thread winders. Most are late nineteenth century. top row: 1, & 2, French.
3. English.
Middle row: 1. & 2. Dutch.
3. American.
4. & 5. Dutch.
Bottom row: 1. English.
2. French.
3. Maltese hallmark with Maltese Cross. *Photo: Diane Pelham Burn*. $35-50.

Two knives, crossed— scissors

"A pair of scissors is essentially two knives, crossed in the middle and held together with a pin." So wrote Estelle Zalkin in her *Handbook of Thimbles and Sewing Implements*. That definition might be oversimplified, but it does offer a clear picture of what scissors were in Roman times. From antiquity to the early nineteenth century, scissors were made by hand. The Industrial Revolution provided a way to manufacture many diverse types of scissors, from embroidery scissors which could be very small to large cutting shears used by tailors on heavy fabrics.

While scissors were used in the sewing room or corner from as far away as China, they also were made and used throughout Europe. Germany was known for the superiority of its steel blades and these were exported to be combined with ornate silver handles in England, France and the United States.

The Victorian lady many times carried her needlework with her when she went to call upon a friend for tea. Her scissors, as well as other sewing tools, might have been in a box small enough to fit in her reticule. Such scissors were elegant examples of the art of sewing tools and are treasured today by anyone who specializes in "two knives, crossed in the middle, and held together with a pin."

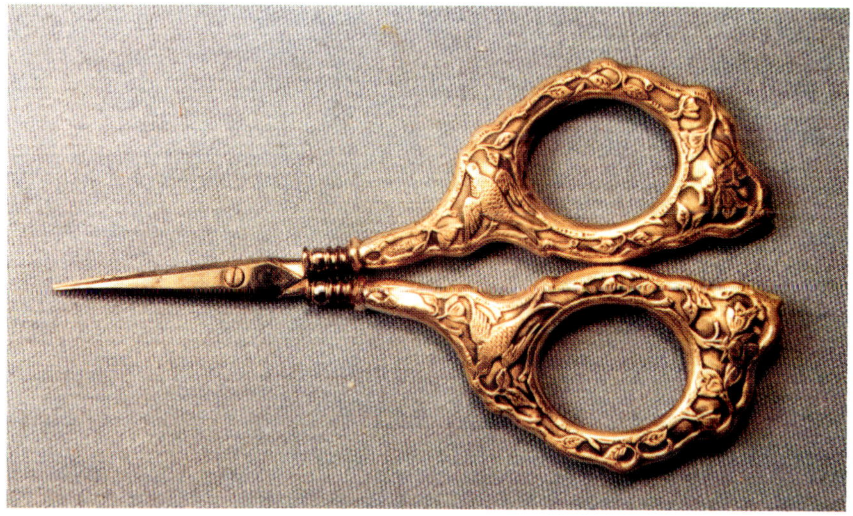

Embroidery scissors. American, sterling with birds and flower motif. c.1890. Measures 3-1/2". *Collection and photo: Frances Graves.* $25-125.

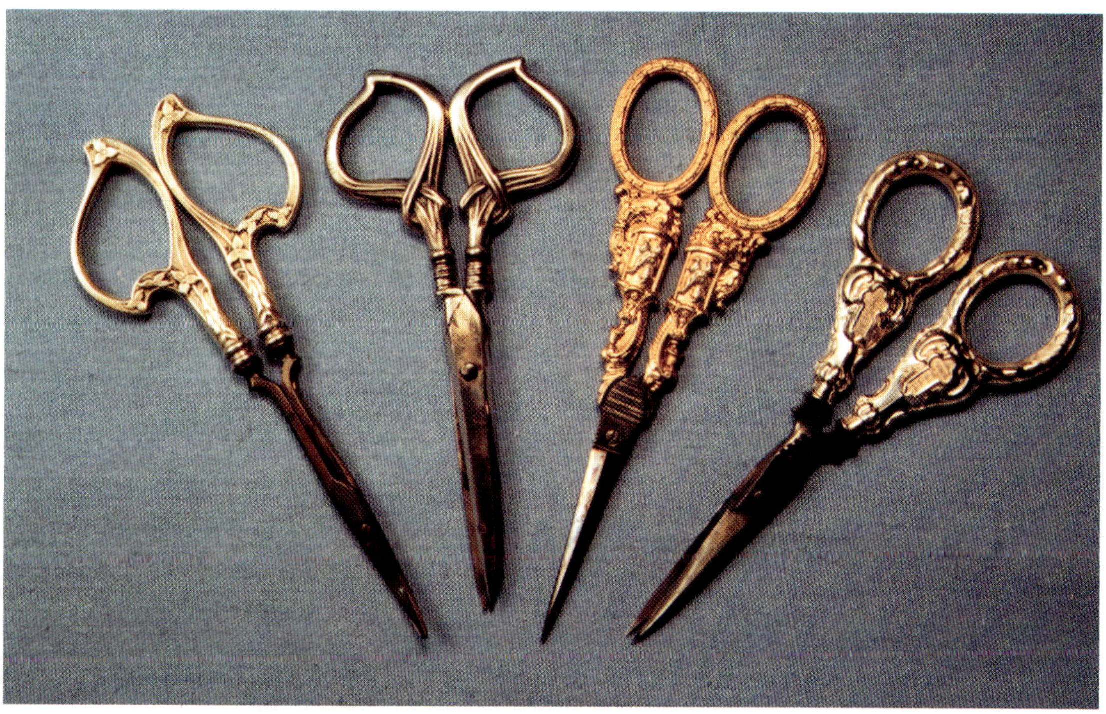

Embroidery scissors c.1875-1900. with four varieties of silver handles. From left: 1. F & B, American.
2. Art Nouveau marked sterling.
3. Silver gilt with French marks.
4. Swedish silver with cat's paw quality mark. *Collection and photo: Frances Graves.* $25-125 each.

Chapter 6. Silver Curios for use...
...in the Study

In Victorian times, the master of the house could go into his library and remain there alone as long as he wished. Neither his wife nor his children could go there uninvited. If the master had a butler, said butler entered only, after knocking, with refreshments from the bar or from the kitchen. The master could shut out the world in his library.

Here was where he sat at his desk and paid his bills. Here was where he wrote letters and, of course, here also was where he kept his books. He usually had a clock, perhaps a small desk clock or an eight-foot tall case clock. This room was truly the Victorian master's space.

Today's library is used by all members of the family. It is here that small children may first learn to read. We learn more and more about how important it is for children to be read to, and also to learn to read for themselves.

Today's library (or study) may also be where members of the family display their trophies won in competitions. Certificates of merit may be placed on the walls for admiration by the whole family. Most of all, the library is the place where each one may retire to read a book on whatever subject is of interest—once each of us has learned the pure joy of reading.

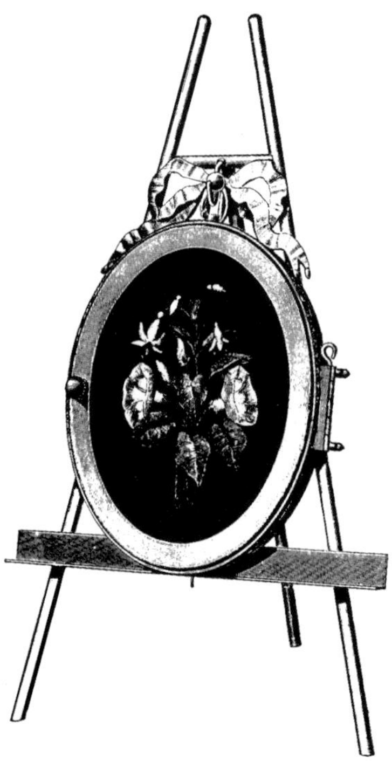

STAND FOR TWO CABINET PHOTOGRAPHS. With Florentine Mosaic Panel.
Illustration shows Stand when Closed.
No. 25. $30.00. (GRASSY)
Gold and Steel Finish, 35.00. (GRATEFUL)

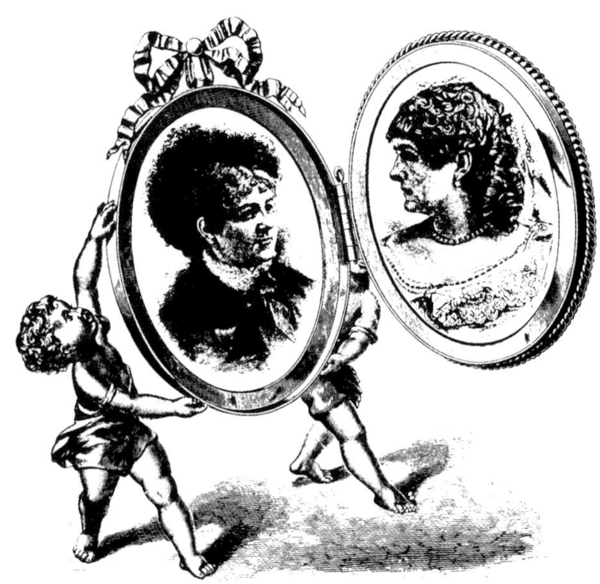

Picture frame on left sits on an easel. On right, two cherubs holding pictures in an open stand. Reed & Barton catalogue, 1885.

Chapter 8. Silver Curios for use...
...at Breakfast

Breakfast, literally "to break the fast," is a meal eaten early in the morning after a night's sleep; in Medieval and Tudor Europe it took place at sunrise. For those who could afford it, breakfast was a substantial meal consisting of bread, cold meats, fish, cheeses, and ale, wine, or beer. In poorer households breakfast was limited to bread with ale, wine, or beer.

During the English Stuart era, breakfast was a relatively light meal including cold meats, salted fish, cheese, bread, butter, and wine, beer or ale. For the poor, there was a popular cereal potage made from local breadcorn. Among the well-to-do the Continental breakfast of rolls, tea or chocolate, spiced bread and cake served around 9:30 to 10:00 AM became fashionable.

At this time the aristocracy and expanding middle class benefited from an improving standard of living. An example is a growing reluctance to accept non-white bread. White bread became scarce and much in demand following several poor wheat-growing seasons. Those who had eaten white bread could not be satisfied with anything else. Therefore bakers began to add lime, chalk and alum which not only bleached the bread but also made the loaves larger. The gentry breakfasted on fruited spiced bread or cake, hot and buttered.

In Georgian homes, breakfast was an informal affair between 9:00 and 11:00 AM. Ladies often breakfasted in their rooms on chocolate or tea with bread and butter. Small mahogany tables were made expressly for the purpose. Slices of bread were buttered and held before the fire to toast. Breakfast parties became fashionable, being scheduled later and later. Eventually they were held in the afternoons.

At the beginning of the nineteenth century, breakfast was taken between 9:00 and 11:00 AM in bigger cities, as in the previous century. But in the country breakfast was a substantial meal served early of cold meats, game, grilled cheese, grilled chops and steak with chocolate, coffee or tea, rolls and cakes. By the late 1840s, as the pattern of "going to the office" developed in middle class and well-to-do households, breakfast was eaten later and became less of a social meal. The amount of meat served at breakfast depended on the wealth of the family. Eggs were served boiled, broiled, or scrambled with lots of butter. Toast and marmalade followed the main course, using white and fancy breads and muffins made fresh every morning. The kitchen maid prepared oatcakes, crumpets (in their season), scones or bannocks all washed down with coffee, chocolate, or tea. As tea had a bad reputation, it was thought to be more nourishing when accompanied by bread and butter or toast with boiled eggs. For those not so affluent, porridge was usually served for breakfast.

In America, where most of the population lived on farms, breakfast was always a hearty meal and tended to follow whatever customs applied in "the old country" from which each community derived. For example, in German influenced Pennsylvania, people were devoted to their scrapple. In French influenced New Orleans, people favored their coffee and sweet rolls while others in the South could not have breakfast without grits and red-eye gravy on biscuits.

Today, many breakfast eaters everywhere are apt to have only toast and coffee on-the-run or skip breakfast at home and grab a pastry and coffee on the way to the office.

Egg cups, cutters, and boilers

In the eighteenth century many articles were produced in silver for the preparation and eating of eggs. There was no concern about high cholesterol or calorie counting; indeed, eggs for breakfast were a staple.

Among the most readily found silver and silverplated objects used for eating eggs are small egg spoons with egg-shaped or tear-drop bowls. Some were made to match flatware patterns and many had gilded bowls to counteract the tarnishing action of eggs on silver.

Egg cups, intended specially for the consumption of soft-boiled eggs, also often had gold-washed interiors. Some egg cups were combined with toast racks.

Cutters were made to remove the tops of soft-boiled eggs. Several types of cutters were employed; some had a scissors-like action.

Egg boilers or steamers are rare today and are mostly found in silverplate. Some Sheffield plate examples from c.1790s were replaced c.1850 by electroplated versions made by Elkington & Company. These vessels for boiling or steaming eggs were of spherical or ovoid shape and varied in size depending on the number of eggs they held. Sizes ran from four eggs to a dozen.

Eggs for breakfast were so important that a great variety of objects were devised for their preparations. Among them were egg coddlers, egg timers (sand glass), egg cups, egg rings (cylindrical receptacle for serving a boiled egg), egg cruets or egg stands (in appearance, much like oil-vinegar type. Many egg-related serving vessels were combined with toast racks.

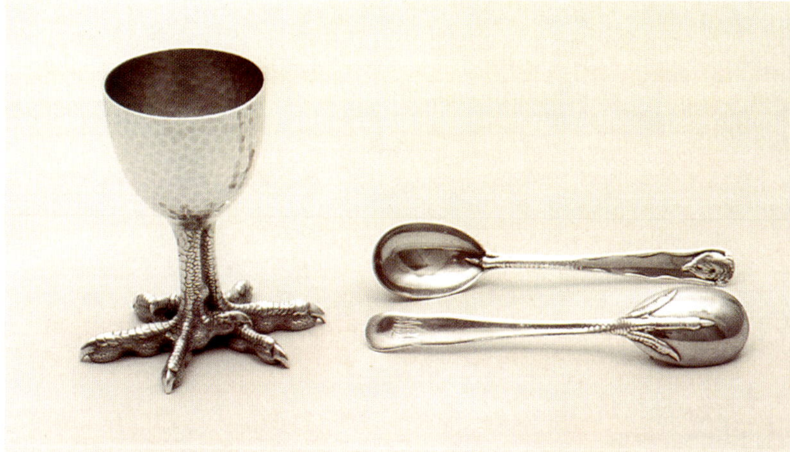

Tiffany egg cup with two egg spoons. Both date to 1880. The hammered cup has stem and base made up of two chickens' legs. The spoons each have a chick's head on the end of the handle while claws grasp the underside of the bowl. Cup measures 3-1/2" in height. Spoons are 4-5/8" long. all are sterling and silver gilt. *Janet Zapata collection. Photo: Richard Goodbody.*

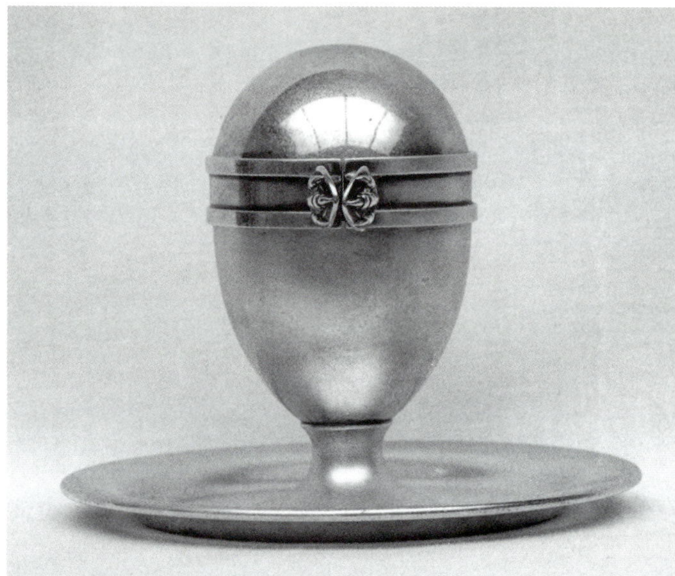

Right:
Egg cup with built-in cutter. Marked "Sterling Pat. Oct. 4, 1910." Height: 3-5/8". *Photo: Courtesy of Silver Magazine Archives*.

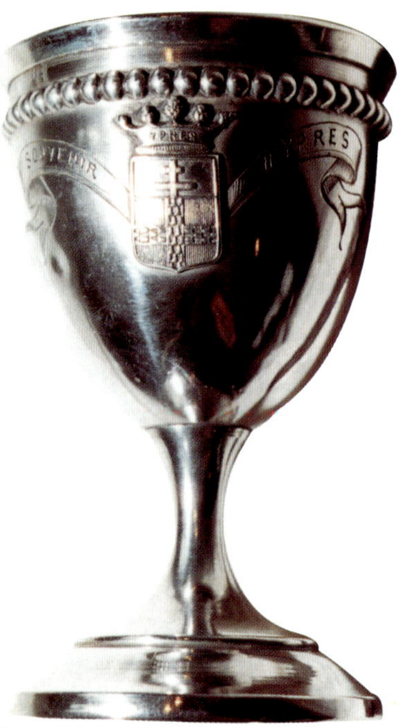

Silver egg cup engraved "Souvenir d' Ypres". 2-1/2" tall. Unreadable French marks c.1930s. *Collection and photo: Anne Jansen.*

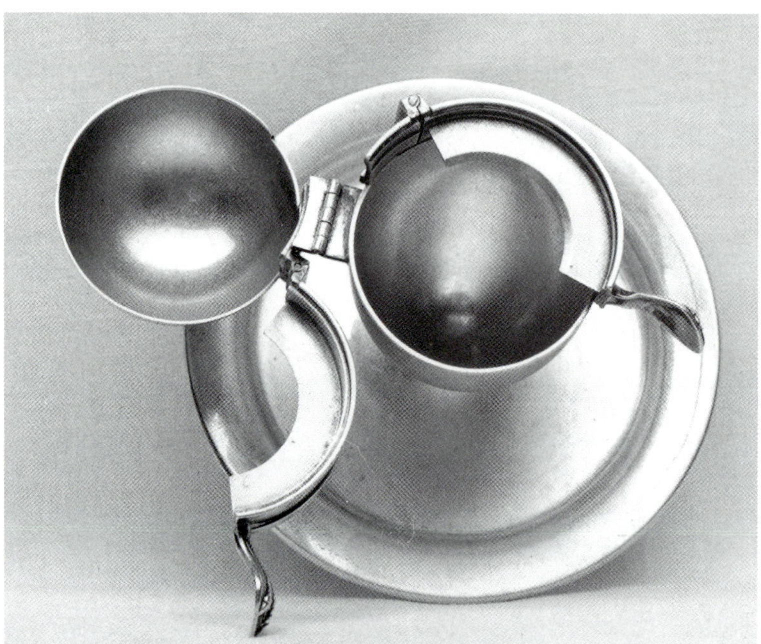

Another view of the egg cup with the lid folded back and blades of cutter shown. *Photo: Courtesy of Silver Magazine Archives*.

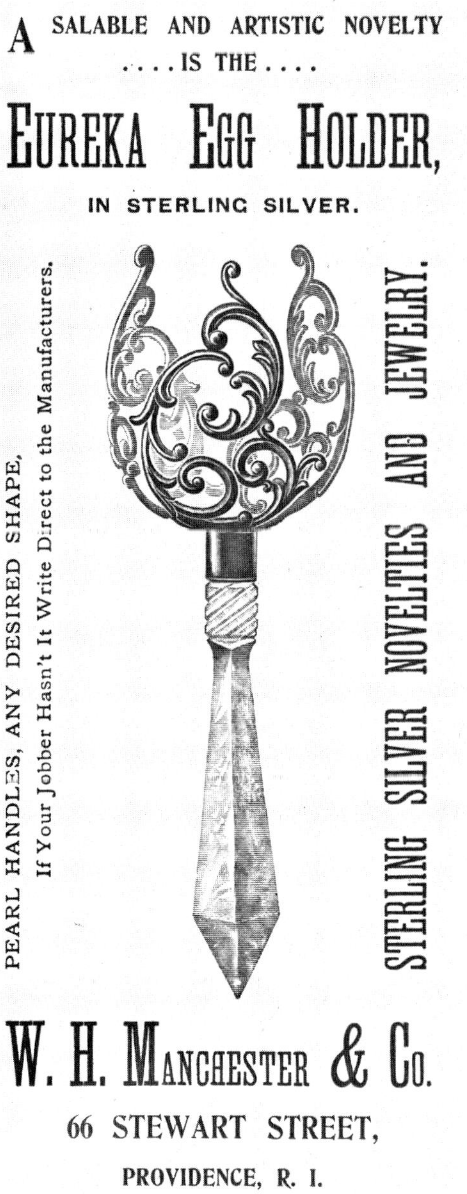

Eureka egg holder from *Jewelers Circular & Horological Review*. Aug. 29, 1894, page 29.

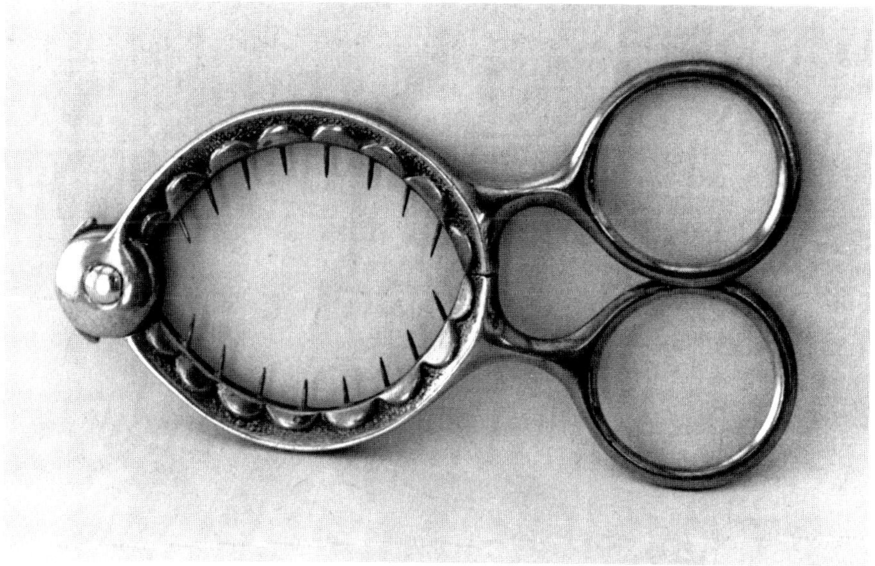

Gorham sterling egg scissors with 16 iron spikes for splitting the shell. Marked: "B.M." with the year code for 1903. Length: 4-1/8". *Photo: Courtesy of Silver Magazine Archives.*

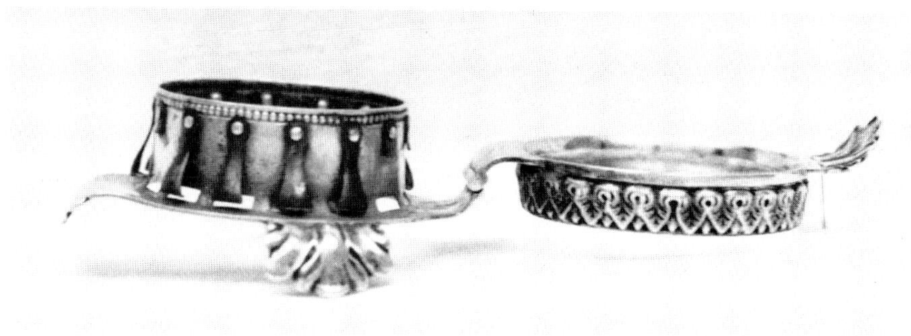

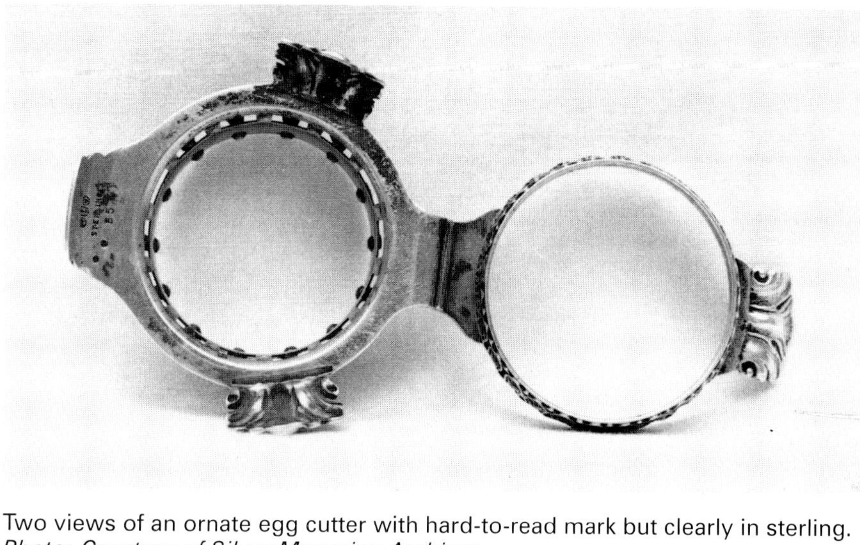

Two views of an ornate egg cutter with hard-to-read mark but clearly in sterling. *Photo: Courtesy of Silver Magazine Archives.*

Napkin rings

In England until the Restoration (1660), the only items of cutlery in common use were the knife and fork. Though napkins of cloth were used as early as Roman times, until the introduction of forks for individual use in the seventeenth century, there would have been little use for napkin rings. Food was eaten with the fingers, which were washed frequently during the meal. Napkins, larger than are ordinarily used now, were treated as towels and were removed from the table after their use.

With the introduction of napkins for individual use, early silver napkin rings were sometimes engraved with initials, names or numbers to make sure that *EACH* person received his own.

Paintings through the centuries show napkins in use, but napkin rings made their first appearance in literature in 1838 in *Work-Woman's Guide*, a magazine devoted to needlework. Directions were given for knitted rings to be stiffened with wire or buckram. Napkin rings may be considered a product of the Victorian age.

The Meriden Britannia Company catalogue of 1860 first listed three types of napkin rings, but did not illustrate them. The August 1, 1867, issue illustrates fifteen designs. Of these, nineteen had figures or raised ornaments. The Reed & Barton catalogue of 1877 devoted four pages including fifty-one designs. In 1886, Meriden Britannia Company assigned seven pages to napkin rings; thirty-five were figurals and fifty-one were round, rectangular, or triangular designs. Reed & Barton's catalogue of 1885 devoted ten and one-half pages to its forty-three figural napkin rings and eighty-six round, square or rectangular bands. Numbers in succeeding catalogues fell off sharply near the turn of the twentieth century and disappeared almost entirely when supplanted by celluloid ones early in the 1900s.

While plain, round napkin rings would undoubtedly hold a napkin efficiently, it is the figural ones that appeal to today's collectors.

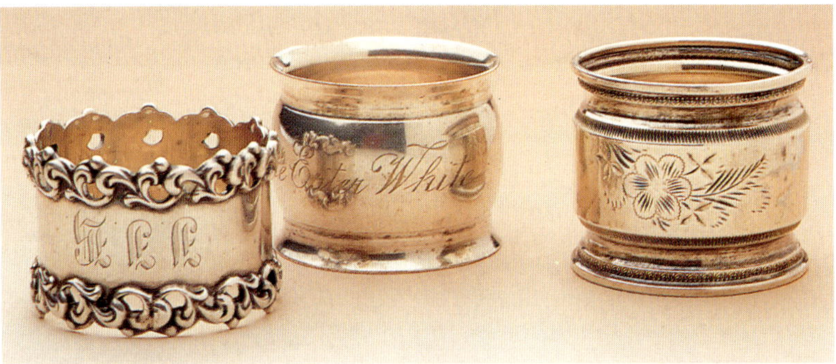

Napkin rings. Left to right. Towle trademark, STERLING, 108. The design is very much like Towle's "Diana" (1885) flatware.
Middle: Inscribed Lee Ester White. No trade-marks.
Right: Marked: STERLING, 156. A six-petaled flower and leaf design inscribed twice. They average 1-5/8" (4.2 cm) in diameter. *Photo: Bruce Waters*.

Combination napkin ring and place card holders. Marked: Nichols & Whitney, Pat. Inscribed Dec. 22, 1985. *Almgren collection. Photo: H Ivan Rainwater*. $160.

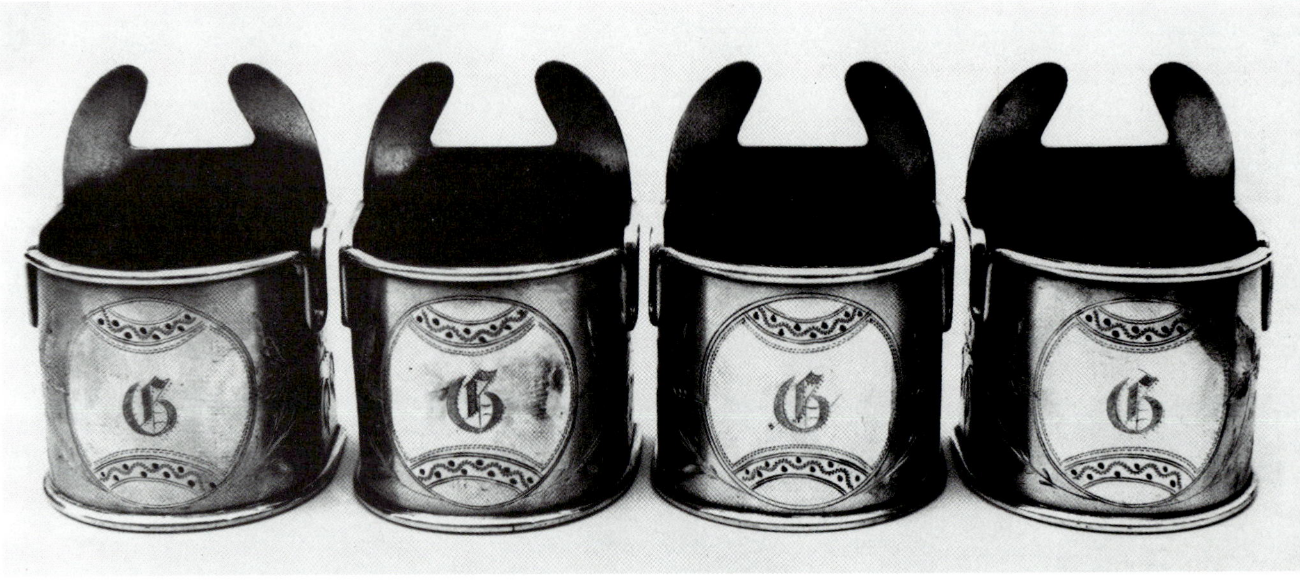

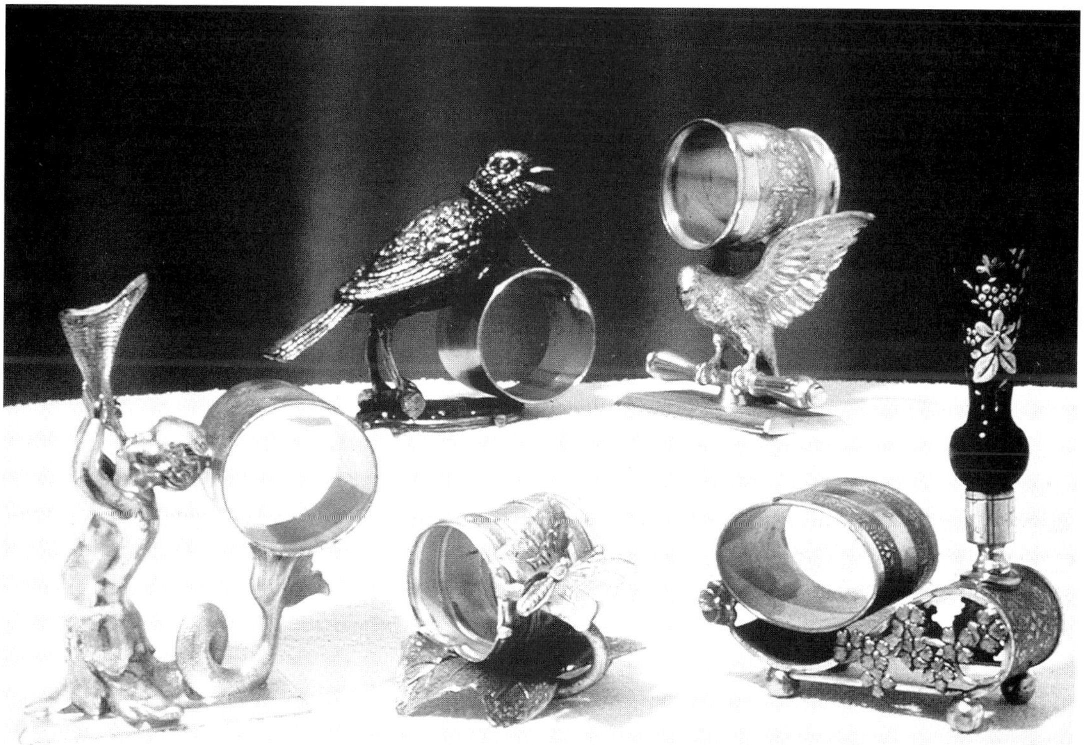

Left and below: Figural napkin rings by various makers. *Photo: International Silver Company.* $55-140.

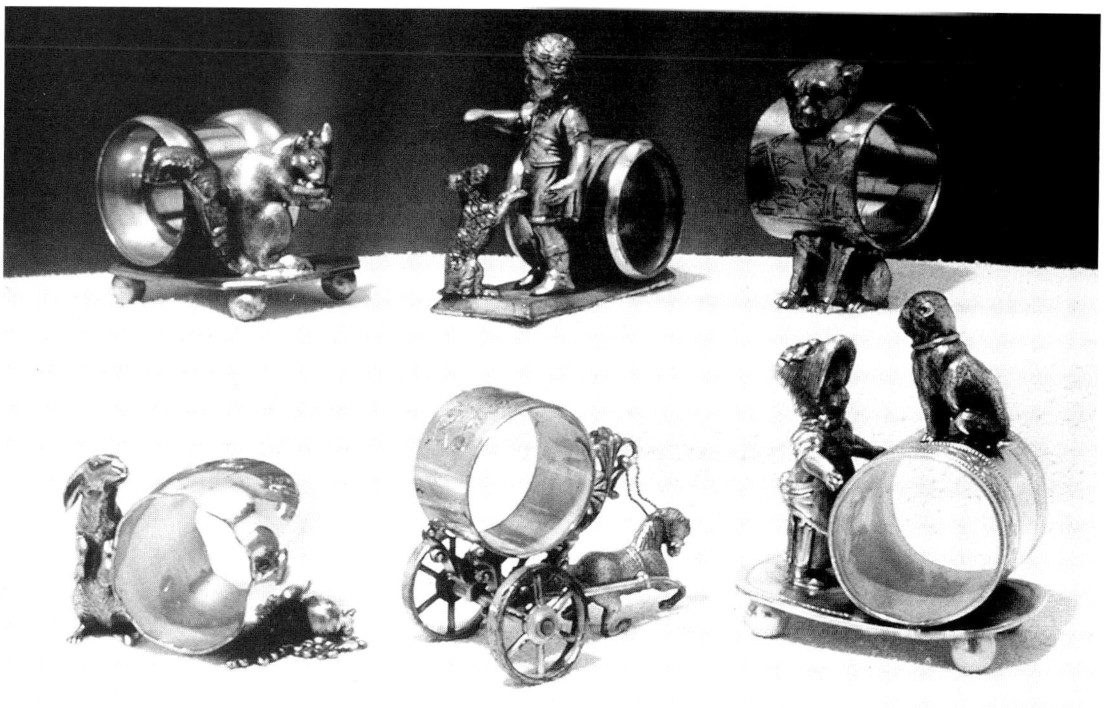

Figural napkin rings are American in origin. Animals such as cats, dogs, chickens, rabbits, squirrels, goats, birds, turtles and dolphins are just a few of the motifs used. Children at play made another favorable motif, especially those inspired by the figures of Kate Greenaway and illustrated in her book, *Kate Greenaway Birthday Book and Under the Window*.

Napkin rings with small glass bud vases attached are quite rare today. They are often sought for the glass vase which is usually hand enameled. An exchange of various articles of silverplate among manufacturers make it possible to find identical napkin rings, or sometimes the same ornaments, bearing different trademarks. Some napkin rings are not marked at all.

Caveat Emptor! A few of the manufacturers brought out some reissues which were not always as carefully made as the originals. Also, reproduction napkin rings from Japan have been noted. Non-figural napkin rings to match sterling silver place settings were also made by manufacturers of sterling flatware. No sterling figurals have come to our attention.

Orange peelers

Was it a bumper crop of oranges at the end of the nineteenth century? Was it an "orange cure" prescribed by physicians which required the patient to consume three dozen oranges daily? We do not know but something inspired several silver manufacturers to produce a number of "dainty devices for the proper way to eat an orange."

Orange peelers, orange cups and orange spoons all became a part of the silverware used at the end of the Victorian era. Some were made in sterling silver while others were offered in silverplate. Some became souvenirs of a trip. Once the collector has used an orange peeler himself, he'll declare it the only way—nay, the *proper* way to eat an orange.

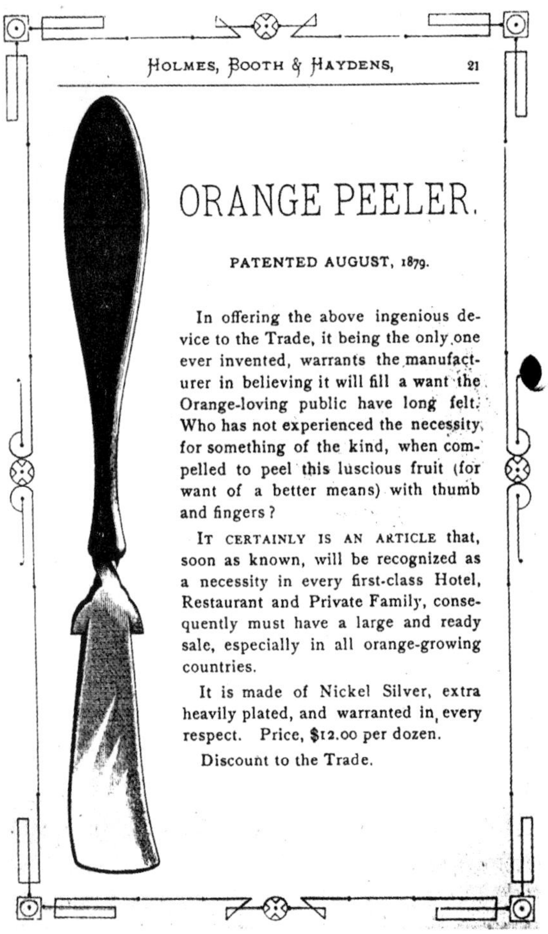

HOLMES, BOOTH & HAYDENS, 21

ORANGE PEELER.

PATENTED AUGUST, 1879.

In offering the above ingenious device to the Trade, it being the only one ever invented, warrants the manufacturer in believing it will fill a want the Orange-loving public have long felt. Who has not experienced the necessity for something of the kind, when compelled to peel this luscious fruit (for want of a better means) with thumb and fingers?

IT CERTAINLY IS AN ARTICLE that, soon as known, will be recognized as a necessity in every first-class Hotel, Restaurant and Private Family, consequently must have a large and ready sale, especially in all orange-growing countries.

It is made of Nickel Silver, extra heavily plated, and warranted in every respect. Price, $12.00 per dozen.

Discount to the Trade.

Reprint from the Holmes, Booth & Haydens catalogue, stating that this is the only one ever invented.

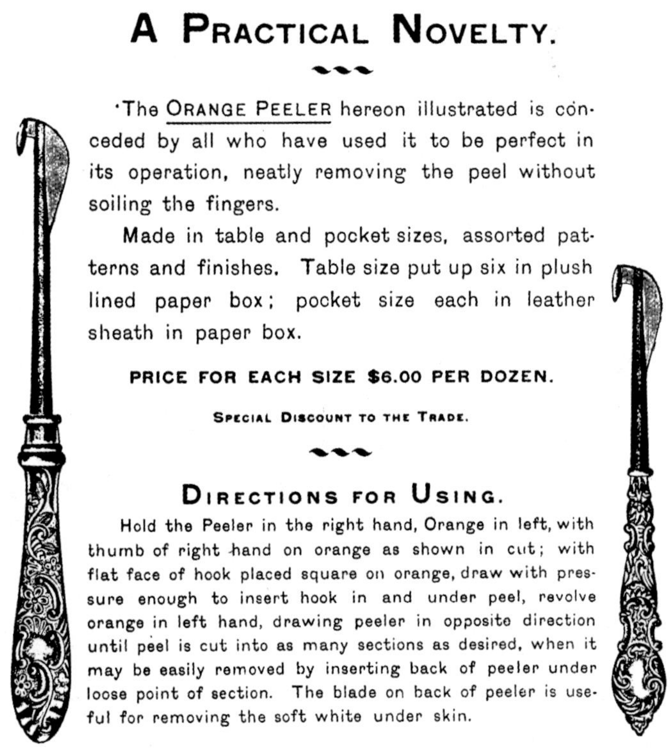

A PRACTICAL NOVELTY.

The ORANGE PEELER hereon illustrated is conceded by all who have used it to be perfect in its operation, neatly removing the peel without soiling the fingers.

Made in table and pocket sizes, assorted patterns and finishes. Table size put up six in plush lined paper box; pocket size each in leather sheath in paper box.

PRICE FOR EACH SIZE $6.00 PER DOZEN.

SPECIAL DISCOUNT TO THE TRADE.

DIRECTIONS FOR USING.

Hold the Peeler in the right hand, Orange in left, with thumb of right hand on orange as shown in cut; with flat face of hook placed square on orange, draw with pressure enough to insert hook in and under peel, revolve orange in left hand, drawing peeler in opposite direction until peel is cut into as many sections as desired, when it may be easily removed by inserting back of peeler under loose point of section. The blade on back of peeler is useful for removing the soft white under skin.

Rogers & Bro. advertisement of their new practical novelty, an orange peeler. Patented January 5, 1893.

Orange peeler, souvenir of St. Augustine, Florida

The discoveries of Columbus inspired a generation of explorers who crossed the Atlantic to find that Columbus had been wrong; he had not discovered Asia but had found a wild and impenetrable barrier to it. In 1513 the Spanish explorer Juan Ponce de Léon, while searching for the mythical Bimini Island and the Fountain of Youth, discovered Florida.

In 1565 Don Pedro Menéndez de Avilés, Captain General of the Spanish fleet, founded St. Augustine, the first white settlement on the continent of North America.

The only walled city in the United States, St. Augustine remained under Spanish control until 1761, when, with the rest of Florida, it was ceded to England. The Old City Gate is the sole remains of the city walls built in 1620 of qoquina stone.

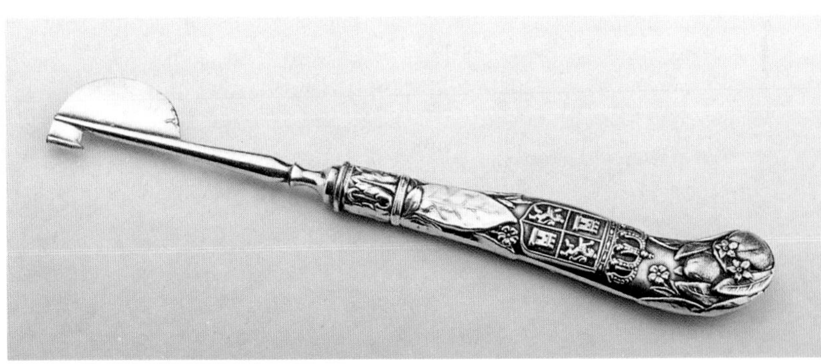

Orange peeler. Souvenir of St. Augustine, Florida with Spanish crest on one side and gates to the walled city on the other. Marked: Sterling. Measures 6". *Photo: Bruce Waters*.

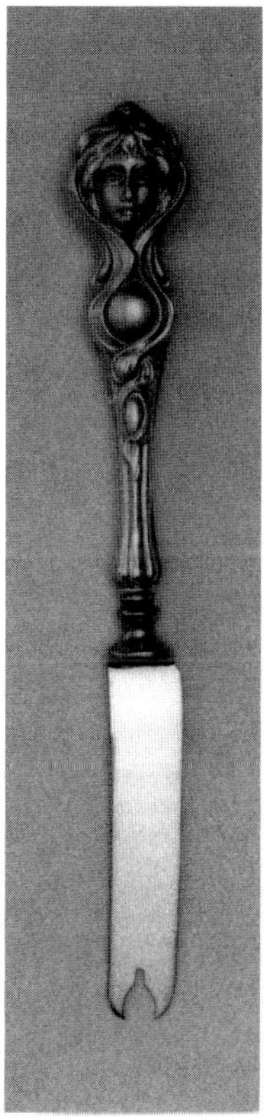

Left:
Art Nouveau orange peeler with lady's tresses forming the handle. No marks. *Photo: H Ivan Rainwater*.

Right:
Revolving sterling silver grapefruit holder. Maker unknown. *Courtesy of Gwen Kelso. Photo: Courtesy of Silver Magazine Archives*.

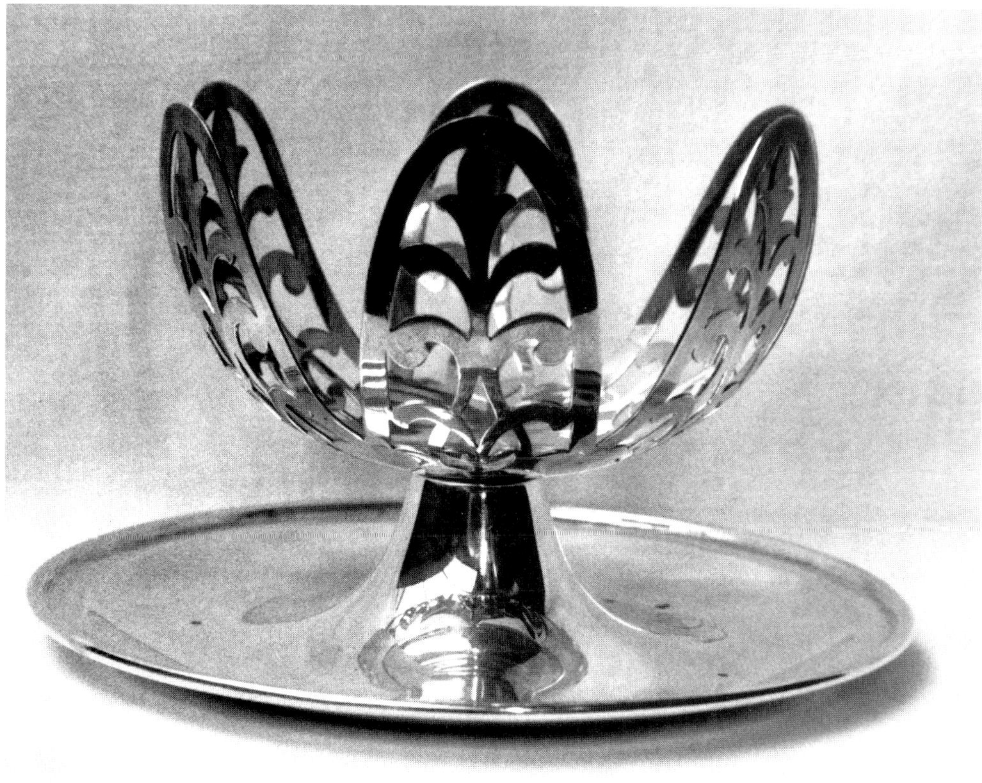

Syrup pitchers and drip plates

Small silverplate syrup pitchers such as this still serve in a very functional way as table items for dispensing maple syrup or other liquid toppings.

Pitchers with drip plates were made in great quantities from the 1870s to around 1910. Some have built-in cut-off arrangements to stop the drip. Later models eliminated the drip plate. Pitchers made after 1912 usually do not have Quadruple Plate markings.

In spite of having a built-in cut-off, some pitchers came with a drip plate. Later models eliminated them. Few companies actually made complete lines of flatware or hollowware but bought what they needed to complete their lines.

Syrup pitcher and plate shown here were *not* made by the same company. The drip plate is marked Barbour Silver Co., while the pitcher is marked Hartford Silver Co. Both are stamped Quadruple Plate indicating that they were of best quality. Diameter of the plate measures 5-3/4". Height of pitcher is 5". *Photo: H Ivan Rainwater*. $165.

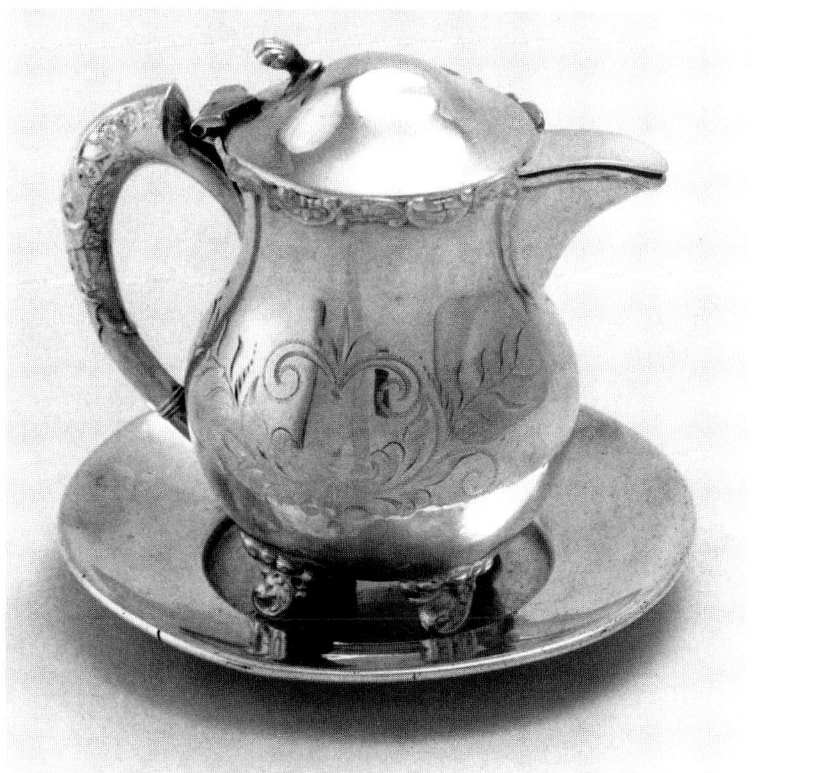

Muffineers or casters

Castors, also spelled caster, are often called sifters, shakers, or muffineers. They originated in France in the mid-1600s and their popularity spread to England by the 1670s and reached America about thirty years later. They ranged in height from 5 or 6 inches to 10 inches. Many castors were made in sets of three or more for the dining table. They held spices, black pepper, and sugar as well as other condiments.

Muffineers are small castors, usually single, used primarily for sprinkling ground spices, pepper, sugar, salt and mixtures such as cinnamon and sugar.

Containers with pierced lids for casting pepper were found forming the upper parts of bell-shaped salts of the Elizabethan and Jacobean periods. Castors as separate articles in English silver appear not to have been generally made before the latter part of the seventeenth century. The first American examples were made about the beginning of the eighteenth century.

Early castors often were made in sets of two or three for the service of mustard, pepper, and other spices. In sets of three one was larger and was intended for sugar. These containers for "casting" condiments on food were often combined with cruets for oil and vinegar and fitted into castor or cruet frames. During the middle of the eighteenth century the two castors were used for Jamaican and cayenne pepper. Some sets also contained an additional castor for sugar or salt.

American silverplate catalogues of the 1880s show only pepper castors, or pepper boxes as they are called.

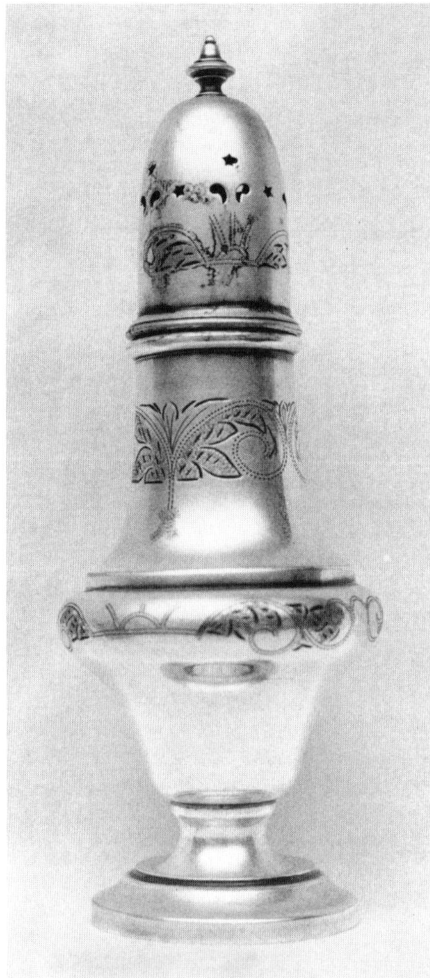

Caster for holding various condiments—ground spices, black pepper, sugar, etc. A gourmet delight was the caster which held sugar and cinnamon for sprinkling on hot buttered toast, children's delight. Silver on copper. No marks. *Photo: Courtesy of Silver Magazine Archives*. $35-350.

Spoon warmers

In many English Victorian homes breakfast was served from a sideboard. Each family member who partook of the meal helped him or herself to a portion of what was there. But the hot foods brought in from the kitchen cooled quickly. Eating with a cold spoon cooled the food even faster, hence, the spoon warmer.

The spoon warmer is a vessel containing hot water. Spoons were placed in the hot water to be kept warm until used for the meal. For the most part, spoon warmers were made of silverplate or Britannia ware and of porcelain. Some sterling ones have also been reported but these were rare. The popular nautilus design was made in several sizes.

The size and capacity of spoon warmers varies. A large spoon warmer holds about a quart of hot water; a very small one holds only one or two cups. The average size spoon warmer holding a quart of hot water measures approximately 5-1/2 inch and 6 inches high.

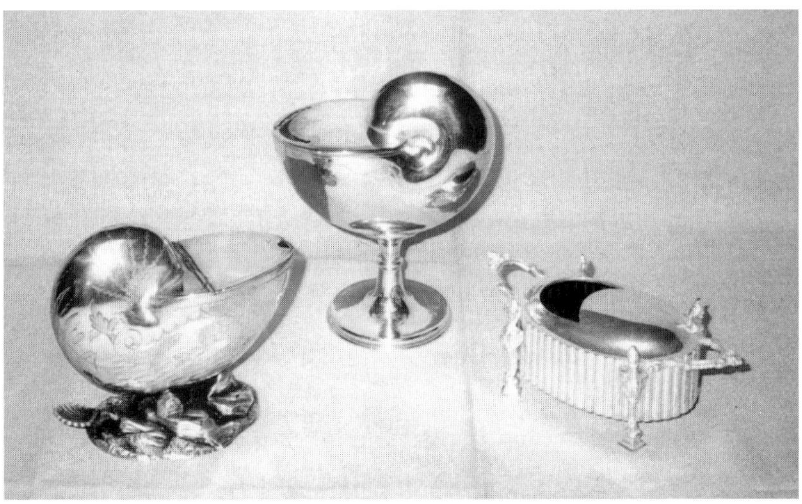

Spoon warmers. Left to right: nautilus shell with fish and seaweed design. 6".
Nautilus shell on stand. 8" tall.
Oval ribbed griffins with handles. *Private Collection.*

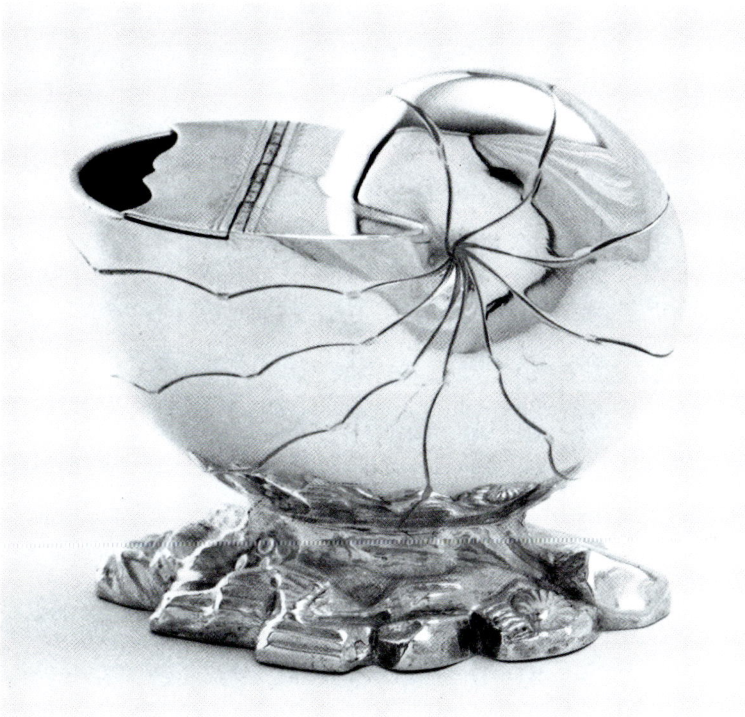

Silverplated spoon warmer in the popular nautilus design. The nautili shell motif was used either plain, fluted or engraved. *Photo: H Ivan Rainwater*.

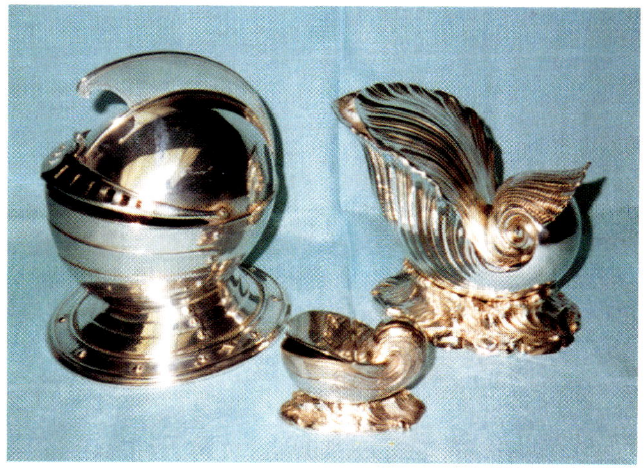

Knight's helmet spoon warmer with hinged visor and English Registry date of December 1864. Decorative nautilus shell at right is for teaspoons. Was the small shell at center front used for demitasse spoons? *Private Collection.*

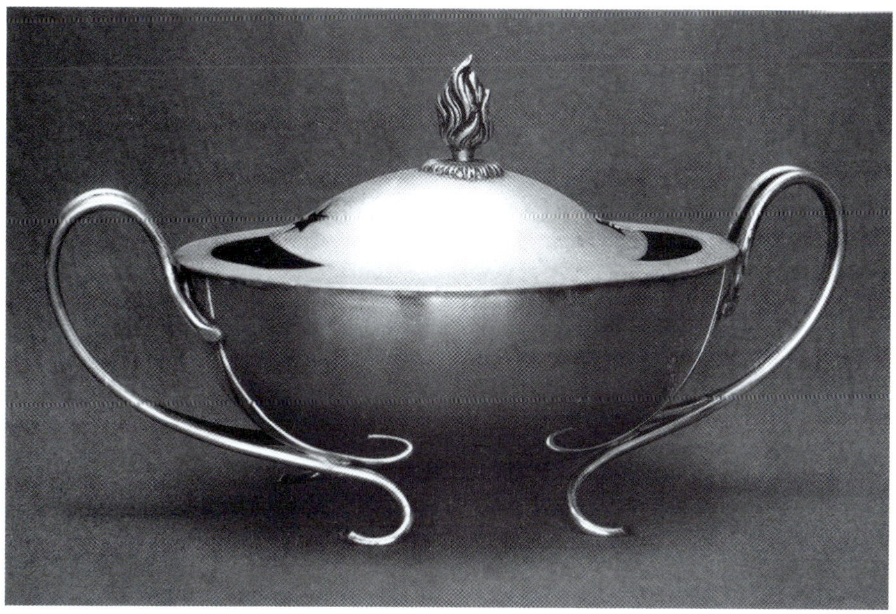

An unusual spoon warmer with openings on both sides. The design is of a Roman lamp with its flame burning. *Donna Felger Collection. Photo: H Ivan Rainwater.*

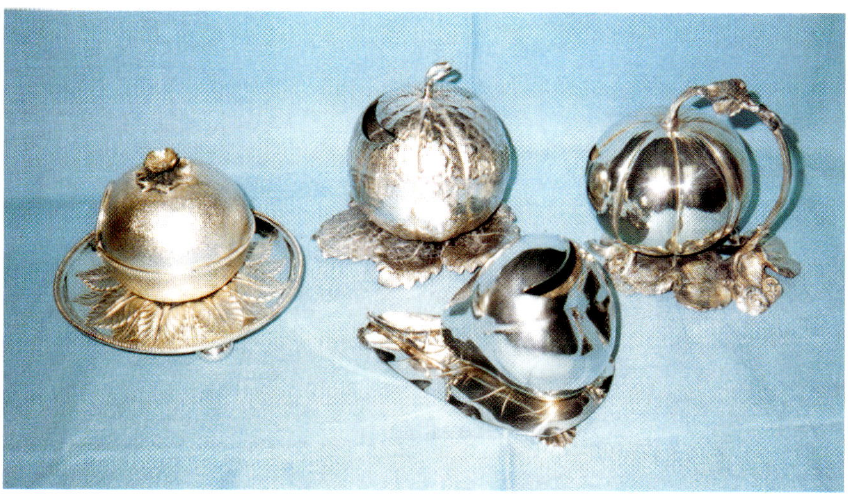

This fruit group of spoon warmers consists of an orange, pumpkin, melon and pear, all approximately 7" tall and all English. *Private Collection.*

Chapter 9. Silver Curios for use...
...with Wine and Beverages

The happy hour

People have always imbibed. The ancient Greeks and Romans did it with great ceremony. Ceremonial events all over the world included drinks from Biblical days to modern times.

Most of the earliest settlers in America were of English, Scots or Scots-Irish descent. They drank little beer. Whiskey and hard liquor were their beverages of choice. These groups of settlers were soon followed by the Germans in Pennsylvania and the Dutch in New York. Each of these groups brought with them their own beverages and the means by which they were produced and served. New brewing methods discovered by the Germans led to a tremendous increase in the consumption of beer.

During the Civil War, Union troops were furnished with beer rations in place of the traditional rum. Each newly introduced beverage meant new collectibles. Many are of silver and/or silverplate. Many bear English hallmarks; others are American and European. Whether in a pub in England or in a gracious private home, corkscrews, ice tongs, swizzle sticks, etc., are needed to serve guests.

Beakers or julep cups

Silver beakers which became a most popular kind of Kentucky silver were not much in evidence prior to 1810. They became a symbol in silver for the State of Kentucky. Their popularity continued through the 1850s, 1860s and 1870s in the South. They were not commonly found in the North and East after the Civil War.

"Perhaps the popularity of the beakers in Kentucky, where it is regionally termed a 'julep cup,' is partially accounted for by its symbolism of a time before the Civil War, a period of romanticized gentility, relaxed wealth and graciousness—an era in which a man's breeding was reflected in his manners and hospitality." (Boultinghouse, *Silversmiths of Kentucky*)

This beaker, or julep cup, was a prize "Taken by William R. Evans for "Best display of silverware" at the Kenton Co. Fair, Kentucky, 1858". Evans was listed in the Cincinnati Directory in the mid-19th century.

The agriculture fairs not only encouraged the farmers, live stock producers and others in food producing areas; they also did a lot to promote the art of silversmithing as they offered prizes of julep cups, silver goblets and other silver articles.

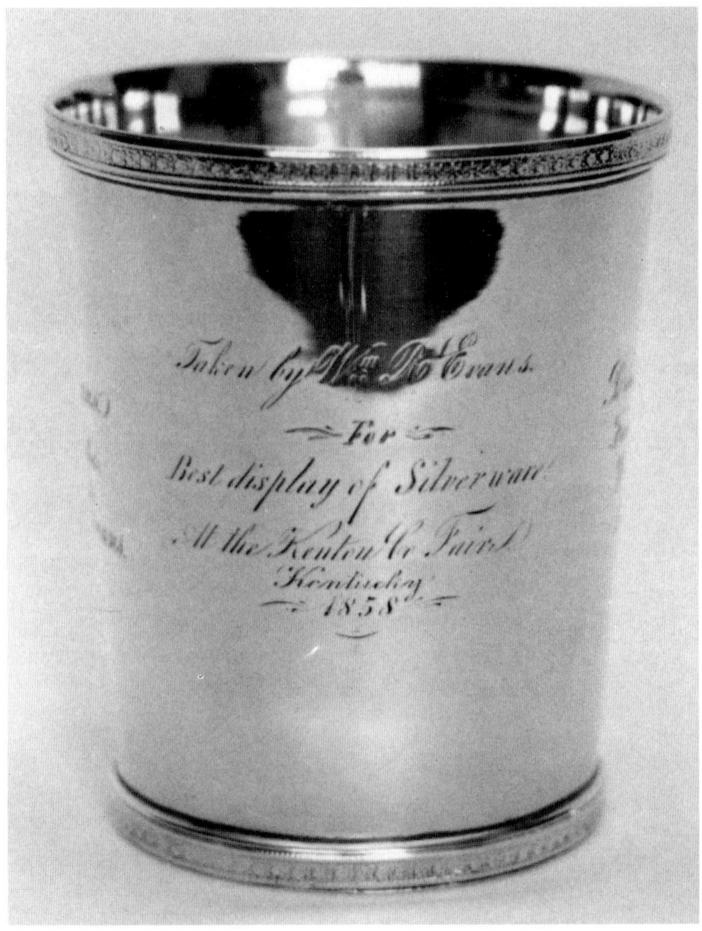

This beaker was a trophy taken by William R. Evans for best display at the Kenton County Fair, Kentucky 1858. Evans is listed in the Cincinnati Directory. *Privately owned. Photo: H Ivan Rainwater.* $325.

Wine funnels

Wine funnels are used to decant the wine into "flint" glass decanters. They appear to have been first made c.1660 and reached the height of their popularity c.1770 when punch became the favored form of refreshment. Early wine funnels were relatively plain. Later ones became very ornate; some fitted with a strainer. Spouts were sometimes curved to minimize the aeration of the wine by causing it to flow down the side of the decanter rather than splashing down into the already decanted wine. Two types were generally made. Each type is provided with a strainer. One has a bowl that is detachable and has a pierced bottom. The other has a removable inner bowl that has a pierced bottom and fits within the outer bowl. In both types a piece of muslin is fitted between the strainer and the spout. This muslin is analogous to the conical muslin strainer (Hippocrates' sleeve) that was fitted into the earlier types of funnels.

Most wine funnels were made in silver and like the strainers, were also made in Old Sheffield Plate. wine funnels of the Victorian period and later are almost without fail very elaborate.

Wine taster

The wine taster shown here with a shallow bowl, a kidney-shaped handle and finger ring is a typical French form made from the seventeenth century onward. To form a wine taster around a coin was a common practice. In England coins were often used in the bowls of small toddy ladles. This coin shows Louis XV and is dated 1726. The marks are the French high standard (.950) used after 1838 (Minerva's head) and the nineteenth century form of the maker's mark. In England pieces made around coins usually are not marked.

Wines are judged by their color, clarity and taste. Small, shallow circular cups called wine tasters were made with a slightly raised bottom which made it possible to judge the color. French wine tasters usually have a chain for wearing around the neck. English forms usually have two twisted handles in the form of snakes.

Similar small round vessels with flat bottoms are probably for the service of wine.

Two views of an elegant silver wine funnel. Maker: Frank W. Smith Co. c.1900. 6" tall. *Photo: Courtesy of Silver Magazine Archives*. $250.

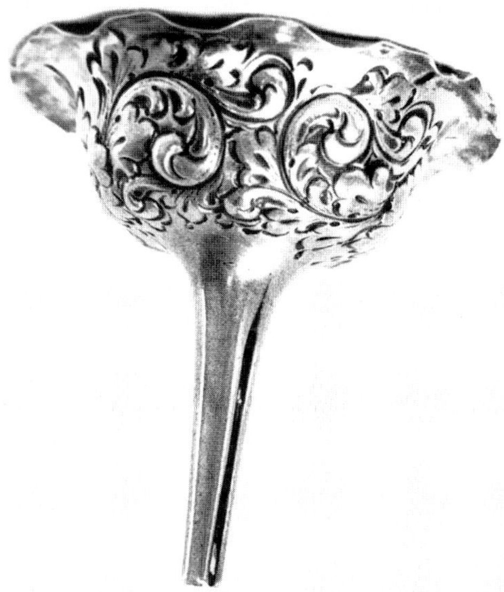

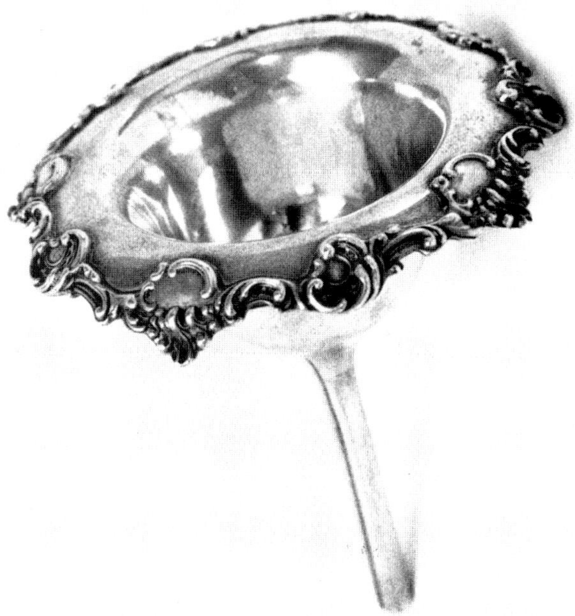

Wine taster with a French coin dated 1726 set into the bowl. The wine taster was made c.1850. *Photo: Courtesy of Silver Magazine Archives*. $200+.

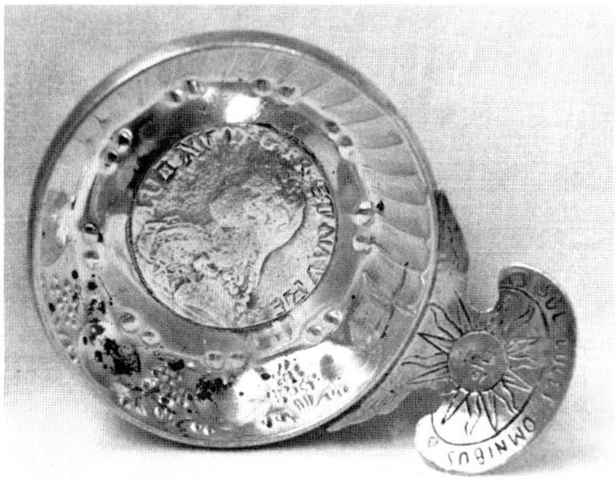

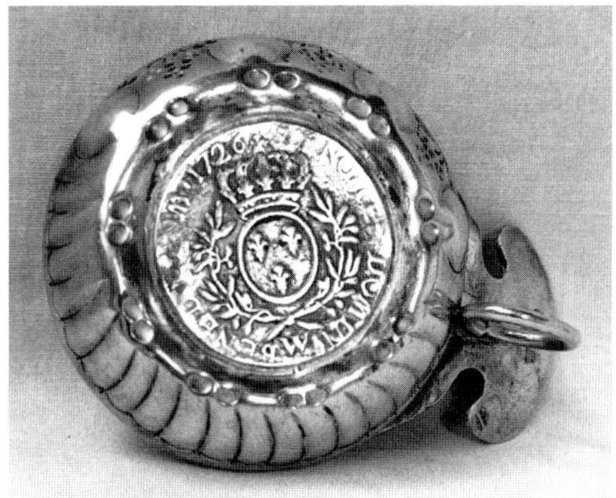

Base of wine taster showing reverse side of coin and the finger ring, a typical French form. Note maker's mark and French high standard mark (.950) used after 1838. *Photo: Courtesy of Silver Magazine Archives*.

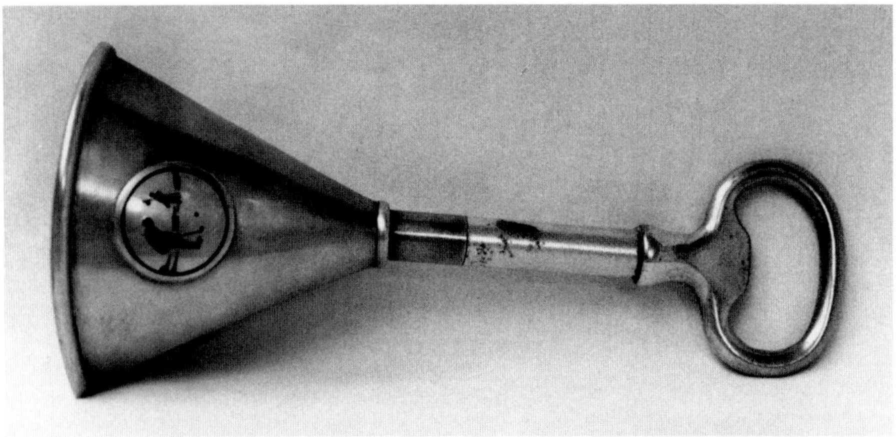

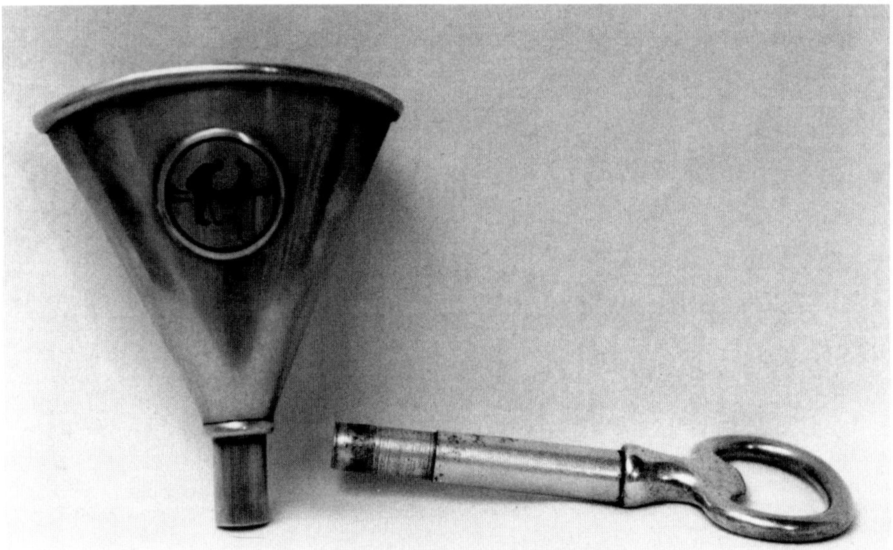

Combination wine taster, funnel and corkscrew. Maker: R. Blackington Co., sterling. Golfer and caddy are black enamel. c.1900. *Photo: Courtesy of Silver Magazine Archives*. $205.

Ice tongs

Ice tongs are useful in transferring cubes or pieces of ice from the ice bucket to glass. Some work on the order of scissors with curved pincer-like or claw-like ends which readily grasp the pieces of ice. Some are bow-like as in the one illustrated here. The end of one arm in this case is more like a spoon.

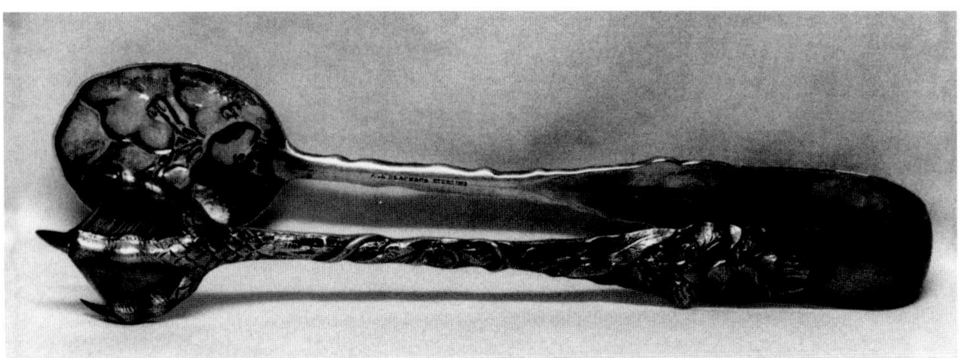

Ice tongs with web foot on one arm and spoon on the other. Sterling. Repoussé. Marked R. G. Black & Co. *Photo: Courtesy of Silver Magazine Archives*.

Punch ladles

Before 1700 punch ladles were mostly of plain round form with wooden or tubular handles set at an angle of 45°. Shaped or fancy bowls began about 1740. By 1760 punch ladles had lost importance and were made of thinner metal. Twisted whalebone handles were used.

The two punch ladles illustrated here have bowls typical of the eighteenth century. Both have twisted whalebone handles, both typical of the eighteenth century. What both have, in addition, are the elements which are not typical of the eighteenth century. The one with the small figure of an Apostle at the tip is a Victorian "improvement" often used. These little figures were cast in great numbers and applied to altered spoons to create a more up-to-date and readily salable item. The other one began as a typical oval bowl with pouring spout. Some time later, probably in Victorian days, the bowl was "improved" by the addition of embossed flowers, etc. There are no marks on the ladle. The marks on the other one are well worn. the maker's marks appear to be Peter and Anne Bateman but are too worn for positive identification. Pap boats clearly marked by the Batemans are identical to the one used here to make the bowl of the punch ladle.

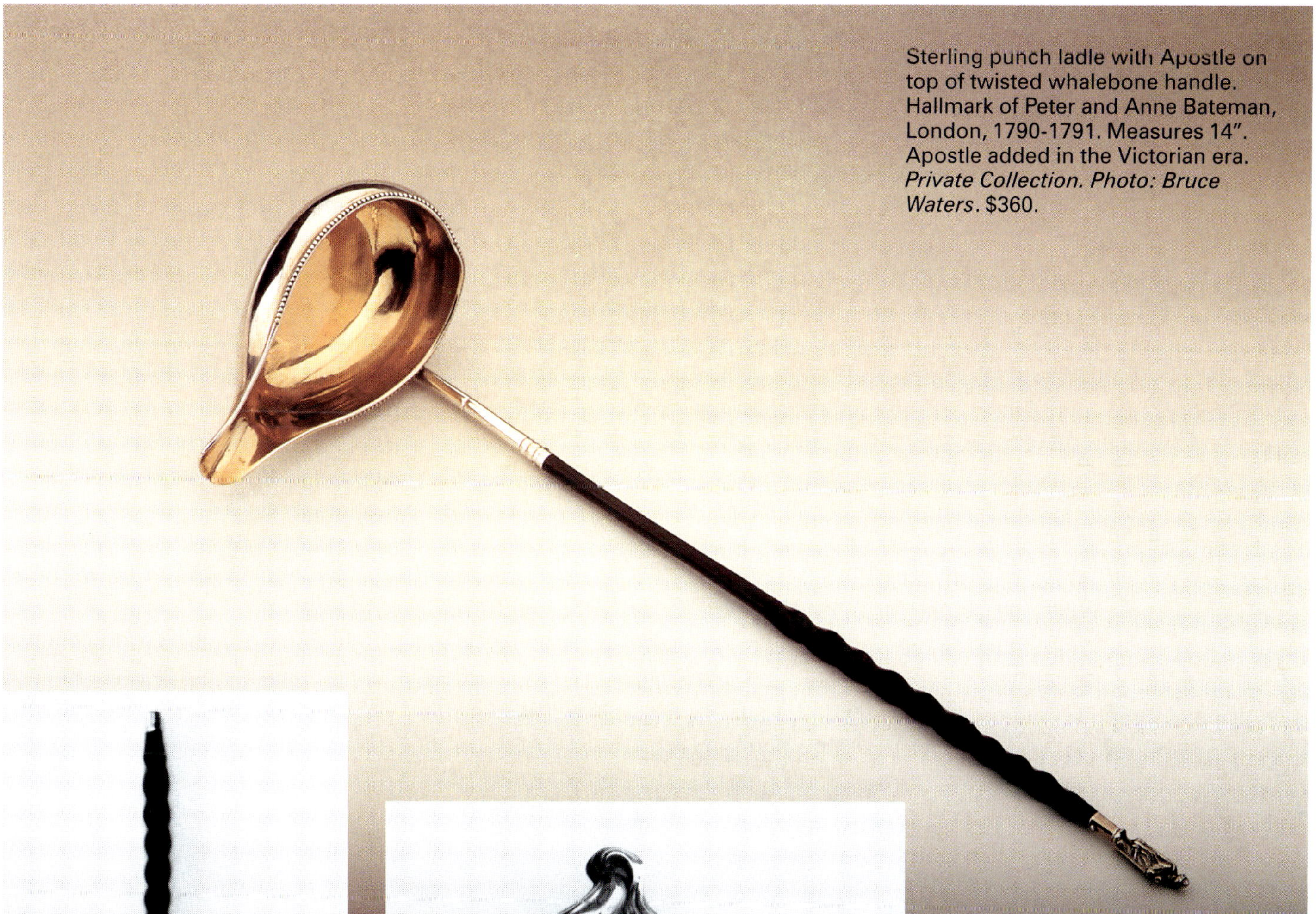

Sterling punch ladle with Apostle on top of twisted whalebone handle. Hallmark of Peter and Anne Bateman, London, 1790-1791. Measures 14". Apostle added in the Victorian era. *Private Collection. Photo: Bruce Waters*. $360.

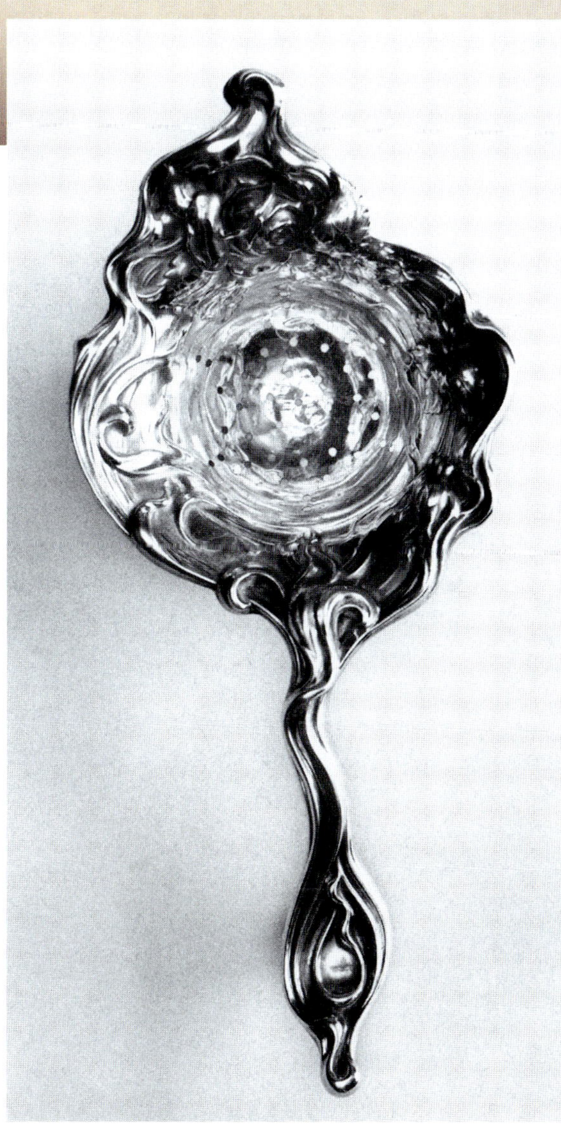

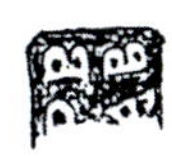

Mark of Peter and Anne Bateman, worn but showing on the above punch ladle.

Far left:
Sterling punch ladle with whalebone handle. Measures about 12". No marks. Twisted handle typical of the eighteenth century. Embossing in the bowl is typical of the Victorian era. *Photo: H Ivan Rainwater*. $300.

Left:
Art Nouveau punch strainer. Marked: Simpson, Hall, Miller & Co. Sterling. c.1895. About 6" long. *Photo: H Ivan Rainwater*. $215.

Strainers

Some strainers were designed especially for straining lemon or orange juice directly into the punch bowl. These have two handles which extend across the punch bowl and rest on the rim. The handles are flat and horizontal. These date from about 1760 in England and America; in Scotland about 1800.

Other strainers have only one handle. Among these, some have a hook that can be clipped to the rim of the punch bowl.

The beautiful example of the rococo style of c.1765 was made in Annapolis, Maryland, by William Faris. Faris is one of the few documented American silversmiths thanks to the survival of his diary, some account books and shop drawings.

Faris was born in London in 1728 and may have trained there or in Philadelphia. He went from there to Annapolis about 1750. Like many other colonial craftsmen, Faris supplemented his income with additional activities including tavern keeping, dentistry, cabinet making and portrait painting. His three sons, Charles, Hyram and William, Jr., trained and worked in their father's shop. (Goldsborough, *Silver in Maryland*). The Art Nouveau period (1880s-c.1910) brought the introduction of countless expressions of new artistic ideas in small articles especially. Strainers, being under no restrictions to design, were an article on which the designer could be as creative as he desired.

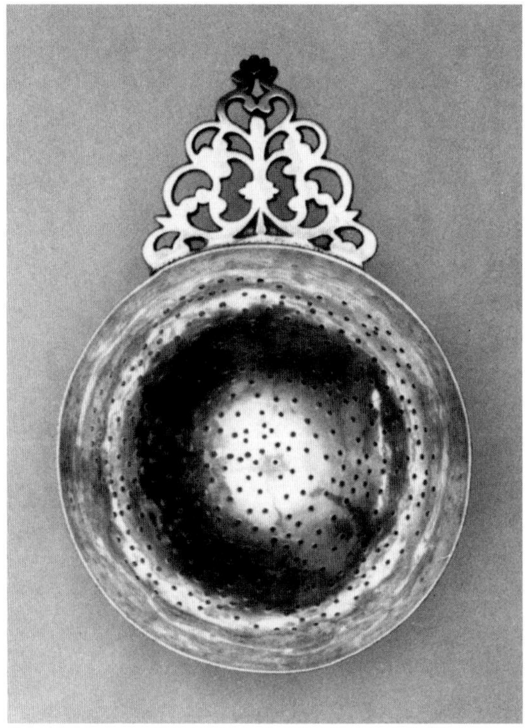

Strainer. Maker: William Farris, Sr., of Annapolis, MD. Overall measure 5-13/16". Marked WF in rectangular punch. c.1765. *Private Collection. Photo: H Ivan Rainwater*. $440.

Corkscrews

Some bottles of bubbly are still sealed with a cork. Because of the increased use in the twentieth century of screw-type bottle tops, corkscrews have become antique collectibles as well as normal bar and kitchen equipment.

Although the Romans were known to use corks in their bottles for storing wine, the use of corks seems to have been lost when the Roman Empire fell in the fifth century. Not until the end of the sixteenth century did the use of corks and corkscrews revive in Europe.

Corks were used in wine bottles to create a strong seal. When dampened by the wine, the cork adhered to the glass. To break this seal, a variety of inventions included such devices as levers, screws, curved gears, and rack-and-pinion gears. Some corkscrew inventions were patented as early as 1750.

Many materials have been used to make corkscrews, silver and silverplate are among them. All corkscrews have in common the worm which goes into the cork. Many times, and especially for pocket corkscrews, the worm was protected by folding it into the handle. Sometimes a pocket corkscrew serves several purposes, such as a corkscrew, a pipe tamper, and a pipe pricker all in one.

The use of a corkscrew in the sickroom was for administering liquid medicine to the patient. Frequently, therefore, corkscrews consist of a worm for the cork on one end and a dose cup on the other end. A specialized type of medicine bottle has a worm that is kept in the cork and a bell on top warns the nurse that the bottle is being tipped, especially when the contents of the bottle was poisonous.

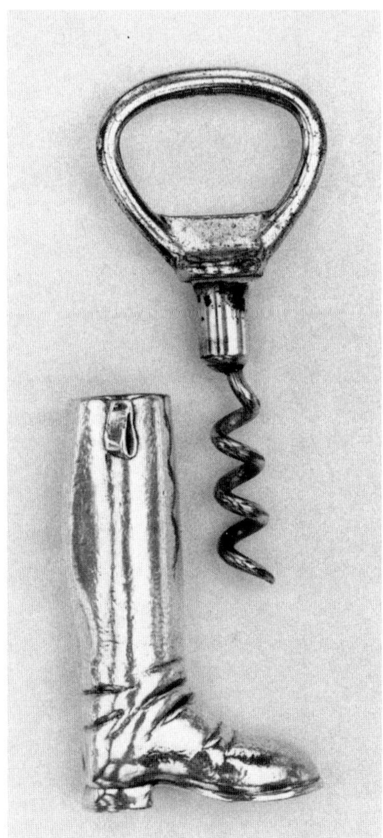

Corkscrew fits into the boot when not in use. Maker: R. Blackington & Co., North Attleboro, MA. c.1900. *Collection of Diane Zinn. Photo: Robert Watkins.* $225.

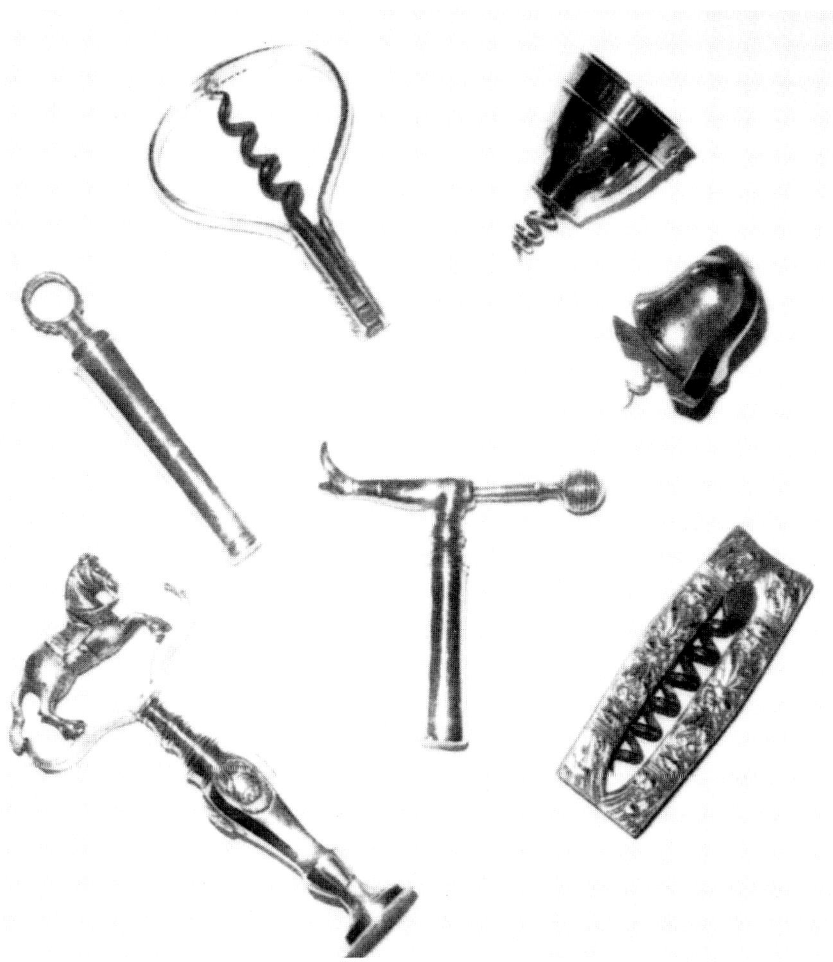

The screw cap for bottles was invented in 1858 by John Landis Mason. Although this invention made the exclusive use of corks as bottle sealers unnecessary, corks often are still in use today. The old-fashioned corkscrews may become items unfamiliar to future generations.

Silver corkscrews from around the world. Left to right: 1. Dutch pocket corkscrew, pipe tamper and pipe pricker. Figural horse on handle. c.1800. 3-7/8". 2. English pocket corkscrew. Sheath unscrews to become handle when slid through ring. c.1780. 2-7/8". 3. Irish folding bow corkscrew marked SINGLETON. c.1780. 2-5/8" 4. American medicine bottle corkscrew/dose cup. c.1880. 1-1/2". 5. American corkscrew bell used for corks in poison bottles. c.1875. 1-1/2" 6. German pocket corkscrew. c.1900. 2-9/16". 7. Center. Dutch pocket corkscrew, pipe tamper, pipe pricker with boot handle. c.1730. 2". *Collection and photo: Milt Becker.* $165-600.

Serving cheese

Cheese has always been an important food worldwide and it is a natural accompaniment to beverages, alcoholic or not. Some varieties of cheese require special servers. The soft cheeses, for instance, require scoops. These appear to have come on the market in the latter part of the eighteenth and early nineteenth centuries. Stilton and brie are two cheeses best served by cheese scoops. The early scoops had straight blades and ivory or wooden handles. Some had attached "pushers" to eject the cheese from the scoop. Later scoops were made with silver handles to match place settings of flatware.

The shape of some cheeses made it necessary to have serving pieces called cheese knobs or cheese ball holders. Various devices were created to hold the ball of cheese firmly in place.

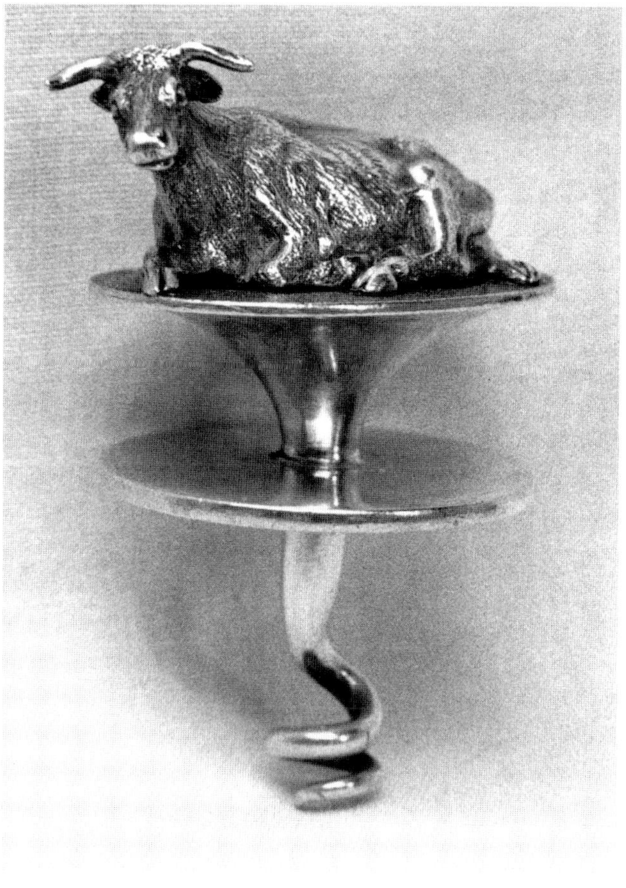

Cheese knob. Maker: Gorham with date letter 1880. These knobs were used in conjunction with a cheese ball holder. The cheese ball was placed in the holder and the knob placed on top. The corkscrew was given a twist to secure it in place. *Photo: Courtesy of Silver Magazine Archives.*

Scandinavians prefer a flat implement with a projecting blade to draw across the surface of hard cheese.

Hard cheeses are served with cutting blades or by implements of stiff wire held in place between two arms. None of this type made in silver or silverplate have come to our attention.

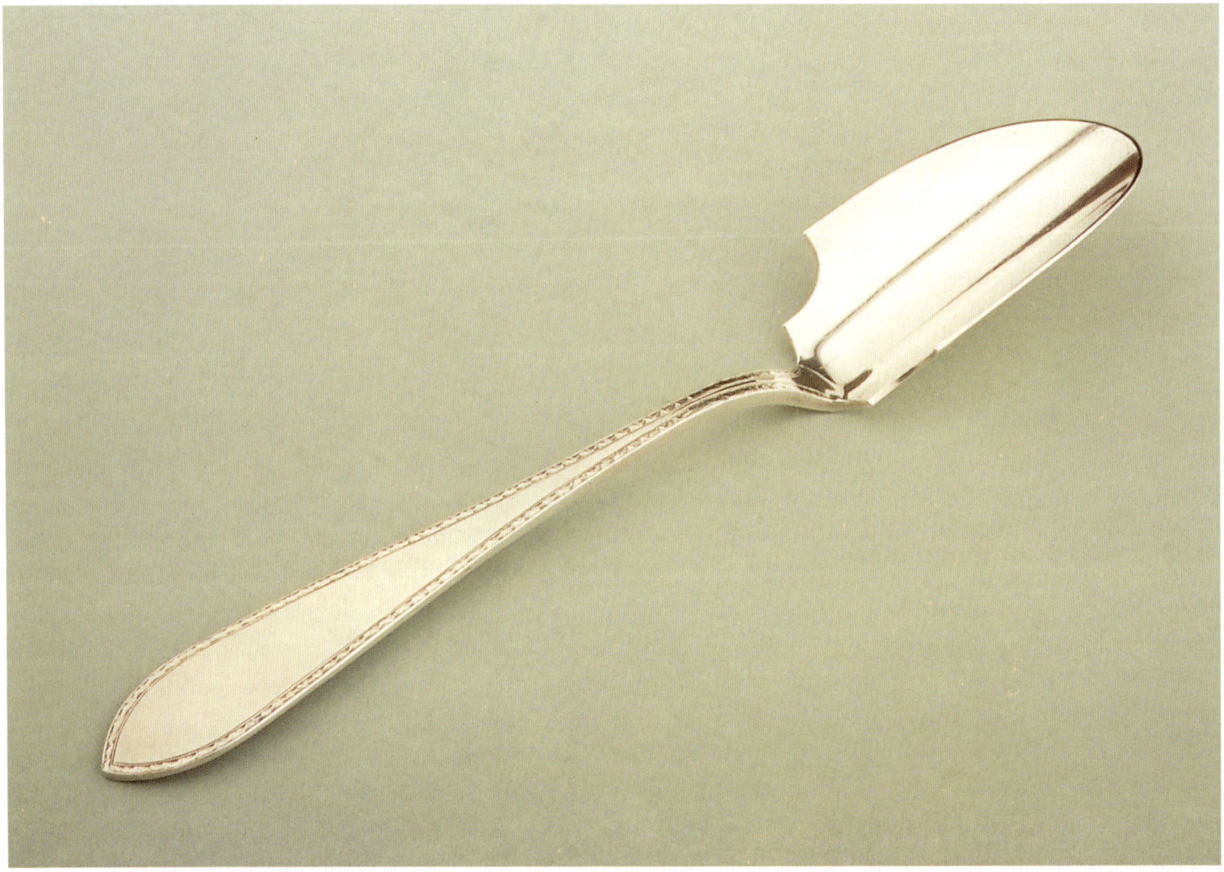

Cheese scoop marked Mealy for Baltimore Jeweler John W. Mealy Son & Co. 8" long. *Photo: Bruce Waters*.

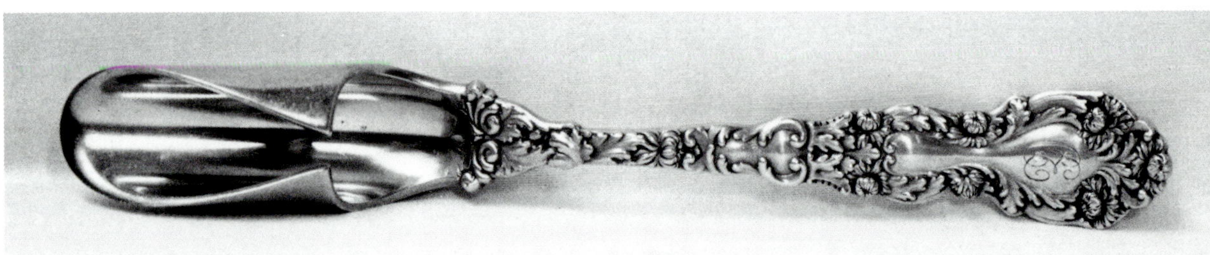

Sterling Gorham cheese scoop. Pattern is Imperial Chrysanthemum. Length: 8-1/4". Scoops such as this were first introduced c.1860 and were used to serve soft cheeses. *Photo: Courtesy of Silver Magazine Archives*. $250.

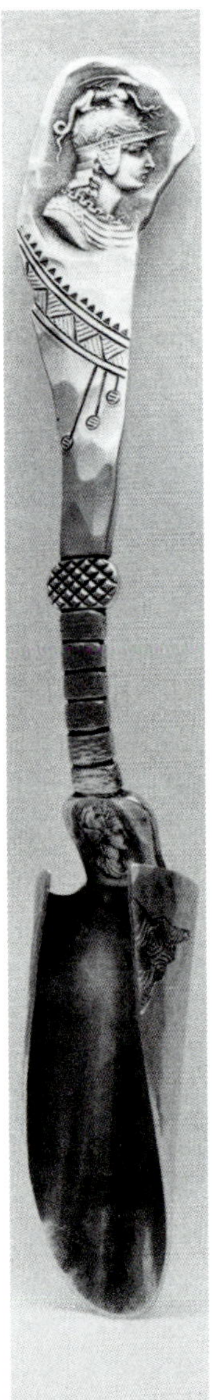

Cheese scoop. Medallion pattern from George W. Shiebler. This Achilles head is often found on Shiebler's jewelry and flatware. *Photo: Courtesy of Silver Magazine Archives*. $225.

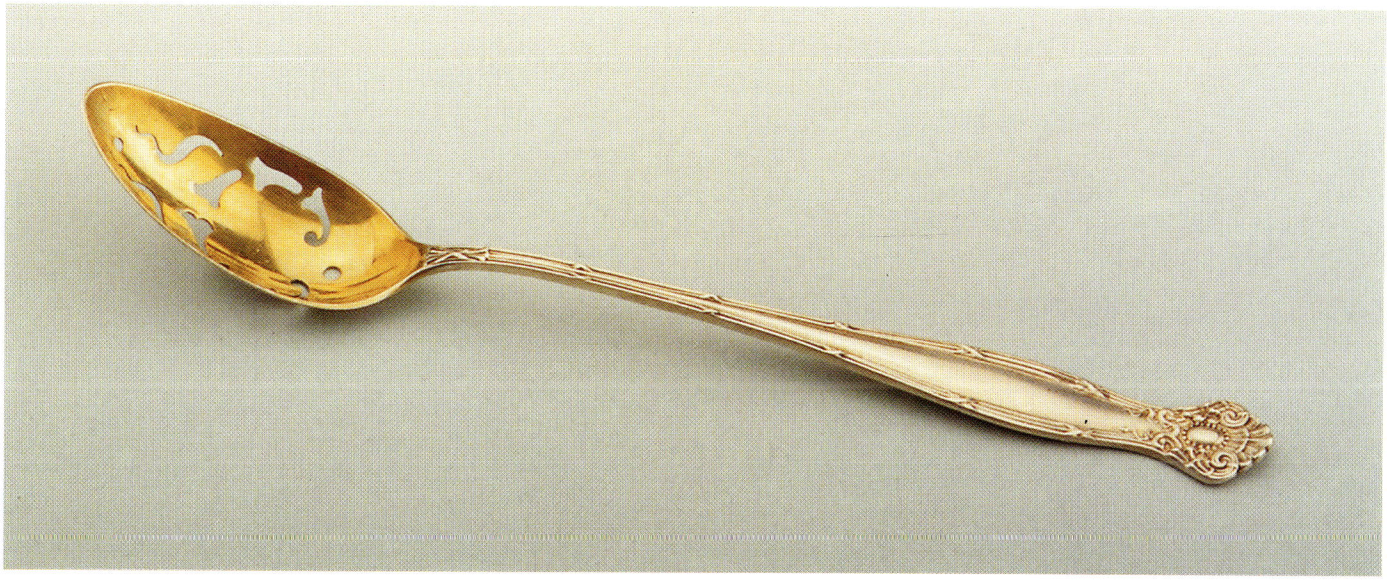

Olive picks and spears

Olvie picks and spears were made in many different styles and with many types of decoration. Most featured a sharp point or pick on one end and a decorative spoon on the other. We have been informed that the long handles were for reaching into the very tall and narrow jars in which olives were sold. Some bear no marks, but all to come to our attention appear to be sterling. A most practical appearing implement for serving olives is the pictured tongs bearing the three gold crowns on blue enamel. A simple press on the top opens the claw-like mechanism. Nut picks are indispensable for scooping out that last bit of kernel.

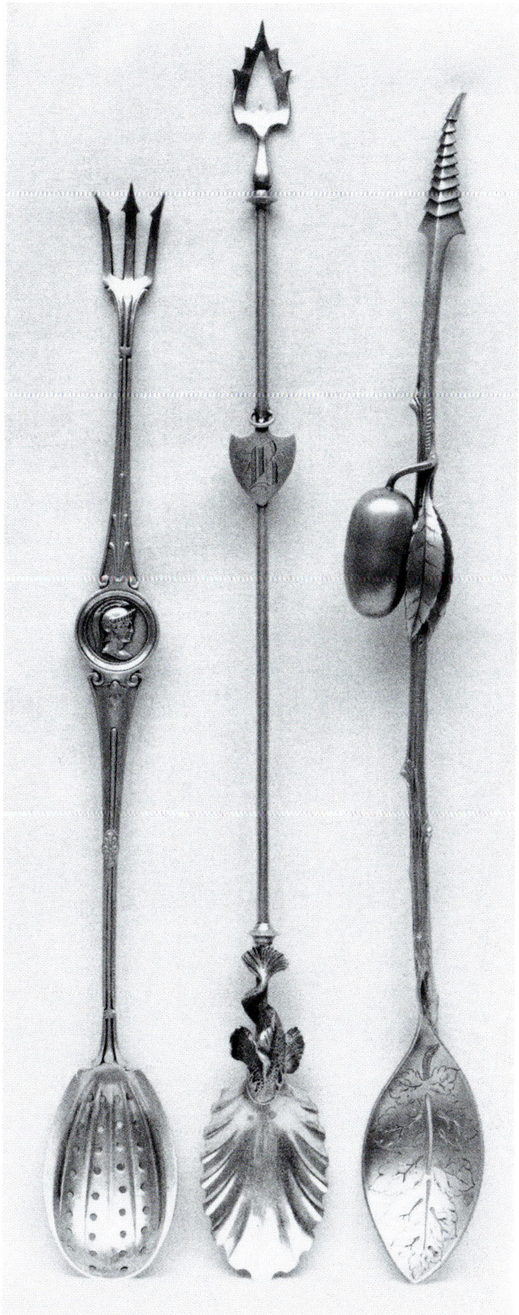

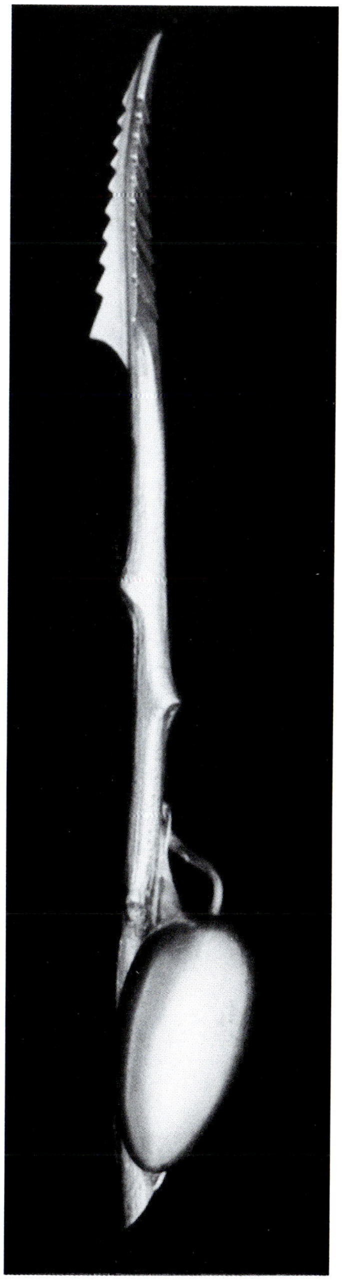

Above:
Olive spoon, Empire pattern by Towle. Patented George P. Tilton. Design patent: 23557 August 14, 1894. Sterling. *Photo: Bruce Waters*.

Right:
Olive spears with spoons for use at the bar. Silver. Left to right: a medallion made by Gorham. c.1860. Center: monogram on shield. An olive and leaves decorate the one on the right. All are between 6" and 7". *Photo: Courtesy of Silver Magazine Archives*.

Far right:
Olive pick. *Photo: H Ivan Rainwater*.

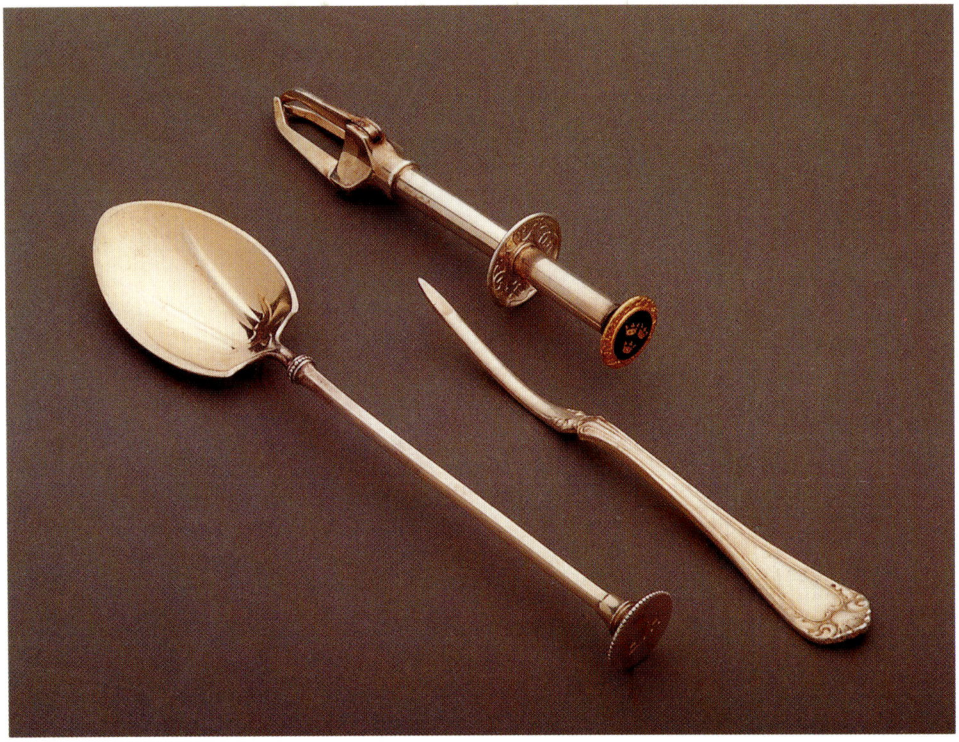

For the bar. Left to right: 1. Sugar mashing spoon. 6" long. Monogrammed. Sterling. Flat surface is used for mashing sugar lumps in a drink. c.1910. $50.
2. Nut pick marked Simeon L. and George H. Rogers Co. Pat. 1906. 4-3/4". Silverplate. $30.
3. Silver olive tongs. Made in Sweden with three gold crowns on dark blue enamel background and gilt on top. To activate the spring, press the top. 4-1/4". $45. *Photo: Bruce Waters*.

Bottle tickets, wine labels, and decanter labels

Small plaques suspended by chains around the neck of a bottle are known as bottle tickets, wine labels, and decanter labels. The identity of the bottle's contents or identifying initial usually is engraved on the plaque. The earliest of these plaques were quite plain, of four basic shapes—oblong, oval, crescent, or escutcheon, and were first known by the term "bottle ticket."

Silver bottle tickets date back at least to the 1730s. The most popular wines were Madeira, from the French *Madére*, port, sherry, and claret. Bottle tickets of old Sheffield Plate date from the 1760s. About 1780 some bore the owner's crest or cipher rather than the name or initial of the contents. Some Scottish examples were known as "pointers," from the outline of fox-hounds "on point." Other forms used were scallop shell, bugle, foul anchor, wine leaf, and tendrils.

The earliest known bottle ticket was for some time thought to have been made by Samuel Bell, but the maker was later identified as Sandilands Drinkwater. Drinkwater was elected an Assistant of the Goldsmiths' Company in London in 1722.

Silver wine labels were first made in the second quarter of the eighteenth century; some prefer the term "bottle ticket" to the more modern term "wine label." Victorian label designers added many of their own refinements. Innovations included the vine leaf with pierced lettering or a ribbon scroll. A label in a shell was used to identify the content of the bottle. These silver labels also enhanced the appearance of the bottle on the table and sideboard.

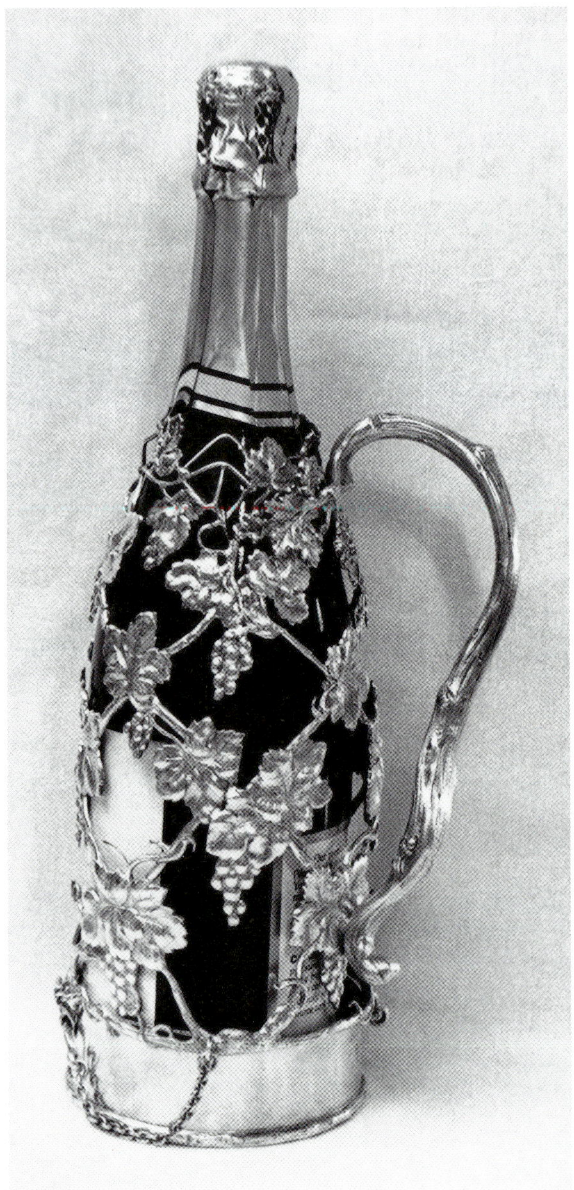

Sterling wine bottle holder by Gorham. Grape clusters and leaves with grapevine handle. *Photo: Courtesy of Silver Magazine Archives*. $750.

Decanter labels differ from wine labels or bottle tickets as they are somewhat larger and more elaborately decorated. Favorite designs were patterns of vine leaves and tendrils along with the foliage and scrollwork. All manner of animals were found on bottle tickets. Among them were elephants, lions and bats. Seashells and anchors often appeared. Bottle tickets were made in other countries where often the spelling of the wine name was in their native language.

Silver wine labels were in vogue in England throughout the 1700s and were made by well-known silversmiths Paul Storr and Hester Bateman and family.

In America, Paul Revere, of Revolutionary War fame in Massachusetts, listed a wine label in 1772 and Lewis (Louis) Boudo of Charleston, South Carolina, listed a wine label about 1810.

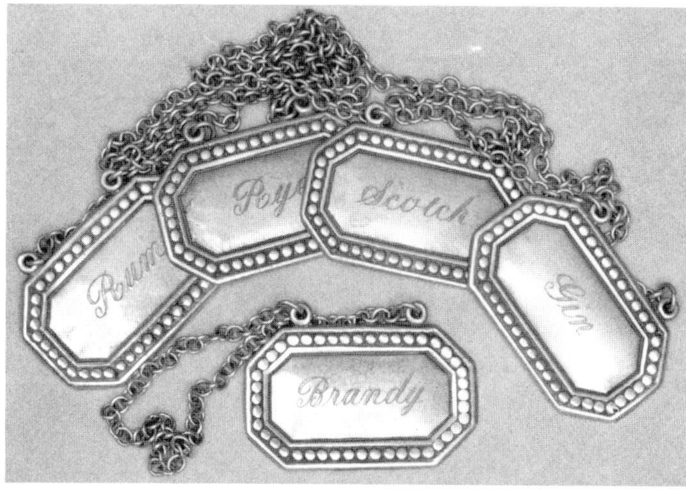

Set of five matching bottle tickets made by Tiffany. Sterling. Price of set was $475 c.1890. *Photo: Courtesy of Silver Magazine Archives.* $162-600.

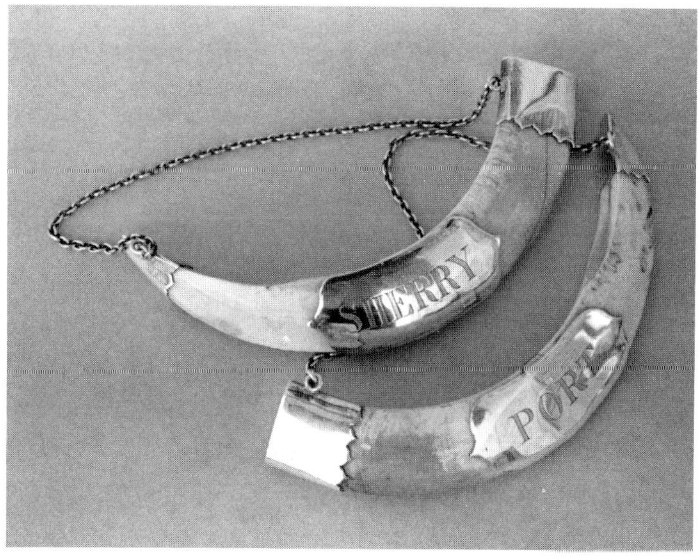

Bottle tickets made of coin silver on bone. Descended in the family of John Tyler. Made c.1840. *Courtesy D. Bigda Antiques., Charleston, South Carolina. Photo: David Bigda.* $162-600.

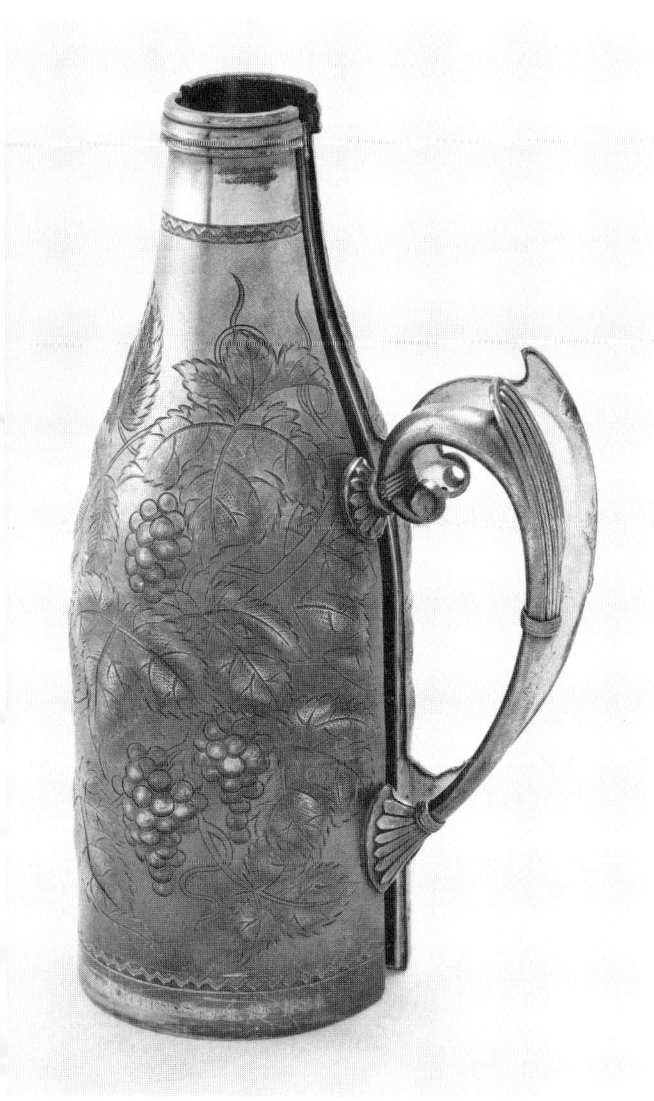

Wine bottle holder in silverplate. Made by American Britannia Co., 1881. Holder is hinged so that the bottle could fit within and be covered by the holder. A felt lining kept the wine cool and prevented breakage. Useful for picnics. *Photo: H Ivan Rainwater.* $150.

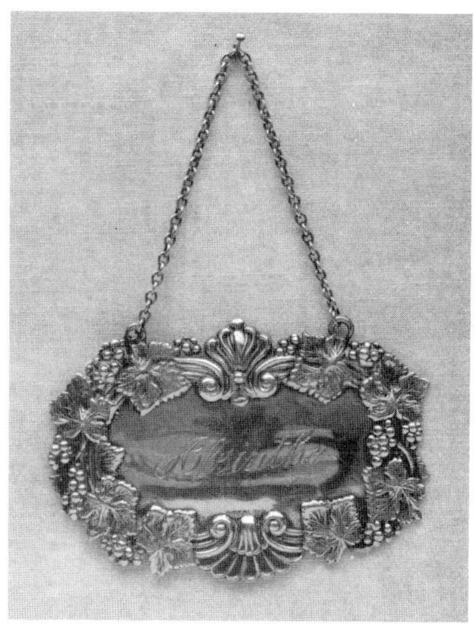

Ornate silver bottle ticket with grape and leaf motif. Engraved with the word Absinthe. American. c.1875. *Photo: Courtesy of Silver Magazine Archives.* $162-600.

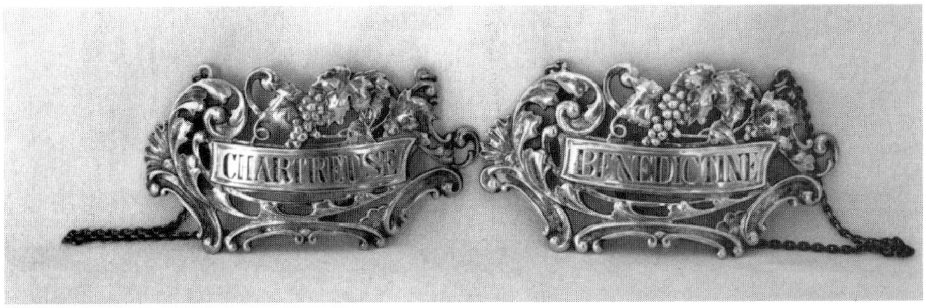

Bottle tickets labeled "Chartreuse" and "Benedictine" with ornate grape motif, American by Gorham. *Photo: Courtesy of Silver Magazine Archives*. $162-600.

Sugar crusher or sugar mashing spoon

These implements usually have straight handles, often hexagonal in cross-section. There may be a spoon on one end with a flat, circular disc on the other. Their purpose was to crush a lump of sugar previously cut from a sugar loaf. Since sugar now is sold mainly in granular form, the crusher is no longer needed. They do turn up occasionally to crush mint leaves or other additions to mixed beverages.

Decision maker and dice

The sterling silver device shown here, known as a decision maker, was made by the Gorham Company. A spin of the top determines whether one goes to work, or hires an assistant, or buys low, or sells high, or— equally important— plays golf. Such decisions are not easily made. And nothing beats a pair of dice for determining who buys the next round of drinks. This pair of sterling silver dice bears the trademark of Lenore Doskow, Inc. This company was founded in 1934 by Lenore and David Doskow to sell specialized items designed and made under the supervision of Lenore. Most of their items are sterling and gold jewelry and novelty items.

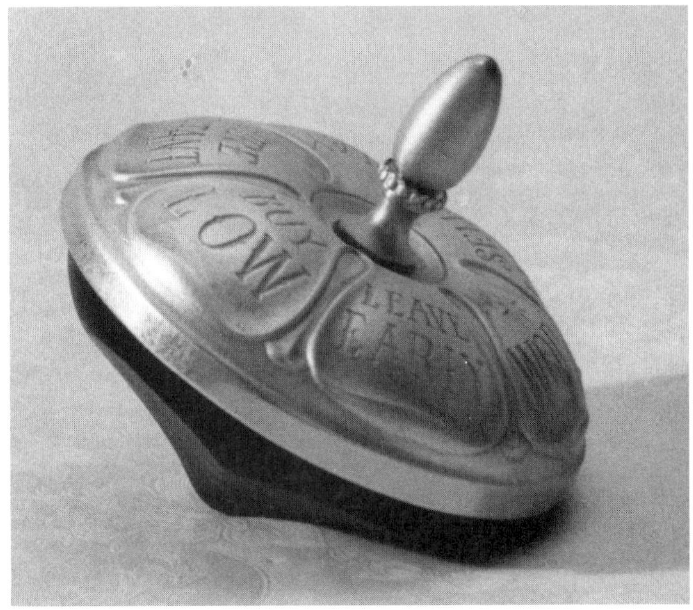

Sterling decision maker. Spin the device to make decisions: "Hire Assistant, Buy Low, Sell High, Play Golf, Work, Leave Early." Maker: Gorham Company. *Private Collection. Photo: H Ivan Rainwater*. $25-40.

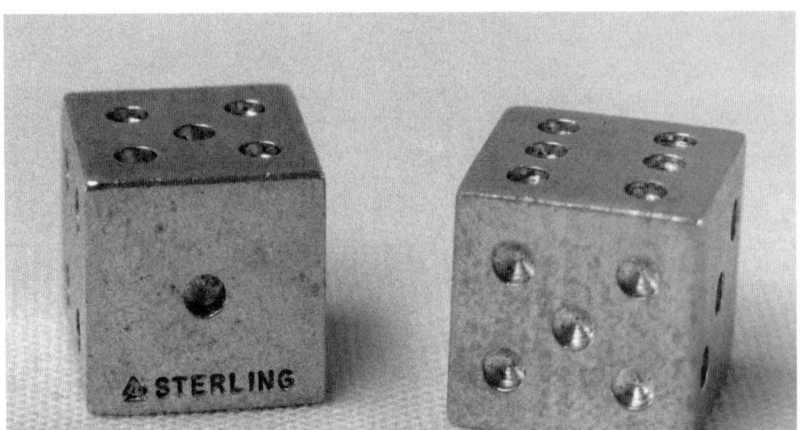

Pair of sterling dice marked with overlapping triangle mark of Leonore Doskow, Inc. American. c.1935. 3/8" square. *Photo: Courtesy of Silver Magazine Archives*.

Swizzle sticks

Swizzle sticks, made for the purpose of stirring a beverage, were made in several styles. They were first made to swizzle a short drink made with crushed ice. Some are made with four or more rounded pierced blades attached to a long handle. Others, made of silver like this one from Japan, are composed of a long, narrow tube which, when opened, shows five or six curved silver wires which stir the contents of the glass.

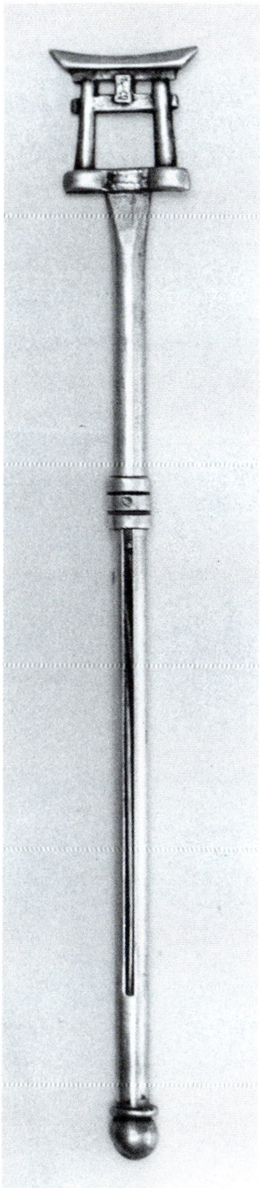

Left and below:
Swizzle stick. Silver. Probably sterling but not so marked. A Japanese Toril decorates the top.
Photo: H Ivan Rainwater. $35.

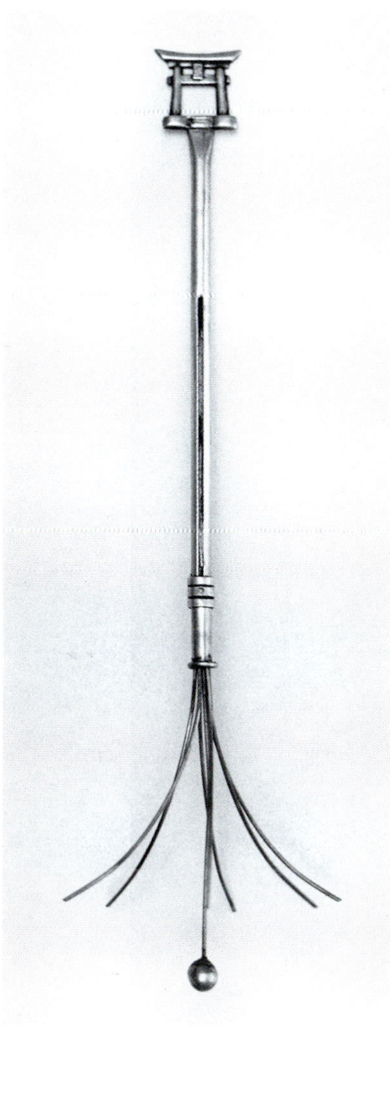

Coasters

Originally, coasters were thought of in connection with the dining room as they first appeared by the name "coaster" about 1887. After dinner, the ladies withdrew to the (with) drawing room and port was placed on the then bare table. The servants had removed the white damask cloth. Men then coasted or slipped the bottle around the table.

Other dining room accessories were called "stands" or "sliders" and were used to protect the table surface from being scarred by the woven osier (willow) covering on some bottles or bottles with rough bottoms.

Today's dining tables are most apt to need protection from ice-filled glassed which "sweat" and leave white rings where the moisture has remained for any length of time.

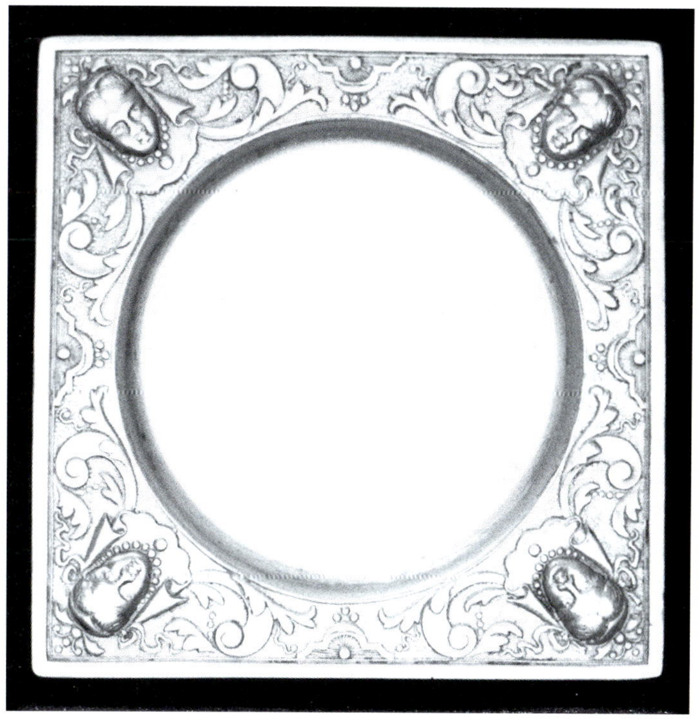

Silverplate coaster made c.1886-1900 by A. A. Webster & Co., Silversmiths, Opticians & Jewellers, 241-243 Fulton St., Brooklyn. Measures 2-9/16" square. *Photo: H Ivan Rainwater*. $35 to 50.

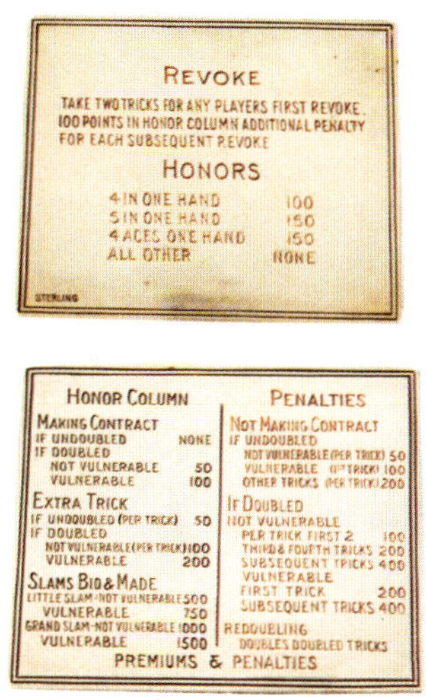

Card game of bridge scoring sheet, front and back, marked sterling. Shows honors and penalties as played c.1920. Honors column engraving is highlighted with black graphite, penalties with red enamel. Measures 1-3/4 by 2-1/4". Conveniently carried in black leather case. *Collection and photo: A. & D. Burstyn*.

Marriage cups, bride's cups, maiden cups, wager cups

These vessels are known by many names. They originated in the Rhine valley in the late sixteenth century. They are double cups formed by a standing woman wearing a long, wide skirt, her arms upraised holding a small pivoting cup supported in a bracket frame. The wide skirt is often decorated with floral motifs. When inverted, the skirt forms the larger cup. Known in German as *jungfrauen becker* (maiden cup), they were part of marriage festivities in German speaking areas of Europe. At a wedding, the bridegroom drank from the larger cup without spilling a drop from the filled smaller cup, which he then offered to the bride. Old marriage cups are rare outside Germany today.

Three examples of wager cups from England made during the Commonwealth period (1653 to 1669) have come to our attention. They all were most certainly made in London, but all records in Goldsmith's Hall were destroyed by the Great Fire in 1666. One is in the collection of the Worshipful Company of Vintners. In drinking a toast to the Master of the Vintners and to the prosperity of the Company, the user is required to drain the larger cup without spilling a drop from the smaller cup. This can be accomplished by drinking from the larger cup first, then reversing the vessel carefully so that the smaller pivoted cup remains upright, and then drinking from that. The other two of these cups are now in the Irwin Untermeyer collection in New York. In 1827 Joseph Anfell II was commissioned by the Company to make replicas. These are still in existence as well as many copies made in the twentieth century.

Another cup, made in London by William Eaton, was donated to the Goldsmith's Company by Francis Boone Thomas who became the Company's Prime Warden in 1881. This cup bears in relief the arms of the Company, as well as engraved details of the donor's career with the Company.

In Holland, these cups are known as bridal or marriage cups.

A few years ago an American company made an electroplated version of a wager cup, as shown here. Design features are well reproduced but the thickness of the metal of the skirt produces an awkward appearance.

The custom of using wager cups spread to many parts of Europe. Today they are found in Switzerland, Norway, England, and Ireland. A wager cup made in Bergen, Norway, and dated 1794, can be seen at the Victoria and Albert Museum in London. This cup shows a lady figure holding a small cup in just one hand, her right, while her left hand is placed over her heart. She wears a *rebato* (stiffened upstanding collar) and a low-cut waistcoat over a farthingale skirt. (R. W. Lightbown, *Catalog of Scandinavian and Baltic Silver*, London: Victoria & Albert Museum, 1975, page 15.)

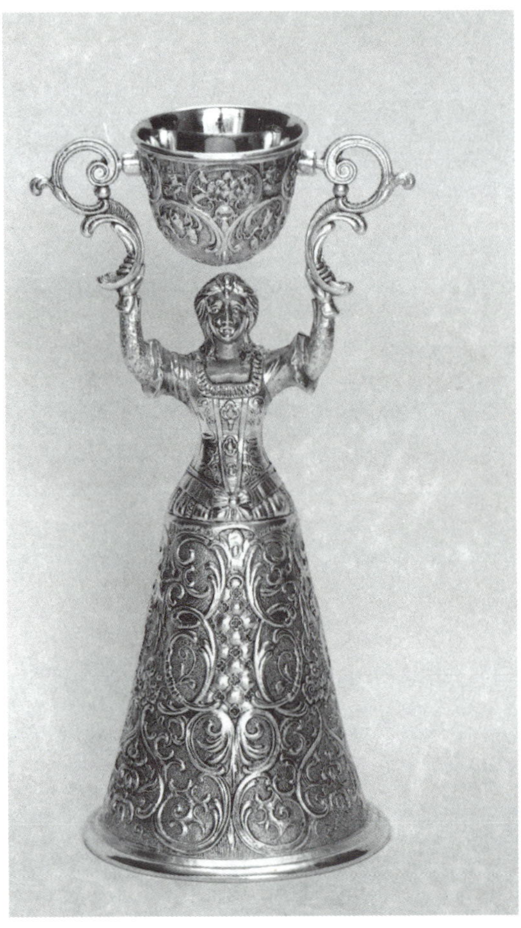

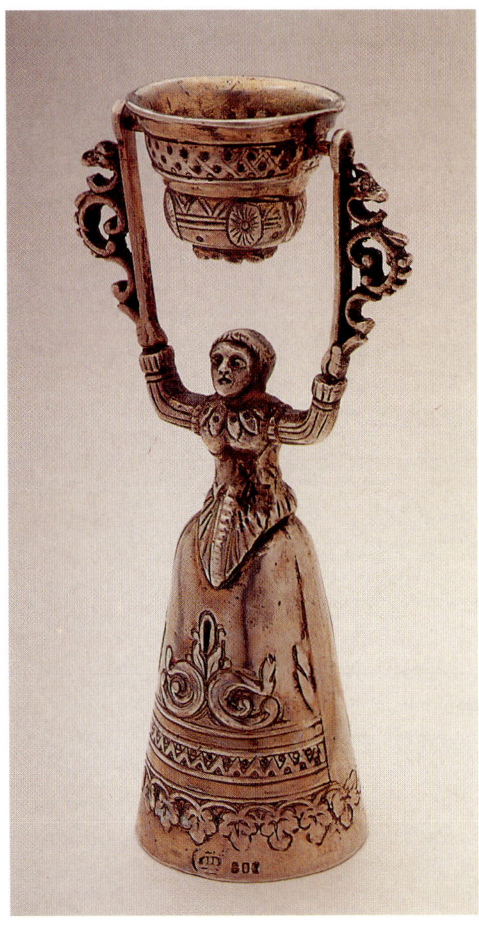

Far left:
Silverplate copy of a German Wager or Bride's Cup. Though the design features have been well reproduced, the thickness of the metal on the bottom of the skirt detracts from the overall design. Made by an American manufacturer of silverplate. *Photo: H Ivan Rainwater*. $75 to 90.

Left:
Miniature Wager or Bride's Cup. Height: 3-5/16". Mark: Crescent & Crown/800. Mark used in Germany since 1 January 1888. *Private Collection. Photo: Bruce Waters*. $95 to 110.

Hanau silver

While attempting to determine when and where the wager cup, now identified as probably from Hanau, was made, the lack of wear expected on a cup from the sixteenth or seventeenth century was noted. This suggested it was not one of the early originals. Also, the marks, though well worn, were poorly struck and impossible to read precisely. One mark was fairly clear and appeared as a possibility for Hanau, Germany.

Hanau silver of the latter part of the nineteenth century is often mistaken for older silver. According to Burstyn (*Silver magazine*, Sept./Oct., 1989), "Hanau produced enormous numbers of the marriage or wager cups... These wager cups were often exact copies of originals. Hanau silver is still often mistaken for old silver, and the spurious marks are a constant source of confusion for many collectors."

> Hanau pieces are not fakes. They were originally sold as old pieces, though now they are frequently mistaken for such. They really attempted to exactly reproduce earlier forms and decoration. Their marks should be considered as in the same category with 19th century American pseudo marks which generally resemble, but do not exactly reproduce, English marks. Hanau silver usually had a great deal of hand work in it, tends to be of moderate to good quality, and is often very attractive to those who prefer highly ornate pieces. As knowledge of these pieces spreads and we learn to appreciate them for what they really are instead of for what we would like them to be, Hanau silver is likely to become a new specialized area for collectors. (Charles C. Williams, "Ask A Question," *Silver magazine*, May/June, 1985. Used by permission.)

Old ideas and legends never die; they simply reappear in revived form, perhaps in a new material. Such is the case with a bride's cup illustrated in the Fall, 1998, catalog *In the Spirit,* published in Hanover, Pennsylvania, where it is called "The Book of Gifts and Collectibles." While earlier bride's cups were made of silver or silverplate, this one is advertised as being solid pewter.

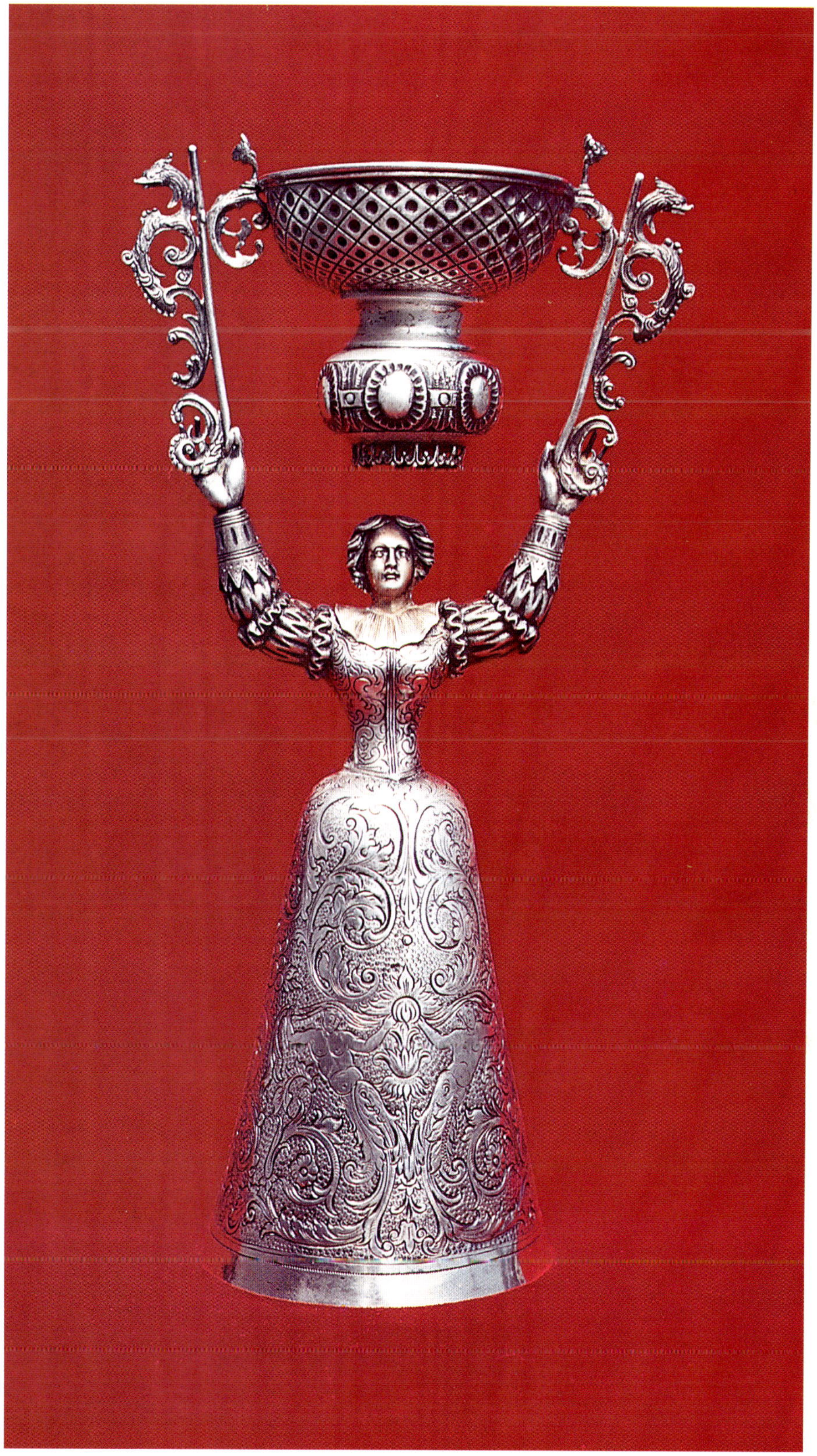

Wager cup or bride's cup of silver. Design on the skirt features Adam & Eve identical to one shown in Schleissner and Neresheimer's model books around 1900. See *Silver Magazine*, Sept./Oct. 1997, p. 45. Marks poorly struck. One fairly clear may be Hanau, Germany. Height: 10-1/8". *Private Collection. Photo: David Arky ©1980, Time-Life Books, Inc.* $1,800 to 2,000.

Chapter 10. Silver Curios for use...

...at Tea

The adoption of the custom of "dinner at eight" in the 1840s led to the mid-afternoon tea time. The time lapse between lunch and dinner was too long for some and ladies began to take a meal of tea and small cakes in the afternoon, around four o'clock. At first, tea was served in the bedroom or boudoir and later in the drawing room. Tea drinking is fully accepted today; ask any Englishman about a sure cure for all ills and the response will be, "a nice cup of tea."

Possibly no one custom has become so widespread as the drinking of tea. It was, of course, the Chinese who first designed and made equipment for the proper storage and serving of tea. In the early eighteenth century, when the Dutch and British East India companies conducted regular trade with China, European people embraced the custom of drinking tea wholeheartedly.

Because tea was an expensive commodity, containers which could be locked were made. Devices for measuring and serving tea were developed and they profoundly influenced the manufacturing of western silver and porcelain, furniture, and other decorative arts. There are many magnificent tea kettles, tea pots, trays, etc., well outside the scope of this volume. A great variety of forms, materials, and style are displayed in the designs of caddy spoons, strainers, infusers, tongs and other small items used for the service of tea.

Tea infusers

Tea infusers are pierced containers for infusing a small quantity of tea in hot water in a cup or in a teapot. "Tea ball" is another term often used. They are of two basic types: (1) hinged or screw top with chain attached or (2) those with extended rigid handle which is hinged.

Tea infusers or tea balls with chains usually have a hook on the end of the chain to be hooked over the edge of the cup or teapot. The type with chains almost always screw together. Those that are hinged have a catch to hold the parts together.

Both the chained type and those with extended handles were made in sterling, silverplate and other metals. The quantity of tea they hold varies greatly. Some are intended to make one cup of tea while larger ones hold enough tea for a teapot.

The introduction of the tea bag has put many tea infusers "on the shelf" or pushed to the back to the kitchen drawer. There are those who still delight in the whimsical design of the tea infusers. There are also those who say they object to the taste of tea bags.

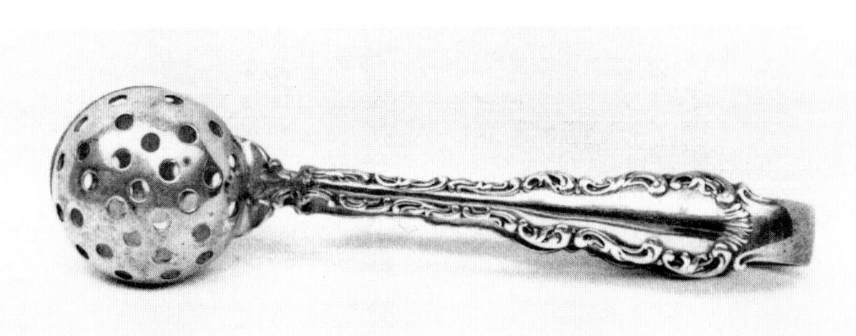

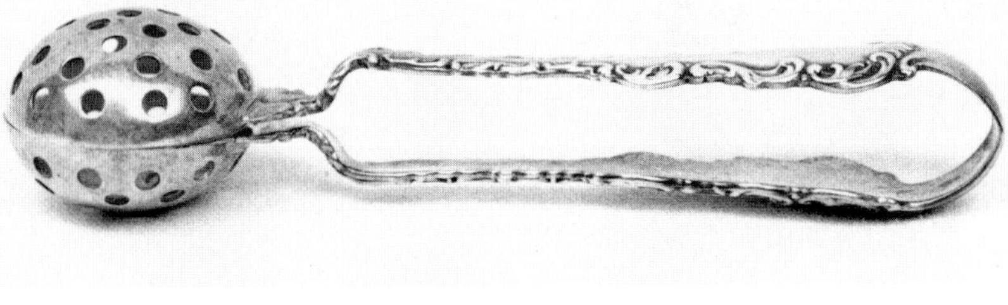

Two views of sterling tea infuser. Maker: Whiting, division of the Gorham Co. "Louis XV" pattern. Patented by Charles Osborne, design patent #20,466, January 6, 1891. *Collection of Peter and Helen Nowell. Photo: Courtesy of Silver Magazine Archives.*

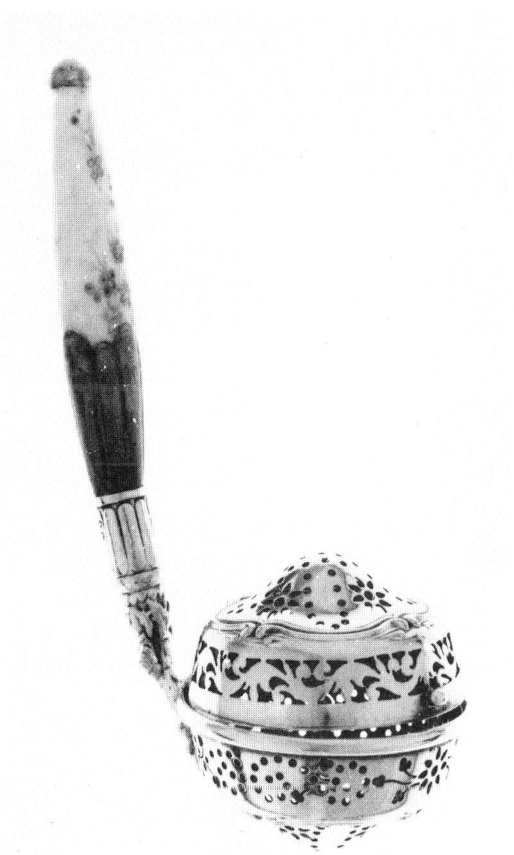

Left:
Stick tea infuser with porcelain handle pierced tea chamber, Gorham Co., c.1900. *Collection of Peter and Helen Nowell. Photo: Courtesy of Silver Magazine Archives.* $95.

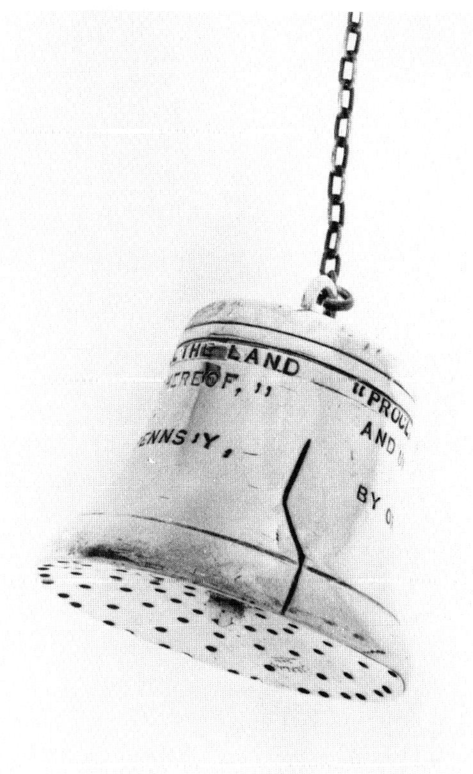

Liberty Bell tea ball. Webster company. *Collection of Peter and Helen Nowell. Photo: Courtesy of Silver Magazine Archives.*

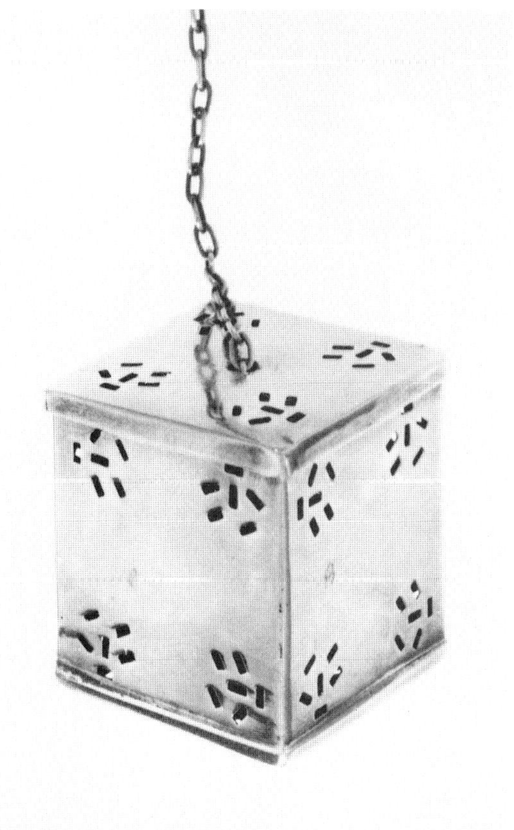

Square tea ball with removable top. Maker: Webster Company. The piercing in the corners has an "Oriental" feeling. *Collection of Peter and Helen Nowell. Photo: Courtesy of Silver Magazine Archive.*

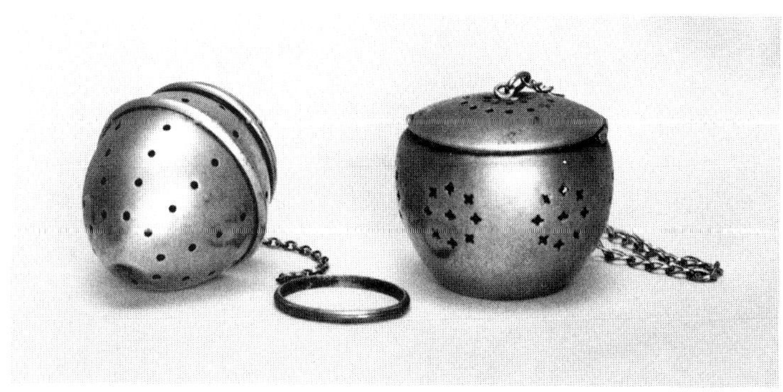

Individual tea balls. Left: no mark. Right: International Silver Company. Both are sterling. To be used in individual tea cups. *Photo: H Ivan Rainwater.*

Tea strainers

Strainers for tea appeared late in the eighteenth century, much later than the strainers for fruit in punch. Small tea strainers with hanging loops and circular, oval, or lozenge-shaped bowls were intended to hang beneath the teapot spout to catch the leaves. These small bowls were only 1-1/2" across and must have required frequent emptying. Stephen Helliwell writes in *Collecting Small Silverware* that these spout strainers were impractical as they allowed drops of tea to fall on the tablecloth. It is assumed that early tea drinkers simply let the tea leaves settle in their cups and emptied the dregs into the waste bowls, which were a standard part of all porcelain and pottery tea sets.

The tea strainers of the type familiar today seem to have appeared late in the nineteenth century. Many ornate examples were made in Holland and Germany. Many bear spurious marks in an attempt to pass them off as antique. Some are very decorative. Some are covered with mythical or historical scenes.

Twentieth century strainers are smaller than early ones. Some stand on little matching bowls designed to catch any drips of tea. Many were copies of earlier fruit strainers.

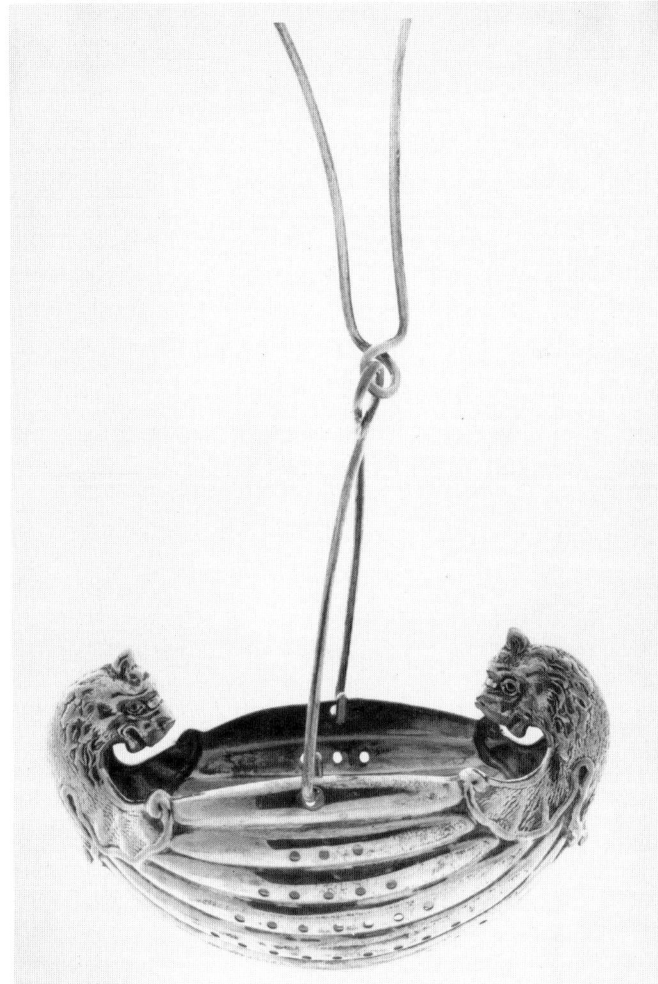

Boat shaped spout strainer with lion's head fore and aft. An interesting variation on the dragon's head so popular in the late eighteenth or early nineteenth centuries. Maker: Gorham Company. Some speculation that the lion's head might be derived from the Gorham trademark. *Collection of Peter and Helen Nowell. Photo: Courtesy of Silver Magazine Archives.* $65+.

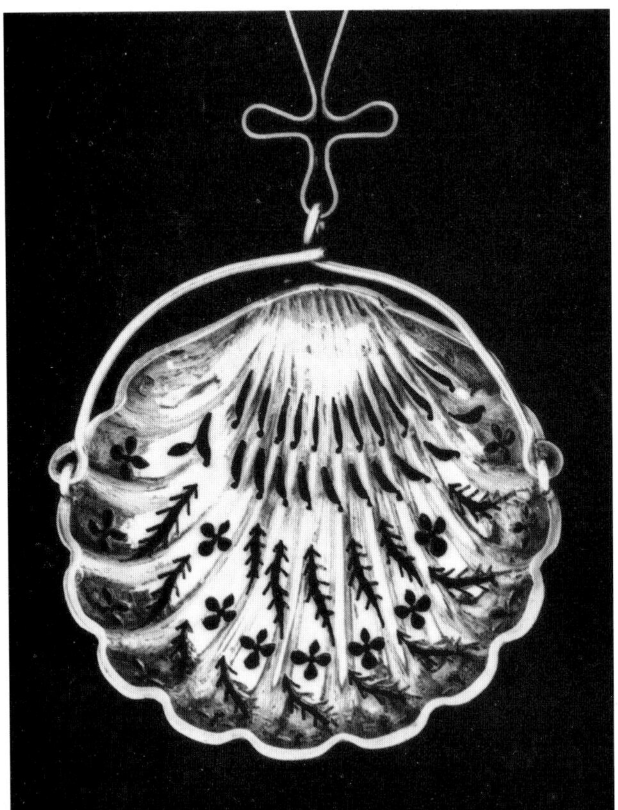

Heavy shell-shaped "Spouter" (spout strainer). French. Nineteenth century. This type was especially popular in France. *Collection of Peter and Helen Nowell. Photo: Courtesy of Silver Magazine Archives.* $65+.

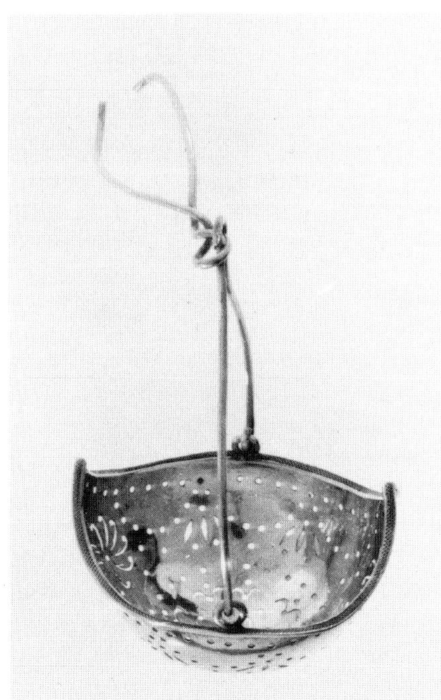

Spout strainer intended to hang beneath the teapot to catch the leaves. *Collection of Peter and Helen Nowell. Photo: Courtesy Silver Magazine Archives.* $65+.

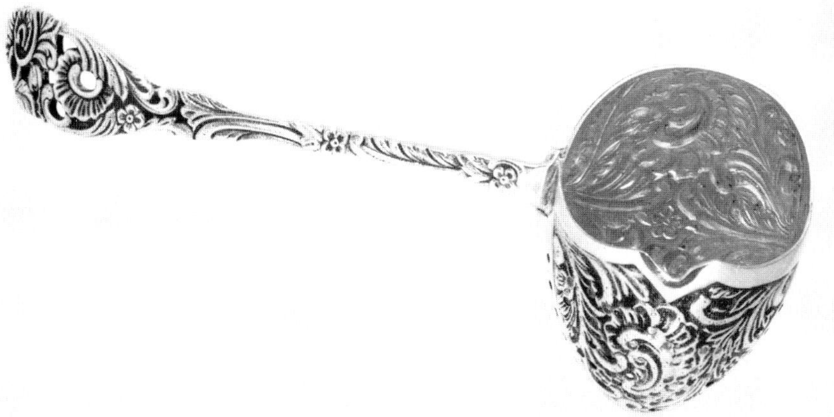

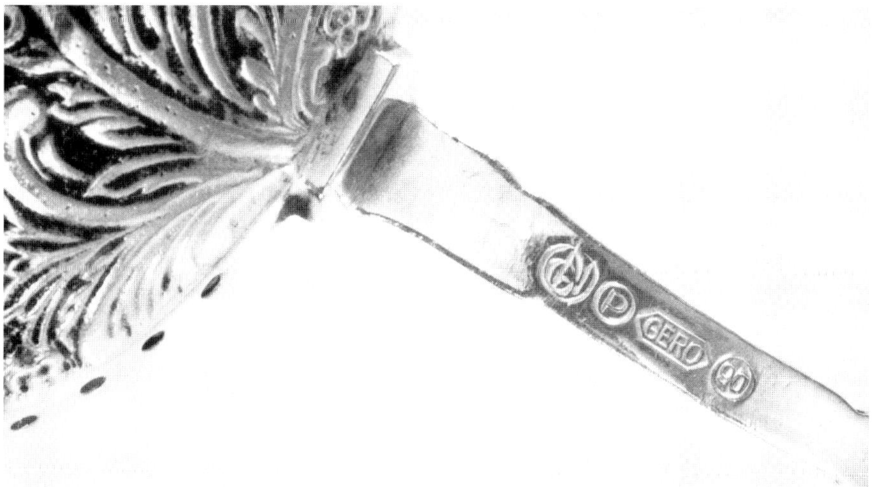

Tea strainer. Egg-shaped bowl with piercing along one side and bottom. Marks are those of the Gero Factory (Geist, Province of Utrecht in Holland). The strainer is 900/1000 silver. c.1920s to 1930. This company was well known for cutlery sets and hollowware. *Photo: Courtesy of Silver Magazine Archives.* $65+.

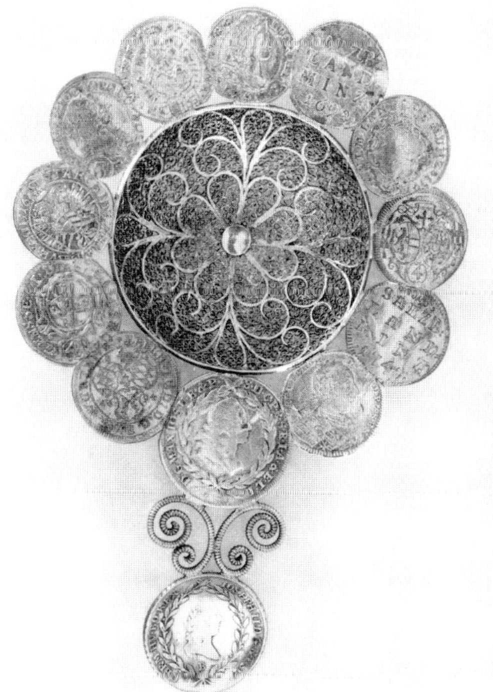

Tea strainer fashioned from seventeenth and eighteenth century German coins from 1673 to 1774. Issued by several of the small principalities that constituted Germany between the Thirty Years' War and the Bismarck Reunification. Presumably, the coins were already 100 to 200 years old when the strainer was made. No marks. Filigree work is quite fine. Measures 5-1/2" by 3-3/4". *Photo: Courtesy of Silver Magazine Archives.* $95.

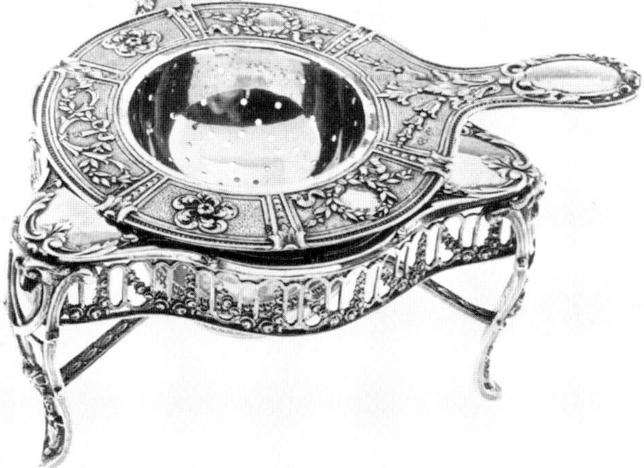

Cup strainer with triangular stand, German, nineteenth century. *Collection of Peter and Helen Nowell. Photo: Courtesy of Silver Magazine Archives.* $65+.

Sugar nips and tongs

Sugar nips are a form of sugar tongs with scissors action. They are modeled after the large sugar nippers with steel pincers, used to nip pieces of sugar from the large loaf or cone shape by which sugar was supplied. The earliest sugar nips with scissors action appeared around 1715 with circular handles and scrolled stems. The grips were sometimes in the form of claws or shells. These early nips often bear no hallmarks but by the 1770s, more were fully marked. Some of the more elaborate of the examples of the rococo period with their cast flowers and foliage were reproduced in quantity in the nineteenth century. Many bear the Continental 800 standard mark. Generally, the workmanship of the reproductions is lacking in detail.

The design of early sugar tongs was based on andirons or fire tongs. Being less expensive to make, they began to replace sugar nips in the 1870s. In the 1760s and 1770s, the cast arms which were made separately were attached to the bow section which had been subjected to repeated heating and hammering to produce the necessary "spring" action. The arms are usually crudely pierced with elaborate rococo details. Most tongs of this type have been repaired with the attendant loss of maker's marks. By the 1780s, sugar tongs were usually made form one piece of metal. Most are fully marked inside the bow. Sugar tongs of the late 1800s and early 1900s were often made so much larger and of heavy gauge metal that they are clumsy to use.

American tongs follow British ones in style and decoration but are much rarer and are, therefore, more expensive to collect.

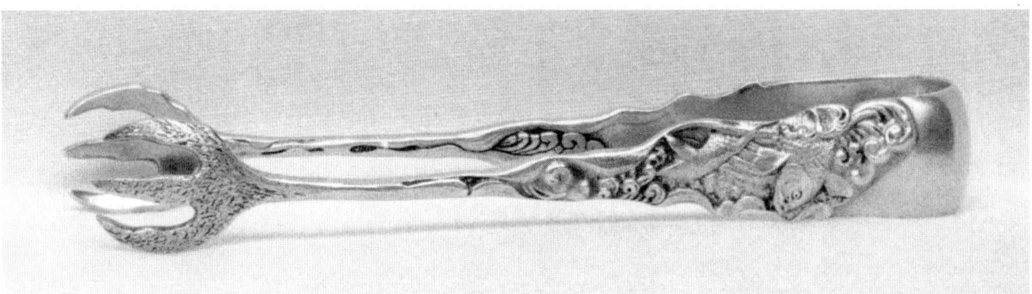

Gorham "bow" type sugar tongs in a pattern called "Hizen" found in the 1888 catalogue. *Photo: Courtesy of Silver Magazine Archives.*

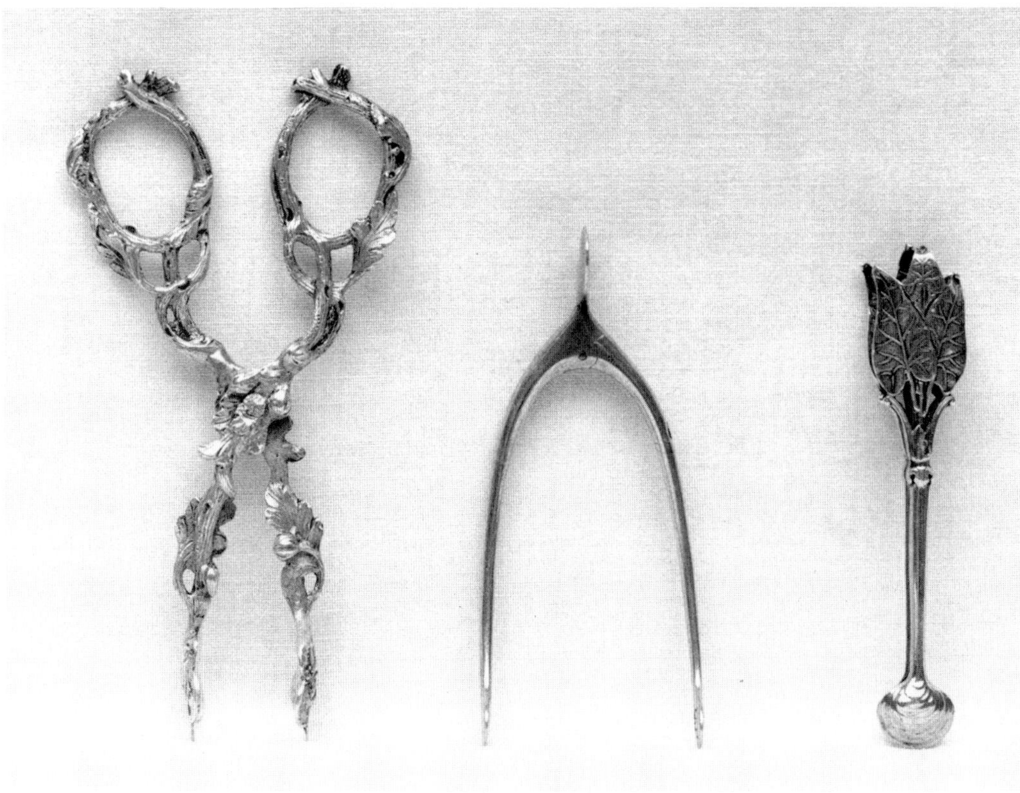

From left to right: 1. Gorham Co. sugar nips, sometimes called sugar scissors. 4-3/8" long.
2. No. H171 Wishbone shape. 3-3/8" long.
3. No. 66 bon bon tongs. 3-3/8" long. *Photo: Courtesy of Silver Magazine Archives.*

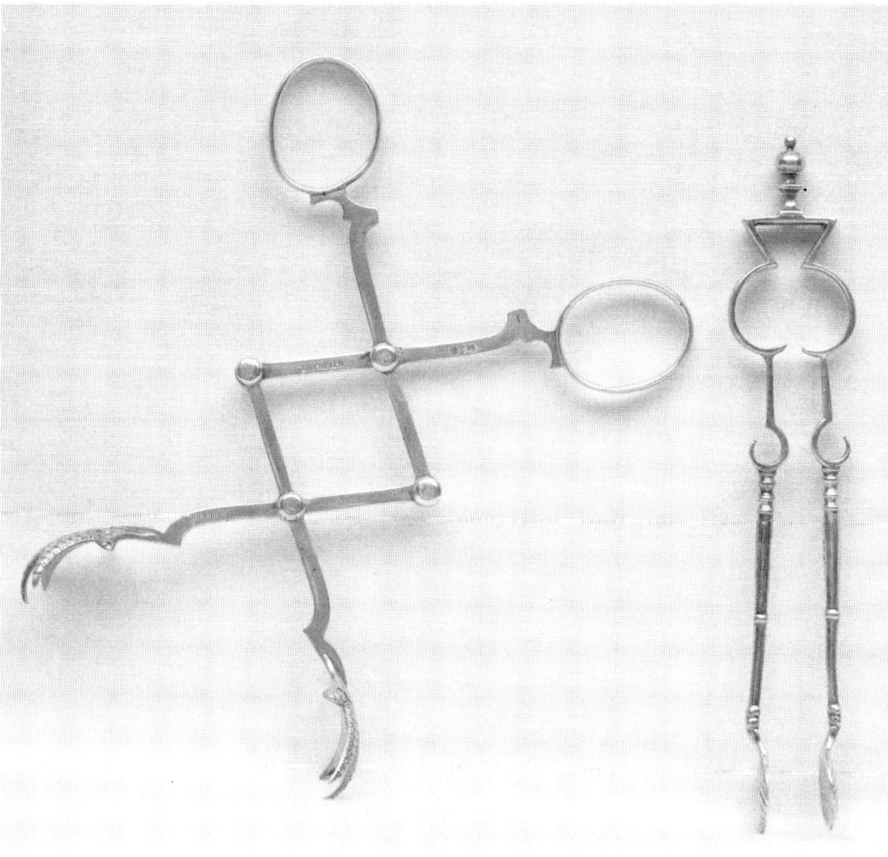

Gorham sugar tongs. Left: based on design of fireplace tongs. Grips are in the form of claws. Extended length: 6".
Right: "Andiron" type of sugar nips. Measures 4-3/4". This design is a Victorian copy of an early eighteenth century style. *Photo: Courtesy of Silver Magazine Archives*.

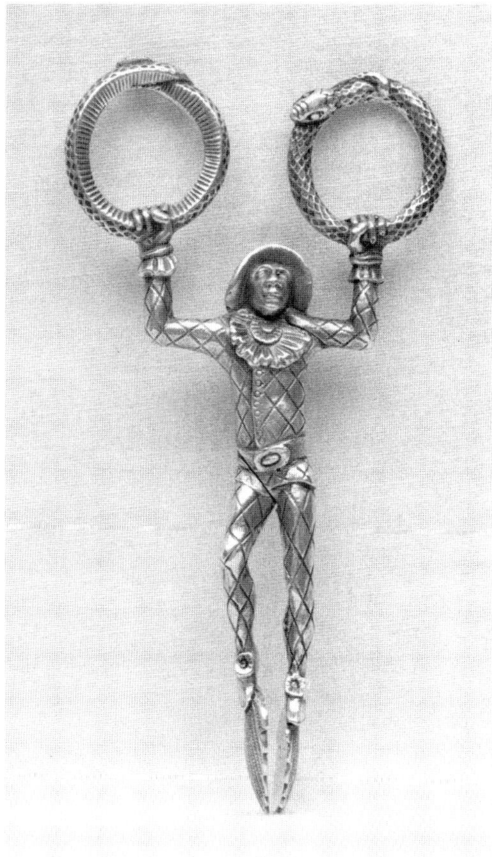

Gorham sugar tongs No. H5 in the form of a monkey dressed in a Harlequin suit hanging from rings formed by two serpents. 4-3/8" long. Gorham began using the H series of numbers after 1900. *Photo: Courtesy of Silver Magazine Archives.*

Tea caddies

Tea caddies were often called tea canisters until the late 18th century. Early ones were made in the shape of the Chinese tea-jars with the high domed cover being used to measure the tea. From about 1800, they were mostly box form with vertical sides. Many types of decoration were used.

Tea was shipped from China in boxes whose name, *caddie,* is a corruption of the Malayan word *Kati*, indicating a measure of weight (1 1/5 to 1 1/2 lb.). Silversmiths created small silver boxes to hold about one-fifth that amount of tea, and to which the term was applied and soon Anglicized to *caddy*. Because tea was so expensive, these boxes often were made with locks on them.

Sandwich servers

The makers of silverplate seem to vie with each other in the production of unusual and very often useful items. The sandwich server is one prominent example that works well also as a server of waffles and pancakes.

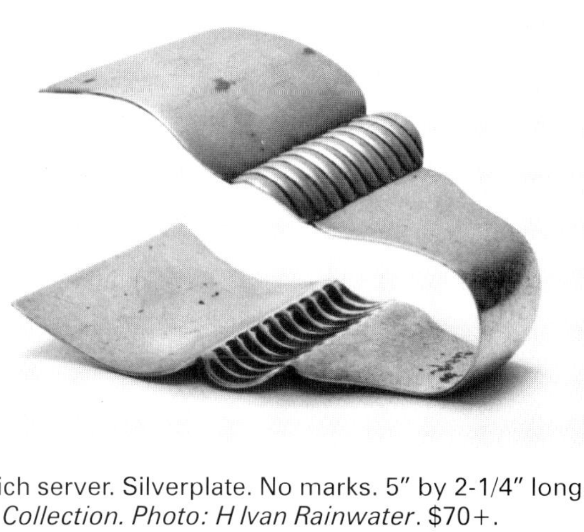

Sandwich server. Silverplate. No marks. 5" by 2-1/4" long. *Private Collection. Photo: H Ivan Rainwater*. $70+.

Waste bowls

One of the necessary components of a tea service has been the waste bowl into which cold tea could be poured in order to have a cup refilled with hot tea. Although they have dropped out of fashion for their first intended use, many waste bowls serve today as flower containers or other adaptive uses to enhance an entry hall, for example. One Reed and Barton waste bowl, larger than most, has been used for many years ceremoniously to serve flaming Cherries Jubilee.

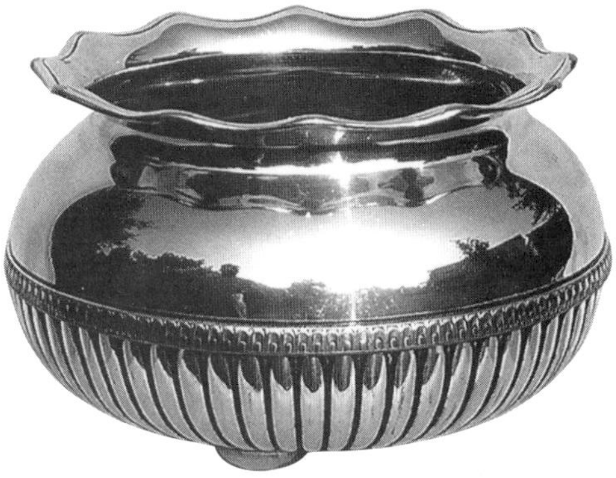

Waste Bowl. A necessary adjunct to the service of tea, here the dregs of cold tea could be discarded. Marked: Gorham Co/0740. silver soldered. Illustrated in the 1888 Gorham catalogue. *Photo: H Ivan Rainwater.* $85+.

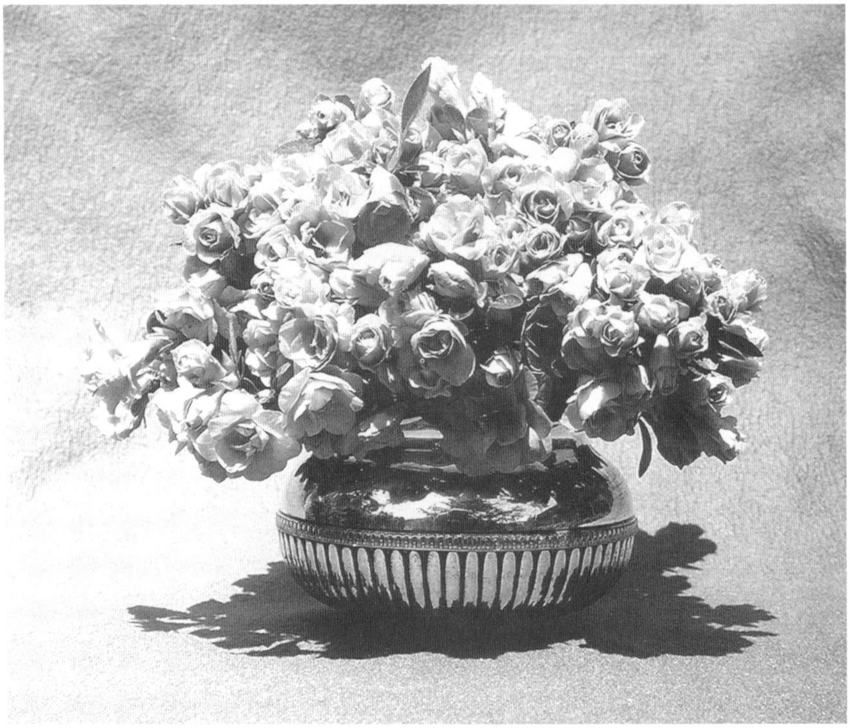

Gorham waste bowl being used to hold a bouquet of azalea blossoms. This is a good example of adaptive use. *Private Collection. Photo: H Ivan Rainwater*. $85+.

Tea caddy spoons

The first spoons made specifically for use as tea ladles were of shell design and originated in Sheffield, England. While London makers copied them and ultimately made more of them, it was in Sheffield in 1777 that the first fully hallmarked shell caddy spoon was made.

The shell motif may have been inspired by the sea shells packed in the tea chests by Chinese importers. These shells were scallop shaped and served as inexpensive and readily available scoops. At least sixty variations of the shell motif have been found.

Some of the other early tea caddy spoons were made with scoop shape or deep oval bowls similar to sugar shells, though they had shorter handles. Decoration was often engraving, and some was bright-cut. These styles continued even after the advent of more elaborate ones. Other fancy shapes were not long in coming and silversmiths vied with each other to see who could product the most unusual design.

The inventive silversmiths of Birmingham, England, put their talents to the creation of a wide variety of tea caddy spoons with a leaf motif, among which were the strawberry, ivy, tea, and acanthus. Other motifs attributed to a Birmingham origin are the "Eagle's Wing," the "Hand" and the "Jockey Cap," all of which were made in many variations. The popularity of the "Hand" and the "Jockey Cap" remain so persistent that they are available today as reproductions.

Large numbers of tea caddy spoons were made of thin gauge silver, probably because heavy gauge metal would not be satisfactory for the die-stamping method of production. Some few appear to have been hand raised from flat sheets of silver.

A cast caddy spoon by George Smith, London, about 1775 antedates others of this method of production by at least fifteen years as the first fully marked cast caddy spoon reported bears the London date of 1790. Other cast caddy spoons followed. Among them is the "Chinese Mandarin" in whose bowl is a portrait of that gentleman. It was made by Edward Farrell, London, 1816.

With the settlement of a colony of Italian craftsmen in the Clerkenwell district of London, there were introduced between 1790 and 1830 the technique of making caddy spoons of filigree. Because of the delicate material used, with only a few exceptions, they bear no marks and are difficult to date except by style. These should not be confused with the Indian and Chinese filigree articles which are generally darker in color and of finer wire. A later development was the creation of a simulated filigree in which the pattern was die-stamped and not made of the delicate wire.

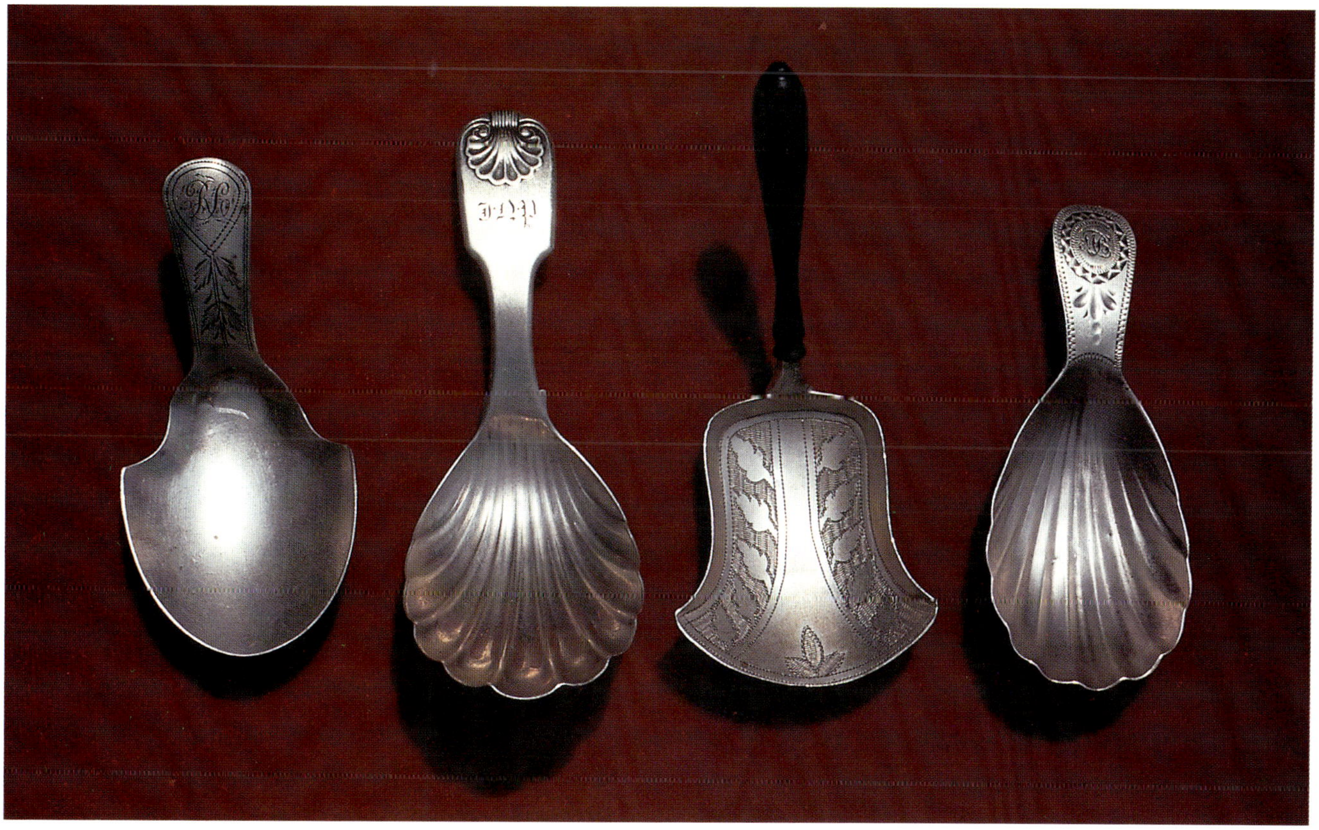

Four tea caddy spoons in silver. From left to right: 1. pastern or hoof-shape bowl. Maker: Joseph Taylor. Birmingham. 1793-1794.
2. Shell-shaped bowl. Maker: WE, London. 1830-1831.
3. Unusual caddy spoon with ebony handle. Maker not traced.
4. Shell-shaped bowl. Marked: London. 1823-1833. *Photo: Bruce Waters.* $115-250 each.

Biscuit boxes

Biscuit boxes, biscuit jars, cookie jars, biscuit barrels, or cracker jars, by whatever name they all serve the same purpose as containers to keep biscuits (cookies in the United States) or crackers fresh. In England, the best-known form is the circular ones of silverplate with tight fitting lids. They stand about eight inches in height. No sterling examples have come to our attention but Carpenter (in *Gorham Silver*, pp. 118-119) does record "a number of whimsical silver cracker jars made in the year 1880." Not inexpensive, one of these retailed for $140!

Most of the English biscuit boxes were silverplate. Though the popular form is the straight-sided circular one, there are folding ones which may have two or three compartments hinged at the bottom. There are those also of Wedgwood jasperware with mountings of silverplate.

In this country some of the most attractive silverware products are the cracker or biscuit jars. Biscuit boxes became quite popular in England in 1865, but American silver manufacturers' catalogues showed few offerings until 1880. At that time, many different types were depicted. Among them were those of pottery, stoneware, pressed glass, cased glass, opal and clear glass, cut glass and molded blown glass. Many of these jars were imported from England and the Continent. From 1876 to 1885, the Meriden Flint Glass

Co. supplied most of the glass. As with many other collectibles where glass was used, the glass is of the most interest. The covers, frames and handles are of silverplate.

A process of offset lithography printing, introduced in 1875, and a new method of embossing and shaping of tin led to the introduction of biscuit tins. Biscuit manufacturers were quick to introduce tins of their own shape and design—and most all bearing the company name. These fancy tins have largely replaced the ones of silver.

Today, one searches antique shops and auction sales for biscuit boxes and jars which still add grace and a touch of charm to the tea table.

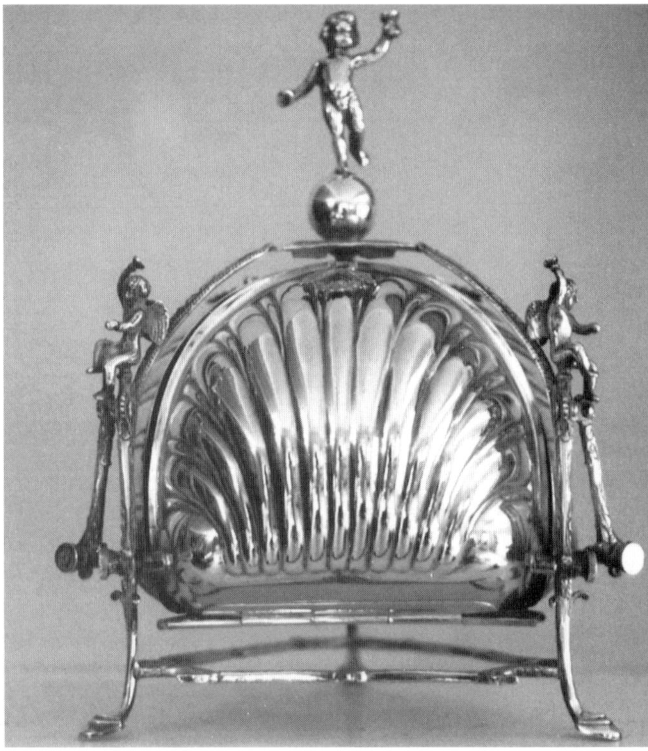

Biscuit box with shell design and three Cupids, one on each side and one on top. Opens into three sections. *Private Collection.* $125+.

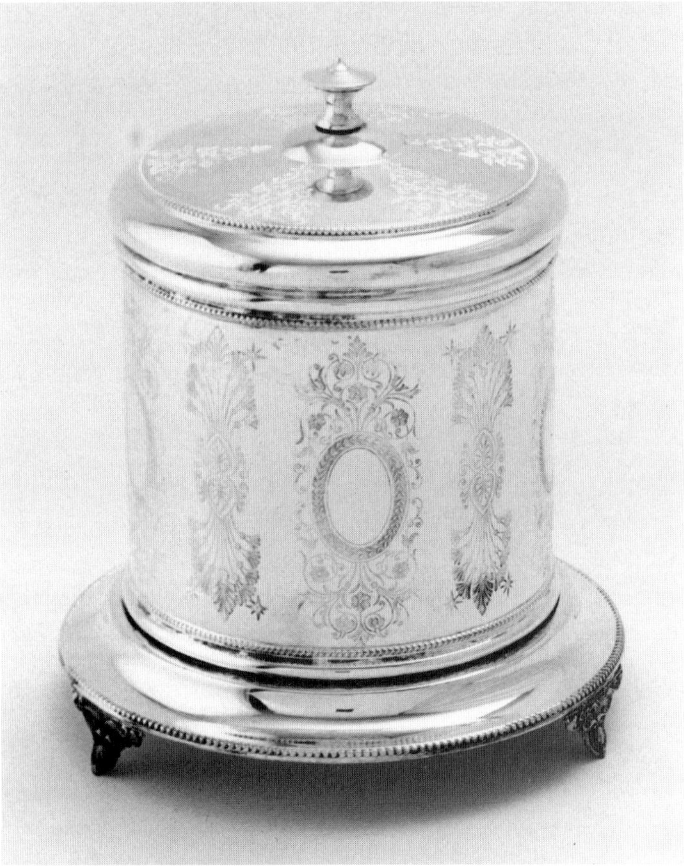

Nineteenth century English biscuit box marked E. P. N. S. (electro-plating on nickel silver). This popular Victorian piece is fairly easy to find. *Photo: David Arky, Time/Life.* $125+.

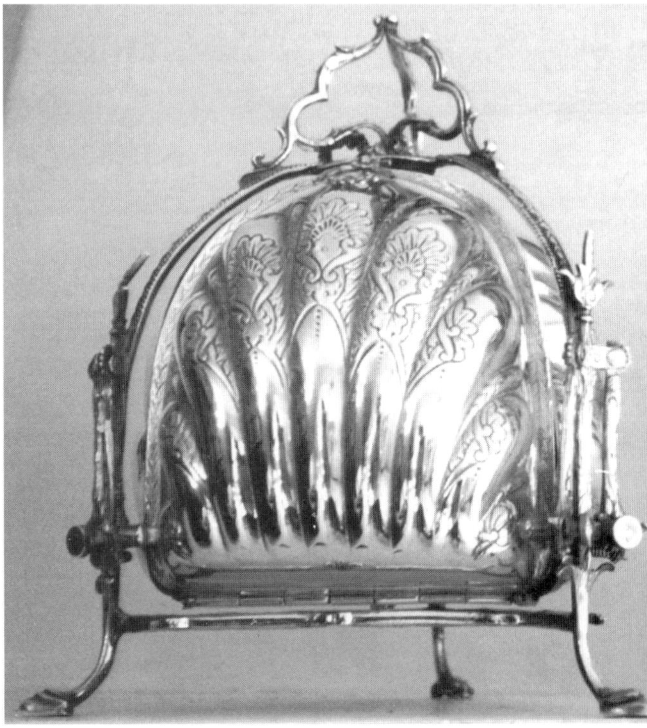

Biscuit box, shell shaped. Opens at the top when handle is released. Decorative etching on both sides. *Private Collection.* $125+.

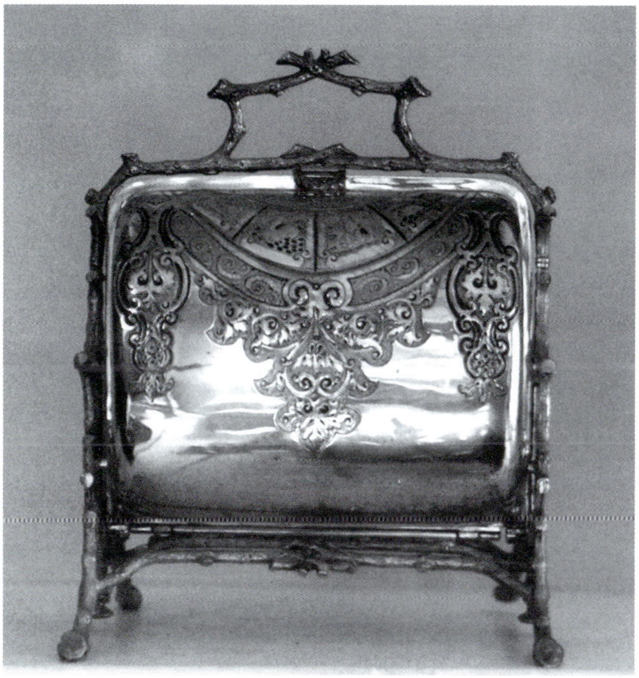

Biscuit box with bark handle and intricate circular design. *Private Collection.* $125+.

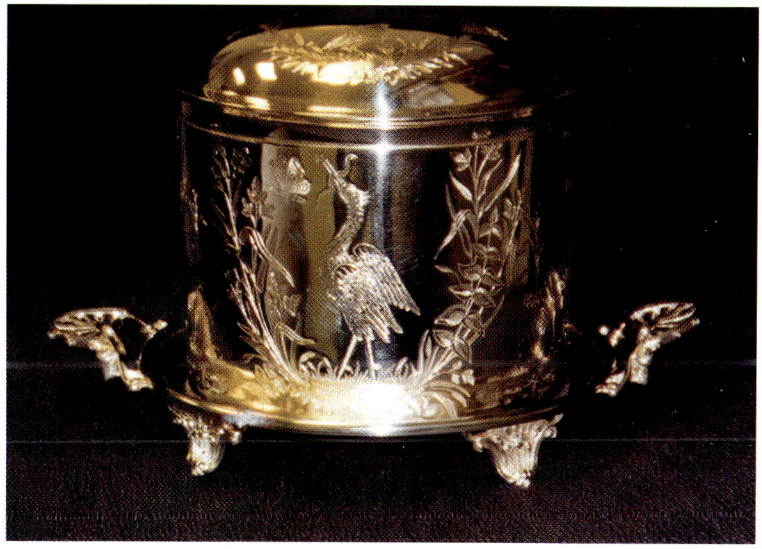

Silverplate biscuit box with ornate design showing egret and butterfly. *Photo: Fortunoff, New York City.* $125+.

Mote spoons

One specialized type of spoon, the original use of which is still debated, is the mote spoon. The handles are long and slender, tapering to a barbed and pointed end. They rarely bear a full set of hallmarks. Early types are pierced with holes and are thought to date from about 1690. Later ones are perforated with elaborate geometric designs. They have been described as olive spoons, strainers, and tea strainers. Some profess that the barbed end was for spearing fruit from hot punch while others believe their most probable use was for clearing loose tea from the spouts of teapots. Mote spoons have been found in three sizes, and the date letters on some indicate that they were made after a fixed strainer had been placed in the spout within the pot, thus doing away with the necessity of a separate strainer. Also, many tea pots of this period were made with s-shaped spouts, through which it would have been impossible to have thrust a straight-spiked stem.

Mote spoons were sometimes accompanied by a set of teaspoons, giving credence to the belief that they were to have been used as tea strainers or to skim the floating tea leaves (motes) from the surface of hot tea in the cup. Separate tea strainers came into use about 1790. American-made mote spoons are extremely rare.

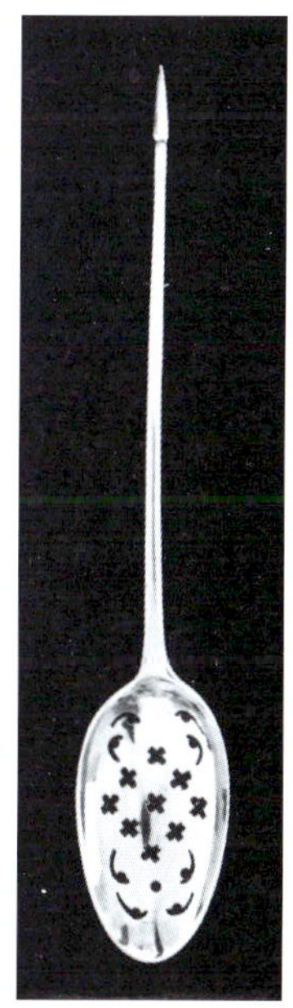

Silver mote spoon. 5-1/2" long. *Collection of Peter and Hellen Nowell. Photo: William Fore.*

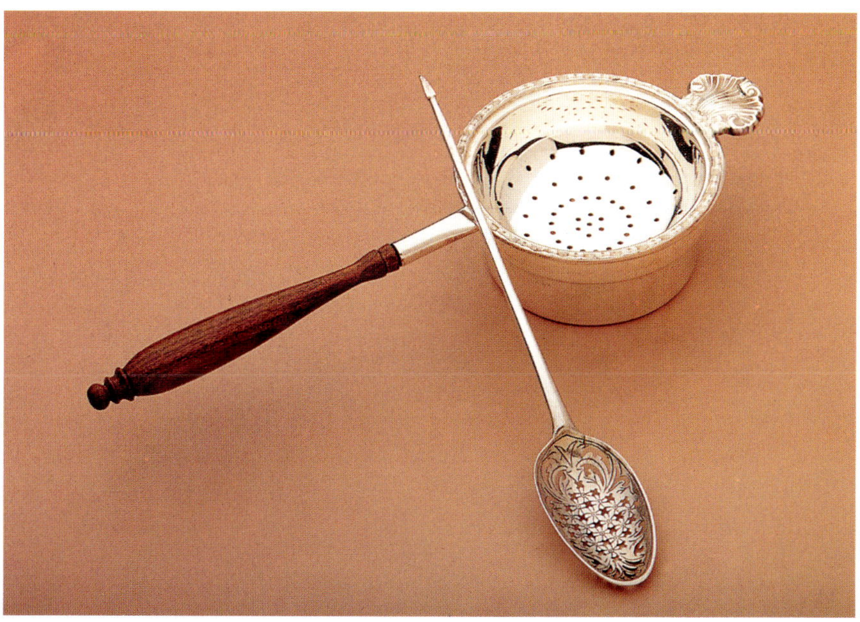

Mote spoon, RCM inscribed on the back. Marked: W.P. Struck twice. Length: 5-3/4". Tea strainer. Marked F H in concentric circles. length: 7-1/4". Three marks: Rose/Lion Passant/O. The Sheffield Crown used for more than two hundred years on silver was replaced with the Rose in 1904 when gold was first assayed. The "O" is for the year 1987. *Photo: Bruce Waters.*

Bonbon dishes

Bonbon dishes, also called sweetmeat baskets, were used to serve bonbons, sweetmeats and, occasionally, even butter. Early ones were of heavy gauge silver and usually had fixed handles; oval shapes were popular. They often bore rococo decorations and scrolls. Pierced designs were introduced in the early part of the eighteenth century. In the 1780s, the central handle (bail handle) was introduced. A few were quite plain but the more ornate ones seem to find favor with most people.

About 1760 heavy rollers were used to produce a lighter weight silver from which bonbon dishes were made. Motifs used then were swags, paterae, bright-cut engraving, and applied rims; all these still cut by hand sawing. Many bonbon dishes from this period were designed to hang from the branches of a table centerpiece.

A serious problem arose when makers of Old Sheffield Plate began to make bonbon dishes and baskets with pierced designs, because the copper showed clearly in the piercing. The invention of the steam driven fly-punch, which stamped out the pierced design with a hardened steel punch, solved the problem. The thin silver layer was stretched enough to cover the thick layer of copper. The ability to produce mechanically that which for years had been done entirely by hand caused production costs to drop dramatically.

By the 1780s, bonbon dishes and baskets were frequently made of drawn silver wire.

In the United States, bonbon dishes and baskets were very popular in the 1890s, both sterling and silverplate being used. Embossing, engraving, chasing and piercing were all used to decorate them.

The sterling bonbon dish by the Alvin Company bears close resemblance to some made by William Comyns, London, 1898.

The heavily decorated repoussé pieces made by Samuel Kirk & Co., and other Baltimore silversmiths have always been favorites.

Unger Bros. featured in their catalogues bonbon dishes with Art Nouveau motifs. Daniel Low catalogues of the early twentieth century often illustrated as many as twenty-five different designs of bonbon dishes.

American bonbon dishes of pierced work, such as the Pairpoint dish with its simple beaded border, were popular as were the type with bail handles.

Victorian bonbon dishes often were reproductions of earlier ones. These reproductions were die-stamped in thinner metal and used foliate, floral, shell or heart-shaped decoration.

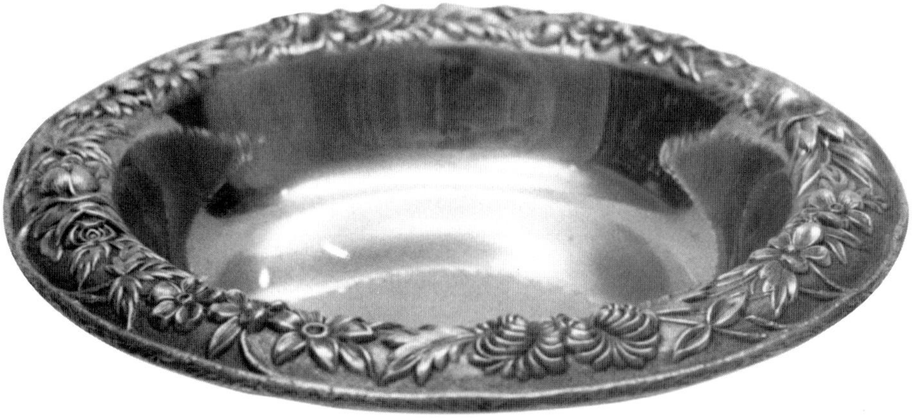

Bon bon dish. Sterling. Maker: S. Kirk & Son Inc. Stock number 409. Dates between 1925-1932. About 5". *Photo: H Ivan Rainwater.*

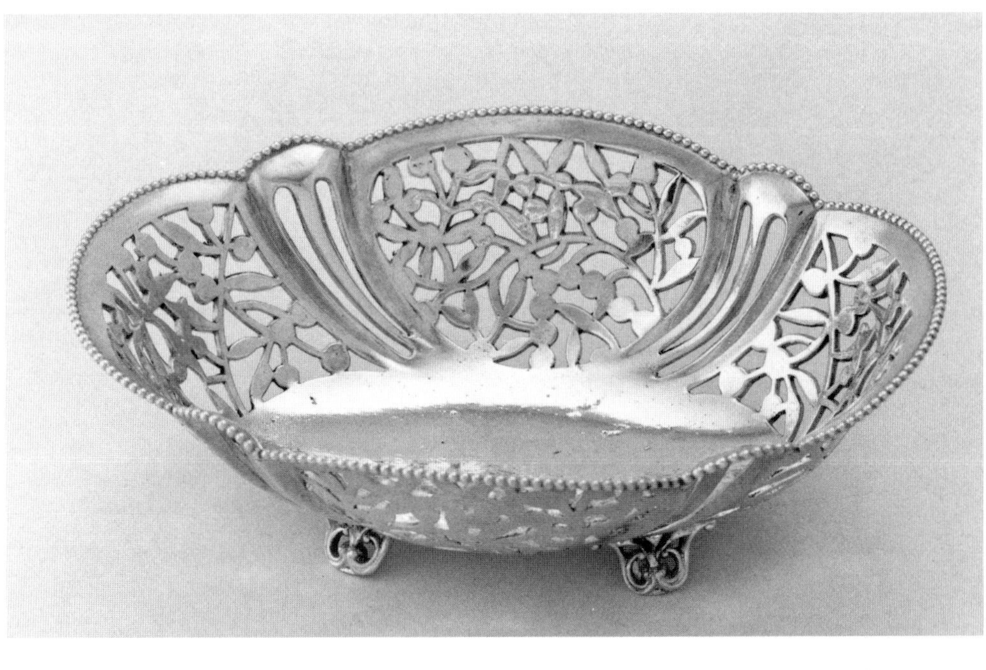

Silverplate bon bon dish. The oval shape and size of 3" both tell that this was for fine candy. Maker: Pairpont, New Bedford, MA. c.1890. *Photo: H Ivan Rainwater.*

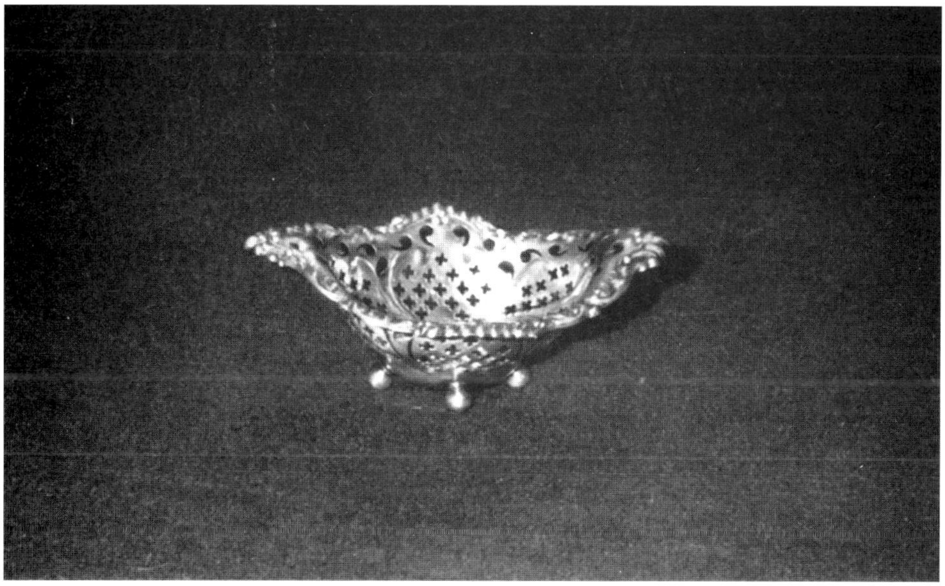

Sterling bon bon dish with pierced sides. Measure 4" by 2-3/4". c.1895. Perhaps used for nuts as well as candy. *Private Collection.*

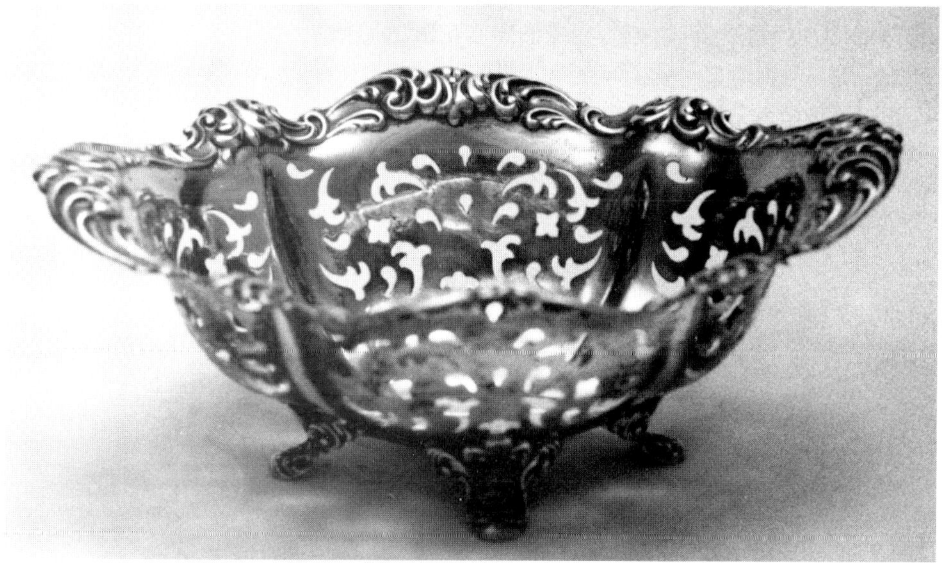

Sterling bon bon dish. Maker: Alvin Co. Trademark 1072. Measures 5" from end to end. c.1915-1920. *Photo: H Ivan Rainwater.*

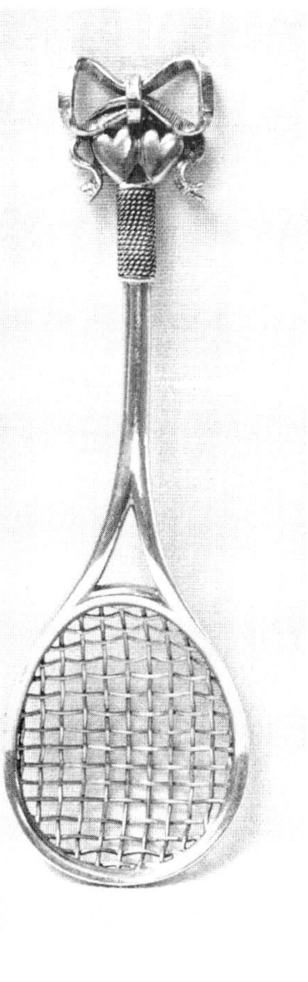

Left:
Bon bon scoop, No. 582, introduced by the Gorham Company 23 June 1891. (Cost Book Flatware 6 p. 80 col. 11) Price per dozen $28.11 or $2.34 each. 4-9/16" long. The bow and hearts finial and the wire band are gilt. *Photo: Courtesy of Silver Magazine Archives.*

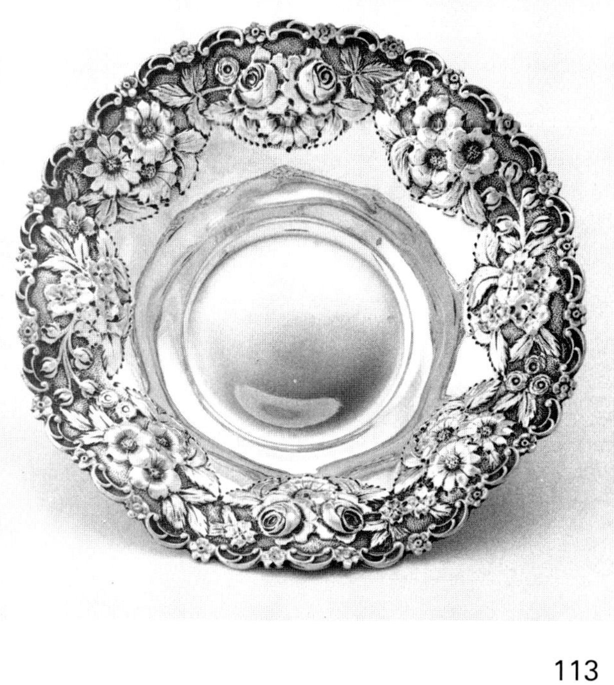

Right:
Sterling bon bon dish with ornate floral design of roses and dogwood blossoms. Trademark of A. G. Schultz plus a hand on underside of dish. The hand indicates a hand made piece, not machine made. Diameter: 6". *Photo: H Ivan Rainwater*.

Chapter 11. Silver Curios for use...
...at Dinner

Until the last quarter of the 18th century, almost no house had a separate dining room. Small tables would be set up in the hall or wherever sunlight was best, where the fire was laid, or in the summer on the cooler and shadier side of the house. Almost all of the furniture used for dining was stored nearby, usually along one wall. For ceremonial use or for other festive occasions, simple wooden boards were laid on an A-shaped trestle frame. This table arrangement would then have been covered with a cloth, often reaching to the floor. This was a protection for the wood. Large napkins were required as diners ate most of their food with their fingers.

The use of forks to convey food to the mouth was introduced in Italy about the first quarter of the seventeenth century by Thomas Coryat, an eccentric traveler. This introduction turned out to be a most significant change in tableware in history.

With the introduction of forks, large napkins were no longer required and were not used in some households. The English were ultra-conservative and did not accept the new Continental fashion of forks immediately. Some visitors to England in 1669 complained that there were no forks and they were expected to bring their own. It was many years before the use of table forks was accepted by the masses.

In many homes, until the beginning of the nineteenth century, dining tables were not left standing permanently in the center of the dining room. Chairs were arranged around the room and small gate-leg tables were kept nearby. Two ends of a large dining table might be placed against the walls as pier-tables and extra leaves were stored elsewhere.

Today's popular lifestyle of informality has meant that the dining room in many private homes once again has been incorporated into a "great room," a multi-purpose room, or eliminated altogether.

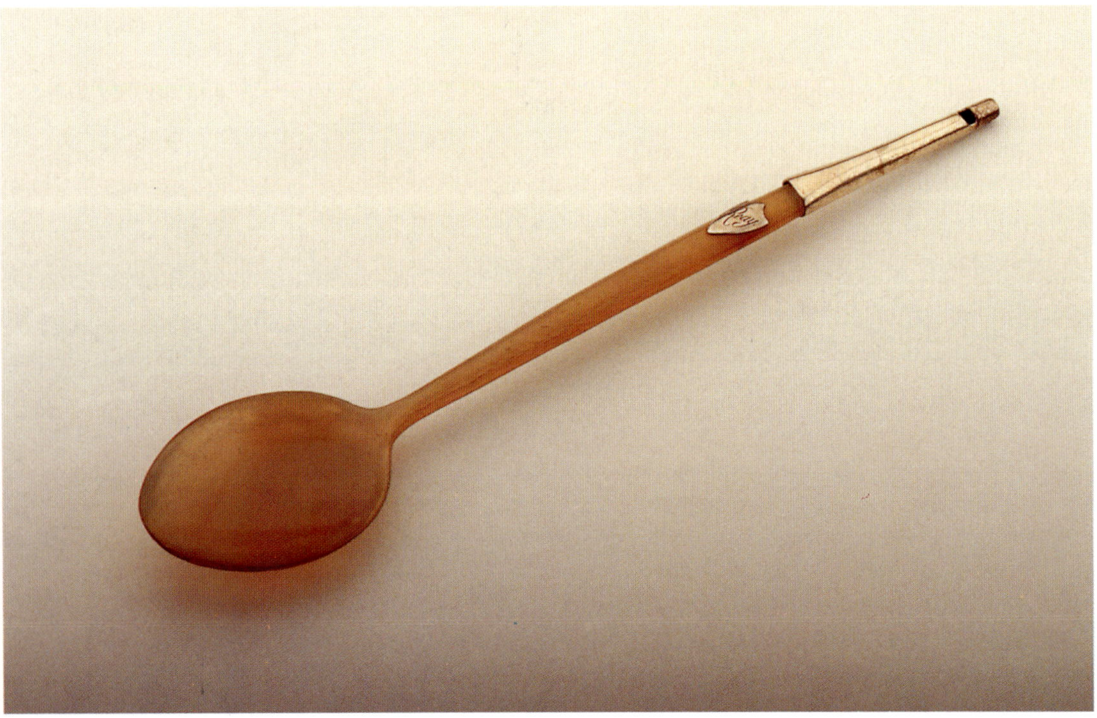

Scottish whistle spoon. Horn and silver. Shield on handle inscribed "Reay." 7-3/4" long. *Private Collection. Photo: Bruce Waters*. $95 and up.

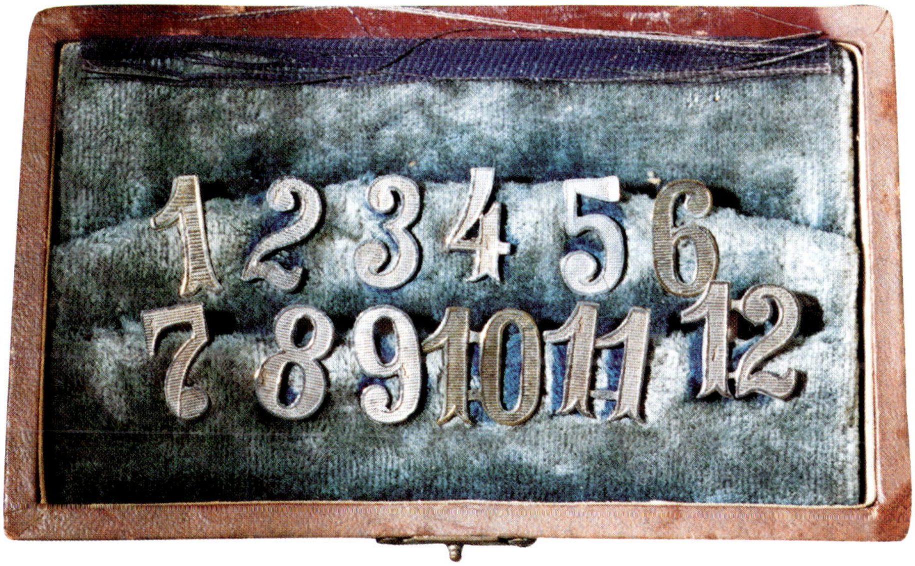

Silver numbers to identify the cup and saucer of each dinner guest. They were attached by means of a hook on the reverse side. Dutch silver mark with dagger used between 1813-1906, c.1900. Each number measures 1". Sets of twenty-four numbers were made. *Collection and photo: Anne Jansen.*

Knife rests

Knife rests are composed of two shaped supports united by a horizontal bar. This bar is used to place the carving knife in a manner that it does not soil the tablecloth. They are made in sterling silver and electroplate, the latter being most numerous. Knife rests have been in widely used in the U.S. since c.1850. Figural knife rests are most popular. Smaller ones were made for individual use.

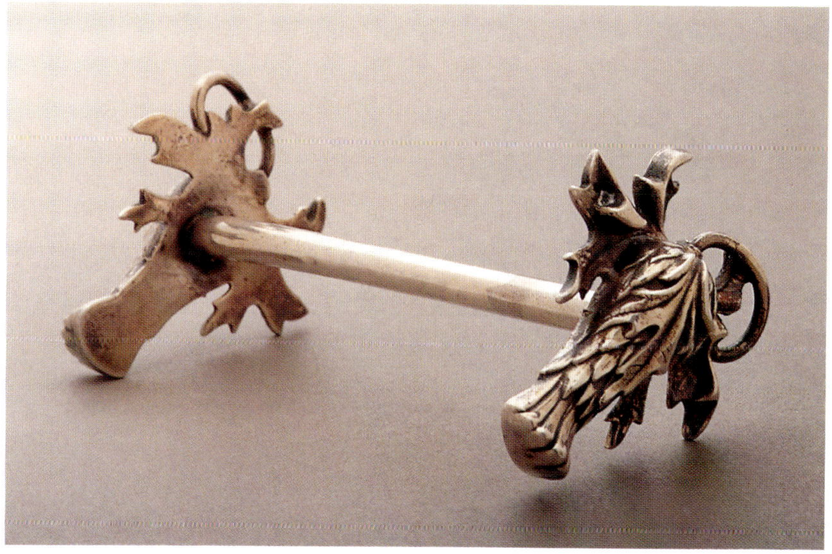

Knife rest with ends in the form of thistles. Marked: STERLING,/ Wm. B. Kerr(?) /767. The middle part of the mark is not clear. Length: 3-1/2" (9.2 cm). *Photo: Bruce Waters*. $160.

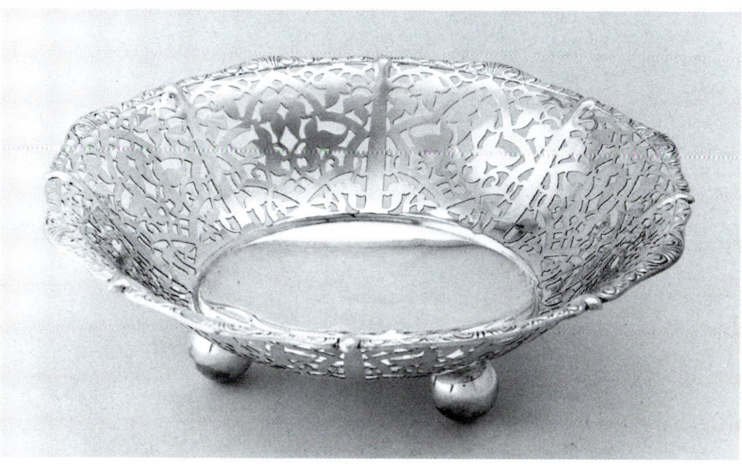

A silver fruit dish of European origin. Marked: 830. Measures 8-1/2". *Private Collection. Photo: H Ivan Rainwater*. $75.

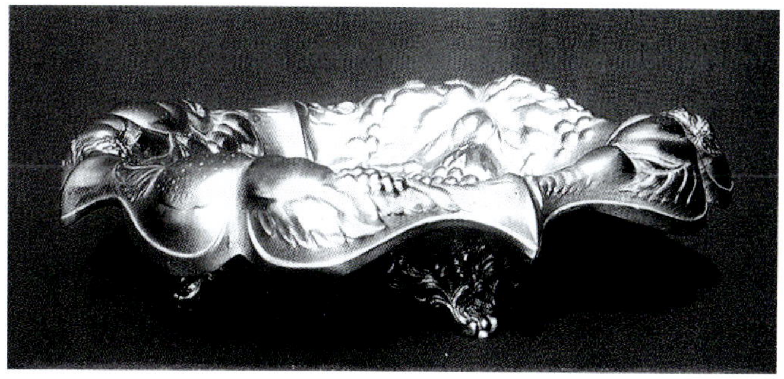

Fruit dish. Silverplate. About 1880. *Private Collection. Photo: H Ivan Rainwater*. $35.

Corn utensils

Corn scrapers, corn slitters, corn scorers, and corn creamers were some of the names applied to the specialized tools used to remove the edible corn kernels from a corn cob. The sharp prongs were scraped across the cob to make a cut in each kernel. Cream-style corn was made by scraping the kernels with the slightly flattened edge. Whole kernels were removed with a sharp knife. Corn scrapers were made by a number of American silver companies; only a few were patented.

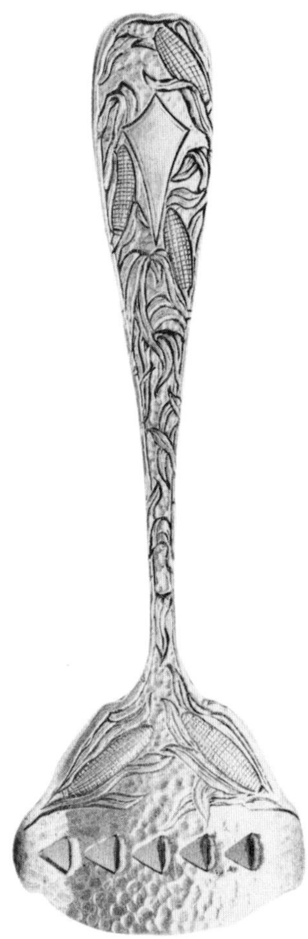

Corn scraper made by Paye & Baker, manufacturing silversmiths noted for their workmanship and variety of unusual pieces. Five tiny ears of corn are in the design for the handle. *Photo: SILVER.* $75.

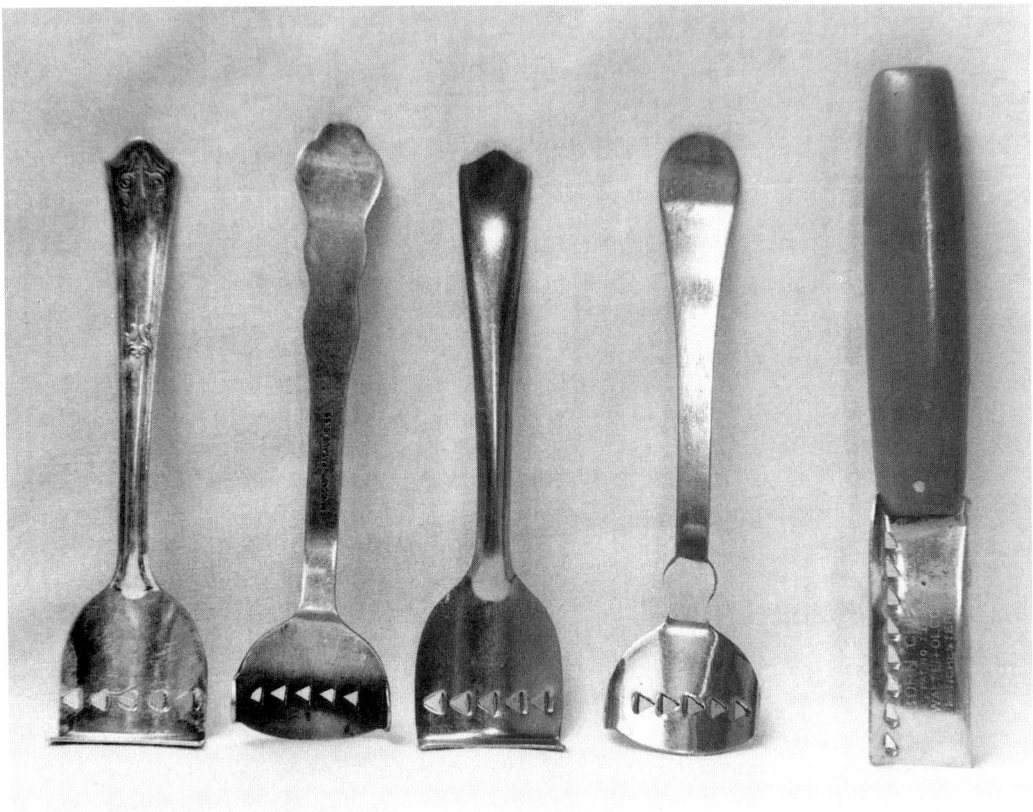

Five silverplated corn scrapers. Left to right: marked H & B Co.; Pancoast Pat. Aug. 15, 1899; unmarked; another Pancoast; marked "corn creamer, Pat. #1345456 made by Walter Olcott co., Manchester, CT." *Private Collection. Photo: Silver Magazine.* $45+ each.

Salt: in Rome it was *sal*

In Roman times salt (or in Latin *sal*) was part of the payment made to the Imperial soldiers. From this source the word *salary* is derived. By the Middle Ages, salt formed an important element in trade as it was used both for flavoring and as a preservative for meat.

Table salt cellars were often elaborate status symbols placed near high-ranking diners. Individual salts, which were used on dinner tables well into the twentieth century, can make a charming collection whether they are sterling, silverplate, or merely have tops of silver.

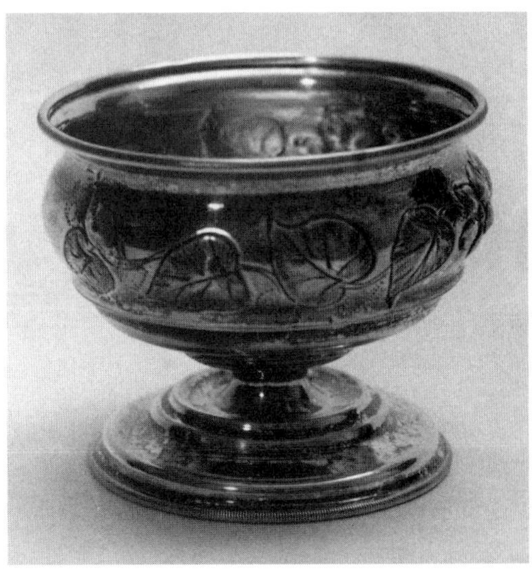

Salt dish with gold washed interior. Sterling but no maker's mark. Height: 2-5/8". Diameter: 2-1/4". *Private Collection. Photo: H Ivan Rainwater.* $75 to 90.

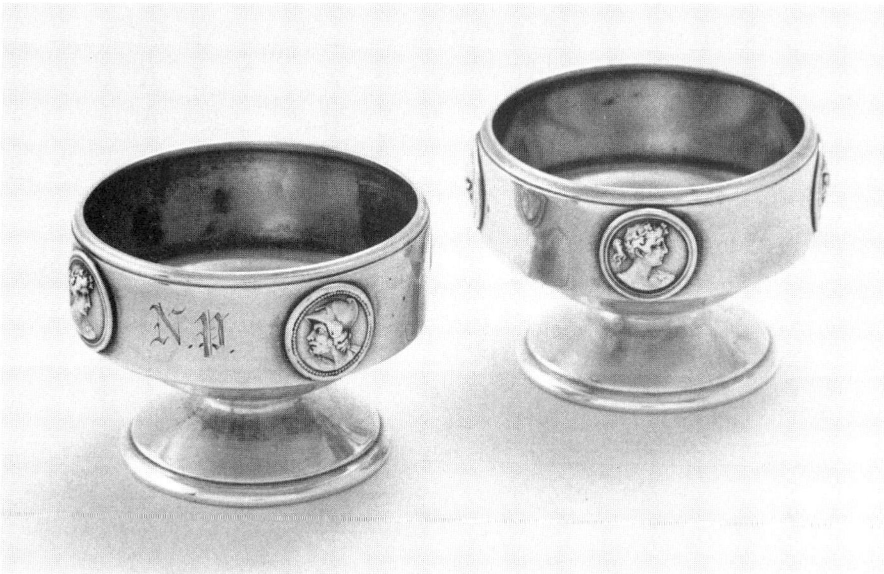

Medallion salt dishes. Marked; Lion/ anchor / G for the Gorham Co. of Providence, Rhode Island. Following the excavations at Pompeii and Herculean, classical medallions appeared on all sorts of silver beginning about 1862. *Private Collection. Photo: David Arky, TIME LIFE.* $95 to 125.

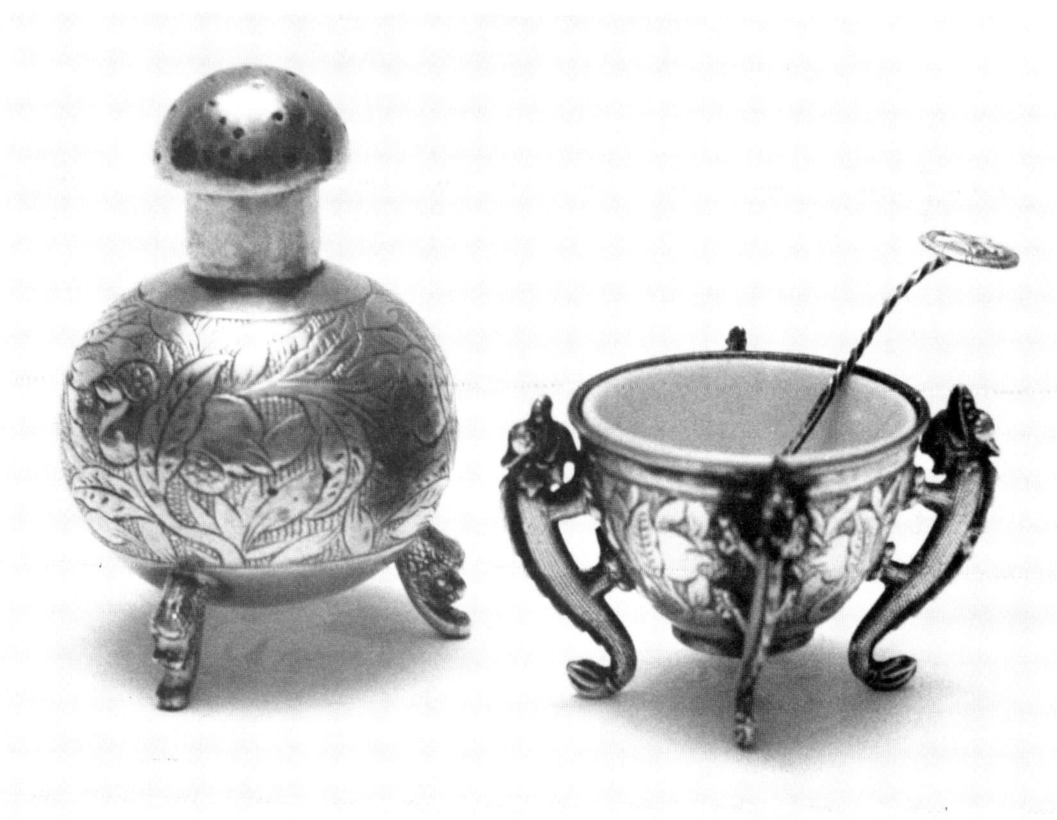

Salt and pepper set with Chinese motifs and Chinese marks too worn to read. *Private Collection. Photo: H Ivan Rainwater.*

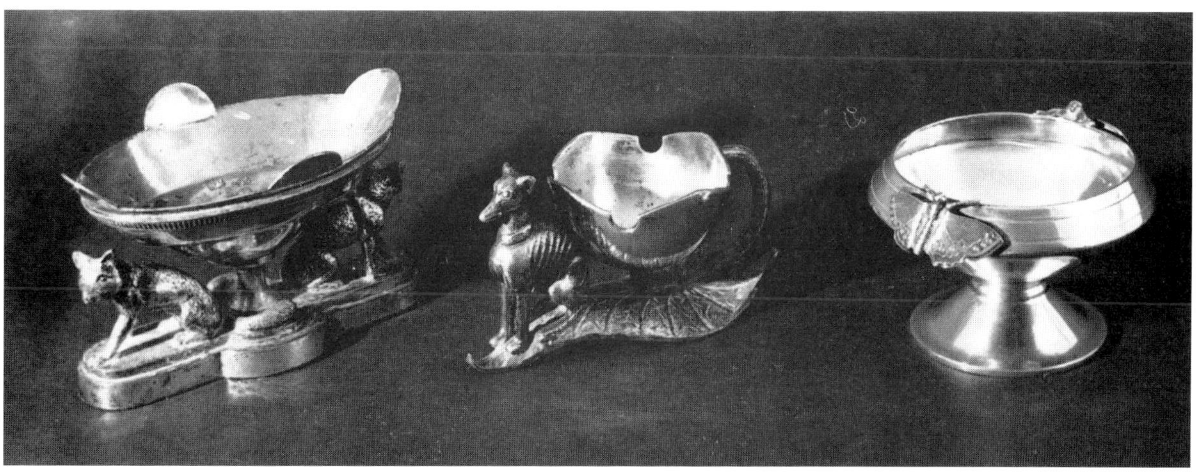

Three salt dishes. Left: Foxes on ball, Meriden Britannia Co. c.1870. Middle: Greyhound seated on a leaf. c.1880. Right: Butterflies on rim. Gorham, 1872. *Photo: Judy Redfield.*

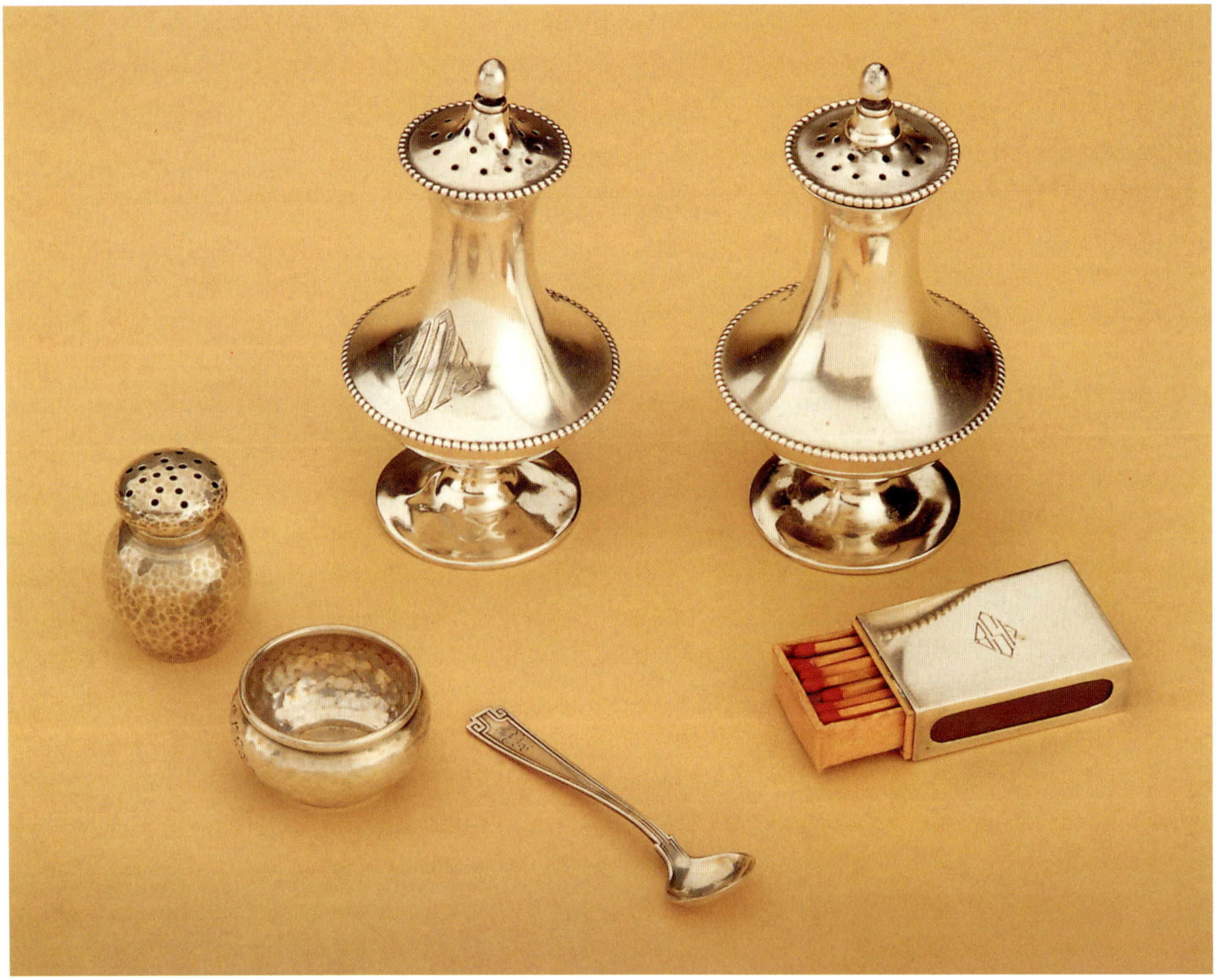

Left: individual open salt and pepper shaker. Both marked S & N Katz (a Baltimore retailer). Salt 1-3/8"d. and pepper shaker 1 1/2" h.
Salt spoon, Gorham Etruscan pattern. 2-3/4" long.
Salt and pepper shakers marked sterling. 4"h. Monogrammed.
Monogrammed match box marked Webster Co., Sterling, 1-5/8" long. *Photo: Bruce Waters*.

Spoon holders and spoon racks

Spoon holders of the two-handled "vase" type were exclusively an American form. Major companies were making them as early as 1850 and many were made to match tea and coffee services. In old manufacturer's catalogues, spoon holders were called spooners. The longer name is more commonly used today.

As the 1870s progressed, more of the fancy types of spoon holders made their appearance. some were made with a bell to serve the double purpose of holding spoons and ringing the bell for help from the kitchen.

Most spoon holders found today rest on a pedestal while a few stand on four feet. Their ornamentation ranges from the very plain and simple to ornate etching and occasionally even a round medallion or two.

Spoon racks could hold a dozen or more spoons. An unusual spoon rack was a combination rack and spoon cup. Slots on an outside rim held eight spoons while a center cup accommodated others. This style of spoon rack is relatively difficult to find today.

Sometimes spoon holders are confused with sugar bowls. Combination sugar bowls and spoon racks made their appearance about 1874. They continued to be made well into the twentieth century.

Still other spoon holders have been confused with small flower containers. They would lend themselves well to holding small bouquets of violets or lily-of-the-valley.

The design on some spoon holders matched tea services. Some were listed in catalogues separately while others could be found with the matching tea sets themselves. In the last quarter of the nineteenth century, spoon holders were used in most homes.

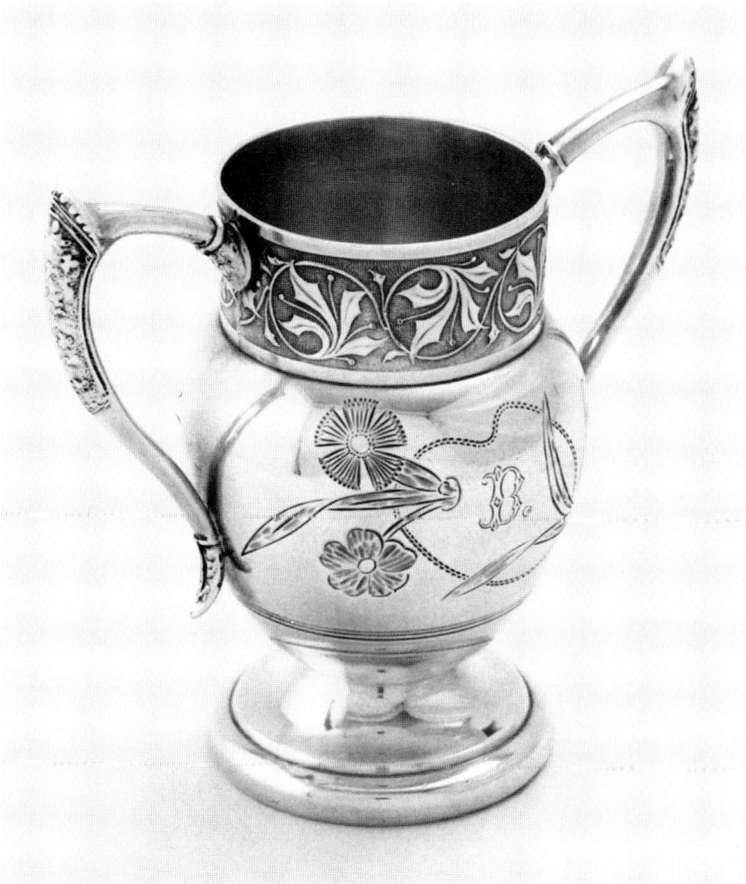

Silverplate spoon holder, commonly referred to as a "spooner," to hold spoons at the dining table or buffet, 6" h. Made by J. A. Eisenhardt of Baltimore which is listed in City Directory of 1887-1888. *Private Collection. Photo: David Arkey.*

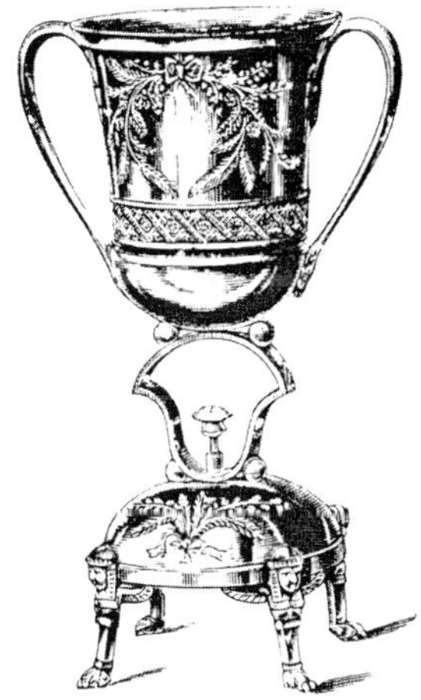

No. 0195. With Bell, $8.50.
Gold-lined, 9.50.

200. Reed & Barton catalog, 1877.

By 1877 spoon holders like these were in the Reed & Barton catalogue for buffet or table use.

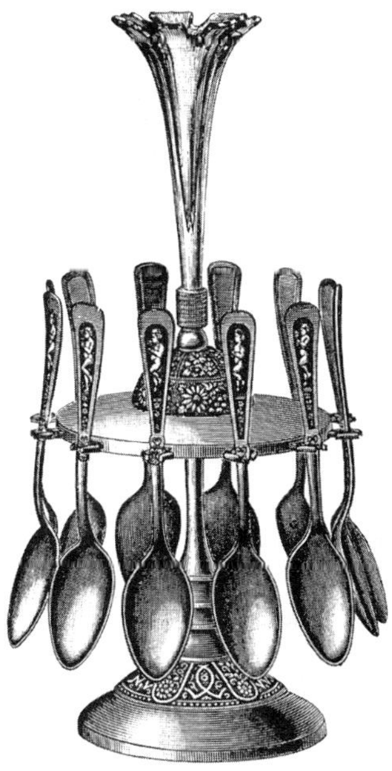

209. Meriden Britannia Co. catalog, 1886.

Spoon rack from the Meridon Britannia Co. catalogue of 1886 took a little more room on the buffet or table but showed the elegant spoons to better advantage. $225.

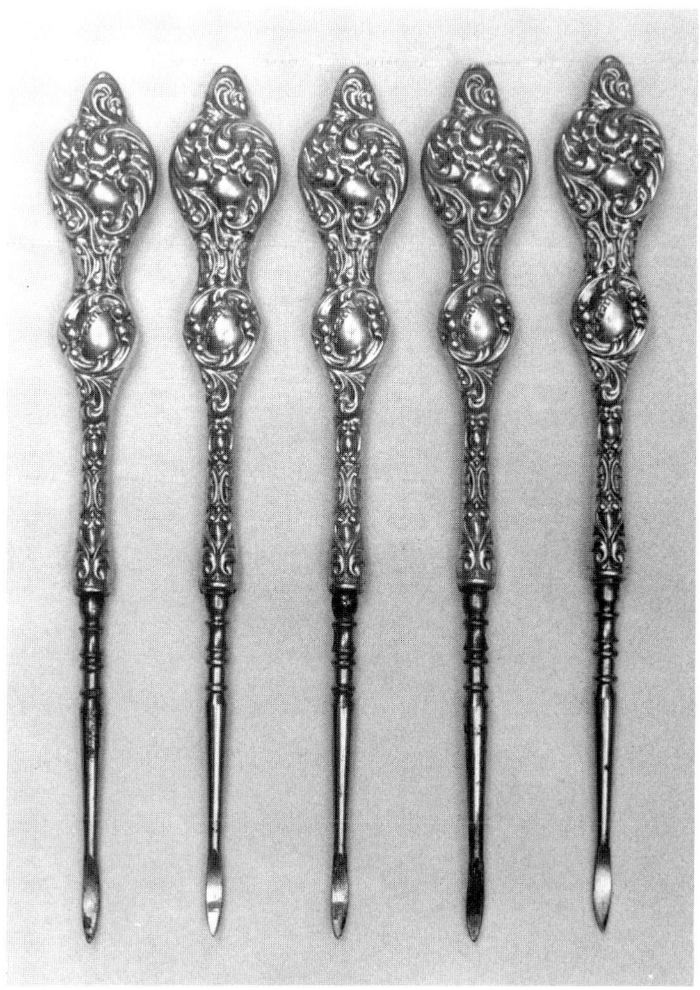

Set of five sterling nut picks in Art Nouveau deign, 5"h. *Photo: H Ivan Rainwater*. $21 each.

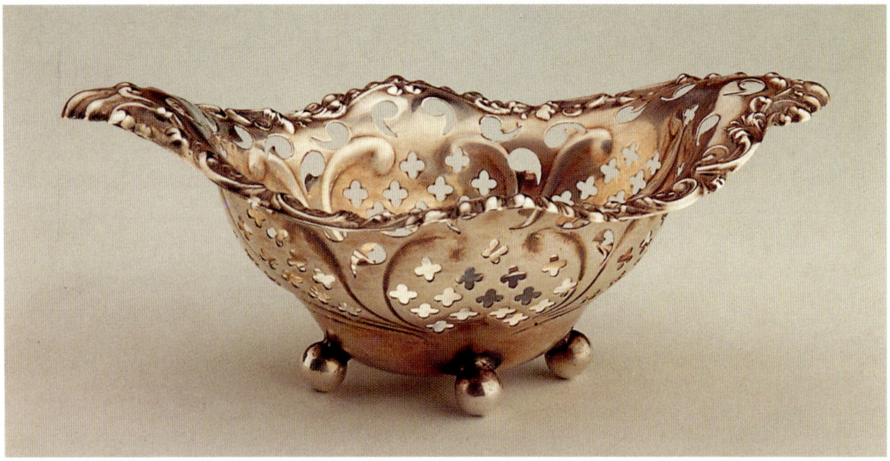

Nut dish marked Sterling but no maker's mark. 4" long by 2-1/2" wide. c.1898. *Photo: Bruce Waters*. $95.

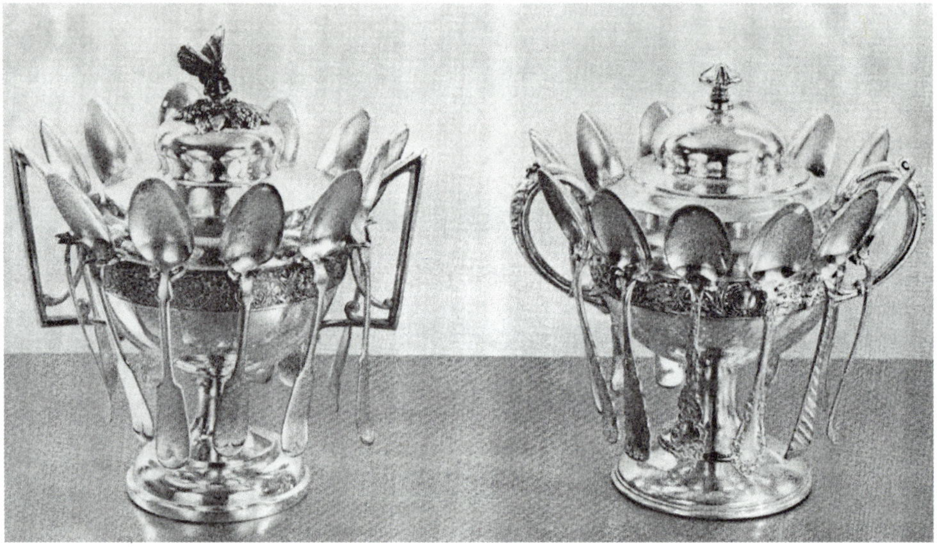

Combination sugar bowls and spoon racks. Left: Middleton Plate Co., 1879; right: Meriden Britannia Co., 1896. $250.

Asparagus servers

The love of asparagus as a cherished vegetable goes back in history to 200 B.C. when the Romans grew asparagus spears in their gardens and brought them to the dinner table as a delicacy. Asparagus was served to Roman emperors, one of whom is reputed to have said, "Quicker than you can cook asparagus."

The earliest implements used to serve asparagus were serving tongs used about 1850, but they generally were not satisfactory as they allowed the asparagus spears to fall, miss the plate, and soil the tablecloth. Other servers were designed as well but they, too, were not successful.

By the end of the nineteenth century, asparagus was served with either a hooded server or individual tongs. Either style worked well but the hooded server allowed the diner to pick up several stalks at one time.

At one time asparagus was used as a medicine thought to prevent heart trouble, dropsy, and toothaches.

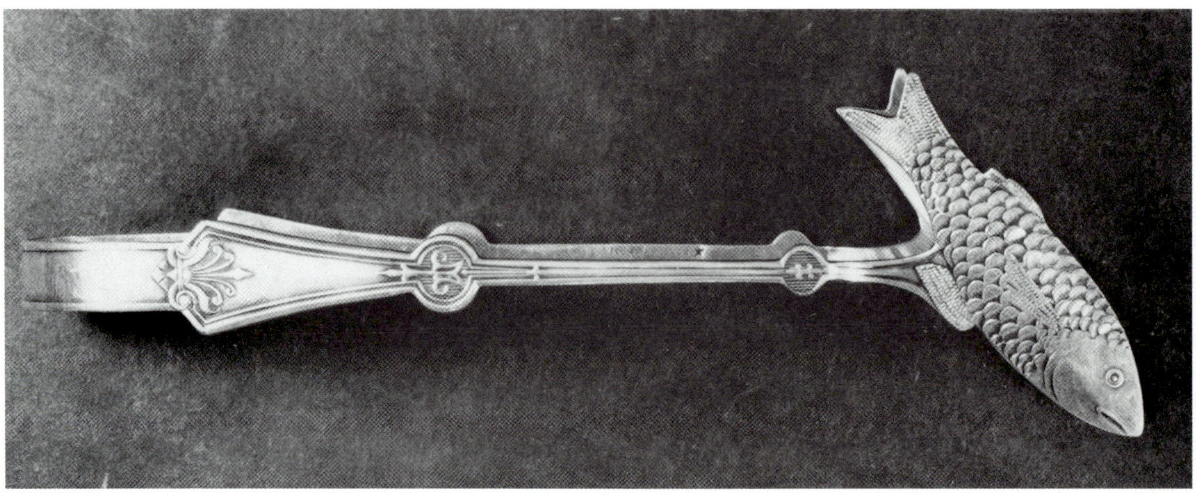

Sardine tongs. Persian pattern designed by Horace C. Wilcox for Meriden Britannia Co. Marked: (Star) Rogers & Bro. Al, c.1870. *Photo: Judy Redfield.* $185.

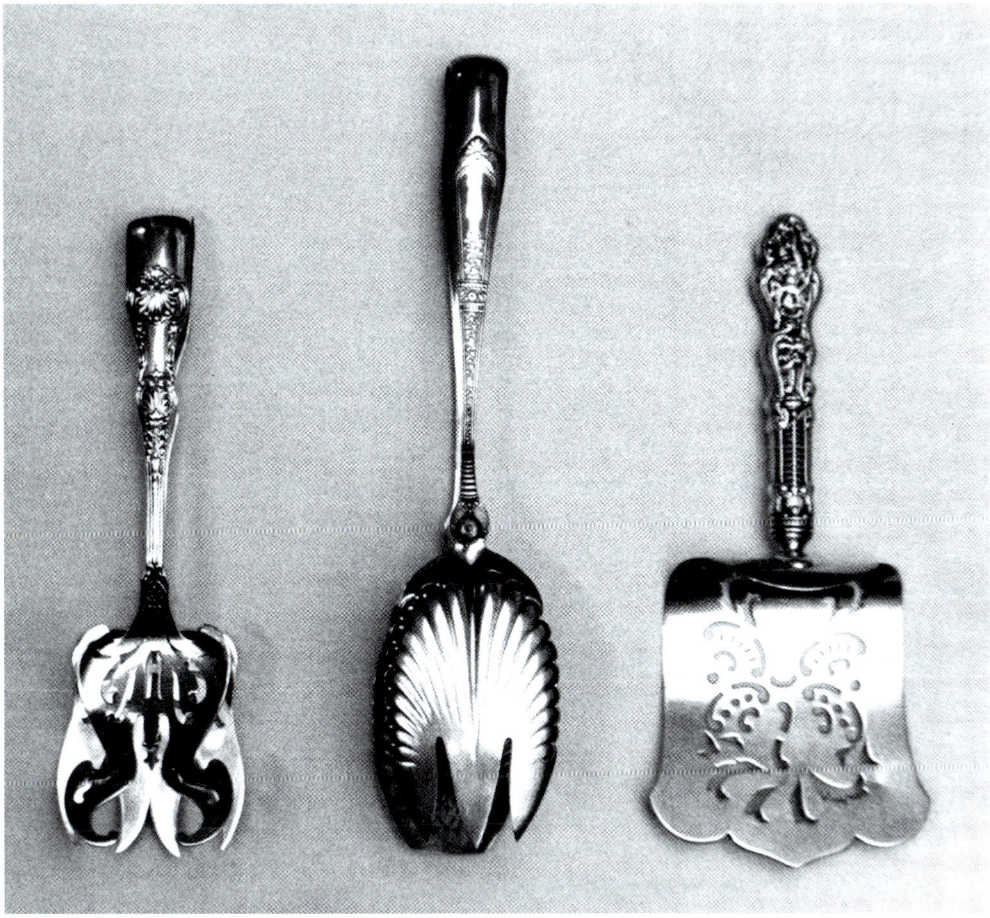

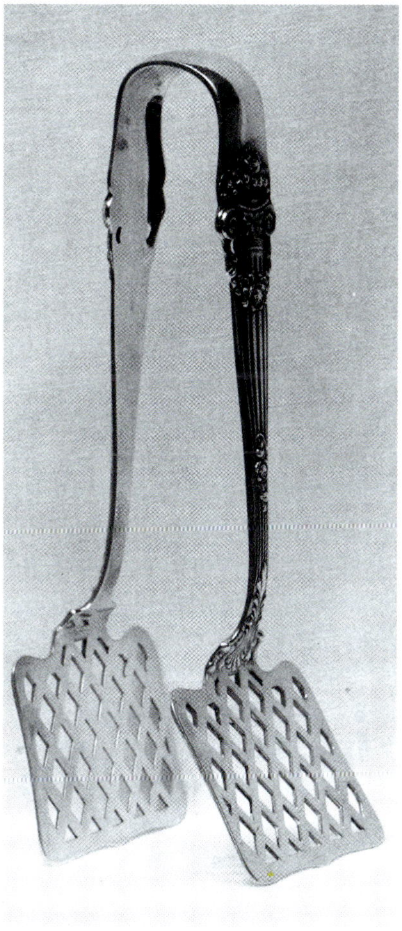

Three asparagus servers by Gorham. From left to right, King George pattern, Domestic (English style, and "hooded" style in Versailles pattern. According to Noel Turner in *American Silver Flatware, 1838-1910*, tongs were introduced in 1850, serving forks in 1855, the "hooded" style in 1890, and individual tongs in 1895. *Photo: Silver Magazine Archives.* $175+ each.

Asparagus serving tongs in Towle's Georgian pattern. since vegetables were known by the Romans as early as 200 B.C., asparagus probably came to the New World with early travelers. *Photo: Silver Magazine Archives.*

Silverplated tongs. No marks. Length 6". $50.

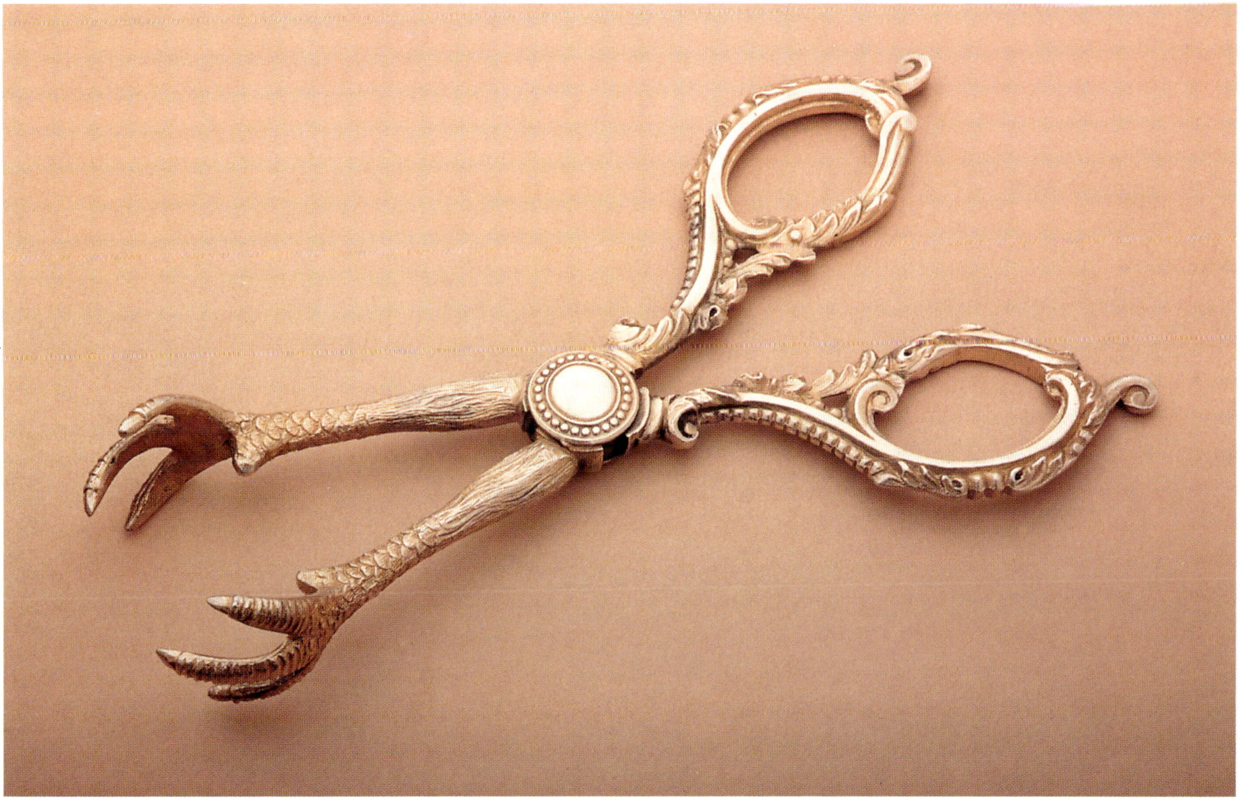

Coin condiment sets

When we hear the words "coin silver," our first thought is of silver coins melted down and then fashioned into useful or decorative objects. There is another use in which the term applies equally, that in which intact coins form parts of spoons, ladles, belts, bracelets, and many other items, such as the condiment set shown here. Coins from many countries were used; and often they were coins which, through changes in government, were no longer legal tender.

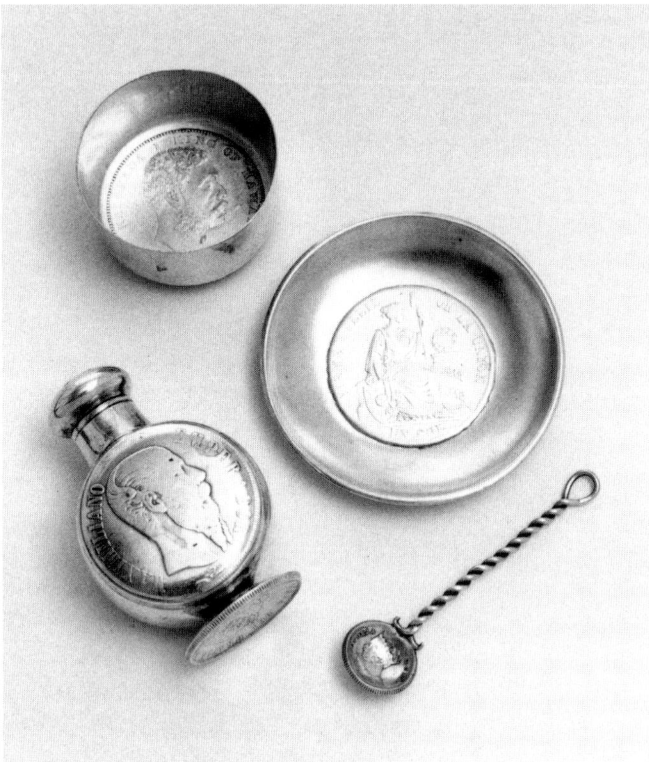

Coin condiment set. Top left: Salt dish with Hawaiian coin in tho bottom, 1-1/8: d Middle: Dish, 2-5/8" d. Lower left: Pepper shaker with coin side. Lower right: Salt spoon with coin bowl, 2-3/4". *Private Collection. Photo: David Arky.*

The tray or dish has an 1882 *un sol* from Peru set in the center of the base. It is marked "9 DECIMOS," and "FERME Y FELIZ POR LA UNION."

One side of the pepper shaker has a coin with the words "MAXIMILIANO IMPERADOR" and a man's head facing right. It is so well worn that no other figures or legends are legible. The other side of the pepper shaker has the words, FERDIN VII DEI GRATIOS," and "18_." The man's head may have a laurel wreath tied with ribbons. It is too worn to be sure.

The base of the pepper shaker is composed of a coin from Canada with the inscription, "DEI GRATIA REGINA VICTORIA CANADA." Only the maple leaf wreath is visible on the other side.

The salt spoon has Queen Victoria in the bowl and "HONG-KONG 1885 TEN CENTS" and some Chinese characters.

The salt dish is composed of an Hawaiian "AKAHI DALA" (Hawaiian one dollar). "KALAKAUA I, KING OF HAWAII," and the date 1883 are on the coin. On the other side is the Hawaiian coat-of-arms and the slogan, "UA MAU KE EA O KA AINA I KA PONO," (The life of the land is preserved in righteousness.) By 1850 Hawaii was flooded with silver coins of many nations. In making remittances to the United States, where Hawaii did most of her buying and selling, loss by depreciation, the expense of shipping coins and the insurance were a strain on the island economy. In 1883 the Hawaiian government minted its own coins. The standard silver coins of the United States and those of the Hawaiian Kingdom became the only silver coins that were legal tender in Hawaii. Following annexation, the problem of silver coins came up again. After many trials and tribulations, an act of Congress provided for redemption of Hawaiian coins in United States' coins. After January 1, 1904, Kalakaua coins were no longer legal tender. Only a small portion showed up for redemption. Hundreds, perhaps thousands, of them were made into souvenirs.

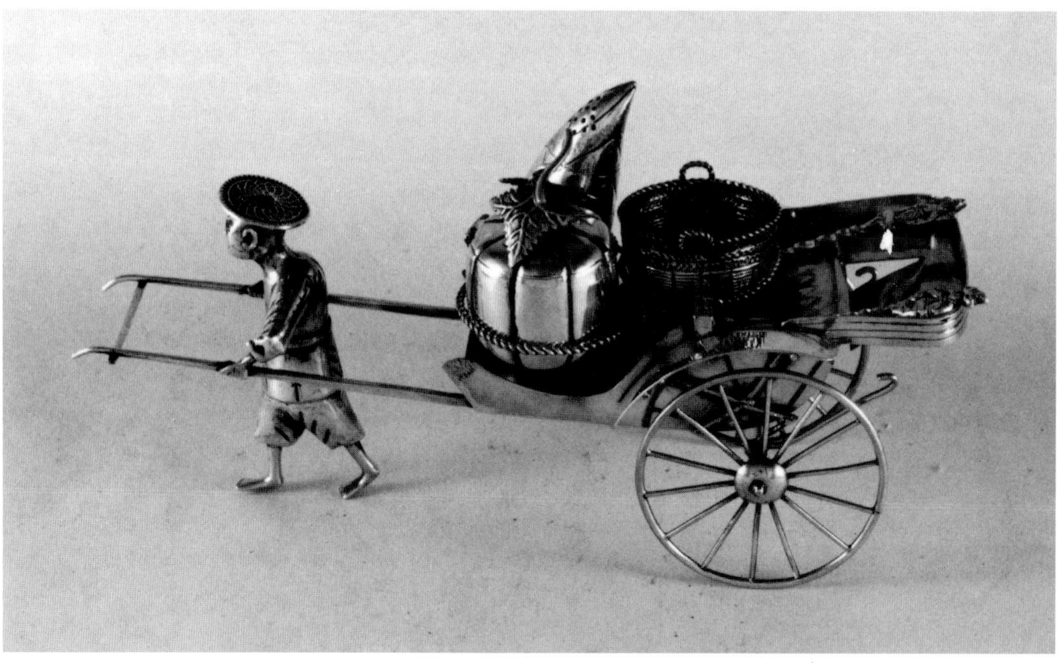

Condiment set designed as a Chinese ricksha marked LH in rectangle, ideogram in rectangle, 90 in rectangle. Made by Luen Hing c.late 19th century. Pepper shaker, covered container, open basket as well as two small spoons for mustard and salt. Set is completed with two wheels, shaft and coolie. Length 8-1/4". Height to top of pepper shaker 4-3/8". *Courtesy of Gebelein Silversmiths, East Arlington, Vermont.*

Chapter 12. Silver Curios for use...
...with Tobacco and Snuff

A puff of smoke...a pinch of snuff

The habit of smoking tobacco began with the natives of the Americas. The dried tobacco that Christopher Columbus carried back to Europe at the end of the fifteenth century was used mostly for medicinal purposes. It took nearly one hundred years and Sir Walter Raleigh to make smoking a habit in England. The habit spread to most countries in Europe.

The use of snuff, which is finely grated tobacco, became a habit with both rich and poor. It also created a need for snuff rasps and snuffboxes. The snuff rasps were used to grate the tobacco very fine. Snuffboxes with or without rasps soon became ornamental objects which fit into the user's pocket.

Smoking pipes, cigars, and cigarettes were addictive habits by the middle of the nineteenth century. The first manufactured cigarettes were made in Austria in 1865.

At the beginning of the twentieth century, tobacco was being smoked in pipes and as cigars and cigarettes by growing numbers of people. Smokers used silver lighters, boxes for vestas (matches), and cigarette and tobacco cases. Every residence and office had many ashtrays, some of which were silver or silverplate.

Today, at the end of the twentieth century, the habit of smoking is frowned upon by both the medical community and government agencies. It is perceived by many as an addictive habit which kills its users. However, smoking has left us a plethora of silver collectibles from large silver cigar holders to pocket-sized silver snuffboxes.

Tobacco in the form of snuff

The practice of snuff-taking was introduced into Europe from America during the sixteenth century. By the eighteenth it had become quite common on the continent and in England. The capture of a large quantity of snuff by Sir George Rooke in Vigo Bay (Battle of Vigo Bay, Spain, 1792) made it readily available and the practice became widespread throughout England.

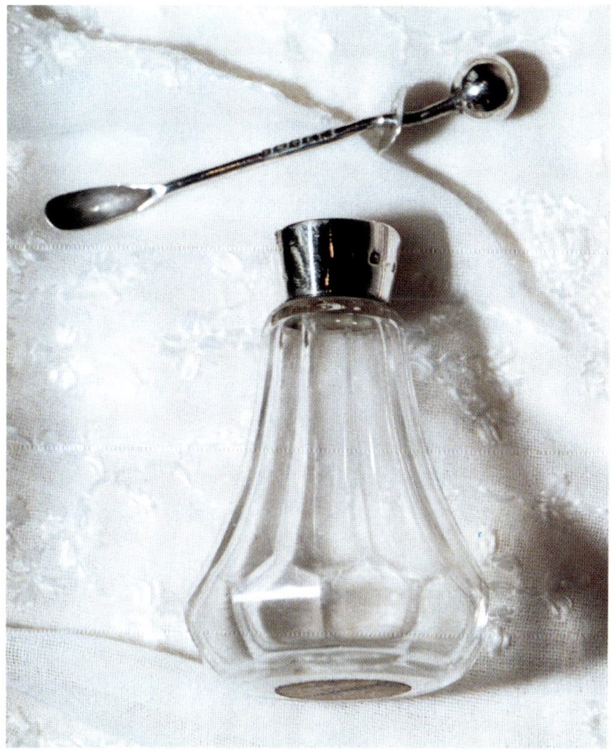

English glass snuff bottle with silver collar and snuff spoon. Closed bottle measures 2-1/4". Spoon measures 2-1/2". Date letter 1906. *Collection and photo: Anne Jansen.*

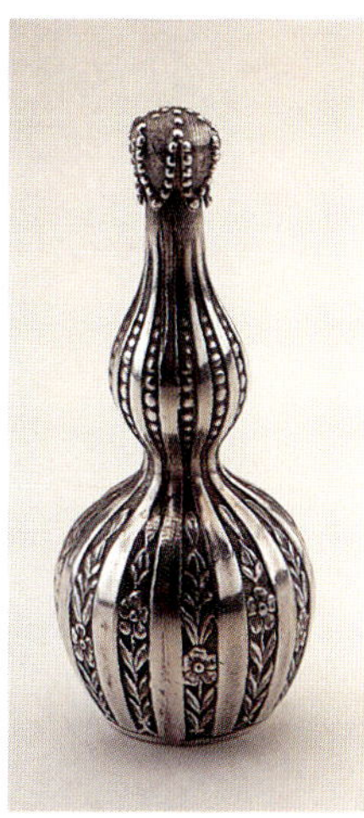

Snuff bottle marked Patent Pending Sterling 925. Another illegible mark in a circle. Take off the lid to reveal a tiny spoon. Measures 2" tall. *Private Collection. Photo: Bruce Waters.*

Snuff boxes were made in great quantities out of silver and gold and were often set with precious stones. Many were small ones to be carried in the pocket. They were often in an *etui* that included a tiny spoon for taking up a pinch of snuff without soiling the fingers. Table-top boxes were also accompanied by small spoon with which one could refill the pocket box.

Snuff boxes had hinged lids to allow the snuff user to perform the one-handed ritual of taking a pinch of snuff. This was done in hopes he could close the lid before be sneezed. The rather complicated ritual was as follows: "After the snuffbox was drawn from the pocket by the left hand, the fingers of the right hand gave the cover three taps, then the box was opened and a pinch of snuff placed on the back of the left hand or on the thumb nail enclosed by the forefinger and so inhaled."

In China, as early as the seventeenth century, the aristocracy carried snuff in beautifully decorated bottles. Each bottle had a spoon attached to the stopper which was used for dipping out the snuff and inhaling. These were made in a wide variety of materials such as jade, bronze, gold and silver and are considered works of art today.

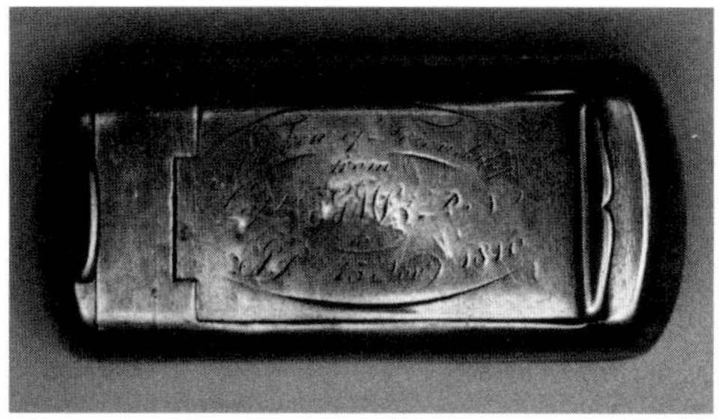

Combination snuff box and vinaigrette. Curved slightly and inscribed, "A Token of Friendship from Capt. G. M. L.(?), R. N. to L. L. 15 Nov. 1810." The hallmarks indicate that it was made in Birmingham in 1808 by Matthew Linwood V.
Matthew Linwood V (1754-?) was the eldest son of the seven children of Matthew IV (a silver plater) and Hannah Meredith Linwood. From c.1766 to 1767 he was apprenticed to Joseph Hunt. Matthew Linwood V was known as the "Box maker." His son, the last Matthew, helped him until 1815 when he left Birmingham and went to London. Matthew V's workshop produced some of the finest boxes ever made in Birmingham. Size: 2-3/8" long. *Private Collection. Photo: H Ivan Rainwater*. $300 to 390.

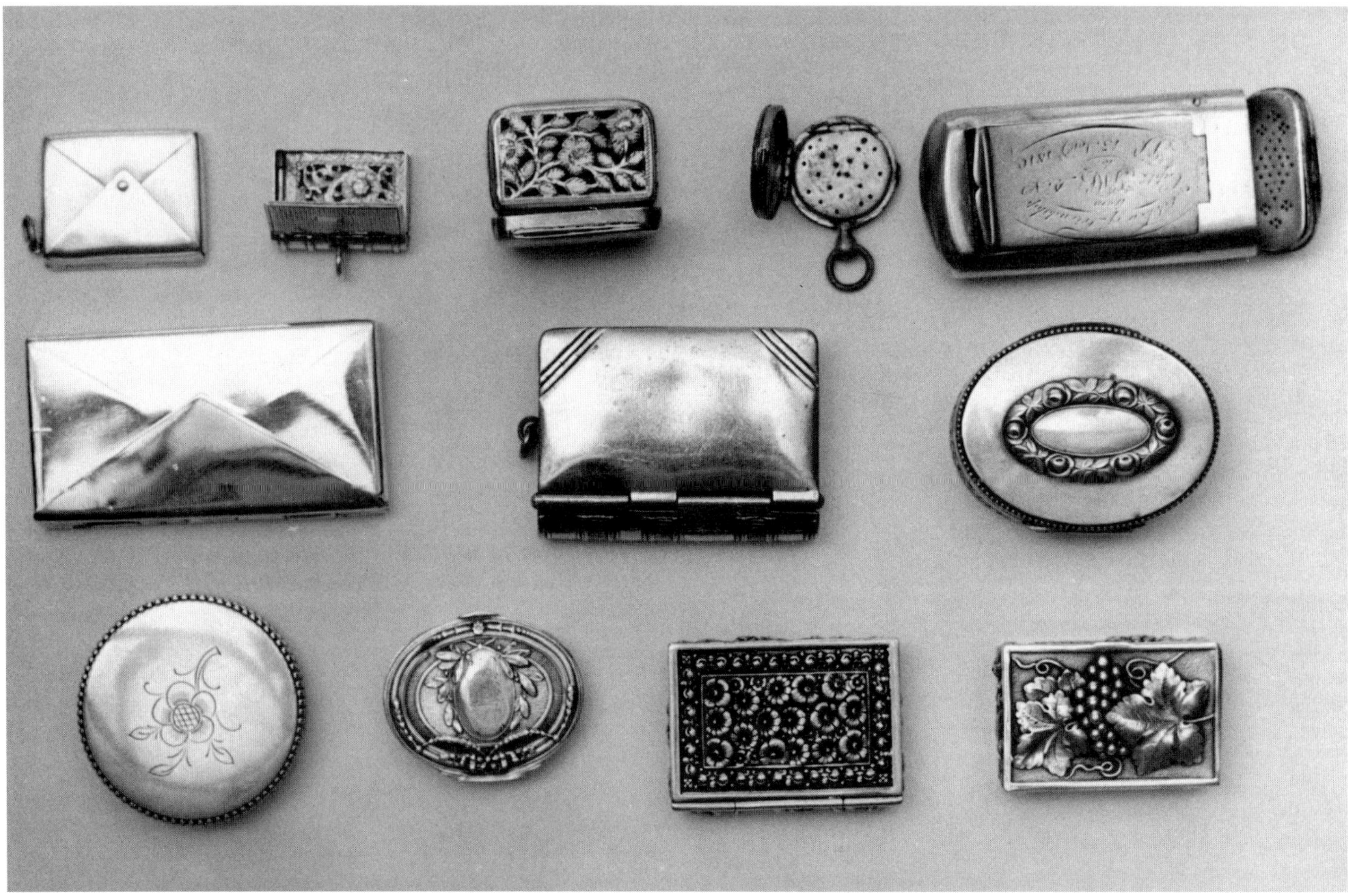

Group of snuff or pill boxes and vinaigrettes. *Private Collection. Photo: H Ivan Rainwater*. Snuff boxes silverplate $65, sterling $500.

Cigar accessories

Cigars are formed as a small roll of tobacco leaf. The people who do this consider themselves experts, not just factory workers.

Certain rituals accompanied cigar smoking. For instance, the cutting off the end of the cigar before lighting up. Until cigar makers made cigars with both ends open, it was necessary to remove a bit of the sealed end in order to draw the smoke into the mouth.

Silver cigar cutters were made by several American silver manufacturers. Unger Bros. made them in rather ornate designs. Daniel Low & Company, not manufacturers themselves, included them in their catalogues alongside court plaster cases, pipe cleaners, cigar box openers, nail file cases, stamp cases, whistles, toothpick cases, pocket combs and smokers' knives. All were made in elaborate designs.

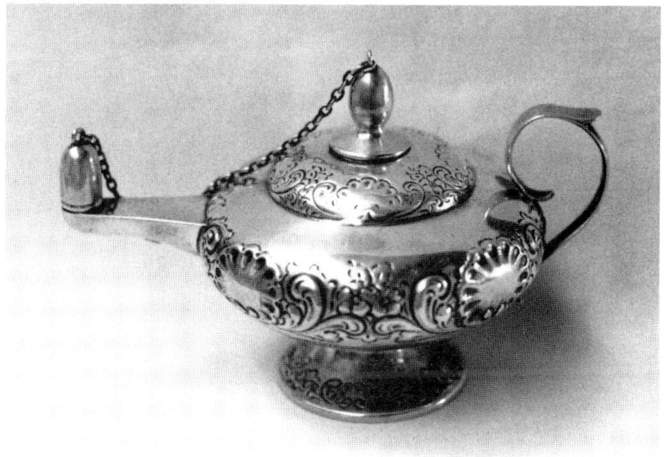

Alcohol lamp or cigar lighter. 2-7/8". Maker: B. Starr c.1890. *Photo: Courtesy of Silver Magazine Archives*. $75.

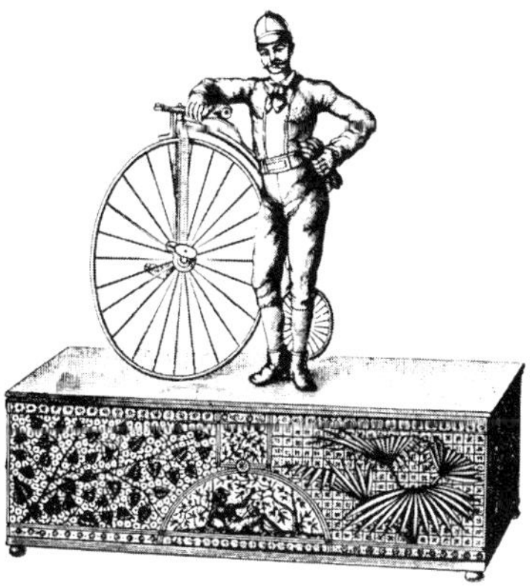

No. 23. For 50 Cigars.

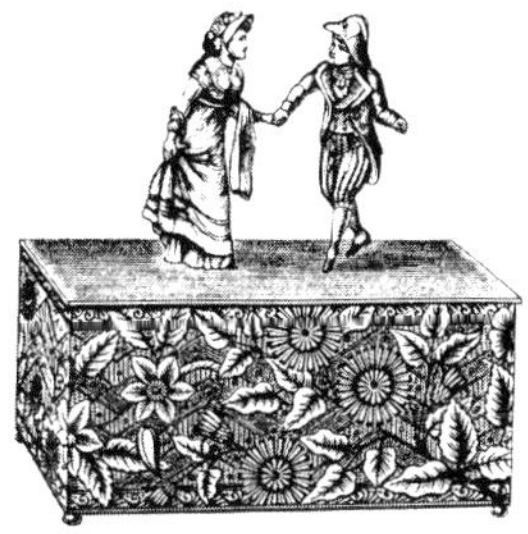

No. 24. For 25 Cigars.
Old Silver, . $12.00 (REAP).

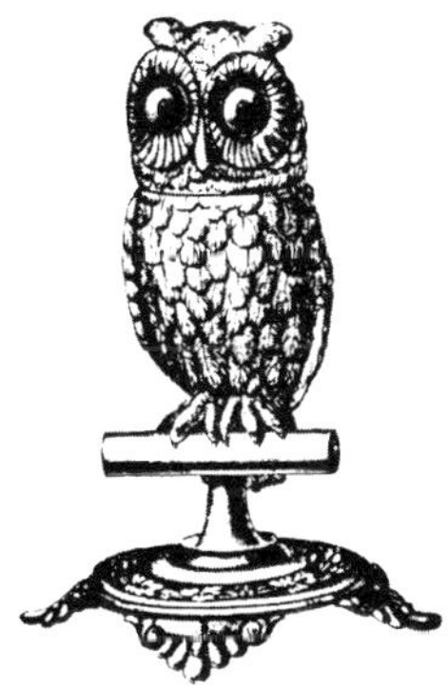

No. 46. CIGAR LAMP.
Old Copper, . $5.00 (PROMOTE).
Old Silver, . 5.50 (PROMOTER).

Cigar lamp in shape of an owl. Available in Old Copper and Old Silver. Meriden Britannia Co. catalogue, 1886. $125.

Silverplate cigar boxes for 25 and 50 cigars. Meriden Britannia, 1886-1887.

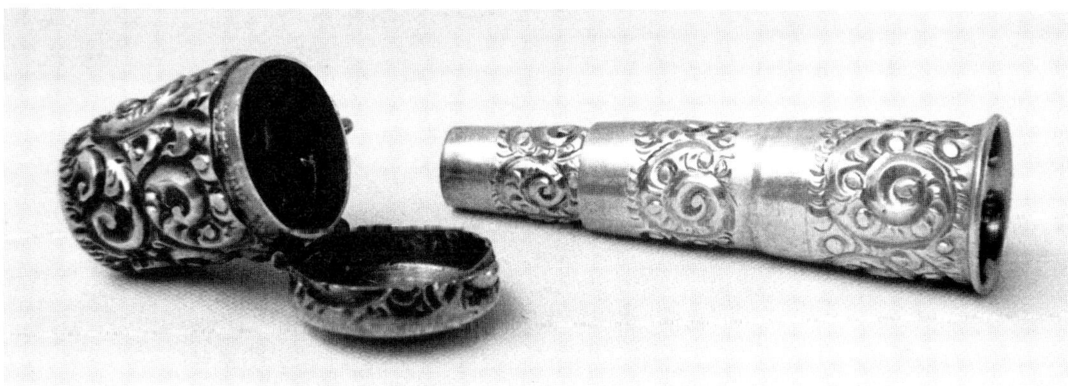

Collapsible cigar holder and case. Pocket sized case has badly worn marks. Probably American c.1910. *Courtesy of Silver Magazine Archives*. $95.

CIGAR CUTTERS

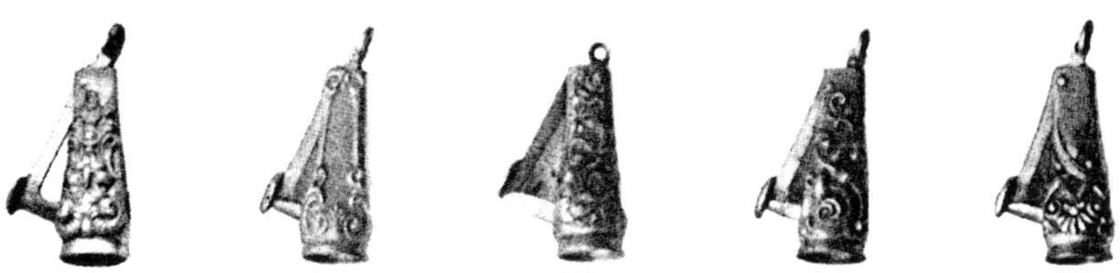

Sterling cigar cutters by Unger Brothers. The ornate designs are typical of the work done by this firm. Cigar cutters were used to make a hole in the end of the cigar for easier drawing. They were produced in both Britain and the United States in the middle of the nineteenth century when larger cigars became fashionable.

Match safes, also known as Vestas or Fuses

The first really practical friction matches were made in Stockton-in-Trees, England, in 1827 by an apothecary, John Walter. Wooden or cardboard sticks were coated with antimony sulfide, potassium chlorate, gum, and starch. The sticks measured three inches long and were ignited by being drawn through a pleat of glass paper.

In 1830, phosphorus was substituted for antimony sulfide as an ingredient for match heads. However, this made matches deadly poisonous. It was not until 1911 that William A. Fairburn of the Diamond Match Company substituted harmless sesquisulphide of phosphorous and this dreadful occupational hazard was removed.

With the invention of the phosphorous friction match, a means of storing and carrying them was a logical development. The two-to-three inch long matchboxes, now called match safes, did not appear in catalogues in great numbers until the 1890s.

Match safes were frequently carried in a pocket by the smoker. They had to be small. However, they could be decorated with cherubs, nude ladies, floral designs or sporting motifs such as the horse and rider at the hunt or the fish that got away. The one thing they all had in common, whether sterling or silverplated, was that somewhere they had a rough surface on which to strike the matches kept inside.

By 1910, pocket lighters began to replace the friction match. Pocket lighters became the way to light up either cigars or cigarettes and the match safe was no longer a smoker's need.

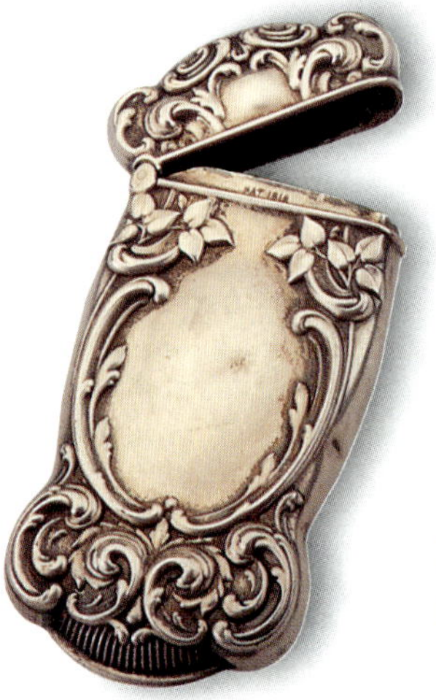

Silver match safe marked PAT 1918. Gorham Co. marks: lion, anchor and G. 2-3/4". *Collection of Antonia Moore. Photo: Bruce Waters*. $165 for silverplate to $275 for sterling.

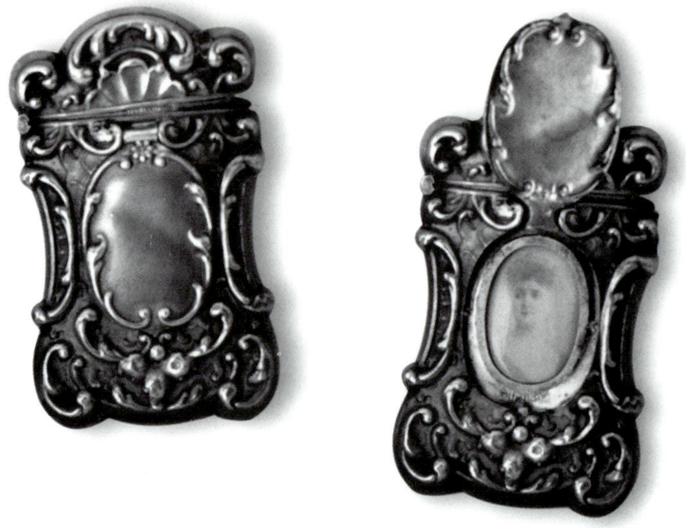

Match safe both closed and open. Pocket size measuring 1-1/2". Place for a lady's picture when open. c.1850. *Photo: Courtesy of Silver Magazine Archives*. $165 for silverplate to $275 sterling.

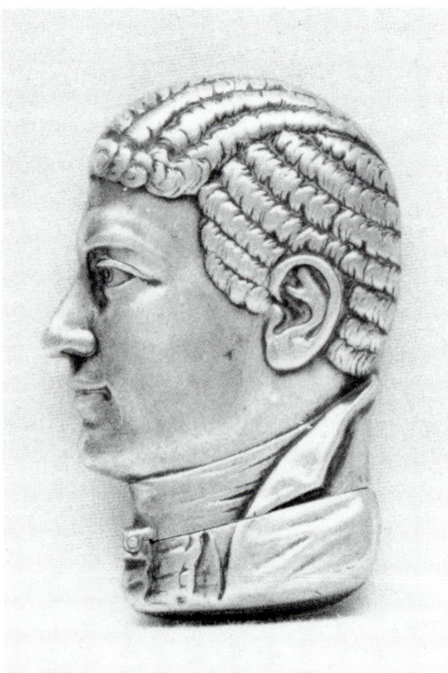

Pocket sized match safe in form of a man's head with striker on the bottom. *Photo: Courtesy of Silver Magazine Archives.* $165 for silverplate to $275 for sterling.

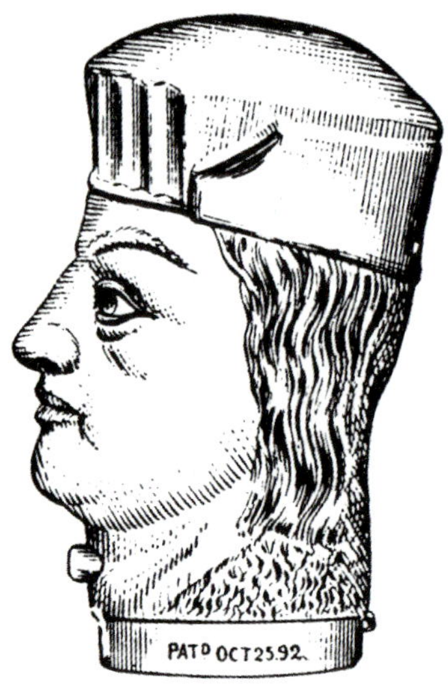

Match safe souvenir of World's Columbian Exposition in Chicago, 1893, as it appeared in *Jeweler's Weekly*, Dec. 7, 1892. Pat' d Oct. 25, 1892. $165 for silverplate to $275 for sterling.

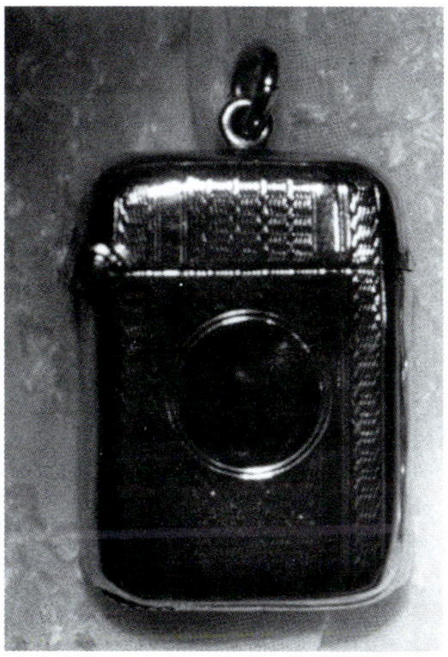

English silver match box, 1-3/4" by 1-1/4". Marked by J.W., Birmingham, 1903. *Collection and photo: Anne Jansen*. $60.

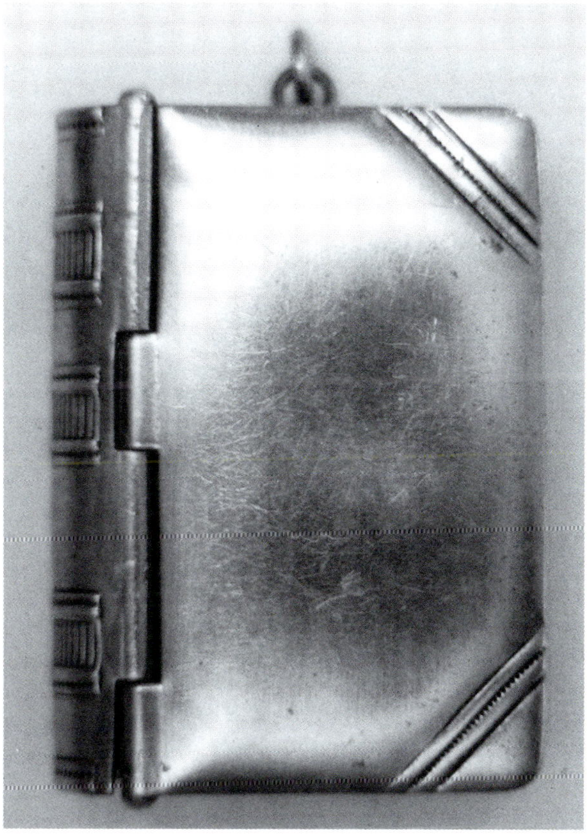

Box with two openings, one for stamps and one for Vesta matches. There is a "striker" on the edge. Silverplate, unmarked. 1-5/8" l. Modern stamps are too large to fit in this box. *Photo: H Ivan Rainwater*. $35 to 50.

Cigarette holders

The dictionary says that a cigarette is a narrow tube of cut tobacco enclosed in paper and designed for smoking. While many people enjoyed that habit of smoking, Queen Victoria did not. She prohibited any smoking within the precincts of Windsor Castle. Although Her Majesty did keep Windsor smoke-free, she did not deter the smokers of the day from indulging in the habit elsewhere.

By 1900, the smoking of cigarettes was a habit of women as well as men in Europe and the United States. As the world headed toward World War I, cigarette smoking increased. Some people used a cigarette holder to protect their fingers from the stain of tobacco.

By World War II, the smoking habit became even more widespread. "Lucky Strike Green has gone to war" did not stop smokers; it only changed the color for the pack they bought. A variety of cigarette holders can be found; many are made of silver.

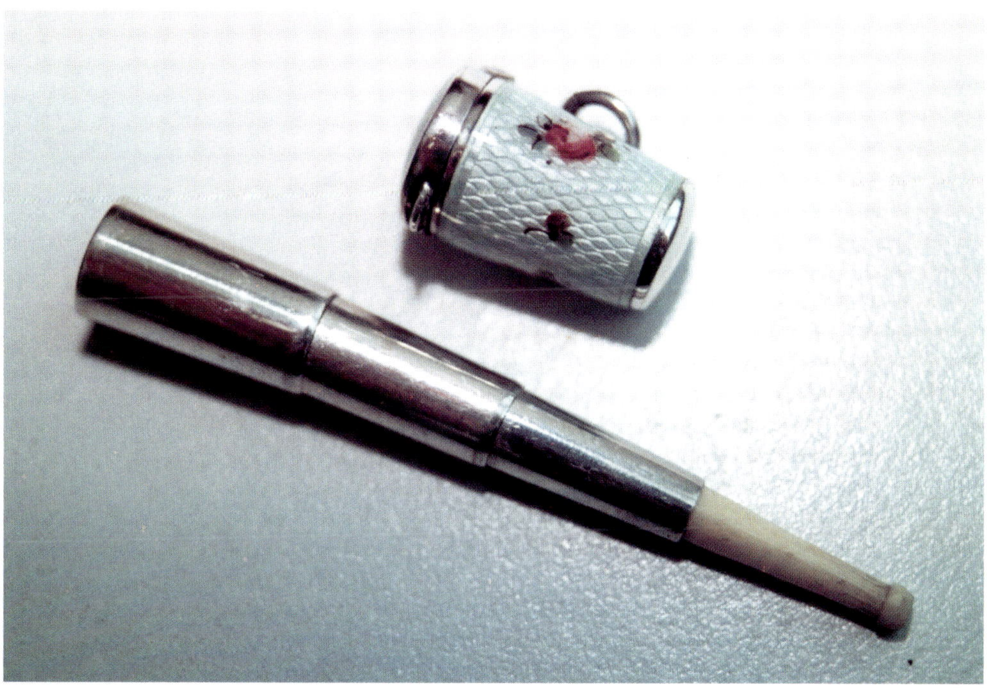

Collapsible ladies' cigarette holder with ivory tip in silver and its own hinged enamel case. Case is 3/4". Open holder measures 2-1/2". Collection of Edie Baker. *Photo: Pat Rich.* $225+.

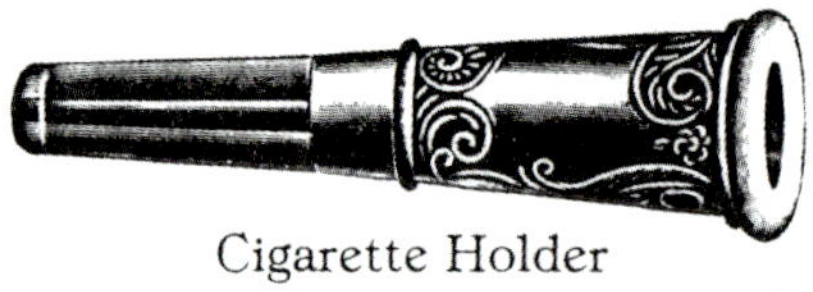

Sterling cigarette holder for the gentleman. From A I Hall and Sons, San Francisco, California. Catalogue of 1895-1896. $225+.

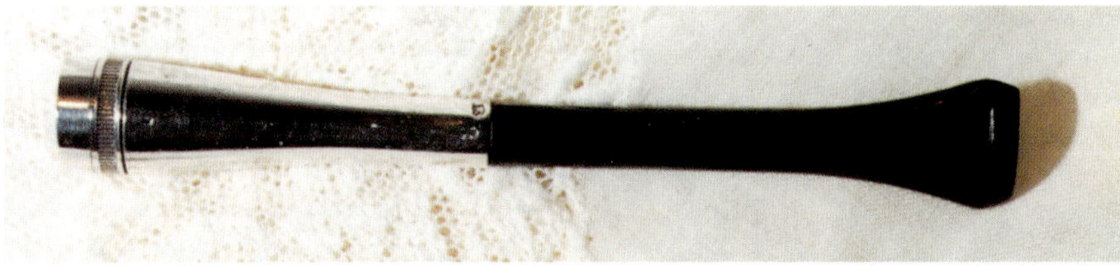

Dutch silver cigarette holder with dagger mark for silver used between 1906-1953. 3-1/4". *Collection and photo: Anne Jansen.* $225+.

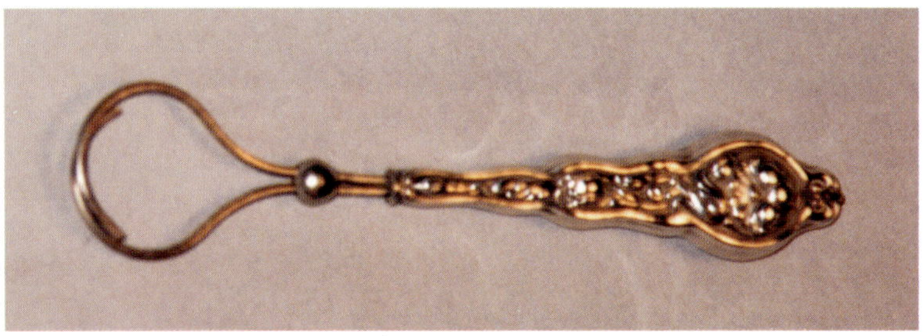

Cigarette holder with barrel slide and high floral relief handle. Sterling. 4-5/8". *Collection and photo: Don Weichert.* $225+.

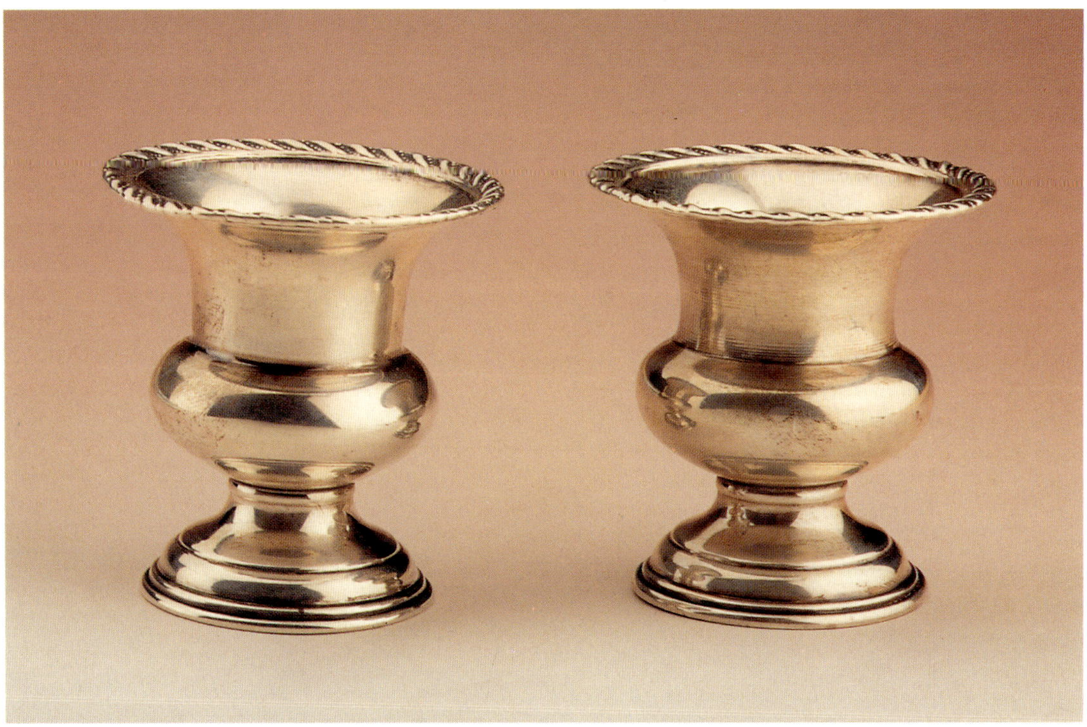

Pair of sterling cigarette urns by P.S. CO., c.1945. Each held ten cigarettes. 2-1/2" h. *Photo: Bruce Waters.*

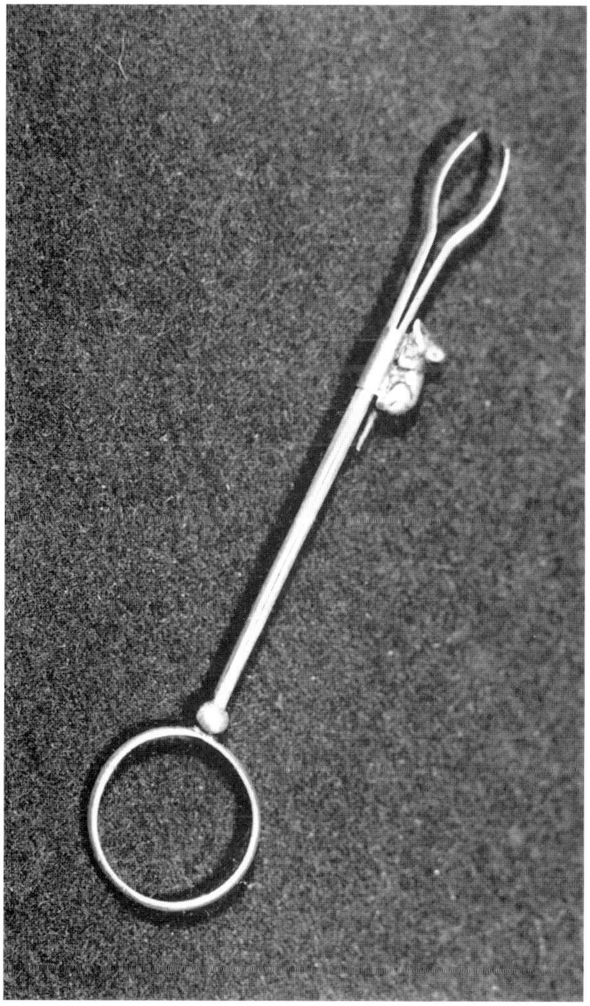

Lady's cigarette holder. Silver mouse slide pushes to open and close the holder. Measures 4". *Photo: Diane Pelham Burn.* \$225+.

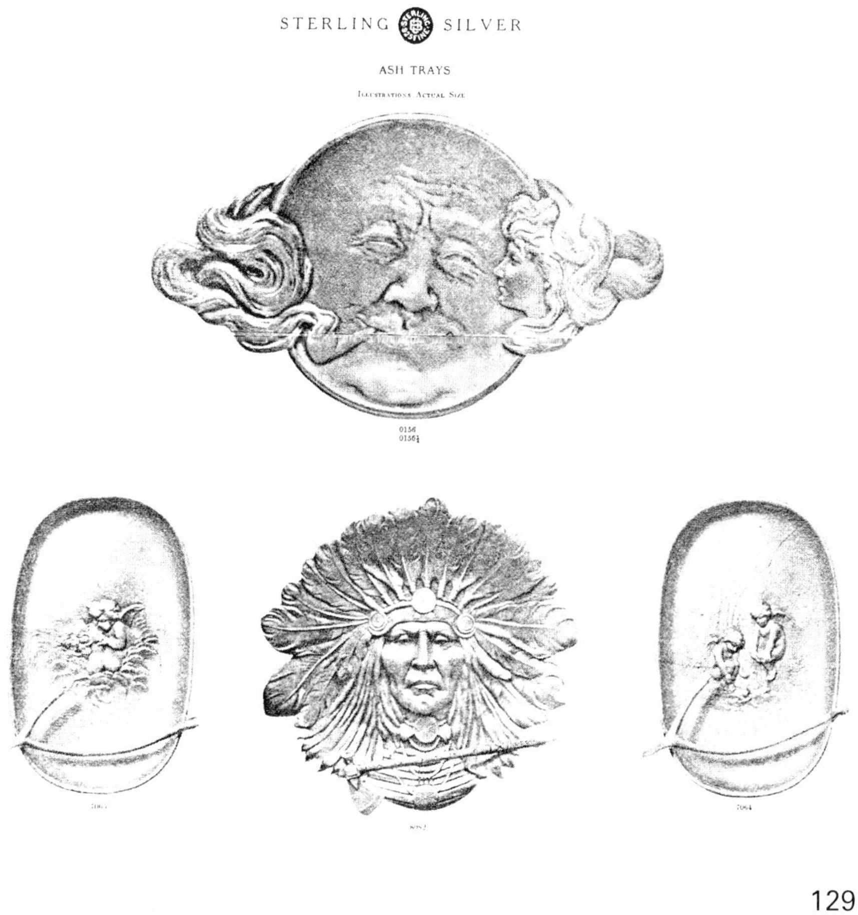

Four silver ash trays made by Unger Brothers Company of New Jersey as shown in their 1904 catalogue. The pipe-smoking man-in-the moon is on other items as well.

Chapter 13. Silver Curios for use...

... in the Nursery

When an heir or heiress apparent appears on the family scene, there is usually much celebration. Family and friends bestow such gifts as baby cups, spoons, and rattle to the newborn. The gifts are often made of silver or silverplate.

Godparents still give silver gifts to their godchildren. The heirlooms of tomorrow are found in catalogues of today. A sterling spoon and fork set with turquoise stone accents is an example. Prestigious firms like Tiffany offer a "baseball" feeding spoon in sterling which measures 5-1/2" long. A little girl might be fed with an Elsa Peretti "Padova" spoon from the same catalogue.

Many old christening sets include three or four pieces. A three-piece American set includes a mug, bowl, and underplate. Little Bo Peep is pictured on the pieces as are birds and letters of the alphabet. It dates to the late nineteenth century.

A christening set from France with a date letter of 1899 includes four pieces. They are a beaker, a napkin ring, a spoon, and a fork, all in a very attractive case. A set with English hallmarks includes a silver knife, fork and spoon all with mother-of-pearl handles and date to the mid-nineteenth century.

Ornate baby rattles come with bells, whistles, and teething rings. Some of these are silver while others are combined with coral or ivory. Nothing is too good for the new baby.

Children's gifts

Baby gifts such as a monogrammed baby cup (sometimes called child's mug) or a set of spoon and fork cutlery may not have been used immediately after the baby's birth. Many cherished spoons bear the mark of baby teeth. The knife and fork sets were used until the child was old enough to use adult silver.

Whether such gifts were silver or silverplate, the baby who used them to beat on a high chair tray had a lot of fun.

Advertisements from the mid-nineteenth century until today bring out the importance of silverware as gifts for children. The Gorham Company, Tiffany, Young and Ellis included "Children's Sets" in their advertising. Towle Silversmiths and Samuel Kirk & Company were among those who advertised children's silverware. Advertisements in the Jewelers Circular in 1878 included: For Children: Cups, napkin rings, bowls, porringers, pap boats, cup sets, plates, knife, fork and spoon. The child's christening set consisted of a bowl and plate, a mug, a spoon, knife and fork, a napkin ring and often an alcohol burner to keep food warm. Through the years other manufacturers have marketed similar articles for children as well as newly developed things such as the curved handle baby spoon by Reed & Barton c. 1888.

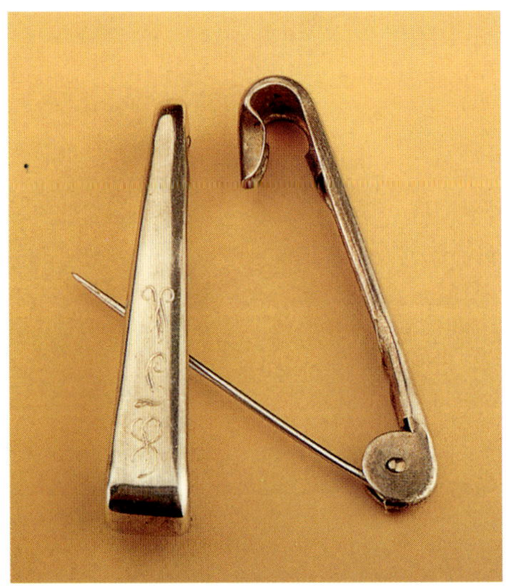

Silver diaper pins. No maker's mark. Both are monogrammed W L B. Measure 2". *Collection of Antonia Moore. Photo: Bruce Waters*. From $90.

Baby rattles

Noises in the form of rattles have been used to distract the crying baby for centuries. Many rattles of yesterday were made of sterling silver with bells attached and some came with a whistle and a piece of coral. It was not unusual for a rattle to be combined with bells, a whistle and a teething ring.

The collector of English silver rattles should look for a complete English hallmark to identify the year that rattle was made. In this country, silver rattles were made by well-known companies such as Gorham, Tiffany, Unger Brothers, and Kerr.

Figural rattles came into vogue towards the end of the nineteenth century. Nursery rhyme characters, animals as well as Kate Greenaway children were only some of the designs used then.

Be wary of reproductions. Silver rattles reproduced today should not command the same price as the earlier, original ones.

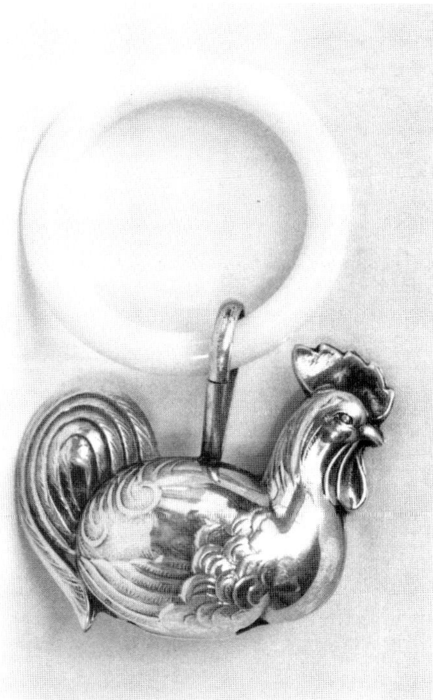

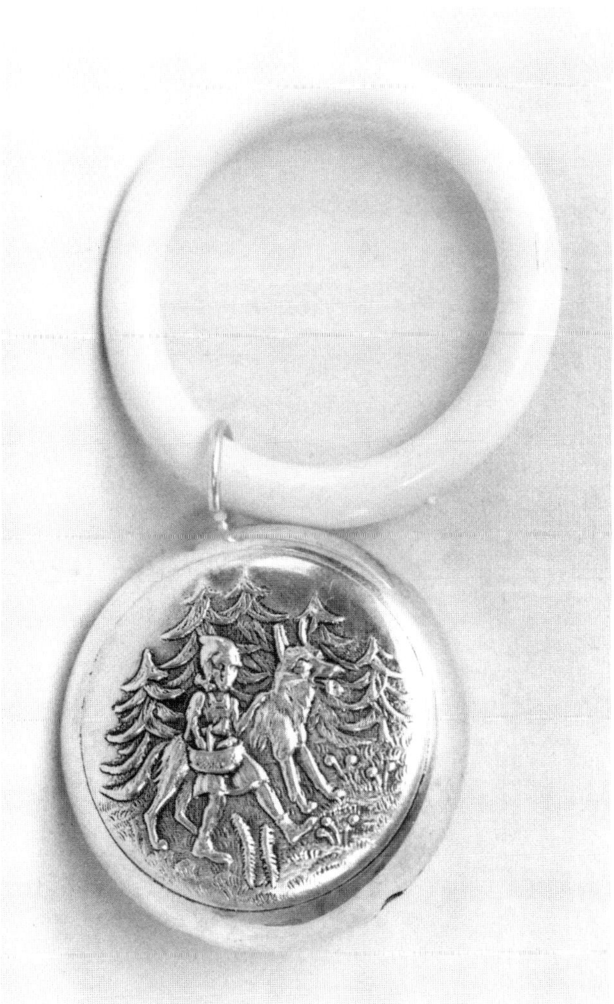

Two silver baby rattles with plastic rings. Left: shows Little Red Riding Hood and the Wolf.
Above: ever-popular rooster motif. *Photos: Courtesy of Silver Magazine Archives*. $75-150.

Children's cups

Cups small enough for use by children are usually of cylindrical shape and have only one handle. Their height is usually not more than 3" to 3-1/2". As christening cups, they have long been favorites of grandparents and fond aunts and uncles. During the early years of the nineteenth century many silversmiths were creating a wide variety of cups suitable for christening presentation. Some became caudal cups bearing a strap handle, soon to be modified to a cast C-scroll. One variation was the spout cup. The long curving spout made them ideal for getting liquid food down

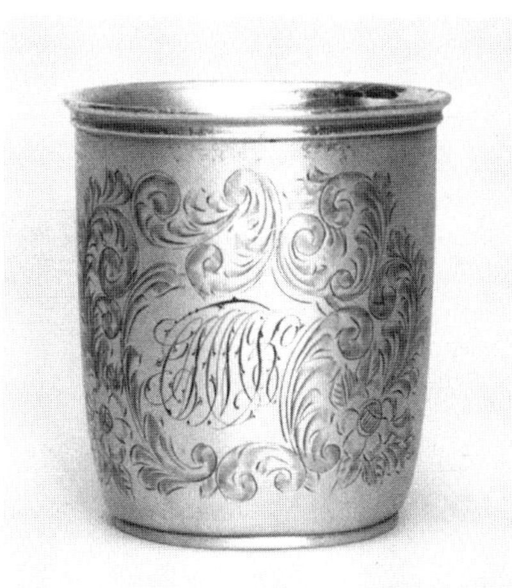

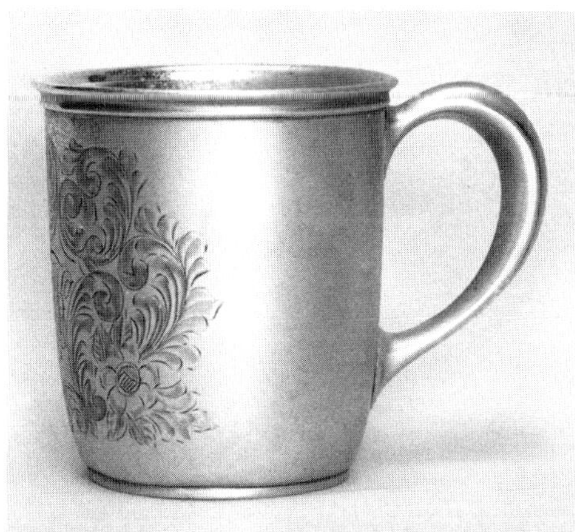

Left and above:
Sterling baby cup. Maker: Unger Bros. Monogrammed. *Private Collection. Photo: H Ivan Rainwater*. $85.

a reluctant child. Spout cups seem to have been primarily a New England form while the South preferred the pap boat.

Accustomed as we are to seeing Unger Brothers wares with their highly ornate rococo and somewhat later Art Nouveau decorations, it comes as a surprise to find a child's cup a model of restraint by comparison. Just the owner's initials are surrounded by feathery C-scrolls.

Another form which has been adapted to the production of children's cups is the basic beaker to which has been added a rim foot band. This nineteenth century form remains as popular today as the famous "mint julep cup" of the South.

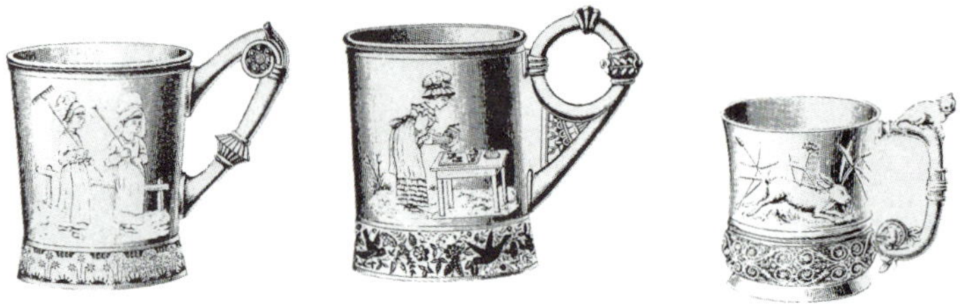

Three silverplate baby cups decorated with nursery rhyme figures. From Meriden Britannia Co. catalogue, 1886. $100.

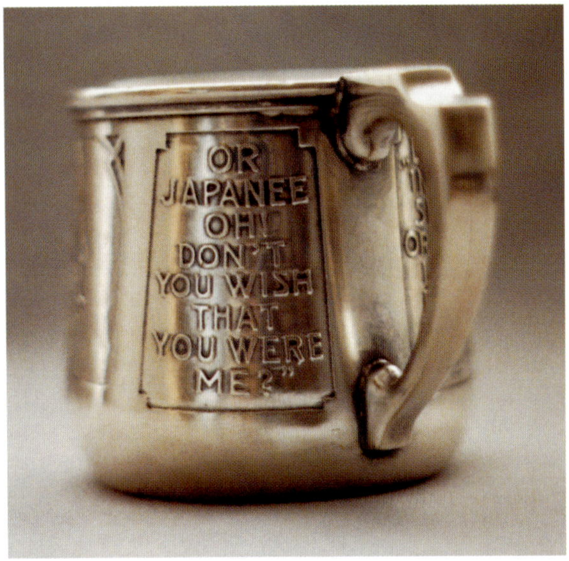

Child's silver mug. Maker: William B. Kerr & Co. Shows five children in their national costumes. Verse said by an American boy in sailor's suit and reads: LITTLE INDIAN, SIOUX OR CROW, LITTLE FROSTY ESKIMO, LITTLE TURK OR JAPANEE, OH DON'T YOU WISH THAT YOUR WERE ME? c.1900. *Silver collection of A. & D. Burstyn.* $110.

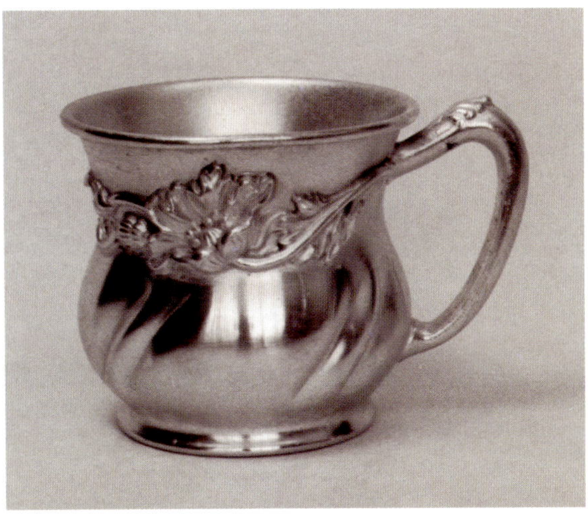

Child's cup made by Columbia Silver Co., Quadruple Plate, Portland, ME./1183. *Collection of Donna Felger. Photo: H Ivan Rainwater.*

This elaborate stork with Moses in the basket was NOT a cutting scissors. Rather, it was used to pick up cotton when needed in the nursery. Elaborate design, probably silver. *Photo: H Ivan Rainwater*.

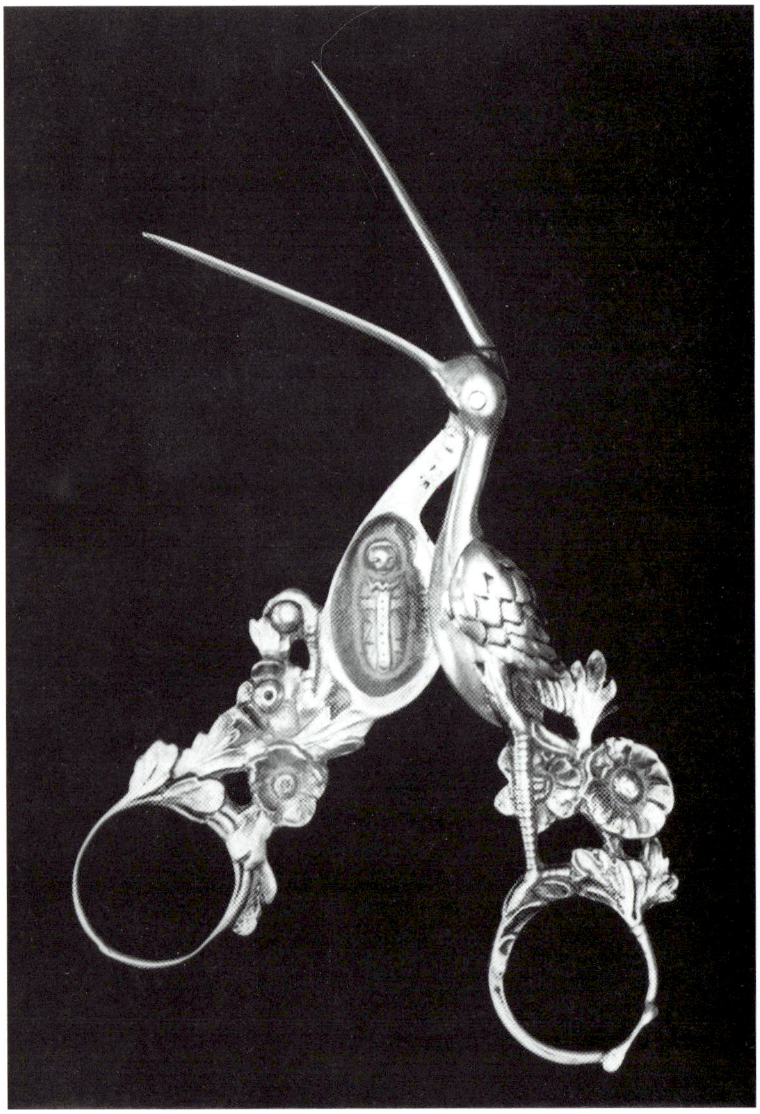

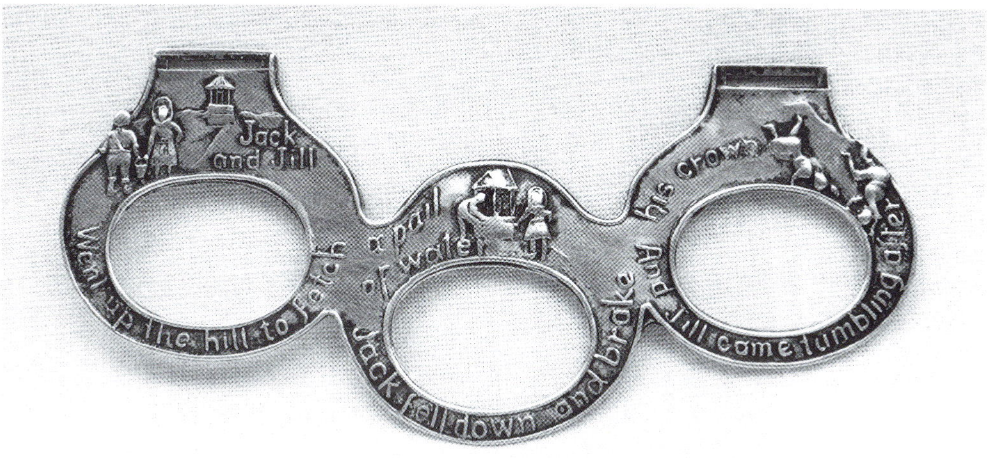

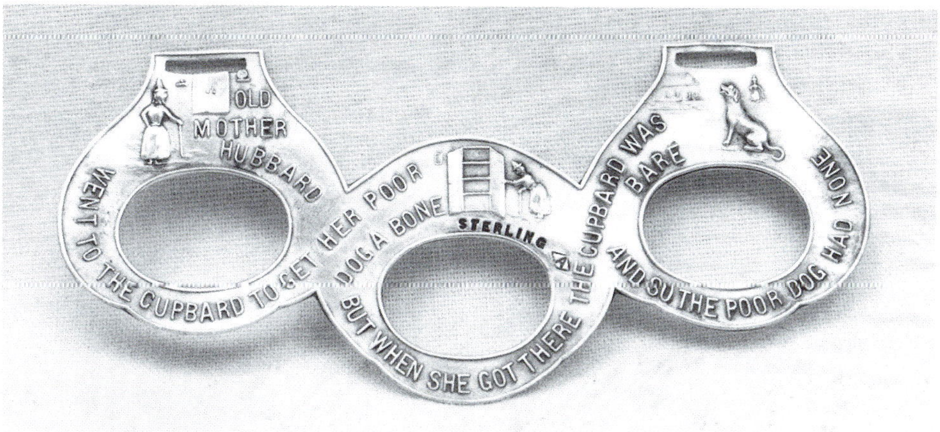

Sterling safety pin holders decorated with nursery rhymes from "Old Mother Hubbard" and "Jack and Jill." cost $1.50 each in Webster Company 1915-1916 catalogue. Width: 3-1/8". Kept the three most common sized safety pins separated for easy access. Were attached to apron or gown with ribbon. Truly a collectible as today's baby is not diapered with safety pins. *Photo: Courtesy of Silver Magazine Archives*.

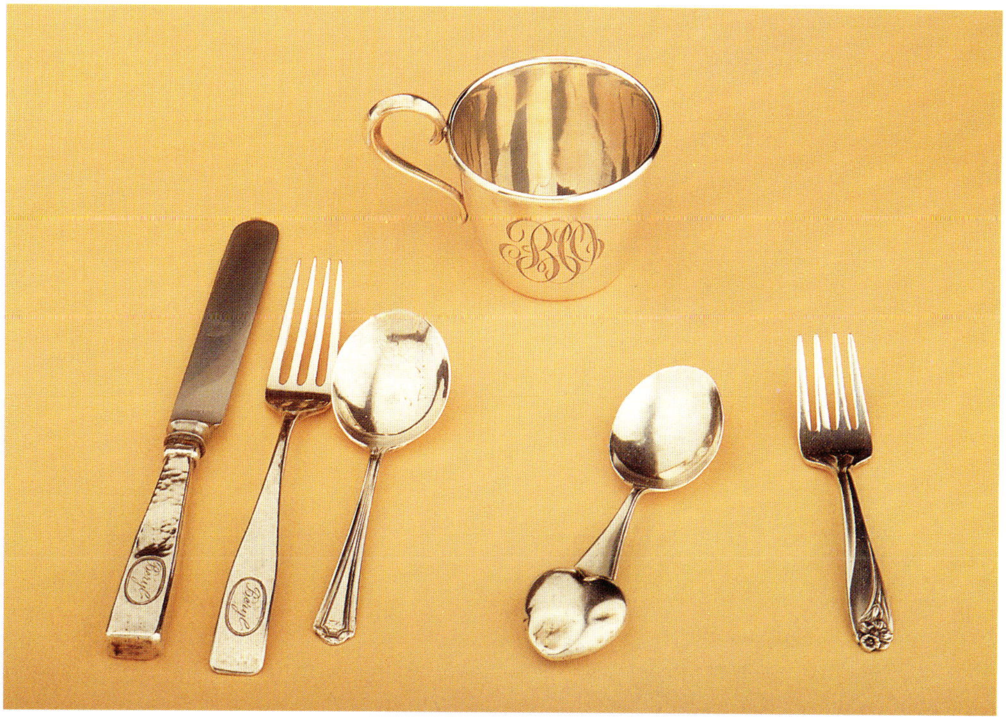

Silver for the fortunate baby. 1. Monogrammed baby cup. Marked Stieff, Sterling. Measures 2-1/2" from base to top of handle.
2. Child's knife and fork set marked Baltimore Silversmith's Mfg. co. Both are sterling 9/25/1000 FINE. Fork is 5-1/2" $35. Knife: 7-1/4" $85. c.1927.
3. Sterling baby spoon. $50. Pattern is possible Fairfax by Gorham. 1951.
4. Spoon with heart-shaped rattle on handle. Marked Webster, Sterling. Measures 4".
5. Baby fork. Marked 1847 Rogers Bros. Daffodil pattern. Measures 4-1/4". *Private Collection. Photo: Bruce Waters*.

Chapter 14. Silver Curios for use...
...to Hold Valuables

Boxes

Webster's Unabridged Dictionary lists the word *box* as derived from the Latin *buxus* which is derived from the Greek *pyxus*. *Buxus* refers to the evergreen shrub boxwood or box-treen which was introduced to Britain by the Romans and is well-known throughout Europe as a medium for spoons, combs, and other wooden carvings. But, many claim that the word really comes directly from the Greek *pyxus*, the shallow circular box which has, from medieval times, served to accommodate the consecrated Host in the Christian communion service. Another famous pyxus is the one used at Goldsmiths' Hall to collect random coins for assay. (See *Silver Magazine,* Jan/Feb. 1978 and Nov./DEC 1989.)

Boxes have been made from silver to serve many purposes. A partial listing includes vinaigrettes, snuff boxes, tooth powder boxes, tobacco boxes, patch boxes, counter boxes, pill boxes, card cases, stamp boxes, bougie boxes, rosary boxes, hairpin boxes, jewelry boxes and vesta boxes.

Early boxes tend to be plainer than later ones. Decoration on early boxes consisted generally in simple engraving of flowers and foliage or initials of the original owner. Later boxes were more ornate; decorations were of chased flowers and leaves, scrolls, fruit, and gems.

About 1830 a ring might be attached so that the box could be worn on a chain or chatelaine. Boxes of the 1840s were sometimes elaborately shaped. Among the box shapes found dating from 1790 to 1875 were acorns, balloons, bags, books, baskets of flowers, bottles, crowns, champagne bottles, cannons, creels, cornucopia, hearts, Maltese Crosses, snails, reticules, scarabs, ship's lanterns, padlocks, roses, shells, strawberries, thistles, turtles, and watches. Eric Delieb's *Investing in Silver* contains an in-depth discussion of boxes, their beginnings and history.

Left: Filigree rosary box. Marks 800 27 GE in a lozenge. Silver-gilt. Right: Oval box with floral swags. Marked: 92 French import mark for 1892. Widest dimension: 1-1/16". *Private Collection. Photo: H Ivan Rainwater*. $40 to 60.

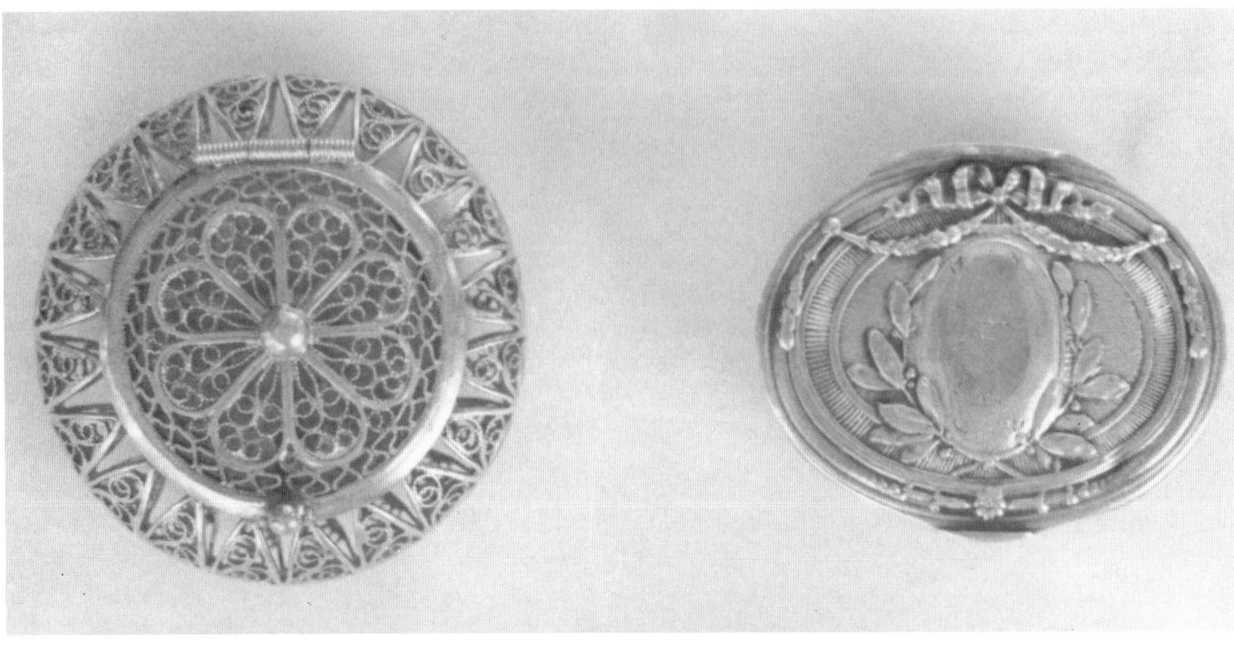

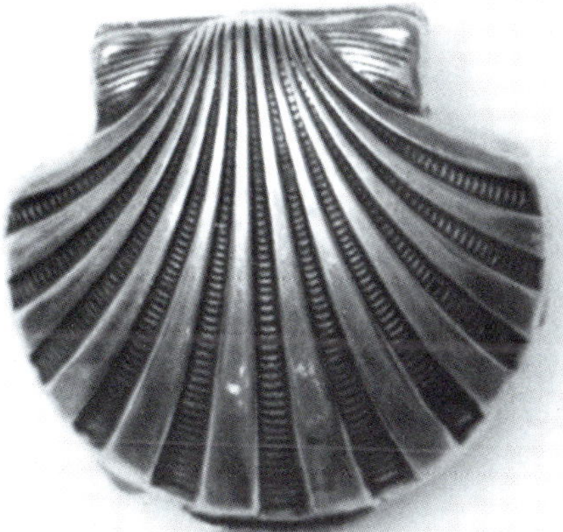

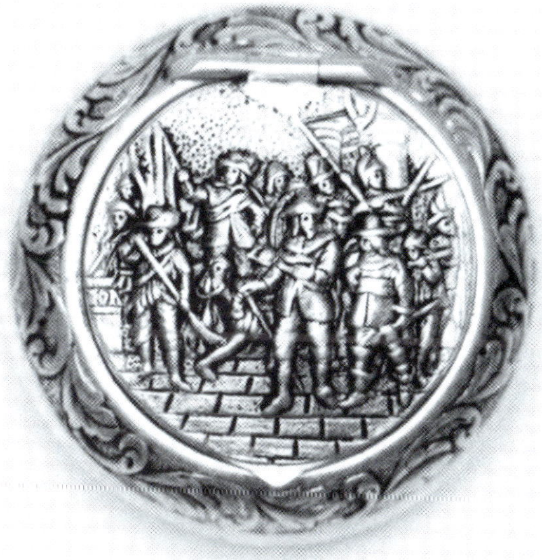

Left: Italian rosary box. Scattered marks 800 0 5. Purchased 1972 at Mondo Cattolico, Piazza Pio. XII. 12 Rome. Widest dimension 1-3/8" 35 mm.
Right: Pill box. No marks. Purchased Amsterdam 1972 1-7/8 48 mm. diameter. Scene is part of "The Night Watch" by Rembrandt *Private Collection. Photo: H Ivan Rainwater*. $35 to 50.

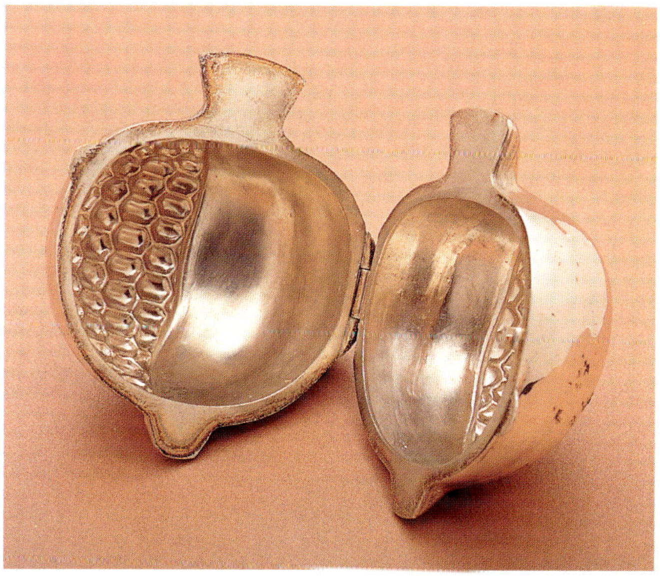

Rosary box in the form of a pomegranate. Diameter: 2". A paper oval tag inside reads, "Made in Italy/Saks Fifth Avenue."

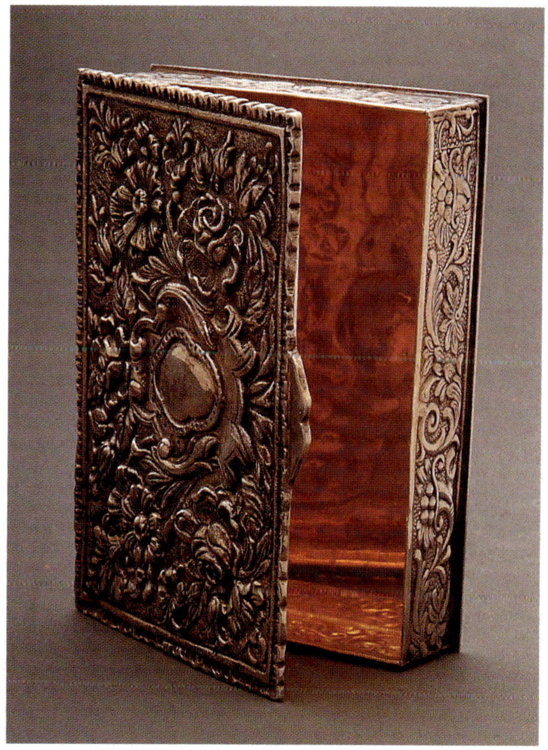

Trinket box. Marked: W Wallace 5831. Interior is gold-washed. Size: 3-1/4" by 2-7/16" by 3/4".

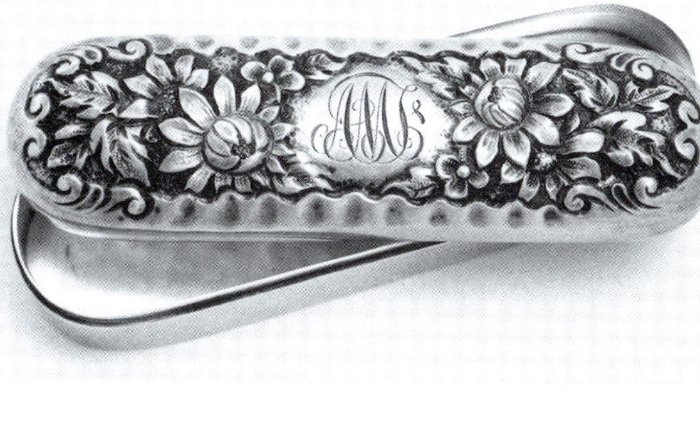

Hairpin box. Marked: Hamilton & Designer Sterling. c.1890-1900. Initials "A M" inscribed. Size: 3-1/2 by 1" by 3/4". *Private Collection. Photo: David Arky.*

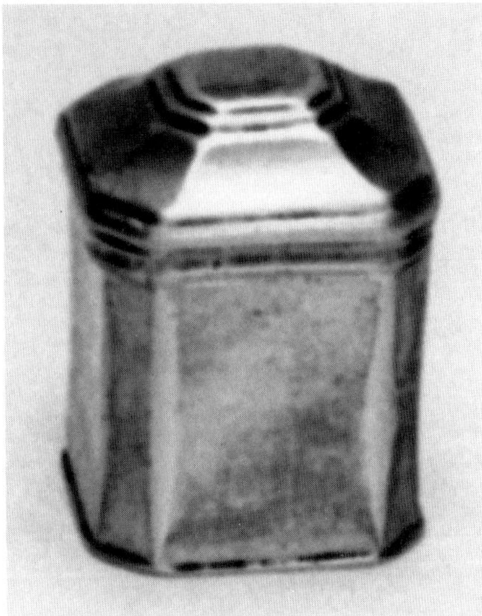

Silver box with hinged lid. Size: Height 1-3/16". Width 5/8". Two poorly stamped marks on bottom. Possibly Dutch. Marks show considerable wear as does the cover. Possibly used to hold game counters. *Private Collection. Photo: H Ivan Rainwater.*

Pomanders

The word "pomander" is from the old French *pomme d'ambre*, *pomme* being an "apple," and *amdre* or *ambergris* meaning "perfume." The original pomanders were scent balls produced by rolling a paste of aromatic substances into balls and wearing them suspended around the neck or at the waist. Men wore them, too, usually on a neck chain. These balls were thought to protect the wearer from the plague and fever, as well as being efficacious against obnoxious smells.

Today the term pomander is generally applied to the box in which the perfume is kept. As a prophylactic, the pomander is recorded as far back as 1800 B.C. in an Egyptian formula which contained various herbs including myrrh, frankincense, cyprus wood, and mastic. There were many combinations, some based on rosemary, roses, bugle-wort, rue, lavender, and lemon.

Some of the most unusual pomanders are the "segmented apple" type originally made around 1580 to 1600. They consisted usually of eight segments opening like the segments of an orange. The lower part was hinged and the ball was held together at the top by a circular cap. Each segment contained a different perfume and sometimes would bear the name of the scent. The lower part often held a tiny compartment holding a small sponge for an aromatic vinegar—in other words, a tiny vinaigrette. Not many pomanders of this type have survived today. The term "collectible" can scarcely be applied to them as there are so few in number and they are priced far beyond the means of most people.

Far simpler types of pomanders were small round boxes made in two parts, an opening across the middle for admission of a ball of perfume. In some cases both sides of the box were pierced to enable the scent to escape.

Pomanders were often carried by ladies through the fourteenth century to the seventeenth, and probably earlier. Men carried pomanders as well, but by the seventeenth century men who did were regarded as effeminate. Of the surviving pomanders, most were made in Holland and Germany. Many were made in England around 1580; they are rare after 1630. Eventually, by the nineteenth century, the pomander gave way in popularity to the vinaigrette.

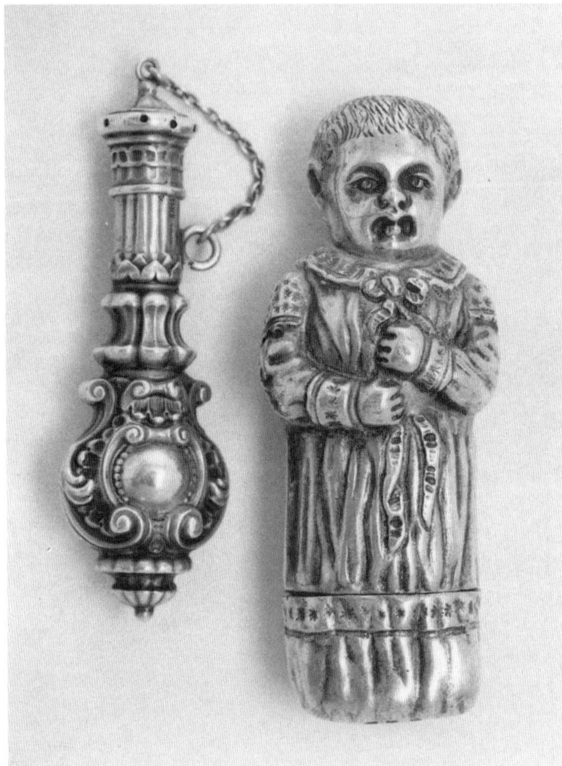

Left: Perfumer with chain to attach to chatelaine. Marked: Fleur-des-lis (mark in use by 1892) for William B. Kerr Co., Length: 2-3/4". $75 to 125.
Right: Pomander in the form of a child dressed in a long gown with ruffled collar and tied at the throat with a bow and long streamers. Sixteen small holes in the form of an irregular pointed oval are on the detachable bottom to allow the escape of the scent. There are traces of two marks. One is a five-pointed star with a pellet inside. The other is badly struck and consists of a hexagon whose interior is not clear. Length 2-1/2". $175 to 225.
England was one of the greatest producers of pomanders. Possibly the pomander reached that country from France. Bearing out this theory is the fact that pomander is a combination of two French words "pomme"—an apple— and "ambre"—ambergris, an often used ingredient. *Private Collection. Photo: David Arky.*

Vinaigrettes

Because of poor sanitation and the foul odors which confronted sensitive noses, an aromatic orange, carried in the hand, was for centuries the only safe-guard against unpleasant odors. These led to the development of pomanders (see above) which began with scent balls of aromatic substances and led to the development of little box-like containers made from a variety of materials.

Vinaigrettes, which evolved from the pomander, were for many years quite small, just one of the compartments of the pomander. Most of them found today were made between 1780 and 1880. The name vinaigrette was first used about 1801. The word itself has been the source of some confusion because of the association today with the kitchen variety of vinegar. In this case, the vinegar used in these boxes was an acetic acid-based liquid enriched with concentrated perfume oils. One composition was 95% acetic, plus oils of flowers and spices, rosemary, thyme, lavender, verbena, cinnamon and cloves. Further improvements were made in commercial aromatic vinegars in the 1820s. While early vinaigrettes were carried in the pocket or bag, by 1830 they were provided with a tiny eye or loop to which was attached a small chain.

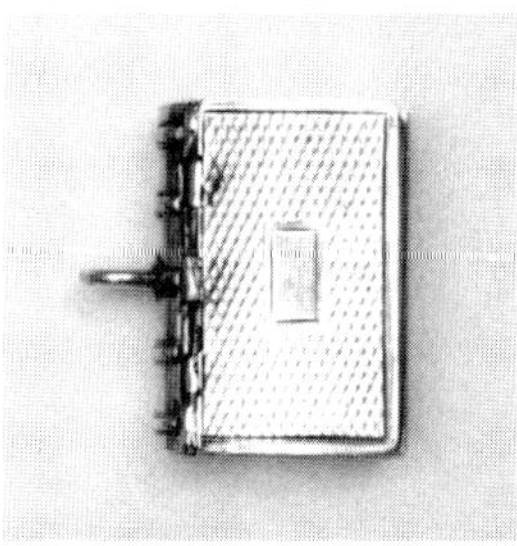

Vinaigrette. Maker: Joseph Willmore, Birmingham, 1834-1835. Measuring only 15/16" in length it is finely detailed both inside and out. The grid is unusual in having a tiny silver-gilt thumb piece by which to raise it. Back and front are finely engine-turned with a diamond design. The edges are enriched with "thread scoring" and the spine treated to resemble a fine leather binding. *Private Collection. Photo: H Ivan Rainwater*. $550

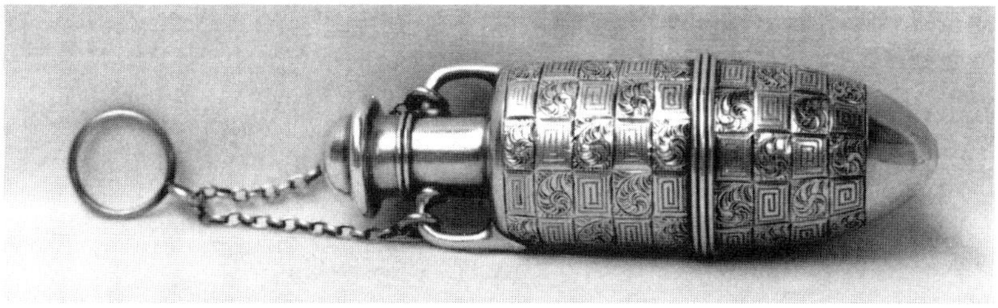

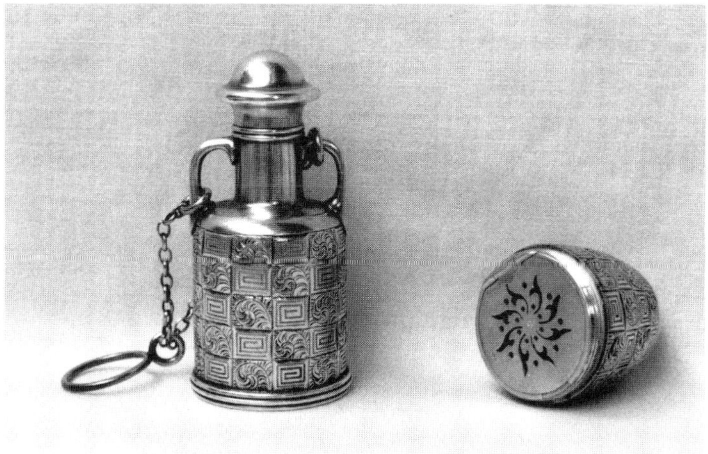

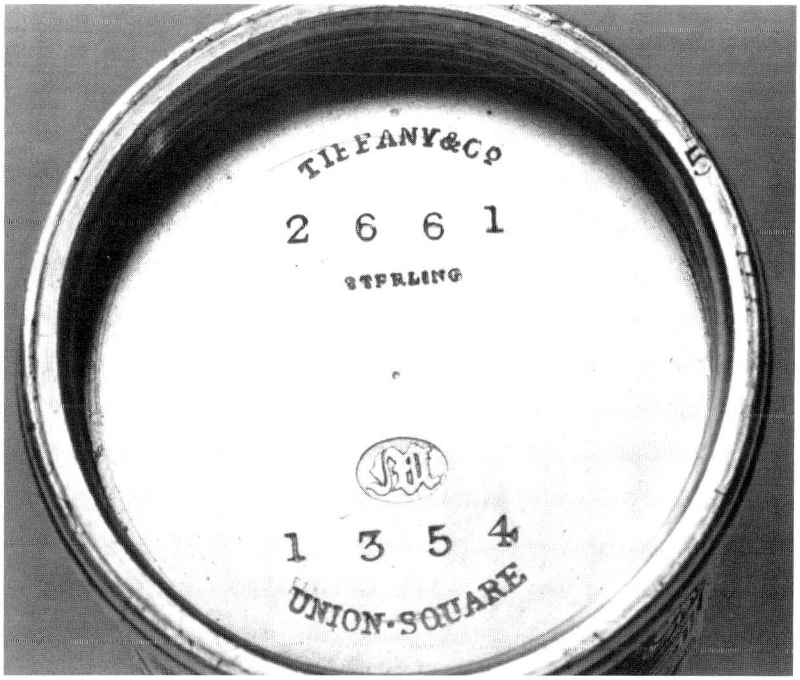

Combination vinaigrette and perfume bottle. Made by Tiffany & Co. with Union Square mark of 1870-1875. Size: 4" tall; 1-1/4" diameter. *Photo: Courtesy of Silver Magazine Archives*.

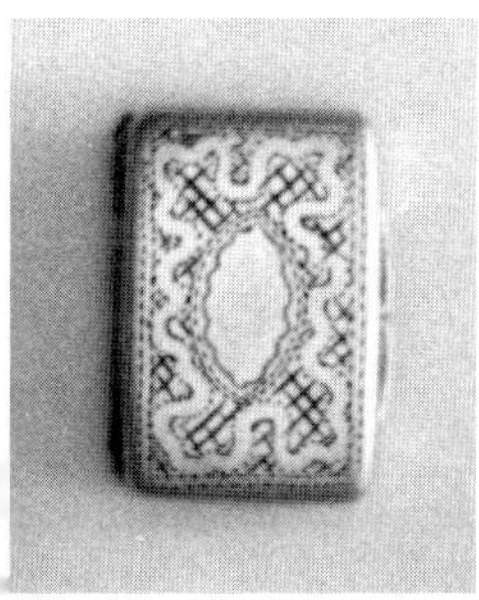

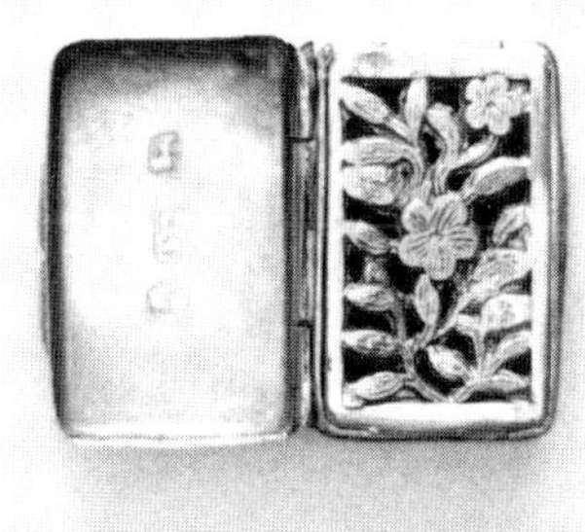

Left:
Vinaigrette. Slight concave curve to fit the body. Marked: Anchor/Duty mark/TS/y(1822-1823). Tiny sponge still inside. L 3/4". Open view shows grid. All interior silver-gilt. *Private Collection. Photo: H Ivan Rainwater*.

The one characteristic which sets vinaigrettes apart from all other box-like articles is that they are fitted with a gilded inner grille which is pierced to enable the aroma of the spiced vinegar to be released. A vinegar-soaked sponge was held firmly in place within the grille. Now and then a vinaigrette is discovered with its tiny sponge still in place.

Until about 1835, vinaigrettes were carried by men and women alike. Frequently, one finds somewhat larger vinaigrettes which were made for men. Until c.1810, chasing, filigree, and repoussé were the usual decorations. Later, other techniques including engine turning, enameling, gem setting and appliqué work were used. Some of the most eagerly sought are the so-called "castle tops." On these, famous buildings are embossed and chased in high relief. The subjects are mostly English castles, cathedrals, and country houses. Around 1790 many novelty shapes of baskets, books, purses, acorns, birds, fish, shells and others appeared.

Notable British makers were Matthew Linwood, Nathaniel Mills, Samuel Pemberton, John Shaw, John Turner and Joseph Willmore.

After the invention of smelling salts, the fashion of carrying a vinaigrette fell into disfavor.

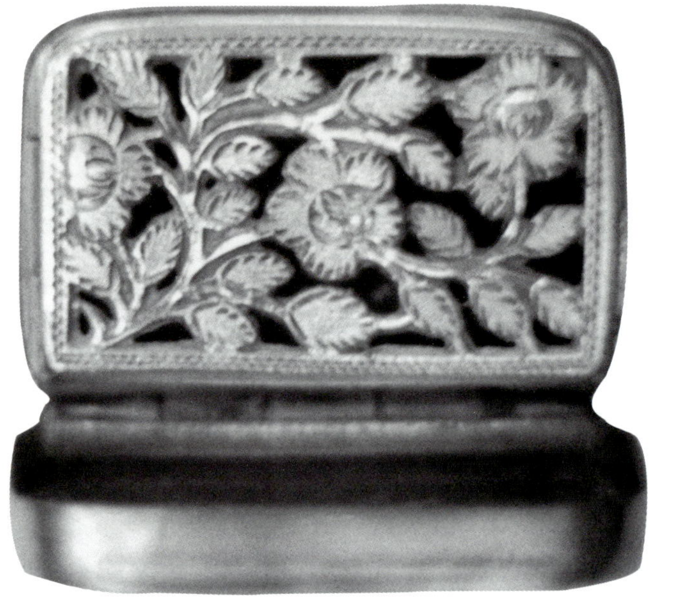

Vinaigrette marked John Shaw, Birmingham, 1907-1908. Monogram on cover "E N." Floral design on cut-out grid. Interior silver-gilt. Original tiny sponge present. Size: 1-3/16" by 3/4" by 3/16." *Private Collection. Photo: H Ivan Rainwater*.

Patch boxes

The oft-told story of how the patch box came into being is of a court beauty who had a disfiguring mole (or smallpox scar) on her face. In order to disguise it she put a small patch of leather over it. Other ladies of fashion took up the craze which soon led to fanciful designs worn just for fashion's sake.

The earliest known hallmarked patch box is from London dated 1669. Patch boxes were mostly sturdy containers about one and a half inches in diameter by half an inch deep. Later patch boxes were rectangular or elliptical, often with tiny mirrors inside the lids.

The earliest patch boxes apparently were raised from flat silver. Later ones, which were less sturdy, were made of circular rims, or bezels, soldered to flat discs. In the 18th century, English Whig ladies wore patches on their right cheeks, the Tories wore them on their left cheeks.

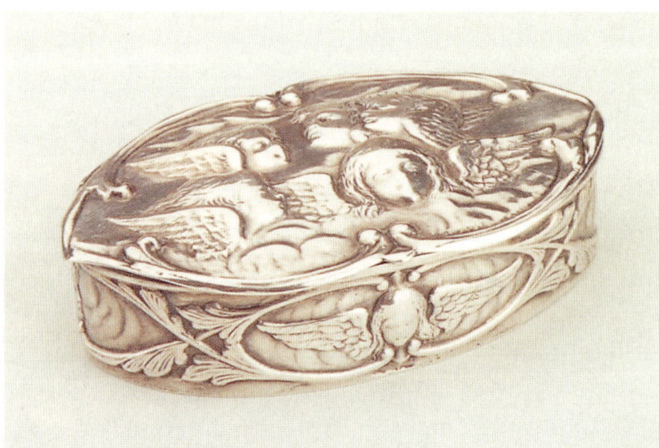

English silver box marked WC, lion passant, leopard head, date letter c.1898. William Comyns died January 16, 1916. The design of cherub heads was after a painting by Romney. Box measures 1 3/4" by 3" . *Collection of Antonia Moore. Photo: Bruce Waters.*

Pill boxes

Medicinal pills came into being for separate dosages in ancient Mesopotamia and Egypt. The Greeks named little balls of medications *katapotia* (something to be swallowed). Grooved tiles and a spatula would have been used to make them. The Romans not only used tiles and spatulas but also employed the first pill machines which were simply grooved stones.

The earliest illustrations and references to a pill machine in Europe appears in Diderot's *Recueil de Planches sur les Sciences* published in Paris in 1763. Many other machines were developed in other countries and some of them were patented.

When pills were made, something in which to dispense and carry them was needed. Small chipboard boxes, used in the sixteenth and seventeenth centuries, did the job adequately. By the nineteenth century, wholesale druggists, using catalogs, offered chipboard boxes; round, oval, or willow and paper boxes; round and covered with bronze or fancy gold and silver paper. Paper boxes were available with the French edge and in many sizes and colors. "Fine glazed paper" was used on some of the boxes. Others, covered with an assortment of fine papers in various colors also had a blank label on top. (Catalogs of the following companies bear these out: Van Schaack, Stevenson & Reid of Chicago, 1875; W, H. Schieffelin & Co. of New York, 1883; and Fuller & Fuller Co. of Chicago, 1883.)

No English-made sterling silver pill boxes have become known to the authors so precise dating cannot be offered. European-made pill boxes of silver appeared in every shape, form and size by the late nineteenth century marked "800" indicating their Continental origins, and others are made of silverplate. Most are round, oval, or rectangular and not deep. Some few are whimsical forms, for instance peanut and clam shell shaped. Unusual pill boxes are the most collectible and least found today.

With so many different types and sizes of pill boxes available, it is not too surprising to find that it was well into the twentieth century before silver pill boxes appeared on the market in significant numbers. Most of the silver pill boxes that have come to the authors' attention are rather flat and were intended to be carried in the pocket or purse. Whatever their form, a nice silver pill box can help banish that queasy feeling of having to take medicine.

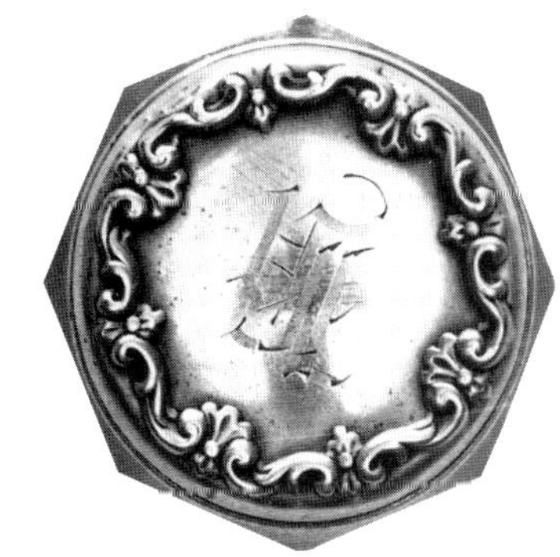

Octagonal monogrammed silver pill box. Marked: Whiting Mfg. Co. c.1895-1900. Diameter: 1-5/8" *Private Collection. Photo: H Ivan Rainwater.*

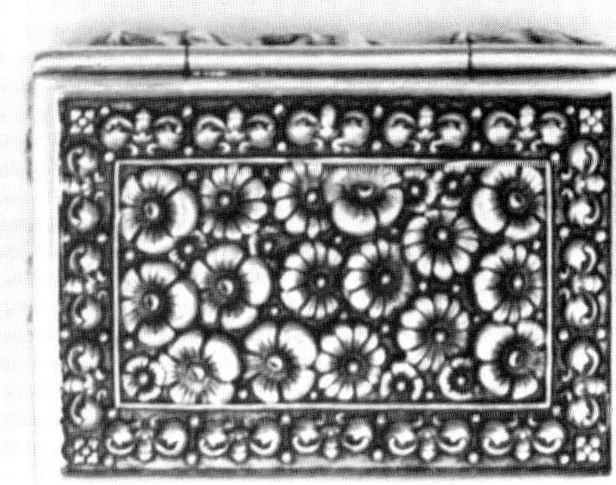

Silver pill box with flower design. Purchased 25 September 1973. Schmuck Passage, H. Schneider, Getreidegasse 23, Salzburg, Austria. Length: 1-1/2". Tiny marks not traced. *Private Collection. Photo: H Ivan Rainwater.*

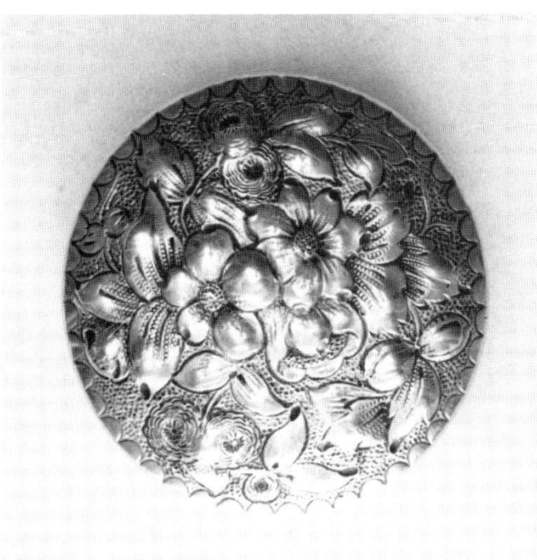

Sterling silver pill box. Made by Dominick & Haff; retailed by M.W. Galt & Co. Inscribed: AMK, from her mother, Dec. 25, 1885. Diameter: 2". *Private Collection. Photo: H Ivan Rainwater.*

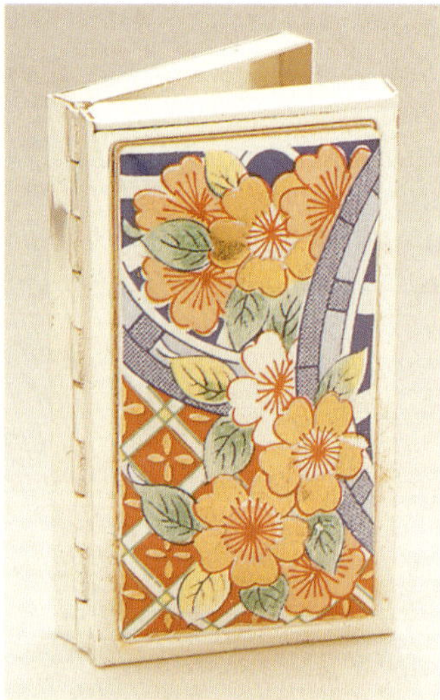

Pill box with floral design multi-color enamel with an Art Deco aspect. No marks. Silverplate. Size: 2-1/6" by 1-3/16".

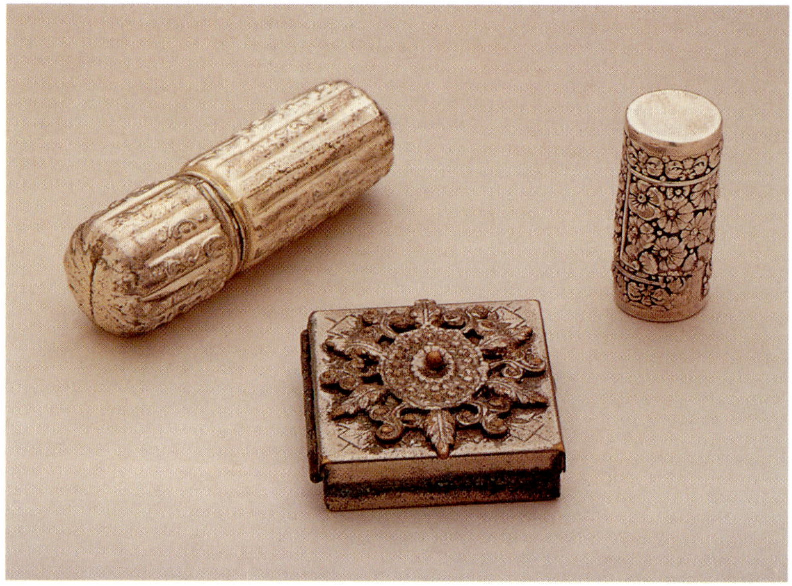

Pill boxes. Left: marked STERLING. Has a loop so it can be attached to a chatelaine. Lift-off cap. 2" long.
Center: silverplate with worn spots that reveal the copper base. 1 1/4" by 1 1/8".
Right: marked STERLING. Lift-off cap. No loop or other means of attaching it to something. 1" long.

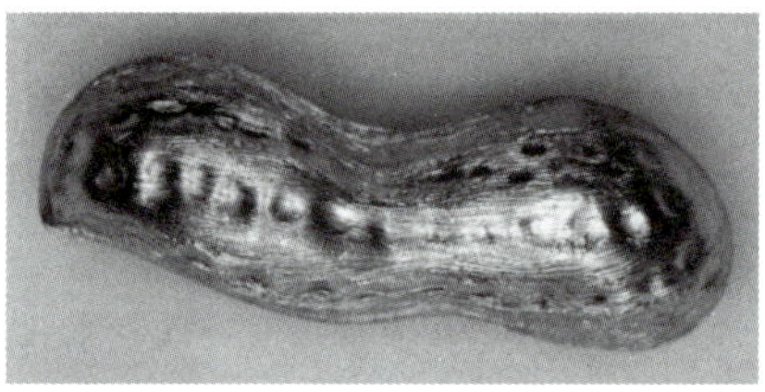

Pill box in the form of a peanut. Marked STERLING MEXICO on the inner band that locks the two parts together. 2" long. *Private Collection. Photo: H Ivan Rainwater*.

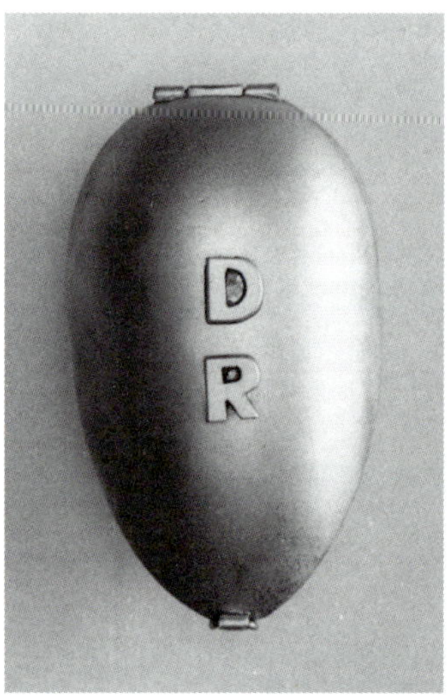

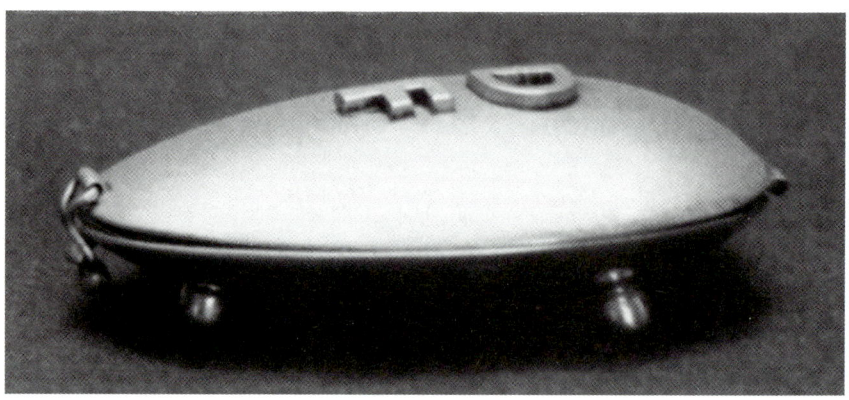

Two pill boxes, each made of two sterling spoon bowls. Each has three feet so they can stand on the table. The measure 2-1/6" by 1-3/8". They were made c.1970-1980. A spoon collector's gift to the two good friends.

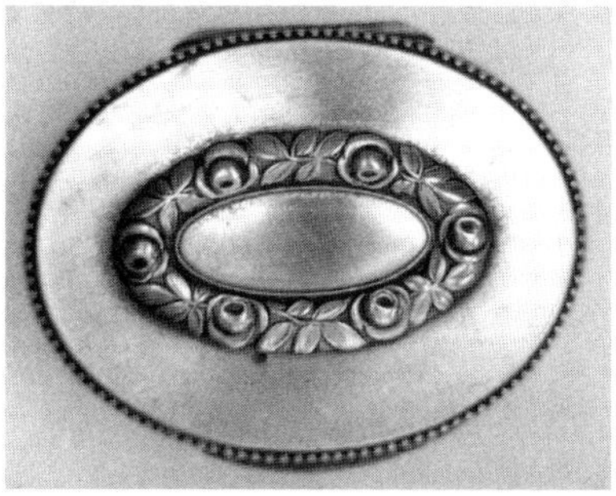

Oval pill box. Marked: M M & Crescent & Crown 800. Measures 1-3/4" by 1-3/8" by 5/8". *Private Collection. Photo: H Ivan Rainwater.*

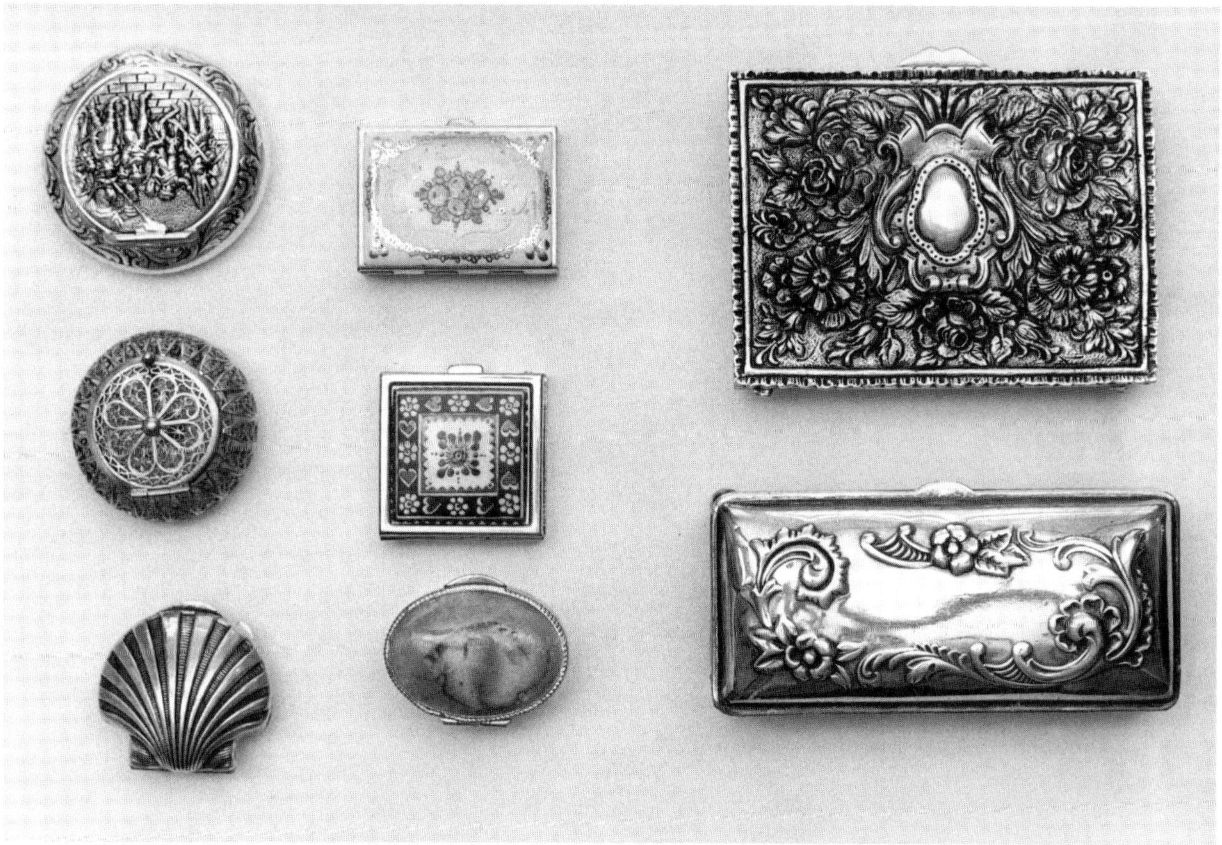

Group of eight small silver pill boxes, late 19th and early 20th century. *Photo: H Ivan Rainwater.*

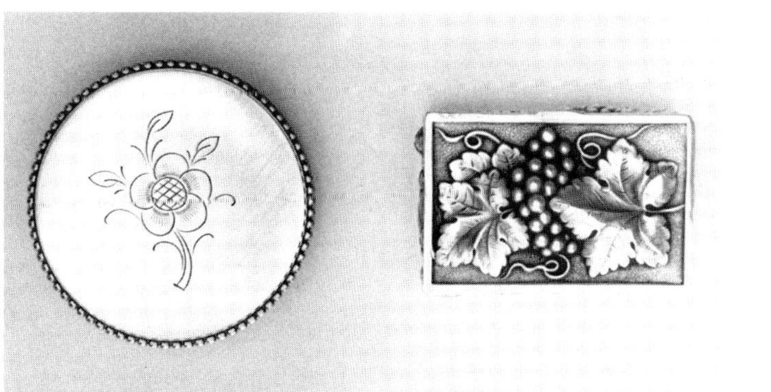

Two pill boxes in sterling. Left: marked 925 S DENMARK, sterling. Measures 1-9/16" in diameter. The top rotates to make an opening on the side.
Right: made in Austria. Grape and grape leaf design. Measures 1-3/8". *Photo: H Ivan Rainwater.*

Chapter 15. Silver Curios for use...
...while Traveling

On the go

The modern traveler is concerned with airline tickets and possible trips to outer space. Victorian travelers prepared for a trip with carriage sets which included knife, fork and spoon in a compact case. The eating utensils were made of silver.

From the mid-nineteenth century, Tiffany & Co. of New York sold and made traveling inkstands using a combination of leather and silver. They ranged from plain to quite ornate in style and were priced from $1.50 to $36. The portable inkstand enabled the user to write while traveling.

Another item which Tiffany & Co. sold was a traveling candlestick lantern made of silver that was suggested for use in the stateroom of a ship. The description from Tiffany's advertising includes, "Closes compactly." The price was $50.

While many travelers may indeed have bought from fine stores, a great many others bought from catalogues such as that of Daniel Low & Co. of Salem, Massachusetts, which offered an ornate silver shaving brush for travel at a cost of around $3. A travel mirror which was made to stand or hang cost $4.25 from the catalogue.

The traveling collapsible cup would not have been needed on the long trip across the ocean on a luxury lines. However, it would certainly have been used frequently when traveling by horse and carriage.

Travel accessories have changed from the days of Queen Victoria. For example, plastic, light weight toothbrushes have replaced the ones with silver handles. Most eating establishments on the road offer stainless steel cutlery or wrapped, throw-away plastic utensils. Luggage tags are still used on suitcases, but now are made from plastics. Pocket-sized razor sets have been replaced with cordless electric shavers.

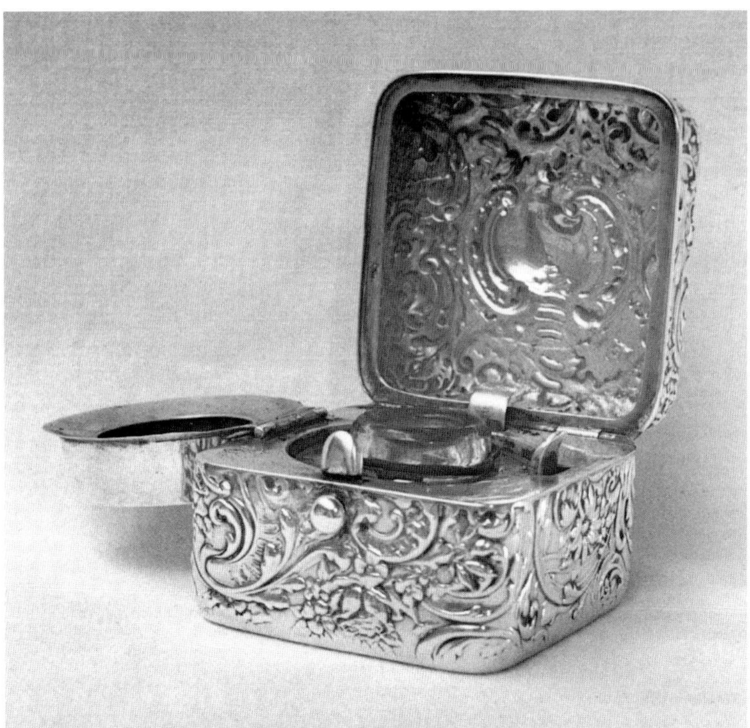

Traveling inkstand shown closed on right and opened on left. Number 280 in the Gorham cost book (vol.8 p.25) June 1893. Height 1-9/16. Width 2-1/4". Hand chased. An inner silver lid kept the ink from spilling. Factory price in 1893 possibly $14.25. Hand chasing and silver gilt both optional. *Private Collection. Photo: Silver Magazine Archives.* $950.

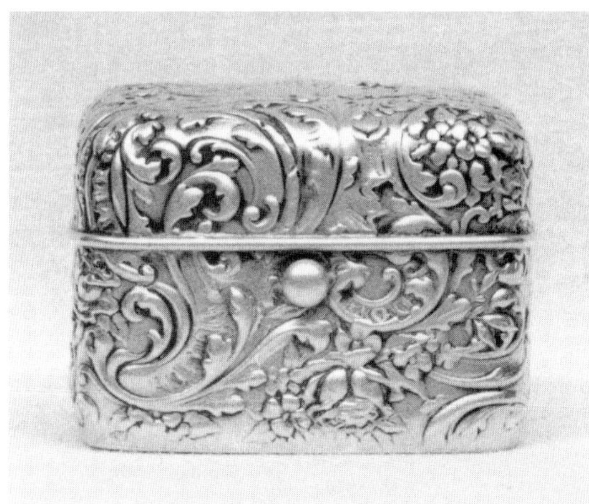

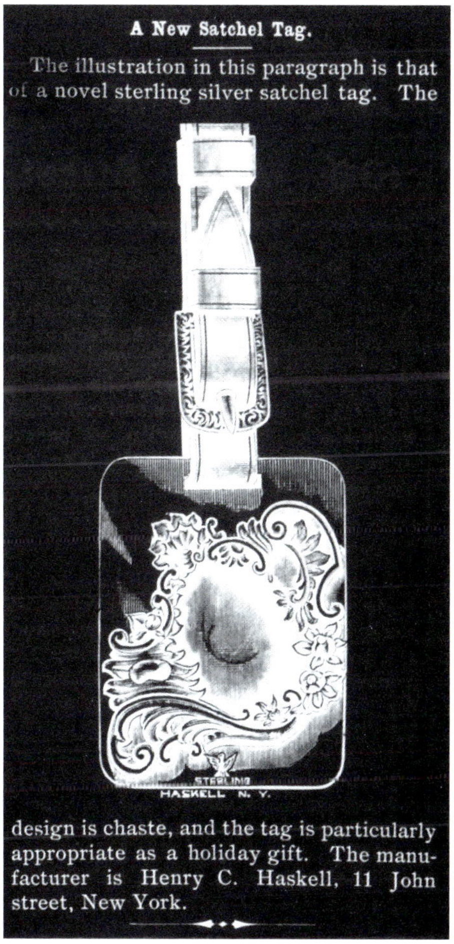

A New Satchel Tag.

The illustration in this paragraph is that of a novel sterling silver satchel tag. The

STERLING
HASKELL N. Y.

design is chaste, and the tag is particularly appropriate as a holiday gift. The manufacturer is Henry C. Haskell, 11 John street, New York.

Jewelers' Weekly, December 6, 1893

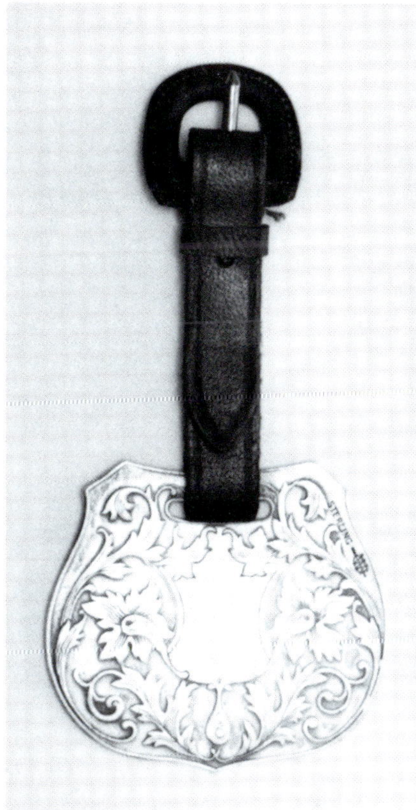

Sterling luggage tag with leather strap. Maker: Webster Co., 3-3/8". *Photo: H Ivan Rainwater*. $50-70.

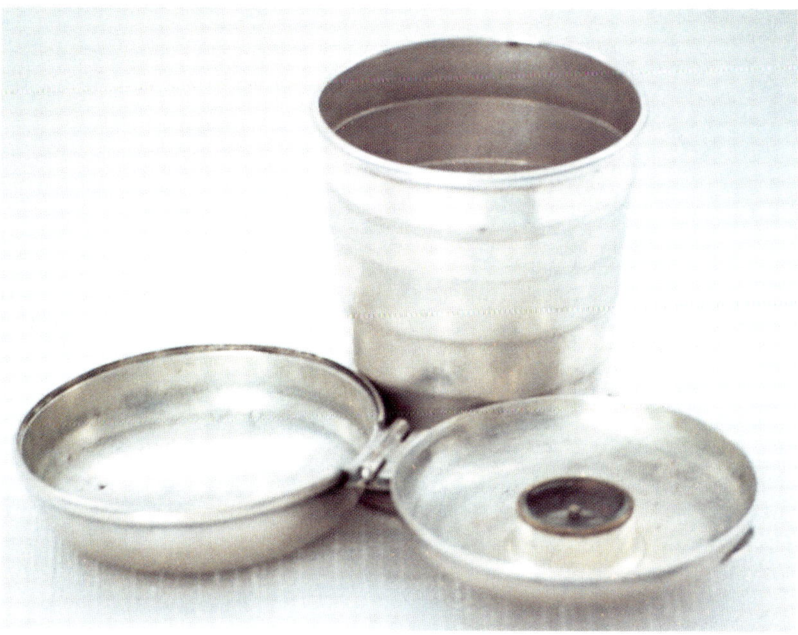

Silver circular case which opens to reveal a fixed compass in the top and removable telescopic cup. Gorham Mfg. Co., Providence, Rhode Island., 1891. *Collection and photo: Dorothea Burstyn.*

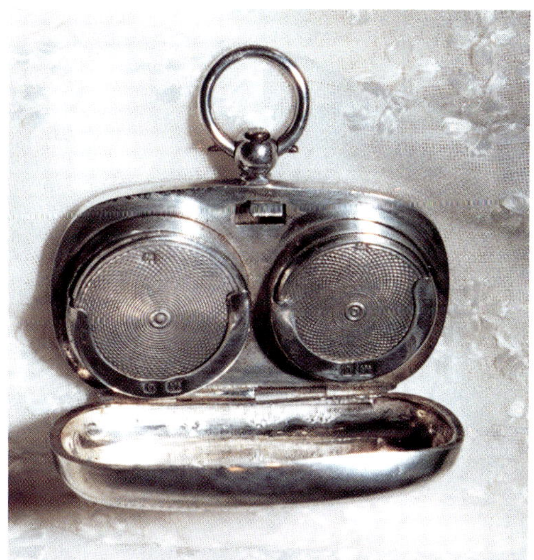

English sovereign coin money case. 2" by 1-1/4". Marked: Birmingham, 1913. *Collection and photo: Anne Jansen.*

Travelers' forks and spoons

Many types of spoons had their beginnings on the Continent. Among them was the folding spoon which could be carried in the pocket. Those that have survived are mostly of French, German, or Low Countries origin. Few are of precious metal; the majority are pewter, platten, or copper. Spoons of bone, bronze, and wood have also been found in association with sites of Roman military establishments.

Though there is evidence that forks were also used by the Romans, their use was not universal until they were introduced from Italy about the first quarter of the seventeenth century. They did not come into general use until about 1660; individuals carried their own. Traveling forks were often combined with a detachable spoon bowl and a toothpick, which was screwed into the end of the handle. The fork tines were fitted into loops on the back of the spoon bowl and the handle was made to fold so that the whole could be carried in the pocket. A sliding sleeve kept the handle rigid when in use.

Early examples of these utensils are rare. Some of those appearing on the market today may be products of the silversmiths of Hanau, Germany (see Chapter 10) who became noted for their fine reproductions of silver.

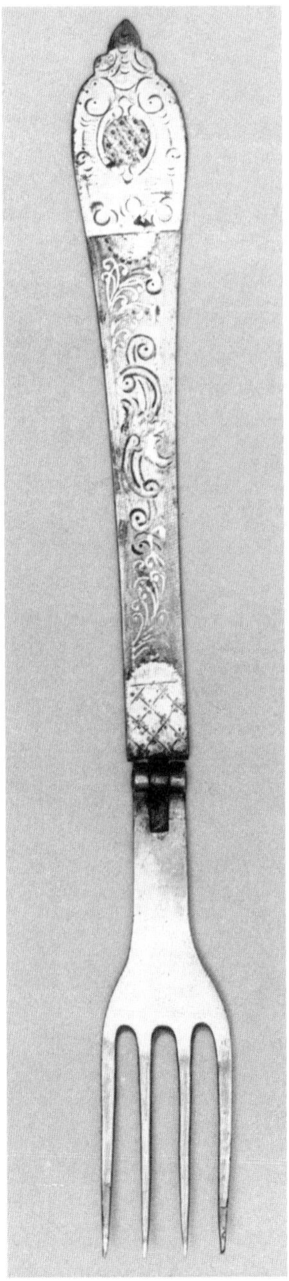

Silver folding fork for use when traveling. Probably made in Spain. *Photo: H Ivan Rainwater*.

One simple type of spoon, found almost exclusively in Britain, is a small rat-tailed spoon with a two-pronged fork on the other end.

The carrying one's own cutlery is said to have survived in numerous European peasant areas until the beginning of the twentieth century. Though the need of carrying one's own cutlery for dining has faded, folding spoons for taking medicine persist today.

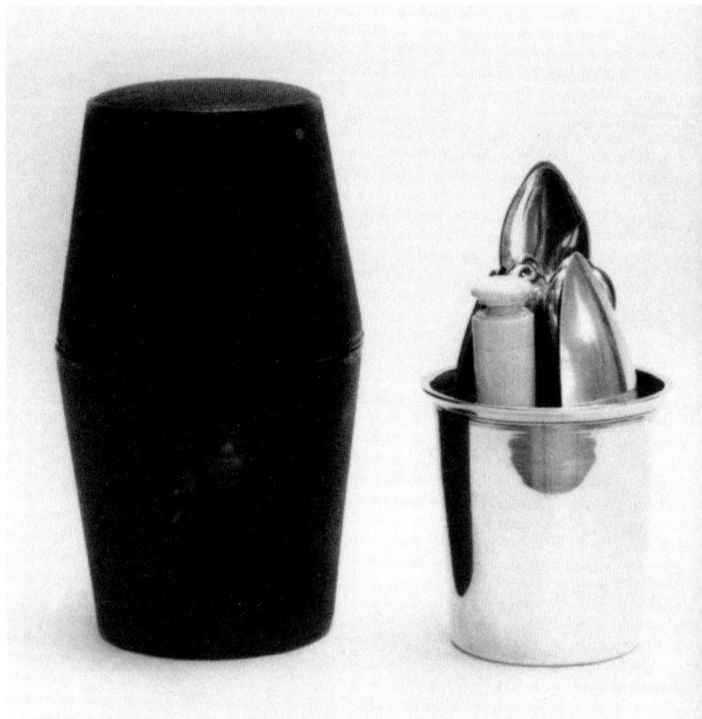

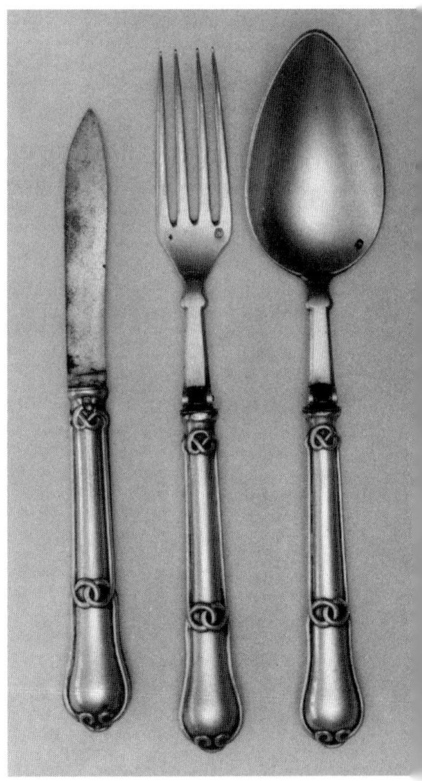

Above and right: French carriage utensil set including knife, fork and spoon which fold to fit inside the compact case for the traveler. *Photo: H Ivan Rainwater*. $350+.

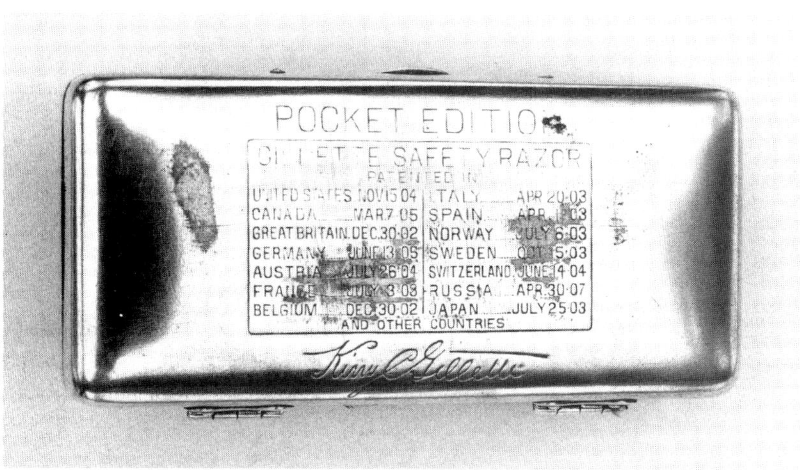

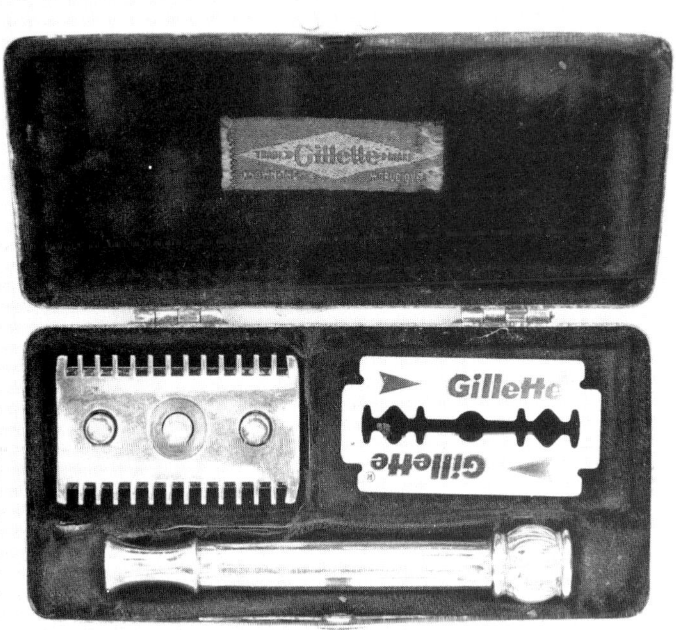

Loft:
Silver cased "Pocket Edition" Gillette razor. Case lined in purple velvet holds double edged blade and 2-part holder. Side of case shows patent dates in many countries from 1902 to 1908 and the facsimile signature of King C. Gillette. *Diane Zinn collection. Photo: Robert Watkins.* $95.

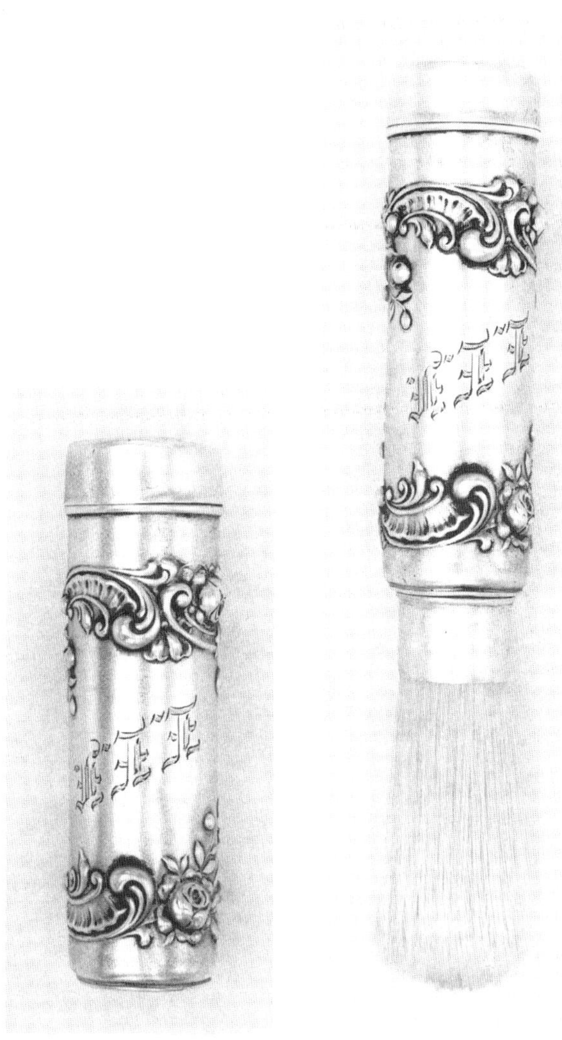

Shaving brush for travel. Sterling. Monogrammed. Maker: Gorham Co. with lion, anchor and G trademark. c.1880. *Diane Zinn collection. Photo: Robert Watkins.* $75-125.

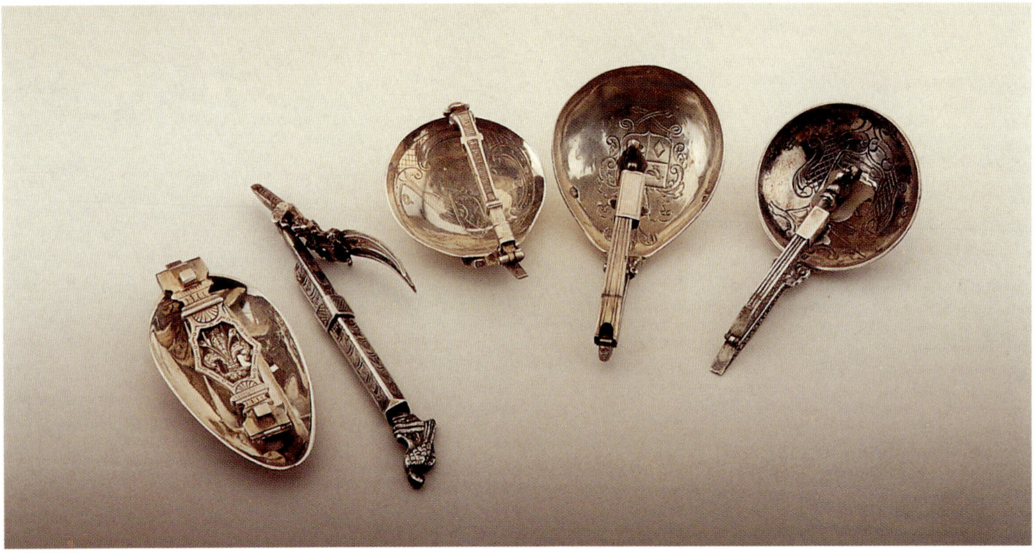

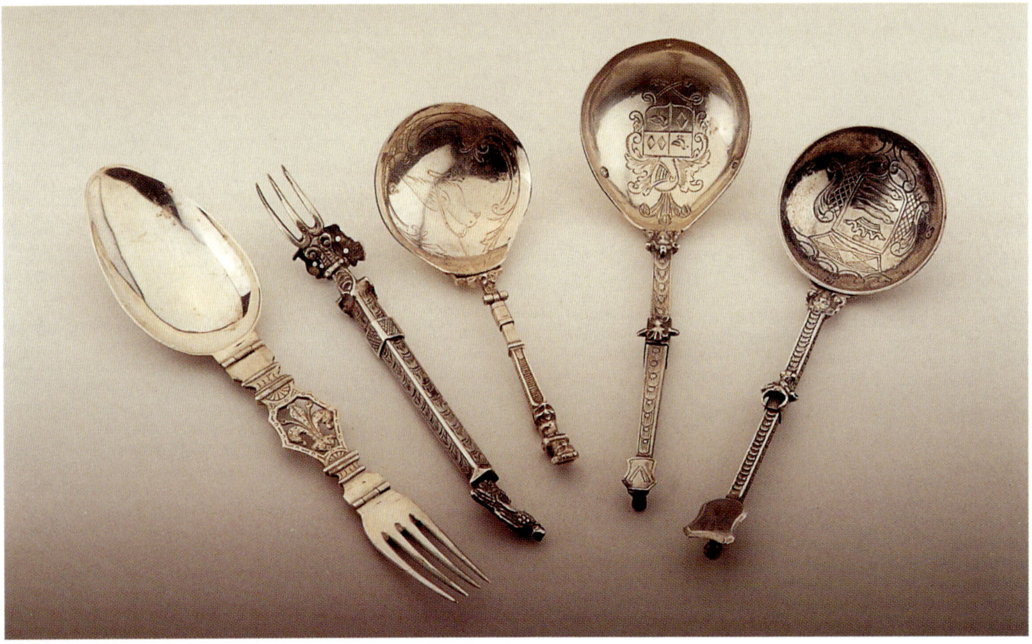

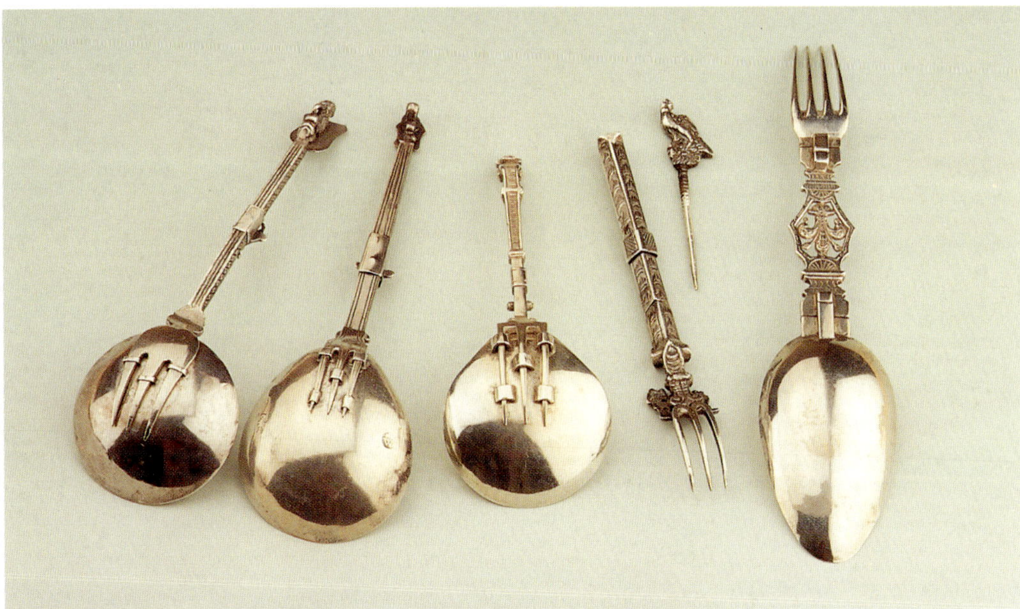

Folding silver utensils for the traveler, each set including a spoon and fork. The largest 7 1/2" long. *Private Collection. Photo: Bruce Waters*.

Chinese Silver Bottles

Victorian gentlemen were not the only travelers at the end of the nineteenth century. A traveler from China could put medications in folding silver bottles such as the ones shown with a floral design on one side and Chinese names of the medication on the other: *Ping An San, Wuo Long Ban, Wan Ying Ding* and *Sa Yan Wan*. Each bottle was marked for a different medicine. Unfortunately, the tops of the bottles are missing, but they were probably made with a spoon attached, similar to the spoons on snuff bottle lids.

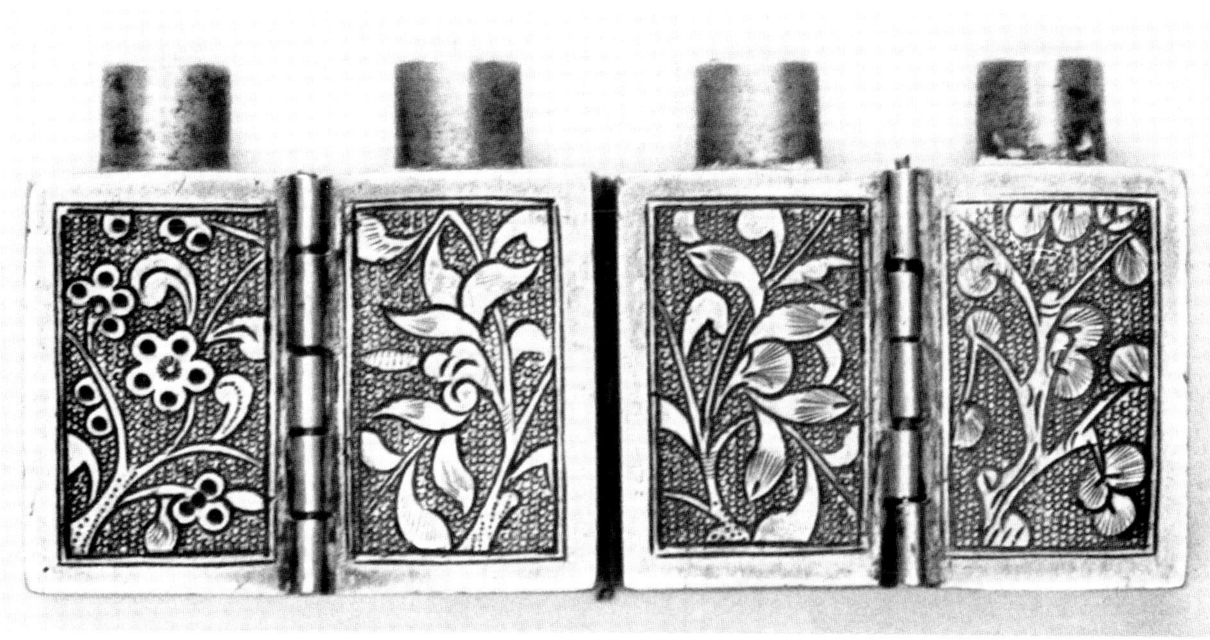

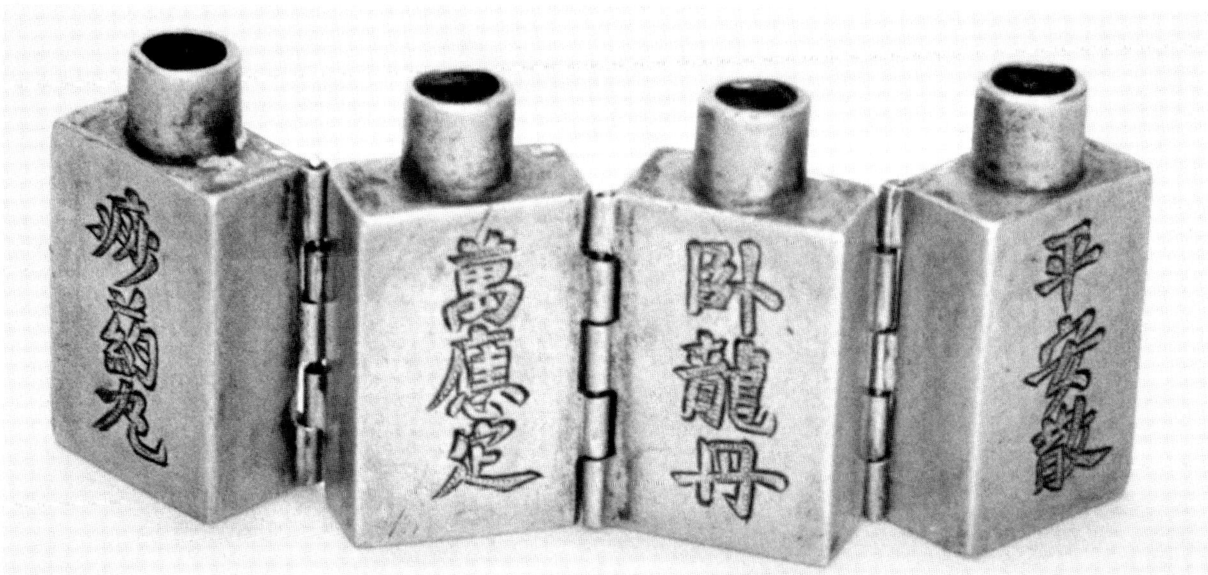

Four Chinese medicine bottles in silver, all hinged together. When folded, measures approximately 6". *Photo: H Ivan Rainwater*.

The Queen's Silver Jubilee

Elizabeth the Second was the fourth sovereign of the House of Windsor to ascend the throne of the United Kingdom. On the death of her father, King George VI, she became the queen on February 6, 1952.

The following year, on June 22, 1953, Elizabeth was crowned in Westminster Abbey. Though the coronation did not take place until more than a year after she became Queen, her reign dates from 1952 and, therefore, 1977 was the 25th Anniversary, or Silver Jubilee, and an occasion for many celebrations.

The celebration of the Royal Silver Jubilee inspired the production of countless souvenir articles including many in sterling and silverplate. An additional hallmark was added to the usual four on all silver articles which were hallmarked in England during 1977. This Silver Jubilee hallmark, with the likeness of the Queen, was stamped on all silver items weighing 15 grams or more.

So many manufacturers of sterling wares produced various silver articles to commemorate the Silver Jubilee and the demand for these was so great that the Assay Office at Goldsmiths' Hall was unable to keep up with the proper recording of marks. Manufacturers of silverplated wares, on the other hand, were unhampered by such restrictions so their wares were readily available.

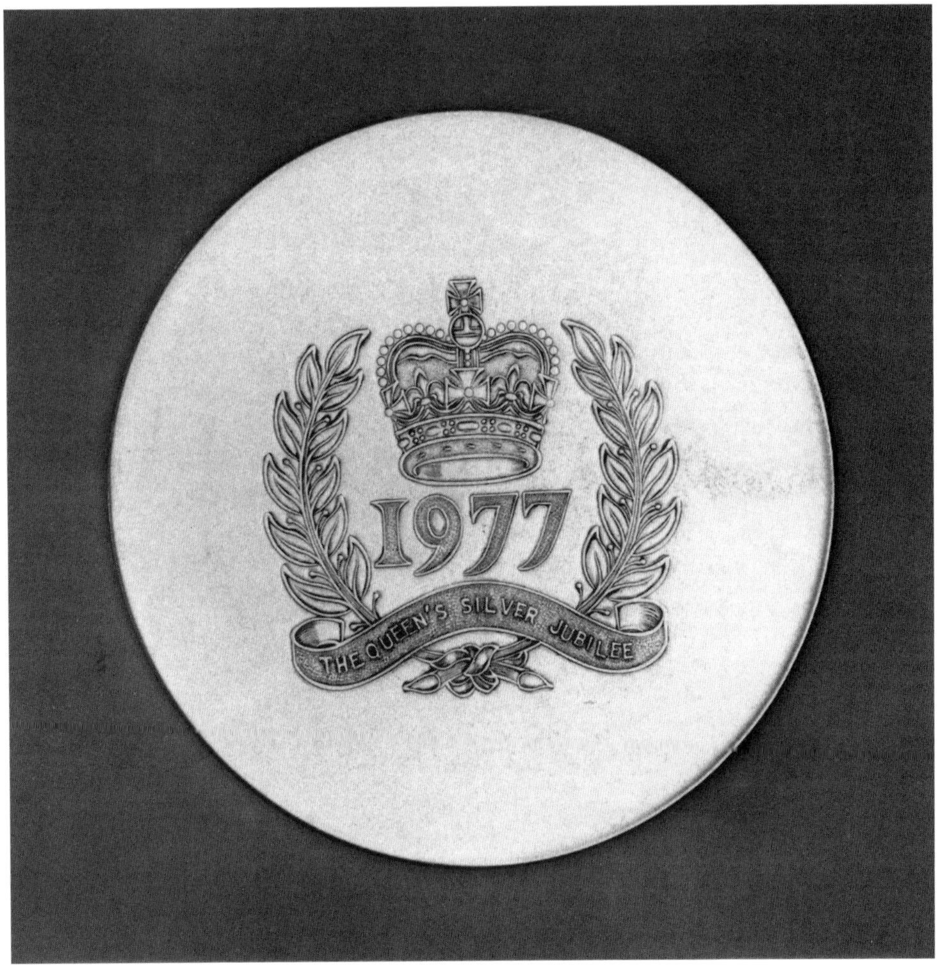

Silverplated hot plate holder bearing the official emblem of The United Kingdom Queen Elizabeth's Silver Jubilee in 1977, 4-13/16" diameter. *Photo: H Ivan Rainwater*. $32.

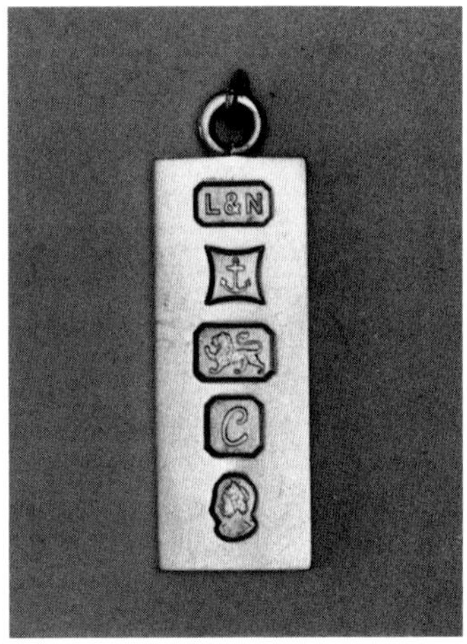

Sterling silver pendant bearing the Silver Jubilee Hallmarks and Birmingham Assay Office stamp. 1-7/16" long. *Photo: H Ivan Rainwater*. $40.

Chapter 16. Silver Curios for use...

...as Miniatures

Though long neglected by dealers and collectors alike, silver miniatures have now become favorites. Clubs whose membership is composed of adult collectors are to be found everywhere and their members seek out prize pieces, swap, and trade eagerly.

There is something about miniatures and our fondness for them that is unexplainable. We react to them as though we were in another world—perhaps that world of childhood when we felt anything was possible. We cheerfully empty our pocketbooks to purchase a tiny coffeepot, too small to be of any practical use, but something we *must* have. As we sit and gloat over our most recent miniature find, we are transported out of our humdrum lives into a world where the impossible is commonplace.

It is probably impossible to know just when the first miniature utensils were made. We do know that miniature bronze utensils have been found in Egypt and Roman iron toys were found in Britain. The Victoria and Albert Museum in London has a large collection of tiny silver objects made during the seventeenth century. But, it is the Dutch who, ever since the seventeenth century, have been the prize producers of miniature silverware. These include a tremendous variety of household articles, often exact working copies of domestic utensils. Dutch silversmiths also have excelled in the production of numerous miniature toys modeled on articles which would not have been made in silver in the normal size.

The first silver miniatures made in Holland were military figures, soldiers with all their paraphernalia. Because of the great expense of producing these little soldiers in silver, they were soon replaced by soldiers made of lead.

Dutch silversmiths created a great variety of miniature furniture—such as chairs, chest of drawers, tables, beds, dining room furniture, and chests.

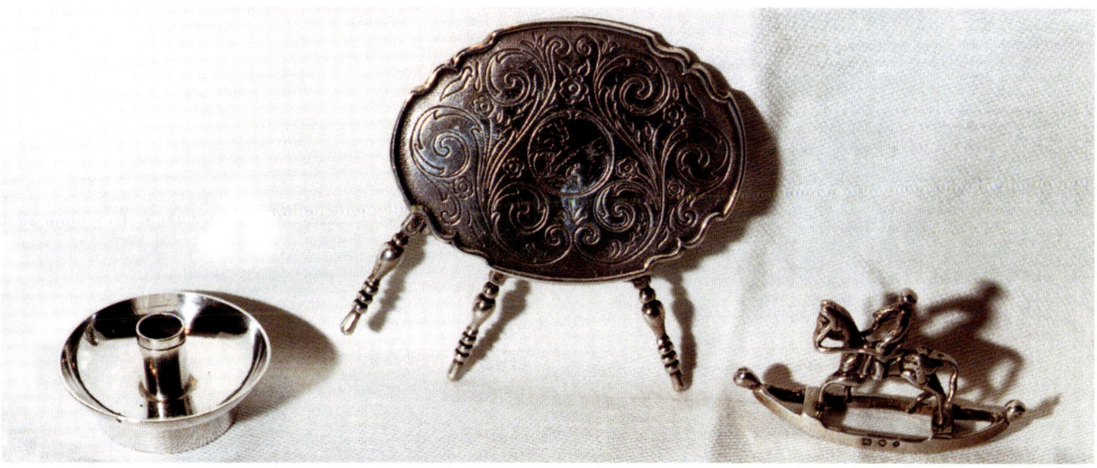

Miniature Dutch silver toys. Left to right: candle holder by Amsterdam silversmith William B. Strandt, second half of 18th century; folding table, 1978; rocking horse, 1978. *Collection and photo: Anne Jansen.*

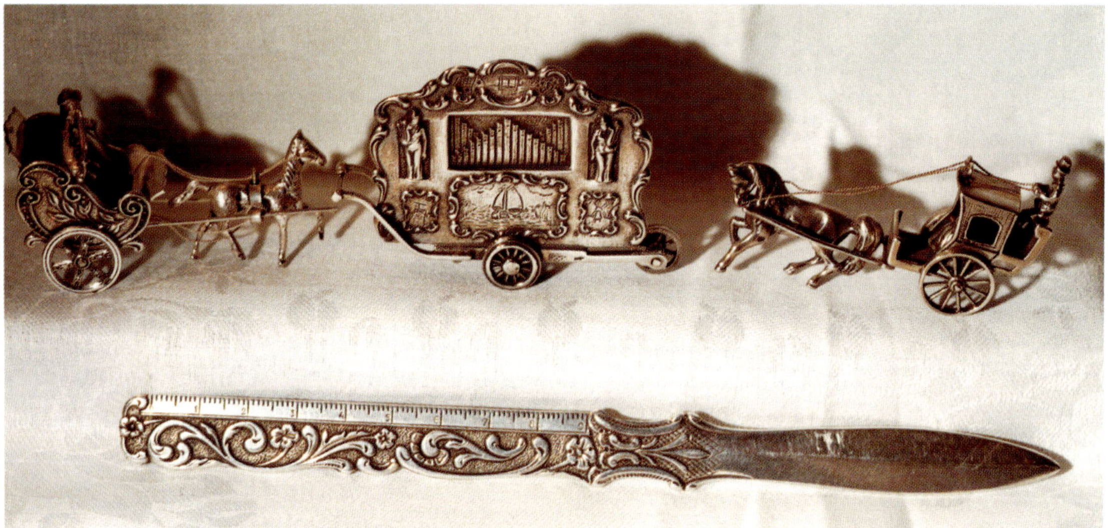

Dutch silver toys of sterling silver. Made c.1978. Shown for scale with a silverplated German letter opener with calibrated centimeter marks. Art Nouveau style, 7 1/2" long. *Collection and photo: Anne Jansen*.

The miniature silver made in the Netherlands was of intricate design and fine workmanship. This interest coincided with the production of doll houses for adults rather than as playthings for children. These doll houses, called "baby houses," were filled with beautifully crafted silver candlesticks, chandeliers, tea and table ware. Miniature silver became popular in England after Charles II returned to England from his exile at The Hague. Silver was fashionable in his Restoration Court and between 1670 and 1760 production of silver miniatures was high in England.

Elsewhere dolls houses were made as children' s toys. Most were filled with furniture and other objects made of copper and pewter. In many cases they were used to teach young girls in the art and practice of housekeeping. Lesser numbers of dolls houses and their contents were made in France, Italy and Russia. They were quite unlike and never as popular as the elaborate Dutch and English dolls houses with which the wives of well-to-do merchants filled their leisure time.

English silver miniaturists

Six prominent English silversmiths made miniatures between 1684 and 1740. George Middleton worked between 1684 and 1697 to produce beakers, bowls, cream pitchers, sugar bowls, candlesticks, montieths, posset pots, snuffers, spoon racks, trifid spoons, and tankards. His Charles III style chairs have caned backs and seats and his fireplace tools include firedogs (andirons), fenders, shovels, and tongs. Despite rather crude workmanship when compared with later examples, Middleton's work is treasured for its rarity and display of full hallmarks.

An English silversmith known only as "M. A." made miniature kettles, braziers, saucepans on stands, tea canisters, coffeepots, jugs, teapots, and flagons be-

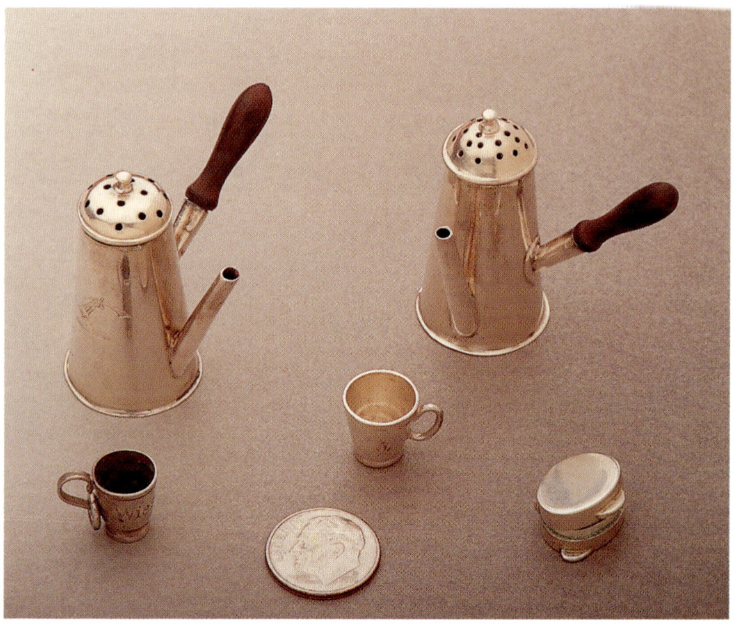

Miniature silver dishes. Top row left to right: individual salt and pepper shakers in the form of chocolate pots, made by CS Star FS in Chester in 1894. One has an engraved crest of an uplifted and mailed hand holding a short sword.
Below: Tiny footed cup with "Weisbaden" inscribed on one side. No marks. Height: 1/2"
Tiny cup. Made by AP (incomplete maker's mark) in Birmingham in 1948. 1/2" high.
Tiny box marked 800 in an oval. Other marks not legible. 1/2" by 9/16".

tween 1697 and 1713. David Clayton entered his mark at Goldsmith's Hall in 1697 and made a beautiful miniature Queen Anne style chocolate pot, just 2 1/2" high, complete with its stirring rod. He was the most prolific English silver toy maker. John Clifton worked between 1703 and 1715 making miniature silver fireplaces, cruets, tea sets, handle-less tea cups, and teaspoons. Between 1708 and 1740, when doll houses were at the height of popularity, Augustin Courtauld made silver miniature tables, fireplace sets, sconces, candlesticks, snuffers, bottles, cruets, saucepans, chocolate pots, covered cups, and plates similar in style to Dutch pieces of the time. His work was not completely hallmarked. Finally, the finest English silver miniatures were made with the same care and detail as full size pieces by John LeSage between 1720 and 1740. Not many of his miniatures have been identified.

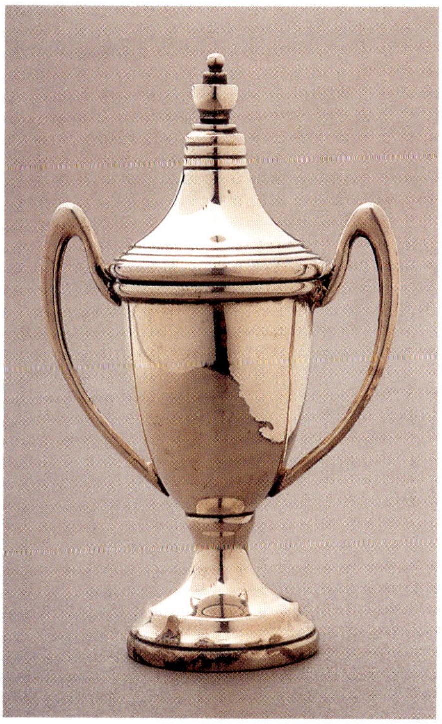

Covered cup. A form sometimes used as a loving cup or one for presentation as an award of merit. Marked: Anchor (Birmingham) 1935/ F. H. Adams & Co., Inc. Height: 2-3/4". $75 to 125.

American silver miniaturists

The earliest documented example of American miniature silver is a tiny silver cup, only one and one-half inches tall, made by John Coney (1655-1722). It is in the collection of the Museum of Fine Arts in Boston. In the same museum is a small cup, slightly larger, bearing the mark of Apopllos Rivoire, a French Huguenot immigrant and the father of patriot-silversmith Paul Revere (who is reputed to have made miniatures, but none have been identified). Other early miniatures in this collection are a cup in the same style by John Edwards (1671-1746) and six miniature spoons by Richard Richardson of Philadelphia, who was active near the end of the eighteenth century. Other American miniaturists of note include Zachariah Brigden and Samuel Bartlett of Boston, William I Jenney and Howard & Co. of New York, and Bradbury Bailey of Vermont. The Museum of the City of New York has miniature tea sets made by Gorham in 1920.

Arthur J. Stone

Arthur J. Stone was born September 26, 1847, in Sheffield, England. In 1861 he was apprenticed to a master silversmith, Edwin Eagle, who is listed in the 1865 Sheffield directory at "Convent Walk" with no assay mark noted. In addition to fifty-nine hours in the shop, Stone spent three evenings each week at the local National School of Design studying mechanical and freehand drawing. By the time his apprenticeship drew to a close in 1868, Stone had mastered the skills of chasing and fluting, and was adept at making and tempering the many small steel tools used in the work. He made a copper "masterpiece" in its original meaning, the work by which a craftsman gained the rank of master from his guild.

Like many young silversmiths, he sought to expand his experience in Edinburgh and after spending a year there, returned to Sheffield. There he joined the venerable firm of James Dixon and Sons, with whom he spent nine years. In 1884, responding to frequent advertisements by American companies,

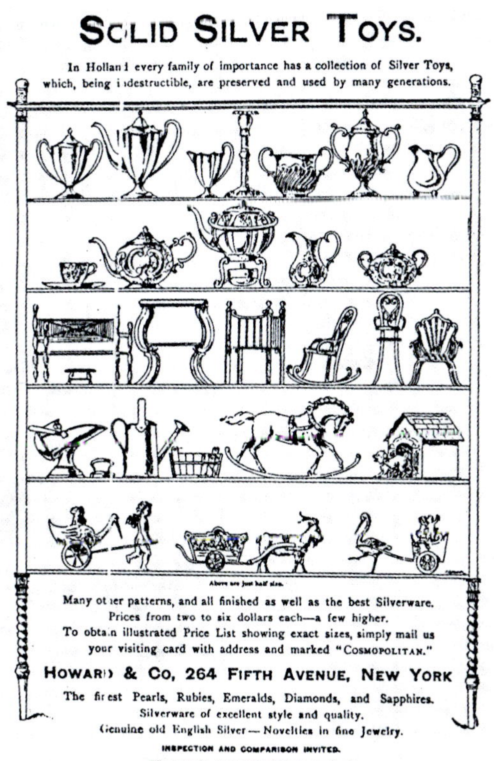

An advertisement for Howard & Co. of New York City from the December, 1895, issue of *The Cosmopolitan* depicting silver miniatures designed by Arthur J. Stone who was a member of the firm at that time.

Stone crossed the Atlantic in the fall of 1884. Shortly after arriving in the United States, he began his employment with the William B. Durgin Manufacturing Co., of Concord, Massachusetts. The commercial nature of the Durgin Company left Stone disappointed and he again sought a new position. In 1890 he applied for citizenship and from that time on was a loyal American.

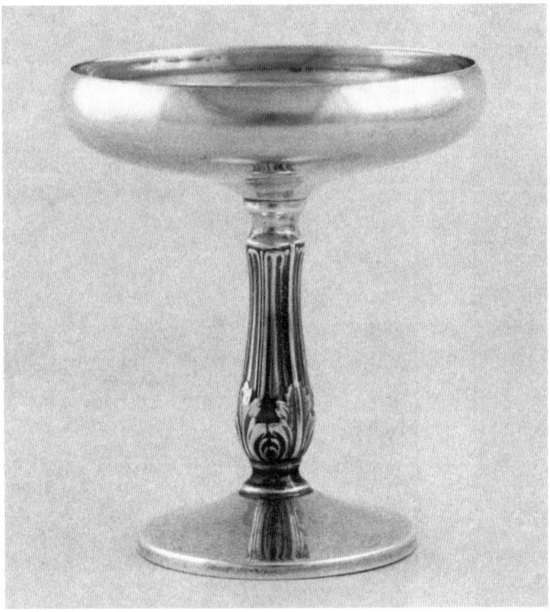

Compote by Arthur J. Stone. Marked. A wreath. Sterling and design number "65" on base. Probably c.1920. 2-3/8" high. *Photo courtesy of Stephen N. Dennis.*

After Tiffany & Co. and Gorham who led the field, the Durgin and the Smith Companies offered the best quality sterling silver available in America. But stamping and spinning, which effectively and efficiently shortened the manufacturing process, again compromised Stone's quest for a shop that allowed him to be involved with every stage of silversmithing. Despite his success with both companies, his predisposition for handwrought work over machine-made silver dictated another move. He terminated his employment with the Smith Company in 1895 and went to New York as a partner of the silversmith and retailer J. P. Howard.

Howard & Company, which had been established in 1866, had a shop on Fifth Avenue in New York and branches in Newport, Rhode Island, and London. The New York City Directory for 1896-1897 lists Stone as a silversmith at 220 Fourth Avenue. A later reference from Stone's biographical data in *Who's Who in America* for 1924-1925 states he was "engaged in mfr. of silver toys with J. P. Howard...1895-1896." In 1896 Howard printed a brochure entitled *Novelties for Christmas/Solid Silver* illustrating full-scale drawings of seventy-five toys, many probably made by Stone, such as a miniature urn pictured. Stone continued to make similar toys and miniatures throughout his life. A piece with the Howard mark can also be attributed to Stone during the Howard partnership on the basis of the chased and applied grape and grapevine decoration. Stone looked to J. P. Howard as his mentor and as a contemporary authority on silver, but apparently once again did not feel himself fully challenged in the partnership. The date of Stone's return to Gardner is not documented but the local directory lists him as a "designer" there in 1898. A letter from Howard dated July 12, 1897, amicably concluded their partnership.

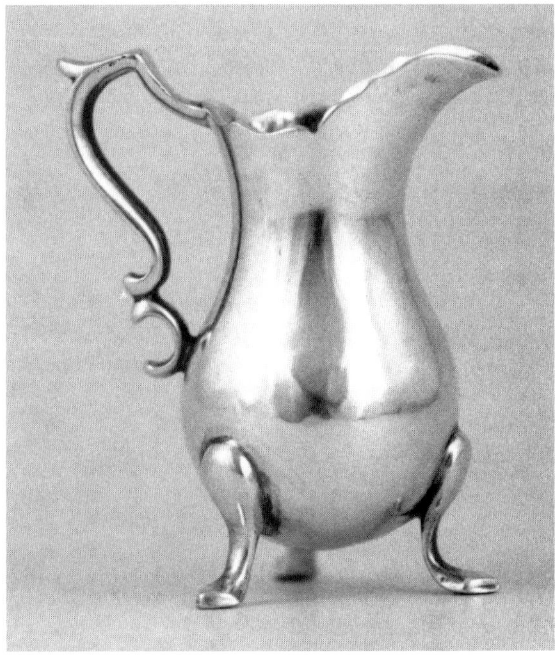

Pitcher by Arthur J. Stone for Howard & Co., 264 5th Avenue, New York City. 1-15/16" high. *Photo courtesy of Stephen N. Dennis.*

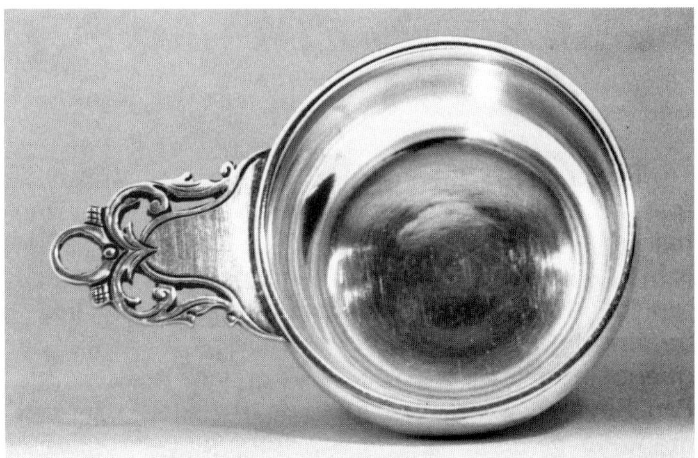

Porringer by Arthur J. Stone for Howard & Co., 264 5th Avenue, New York City. 2" long. *Photo courtesy of Stephen N. Dennis.*

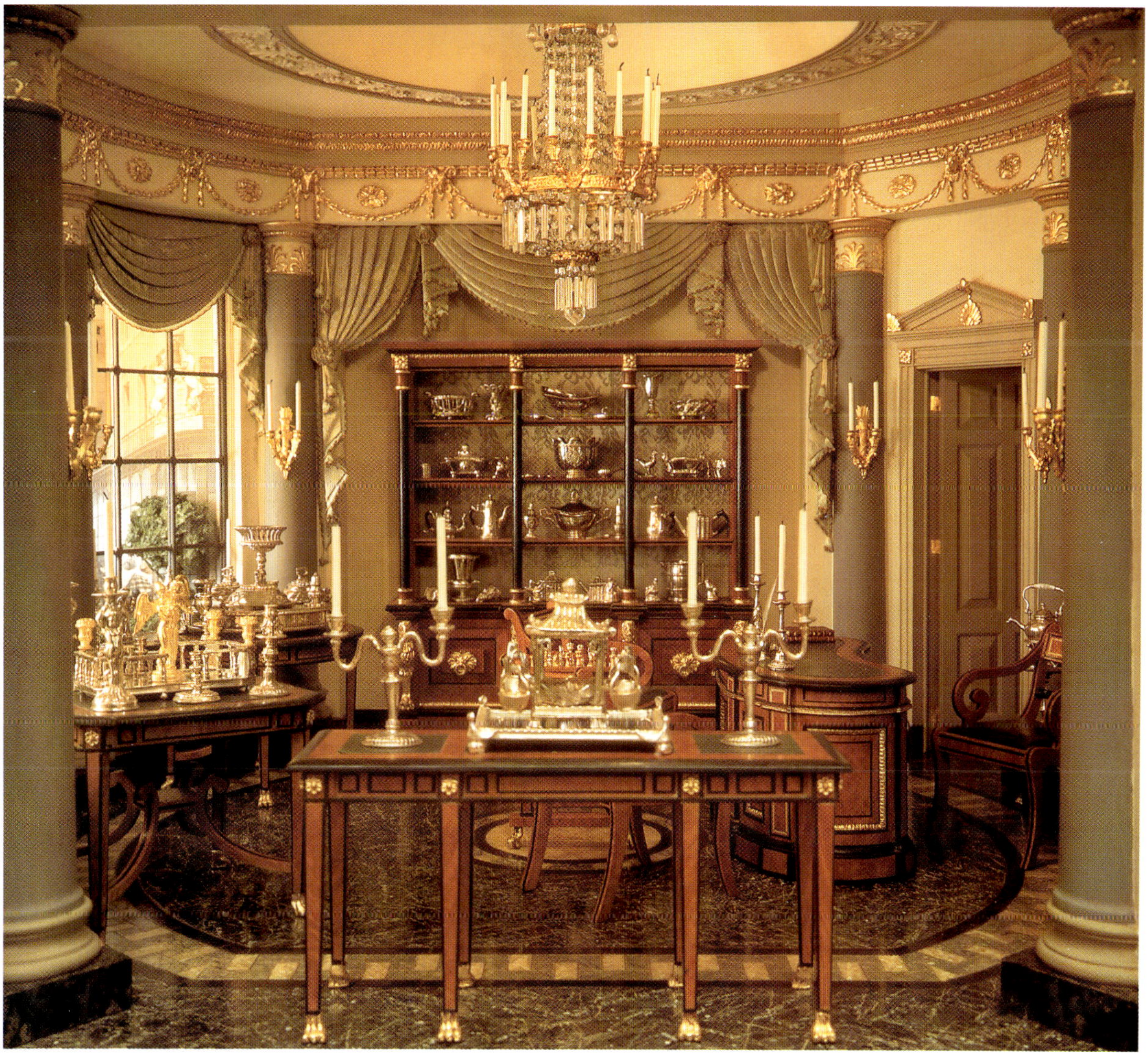

Inch to the foot scale model of an elegant silver shop of days gone by, made by Eugene P. Kupjack. *Private collection. Photo: Jay Kupjack. Copyright Kupjack Studios.*

Eugene P. Kupjack

Miniature silver tableware, based on full-size articles made by some of America's most prominent colonial silversmiths, were made by Eugene P. Kupjack for Mrs. James Ward Thorne's sixty-eight miniature rooms in the 1930s. Many were displayed at the 1933 Century of Progress Exhibition in Chicago. They include designs after John Burt (1693-1746) and Thomas Savage (1664-1750) of Boston, Peter Van Dyck (1684-1750) and Simeon Soumain (1685-1750) of New York, and Joseph Richardson, Sr. (1711-1784) and Joseph Richardson, Jr. of Philadelphia. All sixty-eight of Mrs. Thorne's miniature rooms are displayed at the Art Institute of Chicago. Other museums with outstanding collections of miniature silver include the Philadelphia Museum of Art, the Museum of the City of New York, the Minneapolis Institute of Art, and the Metropolitan Museum of Art. (*Silver Magazine*, July/August, 1979. Used by permission.)

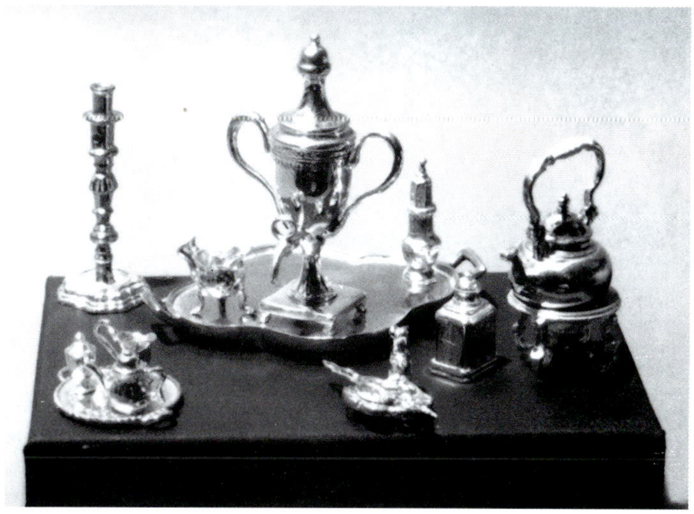

Miniature tea set with candlestick and snuffer by Eugene P. Kupjack. *Private collection. Photo: Jay Kupjack. Copyright Kupjack Studios.*

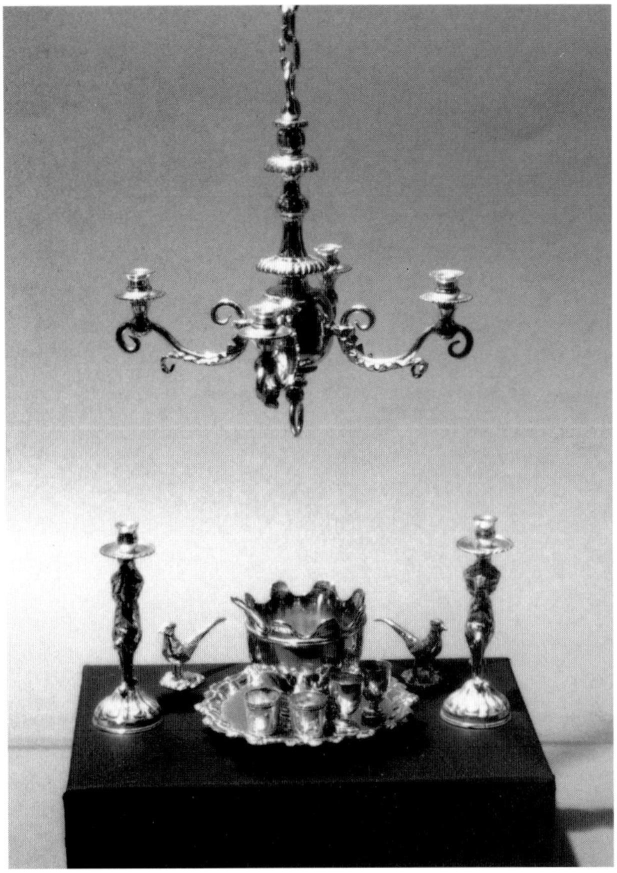

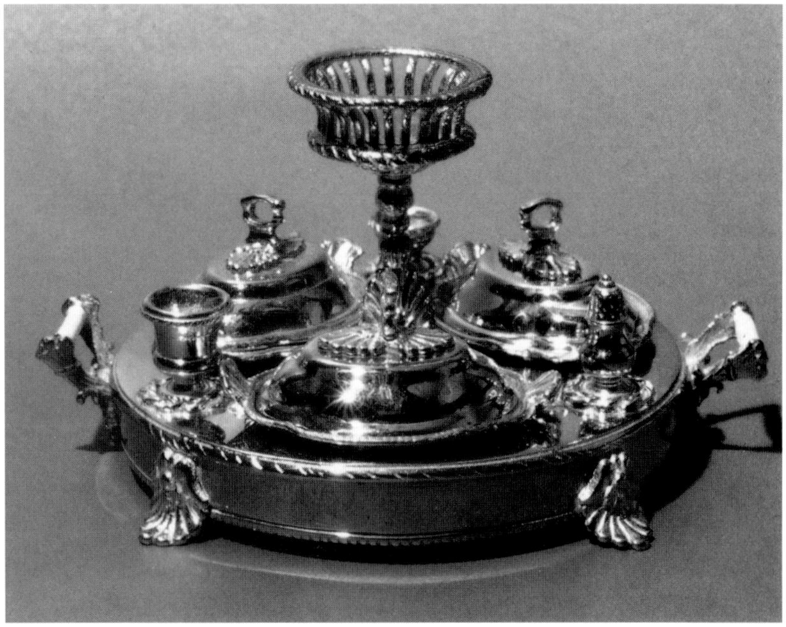

Miniature individual serving set with three covered dishes, salt, pepper, and condiment servers. *Private collection. Photo: Jay Kupjack. Copyright Kupjack Studios.*

Left:
Miniature chandelier, pheasant table decorations, candlesticks, monteith, punch cups, and tray by Eugene P. Kupjack. *Private collection. Photo: Jay Kupjack. Copyright Kupjack Studios.*

William B. Meyers 1887-1958

Following a successful career as part owner, designer, and producer of a firm to make faithful reproductions of antique silver in various museums, William B. Meyers became an outstanding silversmith specializing in miniatures. On learning that the famous silversmith of the Revolutionary War period Meyers was a progenitor, William B. Meyers' interest in handmade silver led him to selling his machinery and establishing a studio (no machinery) working with a se-

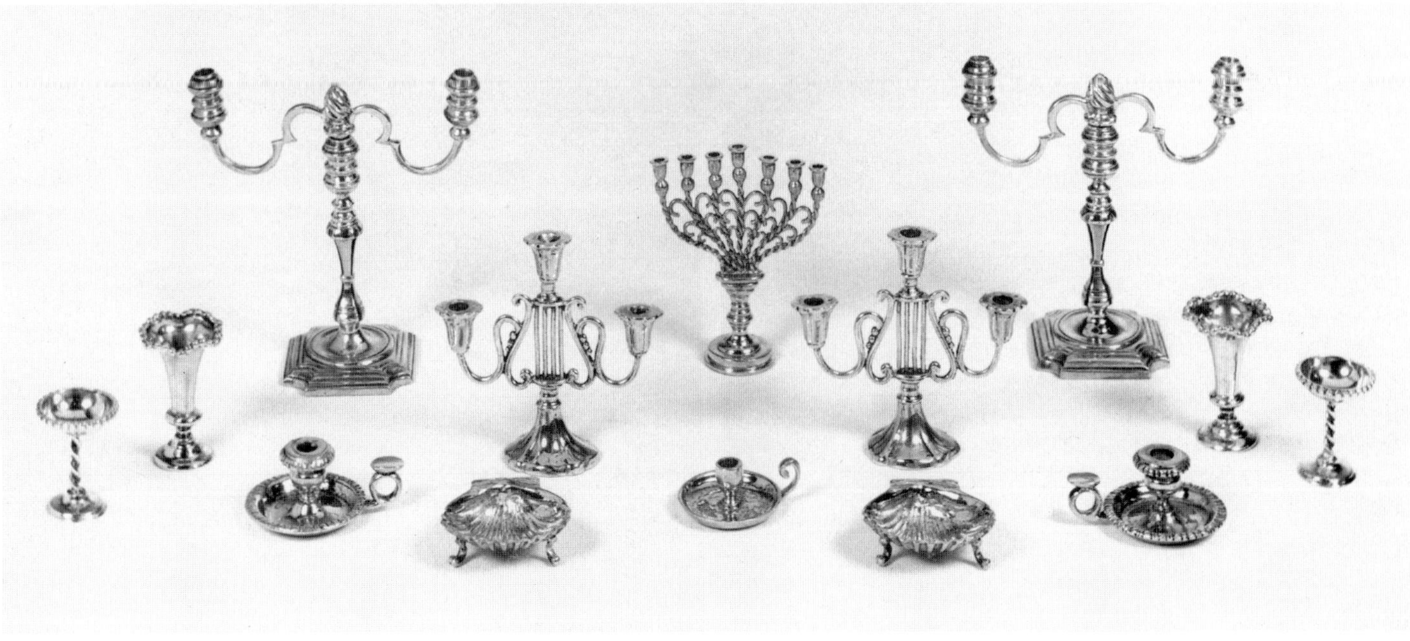

Miniature sterling dining service made by William B. Meyers c.1920. 3" high. *Courtesy of The Newark Museum, N.J./Art Resource, New York, Marion Schaeffer bequest 1964. Photo: Armen Photographers.*

lect group of craftsmen as helpers to produce, by hand, fine, authentic copies of the master silversmiths.

He decided to make miniature scaled copies of the antique silver pieces for his own collection. He scaled them at approximately 1-1/2" to the foot so that he could thus be able faithfully to incorporate every decoration of the original and to make them functional as well.

At first he had no thought of selling any of his silver miniatures, so his early pieces were not marked. An article appearing in *Harper's Bazaar* led to Meyers being so swamped with orders for his miniatures that he trained sixteen of his craftsmen in miniature making. Eventually, the shop made miniatures to the exclusion of any other goods.

After careful consideration, he decided to add to his workshop output miniature wooden antique furniture, which was designed to harmonize and complement the silver he made. The first piece of wooden miniature furniture was a Chippendale dining table. The interest and publicity resulting from a tea, where his pieces were displayed and at which many movie stars of the time were present, created a craze for his miniatures. By then he had around 300 different silver articles in production.

Much of the silver miniature goods made today are cast and are quite crude, compared with the exquisite work of William B. Meyers.

Armada Dish

A miniature silver Armada dish was made in 1977 based on a style (from a set of 22 plates of different sizes) that was taken from wrecked Aramda ships after 1588 (though at least one of them is dated 1581) and presented to Sir Christopher Harris for services rendered. In about 1645 the service was buried by his nephew to prevent its being taken by the Parliamentary Troops. Just before World War II, the service was taken to the London silversmith Comyns for reconditioning. They made copies and miniatures of these so-called "Armada dishes." The marks are those of the Queen's Jubilee (1977) and consist of the Queen' s head, the date letter for 1977, the Leopard's head for London, RC in heraldic shield for William Comyns and Sons (their mark used since 1925), and the figure of Britannia, denoting the .958 standard. The combination of the Jubilee mark and the Britannia mark make it a rare piece. The retailer's mark of Lowe & Son, Chester, is on the underside of the rim. As these marks were punched only at the maker's request, they are not strictly hallmarks.

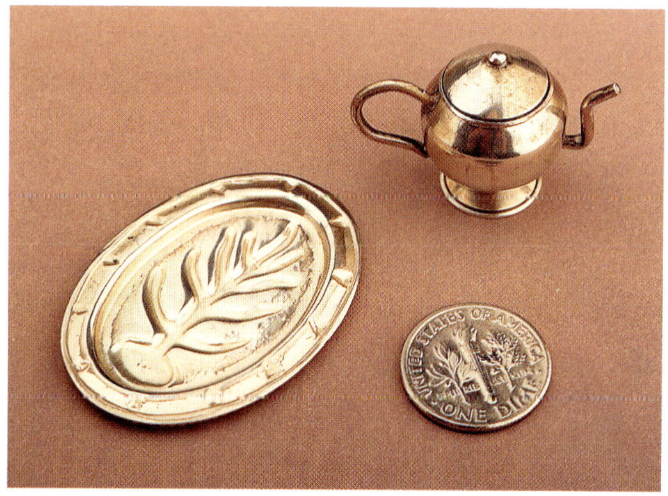

Miniature silver well-in-tree platter 1-3/4" long by 1" wide. Miniature silver teapot on ring base 7/8" tall by 1-1/4" wide. *Photo: Bruce Waters.*

Daniel J. Riccio

Although Daniel J. Riccio has used the ancient technique of lost wax casting for his hand-crafted miniatures, he has designed large sculpture as well. He attend school and worked in New York City for several years making both sculptures and fashion jewelry.

In 1976, he found a location in the country in Glastonbury, Connecticut. There his skills in jewelry and miniatures began to emerge. Large sculptures gave way to miniatures. His work was being enthusiastically received all over the country. Since 1976, he has designed sewing thimbles, bells and jewelry, to name just a few.

Daniel J. Riccio has a unique style which is continuing to evolve. He does one-of-a-kind wood carvings that take on the qualities of the life force itself. His jewelry pieces are fit for a queen and his silver miniatures a delight for any collector.

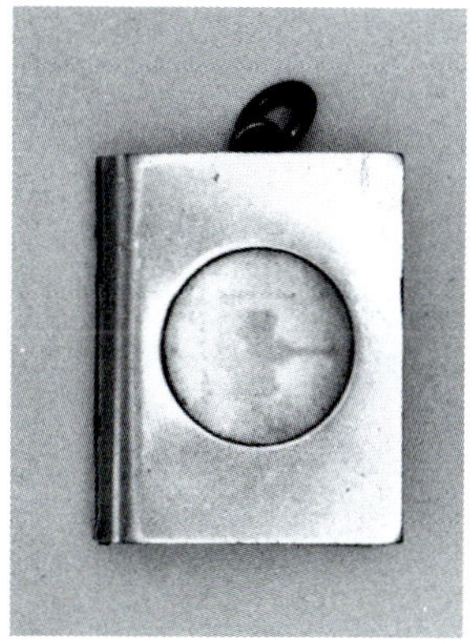

Miniature book-shaped pendant with a magnifying glass set into the front cover. It once held a miniature book—possibly a New Testament or a Dictionary. Height: 1-5/8". *Private collection. Photo: H Ivan Rainwater.*

Bibliography

For further reading

Adkins, Gertrude Dullard. "Silver Buttons". *Silver Magazine*, Sept./Oct. 1972.

Andere, Mary. *Old Needlework Boxes and Tools.* New York. Drake Publishers Ltd. 1971.

Anderson, Robert Charles. *The Great Migration Begins.* Boston. New England Genealogical Society. 1995.

Asimov, Isaac. *Asimov's Chronology of Science and Discovery.* New York, NY. Harper Collins Publishers, Inc. 1994.

Baird-North Company Catalog. 1913 Reprint. Des Moines, Iowa. Wallace-Homestead Book Co.

Baker, Lillian. *100 Years of Collectible Jewelry.* Paducah, Kentucky. Collector Books. 1978.

Beckman, Elizabeth O. *Cincinnati Silversmiths, Jewelers, Watch and Clockmakers.* Cincinnati, Ohio. B. B. & Co. 1975.

Bell, Jenenne. *Gold Jewelry, 1840-1950,* 2nd Edition. Florence, Alabama. Books Americana. 1985.

Bloomingdale's Illustrated 1886 Catalog. Mineola, New York. Dover Publications. 1988.

Boultinghouse, Marquis. *Silversmiths, Jewelers, Clock and Watch Makers of Kentucky 1785-1900.* Lexington, KY. Privately printed. 1980.

Bulfinch Illustrated Encyclopedia of Antiques. London. Little Brown and Company. 1994.

Carlisle, Lillian Baker. *Vermont Clock and Watchmakers, Silversmiths and Jewelers, 1778-1878.* Lunenburg, VT. Stinehour Press. 1970.

Carpenter, Charles H. Jr. *Gorham Silver 1831-1981.* New York. Dodd Mead & Company. 1982.

Carpenter, Charles H. Jr. with Mary Grace Carpenter. *Tiffany Silver.* San Francisco, CA 94126. Alan Wofsy Fine Arts. 1997.

de Castres, Elizabeth. *A Guide to Collecting Silver.* London. Macdonald Futura Publishers. 1980.

Chefetz, Sheila. *Antiques for the Table.* New York. Penguin Books USA Inc. 1993.

Chickering, Elenita C. *Arthur J. Stone 1847-1938 Designer and Silversmith.* Boston. The Boston Athenaeum. 1994.

Clarke, Joan R. & Hinton, David A. *The Alfred and Minster Lovell Jewels.* Oxford. Ashmolean Museum. 1984.

Cohen, Hal. L. *Official Guide to Silver & Silverplate.* New York. NY House of Collectibles, Inc. First edition. 1974.

Collector's Encyclopedia Victorian to Art Deco. New York. Random House. 1974.

Craig, W. D. *Coins of the World.* Racine, WI. Western Publishing Company Inc. 2nd and 3rd editions. 1966 and 1971.

Culme, John. *Directory of Gold and Silversmiths 1838-1914.* England. Antique Collectors' Club. 1987.

Delieb, Eric *Investing in Silver.* New York. Clarkson N. Potter, Inc. 1967.

Drepperd, Carl W. *Dictionary of American Antiques.* Boston, MA. Charles T. Branford Company. 1952.

Druitt, Silvia. *Antique Personal Possessions to Collect.* London. Peerage Books. 1986.

Dry, Graham. *Art Nouveau Domestic Metalwork from Wurtembergishche Metallwarenfabrik.* (The English Catalogue 1906 with an Introduction by Graham Dry.) Suffolk, England. Antiques Collectors' Club. 1988 reprinted 1990.

Eliot, John D. *A Biographical Dictionary of the First Settlers and Other Eminent Characters in New England.* Boston. Cushing and Appleton, 1809. Facsimile reprint by Heritage Books, Inc. Bowie, Maryland. 1995.

Emery, John. *European Spoons Before 1700.* Edinburgh. John Donald Publishers Ltd. 1976.

Encyclopedia of Americans. Danbury, CT. Grolier Soc. 1972.

Encyclopedia of Collectibles. Alexandria, VA. Time-Life Books. 1980.

Ensko, Stephen Guernsey Cook. *American Silversmiths and Their Marks IV.* Boston, Massachusetts. David R. Godine, Publisher, Inc. 1989.

Epstein, Diana. *The Collector's Guide to Buttons.* New York. Walker and Company. 1990.

Fales, Martha Gandy. *Early American Silver.* USA. Excalibur Books. Funk and Wagnalls Publishing Company, Inc. 1970.

Feher, Joseph. Hawaii: *A Pictorial History.* Honolulu, Hawaii. Bishop Museum Press. 1969.

Freeman, Larry, Dr. *Victorian Silver.* Watkins Glen, New York. Century House. 1967.

Goldsborough, Jennifer Faulds. *Eighteenth and Nineteenth Century Maryland Silver.* Baltimore, Maryland. Baltimore Museum of Art. 1975.

Goldsborough, Jennifer Faulds. *Silver in Maryland.* Baltimore, Maryland. Maryland Historical Society. 1983-1984.

Gorham Silver Co. *The Gorham Manufacturing Company Silversmiths.* New York. Cheltenham Press. 1900.

Griffenhagen, George B. "Tools of the Apothecary," *Jour-*

nal of the American Pharmaceutical Association, Practical Pharmacy Edition, Washington, D. C.. American Pharmaceutical Association. 1957.

Grimwade, Arthur G. *London Goldsmiths 1697-1837.* London. Faber and Faber. 1976.

Grover, Kathryn, ed. *Dining in America 1850-1900.* Rochester, NY. University of Massachusetts & the Margaret Woodbury Strong Museum. 1987.

Groves, Sylvia. *The History of Needlework and Accessories.* Feltham, Middlesex, England. 1966 and 1968.

Hammond, Dorothy. *Guide to American Antiques.* New York, NY. Penguin Group. 1995.

Harris, Cyril M. ed. *Dictionary of Architecture and Construction.* New York. McGraw-Hill Book Company. 1975.

Haslan, Malcolm. *Marks and Monograms of the Modern Movement 1875-1930.* New York. Charles Scribner' s Sons. 1977.

Hayden, Arthur. *Chats on Old Sheffield Plate.* London. T. Fisher Unwin Ltd. 1920.

Helliwell, Stephen J. *Antique Collecting.* England. Volume 31, number 6. November 1996. pp. 30-35.

Helliwell, Stephen J. *Collecting Small Silverware.* Oxford, England. Phaidon Christie's. 1988.

Helliwell, Stephen J. *Understanding Antique Silver Plate.* England. Antique Collectors' Club Ltd. 1996.

Historical and Biographical Sketch of the Gorham Manufacturing Company. Reprint of booklet issued 1878.

Hogan, Edmund P. The *Elegance of Old Silverplate.* Exton, PA. Schiffer Publishing Ltd. 1980.

Holland, Margaret. *Phaidon Guide to Silver.* Oxford, England. Phaidon Press Ltd. 1978.

Holland, Margaret. *Silver, An Illustrated Guide to American and British Silver.* London. Octopus Books Limited. 1973.

Holmes, Edwin F. *A History of Thimbles.* Cranbury, NJ Rosemont Publishing and Printing Corporation. 1985.

Holmes, Edwin F. *Thimbles.* Dublin. Gill and Macmillan Ltd. 1976.

Houart, Victor. *Antique Spoons, A Collector's Guide.* London. Souvenir Press Ltd. 1982.

Houart, Victor. *Miniature Silver Toys.* Translated by David Smith. New York. Alpine Fine Arts Collection Ltd. 1981.

Houart, Victor. *Sewing Accessories.* London. Souvenir Press Ltd. 1984.

Hughes, G. Bernard. *Small Antique Silverware.* New York. Bramhall House. 1957.

Hughes, Graham. *Modern Silver Throughout the World 1880-1967.* New York. Crown Publishers, Inc. 1967.

Hughes, Therle. *English Domestic Needlework.* London. Abby Fine Arts. 1961.

Hughes, Therle. *Small Antiques for the Collector.* New York. The Macmillan Company. 1965.

Jackson, Charles James. *An Illustrated History of English Plate.* London. Country Life Ltd. & B. T. Batsford. 1911. Reprint N.Y. by Dover Publications, Inc. 1969.

James, Edward T. *Dictionary of American Biography.* Scribner's Supplement III. 1941-1945.

James, Peter and Thorpe, Nick. *Ancient Inventions.* New York. Ballantine Books. 1994.

Johnson, Eleanor. *Fashion Accessories.* UK. Shire Album 58. 1980.

Johnson, Eleanor. *Needlework Tools.* Great Britain. Shire Publications Ltd. 1978. Reprinted 1980.

Johnston Jewelry Holiday Catalogue. New York. 1895.

Kane, Joseph Nathan et al. *Famous First Facts, 5th ed.* New York & Dublin. H.W. Wilson Company. 1997.

The House of KIRK, Our 150th year 1815-1965. Baltimore: Samuel Kirk & Son, Inc. 1965.

Samuel KIRK & Son Co. 1914 Catalog Reproduction. Baltimore, MD. Michael A. Merrill, Inc. 1994.

The Story of the House of KIRK. Baltimore: Samuel Kirk & Son, Inc. 1914 and 1939.

Knowles, Eric. *Discovering Antiques.* London. De Agostini Ltd. 1996.

Kovel, Ralph & Terry. *Kovel's Know Your Antiques.* New York. Crown Publishers Inc. 1990.

Landale, Catherine. *Vinaigrettes.* Antique Collector. September 1977.

Langford, Joel. *Silver, A Practical Guide.* Secaucus, New Jersey. Chartwell books, Inc. 1991.

Lewer, H. W. & Percival, MacIver. *The Bric-a-Brac Collector.* New York. Dodd, Mead and Company. 1923.

Lightbown, R. W. *Catalogue of Scandinavian and Baltic Silver.* London. Victoria and Albert Museum. 1975.

Low, S. F. *Daniel Low and Co. Catalogue N, 1901.* Reprint. 1998.

Luscomb, Sally C. *The Collector's Encyclopedia of Buttons.* West Chester, Pennsylvania 19380. Schiffer Publishing, Ltd. 1967 and 1992.

McClinton, Katherine Morrison. *Collecting American 19th Century Silver.* New York. Charles Scribner's Sons. 1968.

McClinton, Katherine Morrison. *Complete Book of Small Antiques Collecting.* New York. Bramhall House. 1965.

Mace, O. Henry. *Collector's Guide to Victoriana.* Radnor, Pennsylvania. Homestead Book Company. 1991.

Mackay, James. *An Encyclopedia of Small Antiques.* New York. Harper & Row, Publishers. 1975.

Madigan, Mary Jean & Colgan, Susan, ed. *Prints and Photographs.* New York. Billboard Publications. 1983.

Mahoney' s *Antiques and Collectibles 3rd Edition.* Dubuque, IA. Antique Trade Books. 1995.

Mariana, John. *The Dictionary of American Food and Drink.* NY. Hearst Books. 1997.

Maryland, A Guide to the Old Line State. American Guide Series. New York. Oxford University Press. 1940.

Mason, Anita and Packer, Diane. *An Illustrated Dictionary of Jewelry.* New York. Harper & Row. 1974.

Masterpieces of Cutlery and the Art of Eating. Exhibition at the Victoria and Albert Museum in conjunction with the Worshipful Company of Cutlers of London. 11 July to 26 August 1979.

Miller, Judith & Martin. *Miller's International Antiques.* New York. 1991.

Miller' s *International Antiques Price Guide.* London. Reed Books Ltd. 1995.

Miniature Rooms, at The Art Institute of Chicago. New York, London, Paris. The Art Institute of Chicago. 1984.

Moretz, James. *Posey Bouquet Holders.* Chicago, IL. Flowerian Publishers. 1984.

Newman, Harold. *An Illustrated Dictionary of Silverware.* London. Thames & Hudson, Ltd. 1987.

Osterberg, Richard. *Sterling Silver Flatware for Dining Elegance.* Atglen, PA. Schiffer Publishing Ltd. 1994.

Osterberg, Richard. *Silver Holloware for Dining Elegance.* Atglen, PA. Schiffer Publishing Ltd. 1996.

Paxton-Williams, Sara. *The Art of Dining, A History of Cooking and Eating.* London. National Trust Enterprises, Ltd. 1993.

Paye & Baker Mfg. Co. Catalog no. 50. 1908. (Reprint: Diane Zinn. 1997.)
Peacock, Primrose. *Antique Buttons.* New York. Drake Publishers, Inc. 1972.
Pelham Burn, Diane. *Thread Winders for Collectors.* USA. Thimble Collectors International. 1989.
Perry, Evan. *Corkscrews and Bottle Openers.* U. K. Shire Publishers Ltd. 1995.
The Pictorial Encyclopedia of Antiques. London. Hamlyn. 1968.
Rainwater, Dorothy T. *American Jewelry Manufacturers.* Atglen, PA. Schiffer Publishing Ltd. 1988.
Rainwater, Dorothy T. *American Silver Manufacturers.* Fourth Edition Revised. Atglen, PA Schiffer Publishing Ltd. 1998.
Rainwater, Dorothy T. and Felger, Donna. *American Spoons 2nd Edition.* Atglen, PA Schiffer Publishing Ltd. 1990.
Rainwater, Dorothy T. and Felger, Donna H. *Spoons Around the World.* PA. Everybody's Press, Inc. and Thomas Nelson, Inc. 1976. Second Edition, Schiffer Publishing Ltd. 1992.
Rainwater, Dorothy T. *Sterling Silver Holloware.* Princeton. Pyne Press. 1973.
Ransome-Wallis, Rosemary, Curator. *Matthew Boulton and the Toymakers.* Silver from the Birmingham Assay Office. Catalogue of an exhibition at Goldsmith's Hall. London. 1982.
Revi, Albert Christian, ed. *Antiques for Men.* Hanover, PA. Everybody's Press, Inc. 1974.
Robertson, R. A. *Old Sheffield Plate.* London. Ernest Benn Limited. 1957.
Rogers, Agnes. *The Undimmed Appeal of the Gibson Girl.* American Heritage. December 1957.
Rogers, Gay Ann. *Illustrated History of Needlework Tools.* London. John Murray (Publishers) Ltd. 1983.
Rosner, Bernard and Beckerman, Jay. *Inside the World of Miniatures and Dollhouses*. New York, David McKay Co. Inc. 1976.
Schiffer, Nancy M. *Silver Jewelry Designs.* Atglen, PA. 19310. Schiffer Publishing Ltd. 1996.
Schwartz, Jeri. *Silver and Silverplate*. Sixth Edition. New York. House of Collectibles. 1989.
Schwartz, Marvin D. *Antique American Silver.* Garden City, New York. Doubleday & Company Inc. 1975.
Second World Almanac Book. New York. Ballantine Books, A Scripps Howard Company. 1986.
Silver Magazine (formerly The Magazine SILVER and Silver-Rama). 1968-
Sifakis, Carl. *The Encyclopedia of American Crime.* N. Y. Smithmark. 1992.
Soeffing, D. Albert. *Silver Medallion Flatware.* New York City. New Books, Inc. 1988.
Sterling Flatware Pattern Index. Jewelers' Circular-Keystone. Copyright 1970. Revised 1974.
Sumptuous Surrounds Silver Overlay on Ceramic and Glass. The Collection of Warren Gilson. Milwaukee. WI. Milwaukee Art Museum. 1990.
Taunton, Nerylla. *Antique Needlework Tools and Embroideries.* England. Antique Collectors' Club Ltd. 1997.
Tennyson, Alfred, Lord. "Ulysses." *Bartlett's Quotations*, 11th ed. New York. Garden City Publishing Co., Inc. 1944.
Travers, Bridget, Editor. *World of Invention.* Detroit, MI. Gale Research International Limited. 1984.
Tufts, James W. *Fine Silver Plated Table Ware.* Boston. Press of American Soda Fountain Company. 1903.
Turim, Gayle. *No Postage Required.* Traditional Home. September 1977. Pages 52, 54, 56.
Turner, Noel D. *American Silver Flatware 1837-1910.* Cranbury, New Jersey. A. S. Barnes & Co. 1972.
Victorian Catalogue of Household Goods. New York. Portland House. 1991. (Reprint from 1883 catalogue.)
Von Furstenberg. *The Tables.* New York. Random House, Inc. 1996.
Warman's. *Antiques and Collectibles Price Guide.* 30th edition. Radnor, PA. Wallace-Homstead Book Company. 1996.
Whiting, Gertrude. *Old-Time Tools & Toys of Needlework.* New York. USA. Dover Publications, Inc. 1971.
World Book. World Book, Inc. Chicago, Sydney, Toronto, London. 1998.
World Book Encyclopedia. Volume 15. Chicago. Scott Fetzer Company. 1993.
World Book Encyclopedia. Chicago. World Book, Inc. 1995.
Zalkin, Estelle. *Handbook of Thimbles & Sewing Implements.* U.S.A. Warman Pub. Co. 1988.

Index